Understanding and Managing Tourism Impacts
C. Michael Hall and Alan Lew

Forthcoming:

An Introduction to Visual Research Methods in Tourism
Edited by Tijana Rakic and Donna Chambers

Routledge Studies in Contemporary Geographies of Leisure, Tourism and Mobility is a forum for innovative new research intended for research students and academics, and the titles will be available in hardback only. Titles include:

Living with Tourism
Negotiating identities in a Turkish Village
Hazel Tucker

Tourism, Diasporas and Space
Edited by Tim Coles and Dallen J. Timothy

Tourism and Postcolonialism
Contested discourses, identities and representations
Edited by C. Michael Hall and Hazel Tucker

Tourism, Religion and Spiritual Journeys
Edited by Dallen J. Timothy and Daniel H. Olsen

China's Outbound Tourism
Wolfgang Georg Arlt

Tourism, Power and Space
Edited by Andrew Church and Tim Coles

Tourism, Ethnic Diversity and the City
Edited by Jan Rath

Ecotourism, NGO's and Development
A critical analysis
Jim Butcher

Tourism and the Consumption of Wildlife
Hunting, shooting and sport fishing
Edited by Brent Lovelock

Tourism, Creativity and Development
Edited by Greg Richards and Julie Wilson

Tourism at the Grassroots
Edited by John Connell and Barbara Rugendyke

Tourism and Innovation
C. Michael Hall and Allan Williams

World Tourism Cities
Developing tourism off the beaten track
Edited by Robert Maitland and Peter Newman

Tourism and National Parks
International perspectives on development, histories and change
Edited by Warwick Frost and C. Michael Hall

Tourism, Performance and the Everyday
Consuming the Orient
Michael Haldrup and Jonas Larsen

Tourism and Change in Polar Regions
Edited by C. Michael Hall and Jarkko Saarinen

Fieldwork in Tourism
Methods, issues and reflections
Edited by C. Michael Hall

Tourism and India
Kevin Hannam and Anya Diekmann

Political Economy of Tourism
Edited by Jan Mosedale

Volunteer Tourism
Edited by Angela Benson

The Study of Tourism
Richard Sharpley

Children's and Families' Holiday Experiences
Neil Carr

Tourism and Agriculture
Edited by Rebecca Torres and Janet Momsen

Tourism in China
Policy and development since 1949

David Airey and King Chong

Routledge
Taylor & Francis Group
LONDON AND NEW YORK

First published 2011
by Routledge
2 Park Square, Milton Park, Abingdon, Oxon OX14 4RN

Simultaneously published in the USA and Canada
by Routledge
711 Third Avenue, New York, NY 10017

Routledge is an imprint of the Taylor & Francis Group, an informa business

British Library Cataloguing in Publication Data
A catalogue record for this book is available from the British Library

Library of Congress Cataloging in Publication Data
Airey, D. W.
 Tourism in China/by David Airey and King Chong.
 p. cm.
 Includes bibliographical references and index.
 1. Tourism – China. I. Chong, King. II. Title.
 G155.C55A37 2011
 338.4′79151 – dc22   2010042138

ISBN: 978-0-415-54809-0 (hbk)
ISBN: 978-0-203-82034-6 (ebk)

Typeset in Times New Roman
by Florence Production Ltd, Stoodleigh, Devon
Printed and bound in Great Britain by
CPI Antony Rowe, Chippenham, Wiltshire

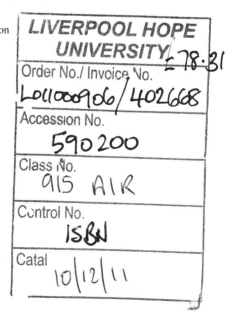

Tourism in China

Tourism in China has grown rapidly since the country started implementing its open-door policy in 1978. Tourism development is now an essential agenda item for the Chinese government's plan for economic and social growth. Policy and policy-making for tourism therefore provide the essential background to understand tourism development in China.

This is the first book to set the development of tourism in China since 1949 in its policy context. Underpinned by a strong conceptual framework, this systematic study of China contributes to an in-depth understanding of how public policy-making for tourism works and how it affects the development of tourism in the real world. The text explores tourism policy during three distinct leadership periods since the creation of the People's Republic of China in 1949: Mao Zedong (1949–78); Deng Xiaoping (1978–97) and the Collective Leadership era (1997–present). The attitudes and values of leaders and central government agencies towards tourism are considered, as well as the interactions of ideological orthodoxies, socio-economic conditions and institutions in their influence on national policy-making and tourism development. A separate chapter is devoted to policy-making in China's two Special Administrative Regions, Hong Kong and Macau, as well as Taiwan due to its political separation from the Mainland, and Tibet, given its distinctive characteristics. Drawing on China's experience over sixty years the book concludes with both theoretical and practical implications for tourism policy-making.

This timely volume offers important insights into China's tourism as well as contributing to a wider pattern of debate about the respective roles of government policy and the market in the past and future. The material draws on exclusive in-depth interviews with key informants in China and on government documents and official sources not generally available in the international literature. This will be of interest to higher level students, academics and researchers within tourism, policy studies, politics, geography and China studies.

David Airey is Professor of Tourism Management at the University of Surrey, UK.

King Chong is Project Fellow at the Public Policy Research Institute, Hong Kong Polytechnic University, China.

Contemporary Geographies of Leisure, Tourism and Mobility

Series Editor: C. Michael Hall

Professor at the Department of Management, College of Business & Economics, University of Canterbury, Private Bag 4800, Christchurch, New Zealand

The aim of this series is to explore and communicate the intersections and relationships between leisure, tourism and human mobility within the social sciences.

It will incorporate both traditional and new perspectives on leisure and tourism from contemporary geography, e.g. notions of identity, representation and culture, while also providing for perspectives from cognate areas such as anthropology, cultural studies, gastronomy and food studies, marketing, policy studies and political economy, regional and urban planning, and sociology, within the development of an integrated field of leisure and tourism studies.

Also, increasingly, tourism and leisure are regarded as steps in a continuum of human mobility. Inclusion of mobility in the series offers the prospect to examine the relationship between tourism and migration, the sojourner, educational travel, and second-home and retirement travel phenomena.

The series comprises two strands:

Contemporary Geographies of Leisure, Tourism and Mobility aims to address the needs of students and academics, and the titles will be published in hardback and paperback. Titles include:

Contents

Illustrations

Figure

Tables

About the authors

David Airey is Professor of Tourism Management at the University of Surrey and Visiting Professor at the University of Central Lancashire. He began his academic career at Surrey in 1975. From 1985 he was with the Government Ministry responsible for education followed by three years with the European Commission. He returned to academia, and to Surrey, in 1997 as Professor of Tourism Management. Professor Airey served as Head of School from 2000–2 and as University Pro Vice-Chancellor from 2001–9. In 2004 he was awarded the EuroChrie President's award for outstanding achievement and in 2006 was recipient of the Ulysses award from the United Nations World Tourism Organization (UNWTO) for his work in tourism education. In 2007 he became co-chair of the UNWTO Education and Science Council. He has a wide range of research interests and expertise, especially in tourism policy, education and organization. He has supervised research and published a number of studies in these areas. Professor Airey sits on the editorial advisory board of the Journal of Policy Research in Tourism, Leisure and Events.

King Chong is Project Fellow at the Public Policy Research Institute, The Hong Kong Polytechnic University. He obtained his Ph.D. degree from the School of Management, University of Surrey in the UK. Apart from working in the tourism industry and in academia, Dr Chong has a substantial amount of professional experience in the public sector. He is a fellow of the Hong Kong Public Administration Association (HKPAA). He has also produced a series of research reports for the Tourism Research Center, Chinese Academy of Social Sciences (CASS) as a guest researcher. Dr Chong is one of the pioneer researchers in studying China's policy-making and tourism development and has published relevant articles in such journals as *Annals of Tourism Research* and *Tourism Management*.

Preface

It is always difficult to identify the reasons for writing a textbook. Reasons often given refer to a 'gap in the literature', 'long-standing interest', 'access to new material', 'important new developments' and 'need for a new approach'. This book on tourism policy and development in China was prompted by a combination of these reasons, but perhaps most importantly it came about as a result of the meeting of the two authors, one a native Chinese in Hong Kong and the other from the UK, both with an interest in tourism policy and policy-making. The fact that one of the authors, Dr Chong, was completing his Ph.D. studies under the guidance of the other author, Professor Airey, not only provided the sparks of interest, but also created the opportunity to generate the ideas, develop the proposal and finally complete the work.

Turning to the precise reasons for preparing the book, the authors were certainly aware of a 'gap in the literature'. Indeed, as set out in Chapter 1, tourism specialists have bemoaned the lack of attention to tourism policy and policy-making for at least thirty years and although there have been some important contributions over this time, there are still very few comprehensive studies of the whole policy-making process. This is one of the gaps that this work is seeking to meet. Given their background, it is hardly surprising that both authors have a 'long-standing interest' in tourism policy issues. Indeed it was salutary to realize that the earliest writings of one of the authors on this topic go back to the beginning of the 1980s. 'Access to new material' initially came from the ground-breaking fieldwork, both interviews and access to original sources, later supplemented by further data collection.

Of course, in the background to all this was the amazingly rapid development of China which is the focus for the fieldwork and for this book. There could hardly be a more remarkable field for 'important new developments' in tourism policy than China, which in the space of thirty years has transformed itself into a major world player in tourism. The importance of China over this period as a setting to consider tourism policy-making cannot be under-estimated and nor can the developments in China be understood without a knowledge of the policy background. In brief, the Chinese state has been the fundamental influence on the development of tourism hence its tourism policy has been of crucial importance. But the important thing is that, as in other aspects of life in China, the involvement of the state and its policies have not been static. Indeed they have gone through massive changes and it is in tracing these changes and their influences that we can learn so much about how tourism policy is made and its influence on tourism development.

The final reason for this book can be summarized under the heading of the 'need for a new approach'. One of the things that has been missing from the writings about tourism policy has been a theoretical framework which can help to bring together the inputs, processes and outputs of policy-making. This book develops and explains an original theoretical framework and then goes on to use it and to some extent to test it in the empirical setting of China. This is a new contribution both in the framework itself and in the setting in which it is explored. The authors found the framework useful in understanding and explaining tourism policy in China over the past thirty years. It will, of course, rest with the readers whether they find it equally useful, and perhaps more importantly whether they recognize its applicability in other settings.

It will also rest with the reader whether the work provides a useful contribution to their understanding of tourism policy-making and of the developments that have taken place in China. For the authors, China has provided a stimulating, fascinating and, in its history over the last thirty years, a unique environment in which to explore one of the key influences on the development of tourism, namely tourism policy.

David Airey
Guildford

King Chong
Hong Kong

September 2010

Acknowledgements

The authors would like to convey their grateful thanks to the many interviewees in government agencies, research institutions and the tourism industry in China and the Hong Kong Special Administrative Region, for their views and insights. The authors also wish particularly to acknowledge the help from Professor Zhang Guangrui, Director of Tourism Research Center, Chinese Academy of Social Sciences in Beijing.

Abbreviations

AD	Anno Domini
ADS	Approved Destination Status
ARATS	Association for Relations Across the Taiwan Straits (Mainland China)
ASEAN	Association of Southeast Asian Nations
ATEATS	Association for Tourism Exchanges Across the Taiwan Straits
BC	Before Christ
BCE	Before Common Era
BTTC	Bureau of Travel and Tourism of China
CAAC	Civil Aviation Administration of China
CASS	Chinese Academy of Social Sciences
CEPA	Closer Economic Partnership Arrangement
CITS	China International Travel Services
CNTA	China National Tourism Administration (its forerunners were the State General Administration of Travel and Tourism and the Bureau of Travel and Tourism of China)
CPC	Communist Party of China
CPCCC	Central Committee of the Communist Party of China
CPD	Central Publicity Department of the Central Committee of the CPC
CPPCC	Chinese People's Political Consultative Conference
CTS	China Travel Services
CYTS	China Youth Travel Services
DPP	Democratic Progress Party (in Taiwan)
DRC	Development Research Centre, the State Council
GDP	Gross Domestic Product
GMD	Guomindang (Nationalist Party of China) (or KMT)
GNP	Gross National Product
HKHA	Hong Kong Hotels Association
HKSARG	Government of Hong Kong Special Administrative Region
HKTA	Hong Kong Tourist Association (forerunner to the HKTB)
HKTB	Hong Kong Tourism Board
HKTIC	Hong Kong Travel Industry Council

IJHM	*International Journal of Hospitality Management*
IVS	Individual Visit Scheme
MoC	Ministry of Commerce
MoCom	Ministry of Communication (now renamed Ministry of Transport)
MoE	Ministry of Education
MoF	Ministry of Finance
MoFA	Ministry of Foreign Affairs
MoFTEC	Ministry of Foreign Trade and Economic Cooperation (renamed Ministry of Commerce)
MoPS	Ministry of Public Security
MoT	Ministry of Transport
MSARG	Government of Macau Special Administrative Region
NDRC	National Development and Reform Commission (its forerunner was the State Development Planning Commission)
NPC	National People's Congress
NTA	National Tourism Administration
NTO	National Tourism Organization (or National Tourist Office)
OCTS	Overseas Chinese Travel Services
OECD	Organization for Economic Co-operation and Development
PATA	Pacific–Asia Travel Association
PRC	People's Republic of China
PRD	Pearl River Delta
RMB	Renminbi
SAFE	State Administration of Foreign Exchange
SAQTS	State Administration of Quality and Technical Supervision
SAR	Special Administrative Region
SARS	Severe Acute Respiratory Syndrome
SDPC	State Development Planning Commission (its forerunner was the State Planning Commission and was renamed the National Development and Reform Commission in 2003)
SEAC	State Ethnic Affairs Commission
SEF	Straits Exchange Foundation (in Taiwan)
SEZ	Special Economic Zone
SGAQSIQ	State General Administration of Quality Supervision, Inspection and Quarantine (its forerunner was the State Administration of Quality and Technical Supervision)
SGATT	State General Administration of Travel and Tourism (its forerunner was the Bureau of Travel and Tourism of China)
SOE	State-owned Enterprises
SPC	State Planning Commission (renamed the State Development Planning Commission in 1998)
SSB	State Statistics Bureau
STMD	Sociedade de Turismo e Diversões de Macau

UN	United Nations
UNESCO	United Nations Educational, Scientific and Cultural Organization
UNWTO	United Nations World Tourism Organization
WHO	World Health Organization
WTO	World Trade Organization
WTTC	World Travel and Tourism Council
Xinhua	Xinhua News Agency

Part I

Theoretical and contextual background

1 Introduction

> It will be clear that where tourism succeeds or fails is largely a function of political and administrative action and is not a function of economic or business expertise.
>
> (Richter, 1989: p.11)

> In the wake of the 2008 global financial crisis, the state's role in the economy may be gaining more appeal throughout the world.
>
> (The United States National Intelligence Council, 2008: p.8)

The role, volume, growth and potential of tourism in China have attracted growing interest since 2000, both from academics and more generally. For example, in 2008 the *International Journal of Hospitality Management* (IJHM) published a special issue on China (R.C. Wang, 2008: pp.323–4); from 2005 there has been a separate journal devoted to tourism in China, *Journal of China Tourism Research*; and since 2003 the World Travel and Tourism Council (WTTC) has produced its country reports on China's tourism. A leading China studies journal based in the United Kingdom, *China Quarterly*, has also started to give attention to tourism (e.g. Donaldson, 2007). But given its scale and complexity, the literature is still relatively scarce. Between the late 1970s and 2007 three of the main international tourism journals – *Annals of Tourism Research*, *Tourism Management*[1] and *Journal of Travel Research* – have only published about fifty papers between them specifically relating to China (Li and Zhao, 2007: p.91).[2] As for books, some nine academic texts about tourism in China have appeared (see the Appendix).

One of the gaps in this literature relates to the ways in which the development of tourism in China has happened and more specifically the public policy context in which this has occurred. Given the sheer importance of the state in any form of development in China this is an important gap. Politics, policy-making and political economy in relation to tourism have come in for increased attention recently with a growing number of books and journal papers. For example the journal *Current Issues in Tourism* published a special issue on this topic in 2001 (J. Jenkins, 2001), and tourism policy studies now appear in dedicated specialist journals (*International Journal for Tourism Policy* from 2007, *Journal of Policy Research in Tourism, Leisure and Events* from 2009) as well as in general tourism journals. Alongside these, recent books have included *Tourism Planning and Policy* (2007) by Dianne Dredge and John Jenkins, and *Tourism Policy and Planning: Yesterday, Today and Tomorrow* (2008) by David Edgell, both with strongly Western orientations. This book adds to this literature by providing a comprehensive account of tourism policy-making during a major period of change and development in a country which has now become a major player in world tourism. In doing so it provides perspective and understanding about how the development of tourism has occurred.

Taking tourism development and policy in China as its key theme, this book explores the experience of China since 1949, and more specifically since 1978, seeking to identify and explain the factors that have shaped China's national tourism policy-making. It sets tourism development within the wider debates about the respective roles of government policy and the market. Above all it seeks to explore and explain how tourism policy-making has changed and developed as national policy has changed and considers the major influencing factors, structures, institutions and players in this process. The book uses a large amount of primary data from key informant interviews as well as open, but not-yet-published (i.e. in the international literature), government documents. The data analysis uses a specifically designed conceptual framework. Overall, the book attempts to contextualize tourism development in China post 1949 from a national policy-making perspective. It focuses particularly on the period from 1978 when tourism shifted from being a political vehicle to its role as an economic activity.

The work is divided into five historical periods which fall within the time frame of three national development models. These are set out in Table 1.1.

As far as territorial coverage is concerned, the focus is on Mainland China, and the theoretical framework and original research findings specifically relate to Mainland China. Included in this is Tibet but given its distinctive characteristics and the worldwide attention that it has received, the experience of Tibet is also included in a separate chapter. Three other territories closely associated with the developments of Mainland China are also included in this separate chapter. These are the two Special Administrative Regions (SARs) – Hong Kong and Macau as well as the island of Taiwan,[3] all of which have significantly different backgrounds and experiences from the Mainland. These are not the primary concern of the book but are included for completeness.

Conceptual background

> Most of the attention of tourism research is devoted to the practical business and marketing of tourism and its economic costs and benefits. Only a few studies pay serious attention to tourism's political dimensions.
> (Belsky, 2004: p.274)

Table 1.1 The five historical periods of national policy-making and tourism
development (1949–present)

The main eras	National development models	Historical periods
Mao Zedong (1949–78[a])	Revolutionary and enthusiastic socialism	Period One 1949–78: tourism as a political–diplomatic vehicle
Deng Xiaoping (1978–97[b])	Evolutionary and pragmatic socialism	Period Two 1978–85: transition of tourism to an economic activity
		Period Three 1986–91: development of tourism as an economic industry
		Period Four 1992–7: development of tourism as an important industry
Collective Leadership (from 1997)	'Public and Harmonious Socialism'	Period Five 1997–present: development of tourism as a multifunctional strategic industry

Notes:
a Mao Zedong died in 1976. 1976 to 1978 was a transitional period leading to China's reform, when the political radicalism of the Cultural Revolution still dominated but eventually declined.
b Deng Xiaoping died in February 1997.

The political dimensions of tourism

There are many conceptions and definitions of politics, in most cases linking it with power, authority, public life, government, state, conflict and conflict resolution. But at its most simple, politics refers to the activities and institutions responsible for public decisions for society as whole (Caporaso and Levine, 2003: p.20). Whatever the conception, tourism as an activity has an important relationship with politics. According to the United Nations World Tourism Organization (UNWTO) (2006a, 2009 and 2010a), international tourism is the largest export earner and an important factor in the wealth of most nations. In many countries it is seen as a major industry and is often ranked as the fastest-growing economic sector in terms of foreign exchange earnings and employment. For these reasons alone tourism should be a hot political issue (Richter, 1983a). As Crick (1989: p.320) suggests, 'international tourism is political, since the state must be involved in foreign relations, the expenditure of large quantities of capital, and large scale planning'. Nevertheless, the political dimensions of tourism are under-explored and not well understood, this despite reminders by scholars since the mid-1970s about deficiencies in the studies of tourism politics. As early as 1975, H.G. Matthews (1975: p.195) wrote 'the literature of tourism is grossly lacking of political research'. Richter

(1989: p.2) remarked that tourism politics 'have been only rarely perceived and almost nowhere fully understood'. Later, in 1994, C.M. Hall (1994: p.1) confirmed Matthews' comments observing that 'today, the same comment still holds true'. He further argued that the mainstream of tourism studies had neglected the political dimensions of the resource allocation for tourism, the making of tourism policy, and the politics of tourism (1994: p.2). Veal (1997: p.27) endorsed these sentiments: 'despite the importance of public policy matters in leisure and tourism, the political dimension of the subject was neglected for many years'. More than ten years later these criticisms still remain valid and notwithstanding a growing number of case studies (e.g. Richins and Pearce, 2000; J. Henderson, 2003; Cooper and Flehr, 2006), the political dimensions of tourism remain under-explored. Belsky (2004: p.274) observes that practical business, marketing and economic impacts still predominate in the body of literature, with relatively few studies that 'pay serious attention' to this area.

Zeigler (1980: p.11) recognized that 'politics is not attractive, even as a spectator sport, to the majority of people. Organized group politics is even less attractive.' It appears there is an apparent resistance to linking tourism that usually represents pleasure, leisure and recreation, with the serious topic of 'politics' that involves conflicting values and interests as well as authority and power. Fortunately, this resistance has not diluted the efforts of a few political scientists and tourism scholars nor has it impeded their inquiries into the political analysis of tourism. Since the first discussion of tourism politics by Matthews in 1975 (cited in Richter, 1989), a few significant studies have been published, including but not limited to those of Richter (1989), H.G. Matthews and Richter (1991), C.M. Hall (1994), C.M. Hall and Jenkins (1995), Elliot (1997), Wilkinson (1997) and Dieke (2000a). The ultimate momentum of these studies rests simply with the indisputable fact underlined by Richter (1989: p.2) that tourism is 'a highly political phenomenon'.

Edgell (1990) suggested that tourism is not only a continuation of politics, but also an integral part of the world's political economy with many facets, including international diplomacy and foreign policy. A few examples amply demonstrate these many facets. The admission of tourists and their travel within a country are political actions that reflect diplomatic relations between states (Edgell, 1978). The encouragement of travel flows between countries provides evidence of favourable bilateral relationships and vice versa. As an illustration of this C.M. Hall (1994) notes that the prohibition of direct travel to Cuba and the Soviet Union by Americans from the early 1960s reflected America's poor relationships with these two countries. Tourism is also used to consolidate the status of a ruling ideology. During the cold war, the encouragement of travel between the socialist regimes of the former Soviet Union, and the states of Eastern Europe, Vietnam, Cuba and China was a deliberate political action to strengthen communist solidarity (C.M. Hall, 1994). At possibly a more fundamental and widespread level, the recognition by the state of tourism as a catalyst for national development, particularly economic development, reflects a salient political attribute of tourism. During the time that it has been a fast-growing sector, governments in both developed and developing nations have sought to ensure that their economies benefited from tourism (Elliot, 1997). As Harrison (1992) has observed, governments in developing countries are keen to promote economic growth, and international tourism is one means to this end.

Tourism as a 'highly political phenomenon' is forged by public policies (C.M. Hall and Jenkins, 1995: p.5) since it has such a widespread involvement in the activities that are of direct interest to governments. C.M. Hall and Jenkins (1995: p.1) indeed suggest that 'tourism has become an integral part of the machinery of many modern governments'. Tourism politics and public policy-making for tourism are thus inextricably linked, and even 'policies determine politics' (Lowi, 1972: p.299). Tourism is characterized by the involvement of a variety of government agencies as well as private and social organizations. So, tourism policy-making is typically a political process involving bargaining, negotiation and coordination. However, Richter (1989) suggests that tourism policy does not fit the stereotype of policy, described as something one must make decisions about. Rather, based on a case study of the Philippines she argues that tourism policy is a 'chosen policy' (p.14). She further observes (1989: p.2) that 'frequently, the politics of tourism are not played according to "the rules"'.

The significance of tourism policy in the development of tourism

> ... the ideological question no longer is whether or not government should be involved in tourism; the question becomes one of 'who benefits from government policy affecting tourism'
>
> (H.G. Matthews and Richter: 1991: p.124)

Tourism has become a significant driver for the development in both developed and developing countries. But whether tourism succeeds or fails is largely a function of political and administrative actions and is certainly not just a function of economic or business enterprise (Richter, 1989: p.11). C.L. Jenkins and Lickorish (1997: pp.186–7) suggest that 'whatever the political system or the changing policies towards market orientation, the state's role is indispensable for successful tourism development'. Harrison (2001b: p.23) also argues that among the major factors in nurturing international tourism, 'one of the most crucial is the state'. This is because there is no industry like tourism that is so wide-ranging and links to so many different industries (Edgell, 1990; D.G. Pearce, 1992; C.M. Hall and Jenkins, 1995; Elliot, 1997). It is only the government that holds the authoritative power to control, plan and guide the growth and development of tourism; and it is largely via governments that international investments, loans and aid for tourism can be agreed and channelled (Mowforth and Munt, 1998). Therefore 'in order to plan for and provide rational order to such a diverse and dynamic industry, it is necessary to develop policies to assist the decision makers in this complex industry' (Edgell, 1990: p.7). Dieke (1993a: pp.280–1) credited one reason for the successful development of tourism in the Gambia during the 1990s to the government's sensible and sound tourism policies for investment that obtained the goodwill of the international lending institutions. Clancy (1999: p.11) also recognizes that the state action of the Mexican government was crucial in the push for tourism during the early years of development. In fact, tourism policy has become increasingly important in driving tourism development. Its position in economic policy has moved from the shadows to centre-stage (Williams and Shaw, 1988). It has been gradually understood that despite governments' role in establishing the broad political and socio-economic framework within which tourism operates, it is also extremely difficult for tourism to develop towards a desirable state without tourism policy (C.M. Hall, 1994). As tourism policy is so important to the tourism industry, many researchers such as Richter (1989), C.M. Hall and Jenkins (1995) and Wilkinson (1997) have called for more studies of the tourism policy-making process. C.M. Hall and Jenkins (1995: p.1) made the point directly: 'tourism has an urgent need for public policy studies'. Although there are a growing number of studies about public policy and state intervention in tourism (e.g. Bramwell and Sharman, 1999; Richins and Pearce, 2000; J. Henderson, 2003; Cooper and Flehr, 2006; Dredge, 2006; Pforr, 2006; Bramwell and Meyer, 2007; Stevenson *et al.*, 2008), most of these are case studies at national or local levels. While recognizing that 'studies of tourism policy-making are moving forward conceptually, theoretically and practically' (p.75), J. Jenkins (2001) also acknowledges that 'tourism policy is an important, yet relatively understudied dimension of tourism research in comparison to such dimensions as tourist decision-making, tourism technology and tourism marketing' (p.69). The possible reason, according to Kerr (2003: xvii), is that 'the majority of tourism policy research is underdeveloped in terms of frameworks, approaches, and theories, to illustrate tourism policy accurately', resulting in an inadequate understanding of the tourism policy-making process (C.M. Hall and Jenkins, 1995). Notably tourism policy studies have borrowed their analytical frameworks (e.g. public choice theory, inter-organizational network, issues network, etc.) particularly from political science and public policy disciplines (e.g. J. Jenkins, 2001: p.72 and 76). Of course, the development of policy-making frameworks specific to the tourism does not deny the value of models from other relevant disciplines; indeed they may be mutually supportive. But there are some important differences. One of these, noted by Richter, is that:

> Tourism is a chosen policy. It is not a policy forced upon a reluctant regime by political pressures like agrarian reform, language policy, or some industrial policies. This may be one of the reasons that tourism policy has been neglected by students of the policy process.
>
> (Richter, 1989: p.14)

The theoretical dimensions of tourism policy-making

C.M. Hall (1994) and C.M. Hall and Jenkins (1995) divided models for studying tourism policy-making into prescriptive and descriptive. The prescriptive model advocates how policy should be made relative to pre-established standards, whereas the descriptive model examines the policy-making process in the real world. Although policy advocacy is important, policy cannot be prescribed or advocated without an understanding of how policy is actually formulated and implemented; the description of the policy-making process needs both prescription and advocacy (C.M. Hall and Jenkins, 1995). Kerr (2003: p.xvii) concurs that the ideals of tourism policy-making 'cannot be realized without an understanding of what actually happens in the formulation and implementation of tourism policy'.

One of the fastest-growing areas of political science is public policy research (Richter, 1989: p.13). Within this, the public policy-making process is a key area focusing on the various factors that affect policy formulation and implementation, as well as the subsequent effects of policy in the real world (e.g. Simmons *et al.*, 1974; Simeon, 1976; Sabatier, 1991; Jenkins-Smith and Sabatier, 1993a, 1993b; Howlett and Ramesh, 1995, 2003; Sabatier, 1999b; Sabatier and Jenkins-Smith, 1999; Sabatier, 2007b; Sabatier and Weible, 2007; Howlett *et al.*, 2009). Simeon (1976: p.555) suggests that 'rather than searching for a very high level of abstraction and one or two "crucial" variables, our conception should allow us to group and make sense out of a wide variety of determinants of policy'. Atkinson and Chandler (1983) also indicate that one of four broad strategies for policy analysis is the study of the determinants of policy-making, that is, to examine how political, social and economic forces shape policy decisions which emerge as successive political bargains are struck by the various participants. This assertion holds true for the present study. Howlett and Ramesh set this out as follows:

> Over the past five decades scholars and analysts working towards the elaboration of a policy science have addressed a series of interrelated questions about the policy process . . . their findings have been remarkably similar and . . . have collectively identified a common focus and set of variables that play a significant role in policy-making processes.
>
> (Howlett and Ramesh, 2003: p.15)

The factors that influence the policy-making process range from broad political and socio-economic conditions to existing institutions and to the values and interests of policy actors (e.g. Simeon, 1976; P. Hall, 1986; Sabatier, 1991; Lindblom and Woodhouse, 1993; Howlett and Ramesh, 1995, 2003; Sabatier, 1999b, 2007b; Howlett *et al.*, 2009). Simeon (1976) views policy as the consequence of the environment, distribution of power, prevailing ideas, institutional frameworks and the process of decision-making. Lindblom and Woodhouse suggest:

We pay at least equal attention to broader influences on policy-making. These include humans' limited capacities for inquiry into complex problems, the frequent conflict between reasoned judgment and the exercise of political power, the central role of business in policy-making, and socio-economic and political inequality.

(Lindblom and Woodhouse, 1993: pp.4–5)

Policy-making for tourism is no exception to this. According to a number of studies (e.g. Airey, 1983; Elliot, 1983, 1987, 1997; Smyth, 1986; Edgell, 1990; Williams and Shaw, 1991; C.M. Hall and Jenkins, 1995; Wilkinson, 1997; Desforges, 2000; Chambers and Airey, 2001), tourism policy-making is also influenced by numerous factors, including but not limited to the political and socio-economic environment, ideology, national policy. For example, C.M. Hall and Jenkins (1995: p.5) summarize that 'policy-making involves the economic, physical and social/political environments in a process of action and reaction over time'. Hall's work, 'Elements in the Tourism Policy-Making Process' (C.M. Hall, 1994: p.50) is assumed to be the first conceptual model to contemplate the forces shaping policy-making in tourism. For this model tourism policy is determined by interaction and competition among policy actors (e.g. institutions, significant individuals and institutional leadership); such interactions and competition are set within the institutional arrangements, values and power arrangements that are seen as the three key explanatory factors (C.M. Hall, 1994; C.M. Hall and Jenkins, 1995; C.M. Hall *et al.*, 1997). Based on these works it is clear that a conceptualization of the factors affecting the tourism policy-making process requires an integrative approach.

Commenting on various factors affecting public policy-making, Simeon (1976: p.566) observes that none alone provides a full understanding; they are more usefully seen as complementary, each making some contribution, with policy emerging from multiple causes. He further emphasizes that the environment can only explain the range of problems or issues that public policies should deal with; it is unable to explain how the problems or issues are perceived. He suggests linking the factors to each other, trying to delineate both their interrelationships and their independent contributions (1976: p.556). The funnel-of-causality model (King 1973; Hofferbert, 1974; Simeon, 1976; Howlett and Ramesh, 1995, 2003; Howlett *et al.*, 2009) advocates that the factors affecting policy-making are intertwined in a 'nested' pattern of mutual interaction in which institutions exist within prevailing sets of ideas and ideologies, ideologies within relations of power, and relations of power within a larger social and material environment. Howlett and Ramesh (1995: pp.111–12; 2003: p.132; Howlett *et al.*, 2009: p.99) go on to suggest that the funnel-of-causality model in fact explains very little as to how these factors actually function in shaping policy-making. They point to its greatest weakness lying in the absence of exact relationships or causal significance. In the tourism context, the interrelationships of factors in shaping policy have not been well explored, either theoretically or empirically. Some previous studies show that tourism policy arises from multiple factors but they do not reveal how these factors interrelate in forming policy. Specific relationships or causalities have not been fully probed. For instance, Desforges (2000) identifies that socio-economic conditions, prevailing ideas, national policy and political institutions contributed to the shift of Peru's tourism policy between 1963 and 1990.

It is the interrelationship of factors affecting tourism policy-making that warrant an in-depth investigation, based on the assumption that any single factor alone cannot shape policy. What is needed is an examination of the inherent processes and underlying causalities, rather than isolating any individual factors or simply describing the various steps (J. Jenkins, 2001: p.71) in the policy process. The interrelationships between the various dimensions of tourism policy-making can help explain the complexities and provide insights. This study focuses on these interrelationships in the context of China. In doing so it uses the concept of the 'idea' (Simeon, 1976; Brooks and Gagnon, 1994; Howlett and Ramesh, 1995, 2003; Howlett *et al.*, 2009; Busch and Braun, 1999; Kerr, 2003) as a starting point. Busch and Braun offer a heuristic introduction to this:

> If we want to understand why social actors act the way they do, their perceptions of the situation they find themselves in, their 'ideas' about their environment have to be taken into account. These perceptions, the subjective reality, so to speak, will differ from objective reality.
>
> (Busch and Braun, 1999: p.1)

The role of ideational factors is at the heart of this. The term 'ideational' (Howlett and Ramesh, 1995: p.109; John, 1998: p.144; Braun, 1999: p.11; Busch and Braun, 1999: p.4; Howlett and Ramesh, 2003: p.127; Howlett *et al.*, 2009: p.51 and 96; Kerr, 2003) here refers to the domain of 'ideas' affecting public policy-making. The constructs within this include, but are not limited to, 'ideology', 'policy paradigm', 'worldview', 'belief', 'value' and 'tradition'. In short, the 'ideational dimension' means the subjective perspective. As Busch and Braun (1999: p.1) comment, 'like any other human action, public policy is only possible within a cognitive framework that relates the goals to be achieved to the available means and other data relevant for a particular decision'. Studying British macroeconomic policy-making, P. Hall (1990, 1993) conceptualized the role of 'idea' in policy-making into a construct 'policy paradigm'. According to P. Hall (1990: p.59; 1993: p.279), the policy paradigm generally refers to an overarching framework of ideas and standards that specify 'not only the goals of policy and the kind of instruments that can be used to attain them, but also the very nature of the problems they are meant to be addressing' which 'policymakers customarily work within'. The policy paradigm is considered by him 'influential precisely' because it is 'unamenable to scrutiny as a whole'. P. Hall (1990: p.59) further suggests that 'it seems likely that policy-makers in all fields are guided by some such paradigm, even though the complexity and coherence of the paradigm may vary considerably across fields'.

P. Hall has perhaps done the most to develop and apply the concept of the policy paradigm (Howlett and Ramesh, 1995: p.190). Since his initial work it has been widely applied and provides 'significant implications' for the research agenda (Menahem, 1998: p.283). On the other hand, as far as tourism is concerned, the ideational dimension has rarely been examined and the applicability of the policy paradigm has been little explored. In short, the momentum in tourism to develop an ideational-based interrelationships framework of the factors affecting policy-making has arisen from the need for further work on existing theoretical frameworks within the tourism policy literature. These include the incorporation, integration and organization of more factors together in explaining the tourism policy-making process as well as exploration of the interrelationships of these factors in driving the policy process. In this, the policy paradigm acts as the focal point. This provides the basis for the theoretical framework for the book.

Methodological design

Using this theoretical framework the study draws upon a range of different sources. As with many studies in political science the primary material is based on qualitative methodology (Miles and Huberman, 1994: p.1). Indeed, many key variables in politics and policy-making, such as ideologies, power, institutions and structure, do not easily lend themselves to quantitative measurement (Belsky, 2004: p.276). As far as data collection methods are concerned, as Snape and Spencer (2003: p.1) suggest, there is no single, universally accepted way of doing qualitative research. Indeed Dezin and Lincoln (1998d: p.3) view qualitative research as a *bricolage* and the qualitative researcher as *bricoleur*; as they say, the 'qualitative researcher-as-bricoleur uses the tools of his or her methodological trade, deploying whatever strategies, methods or empirical materials' they need. The method of inquiry uses Denzin's (1978) 'triangulation' as its strategy. This simply means taking multiple lines of sight (Berg, 2004: p.5), with multiple data collection and analytical methods to maintain integrity (Ritchie, 2003: p.43).

The inquiry of China's national tourism policy-making in fact demanded two main categories of data. The first is the experience and expertise of the political and professional participants in China's policy-making process with tourism. This information was acquired through in-depth interviews with key informants (Marshall and Rossman, 2006). The second are the records of evidence (Wolff, 2004: p.284) about the events, decisions, courses and discourses in the Chinese national tourism policy-making process, which are gathered in the collection of government and official documents (McCulloch, 2004: p.56; Marshall and Rossman, 2006: p.107). The integration of in-depth interviews and documentary studies are commonly utilized both in China studies (e.g. Lieberthal and Oksenberg, 1988; Shirk, 1993) and in tourism policy research (e.g. Clancy, 1999; Chambers and Airey, 2001; Mitchell and Eagles, 2001). This combination seeks to ensure that the weakness of one method can be compensated by the strength of another. The data collection was mainly undertaken between 2002 and 2010. The key informants included senior officials responsible for tourism in the ministerial government agencies, policy consultants within the ministry-equivalent research institution (i.e. the think tank), and experienced industry practitioners. The government officials and policy consultants had had substantial involvement, at a fairly senior level, in national tourism policy-making activities, in decision-making, coordination, administration and advisory capacities over as many as two decades; the industry practitioners had had either an involvement in or a solid understanding of the policy process over a similar length of time. Although China has undoubtedly demonstrated greater openness, investigations about policy-making may still be considered sensitive and for this reason, following the standard international practice in the social sciences (Veal, 1997; Berg, 2004: p.43) and also in common with other similar studies (Lieberthal and Oksenberg, 1988: p.xi; Shirk, 1993: p.20), interviewees are not identified by name. A large number of government documents were also used as well as other official sources and archives, covering policy papers, official speeches, notices, minutes, chronologies and institutional journals. Most of this information has not before appeared in international literature. These sources as well as the scholarly literature are listed in the Bibliography and Sources.

Guided by the conceptual framework, the data were analysed using a set of research procedures (Miles and Huberman, 1994; Strauss and Corbin, 1998a) under the broad approach of interpretivism (e.g. Miles and Huberman, 1994; Denzin, 1998; Patton, 2002; Berg, 2004; Bude, 2004), grounded theory (e.g. Johns and Lee-Ross, 1998; Strauss and Corbin, 1998b; Spencer *et al.*, 2003) and historical analysis (e.g. Berg, 2004; Marshall and Rossman 2006; Towner 1988). The book basically takes an integrative interpretation approach to present the data from the interviews and government documents. This is described by Denzin (1998: p.317) and Marshall and Rossman (2006: p.161) as 'story telling' to facilitate non-specialist access. It aims to bring meaning and coherence to the themes, patterns and categories, establishing a connection and a storyline that make sense of the qualitative information (Marshall and Rossman, 2006: p.161). The findings presented draw from the interviews and government documents, using the broader literature where appropriate. Quotations from interviewees and documentary sources are provided to support particular points but following Rubin and Rubin (1995, 2005) and Kvale (1996) these are used sparingly considering that overuse can easily detract from the clarity of the main commentary (White *et al.*, 2003, p.290).

Theoretical and practical implications

As already noted, policy-making for tourism in China has not been widely studied. This book is one of the first to provide a substantial original inquiry offering an interpretation of tourism development in China from the national policy-making perspective. This provides both theoretical and practical implications and in particular it contributes to an understanding of tourism development from the perspective of the key drivers, namely: politics and policy-making.

Political economy in relation to tourism covers a very broad field. Bianchi (2002) has suggested that there is a lack of substantial outputs although there are important exceptions including, for example, the works of Britton (1982), C.L. Jenkins and Henry (1982), Lea (1988), Wilkinson (1997), Mowforth and Munt (1998), Dieke (2000a), Bianchi himself (2002) and Mosedale (2010). At its heart lies the conception put forth by Caporaso and Levine (2003) which they describe as the state administration in economic affairs (p.1). Using the works of J. Broham (1996) and Clancy (1999) it is this that provides a real focus for an examination of the tourism political economy – the respective roles of state and market in the development of tourism, deriving from general theories (e.g. Evans, 1995; Hong, 1997; B.S. Clark, 1991, 1998). This theme has provided the basis for an ongoing debate both in the general discipline and in tourism. Modernization and neo-liberalism suggest that government intervention in tourism should be low, and limited to maintaining the legal framework and the provision of public infrastructures. By contrast others argue that the development of tourism cannot succeed without a government which specifically favours and boosts its development. The current economic crisis adds a particular poignancy to this long-standing debate. In addressing these issues in the context of China, and its Socialist Market Economy Model, and exploring the development of tourism in China against this background this book provides an understanding of the development of tourism in this important part of the world as well as putting the development of tourism in a wider political and economic context.

As far as practical contributions are concerned, further globalization and the further development of China as a leading tourism destination and generator of tourists will bring further interest in China by outsiders, including international investors. Faced with its socialist regime and a deeply rooted traditional culture, foreign investors have a real concern about accessing formal and informal information, about whether they will be treated the same as indigenous enterprise, and about whether they can effectively engage with the Chinese-styled government-business-social networks (Chinese 'Guanxi'[4]). They want to know 'who is who', 'who does what and how' and 'who to deal with' in China's political economy. Armed with this knowledge, foreign businessmen and practitioners are able to operate. The genesis of Lieberthal and Oksenberg's *Policy-Making in China: Leaders, Structure and Processes* (1988) in fact arose from 'a deeper understanding' of China's energy policy-making requested by the US Department of Commerce to help US firms work effectively in China's energy sector (p.xi). As C.M. Hall and Jenkins (1995) suggest, although policy advocacy is important, policy cannot be prescribed nor advocated without an understanding of how policy is actually formulated. This book goes some way to providing this information for tourism.

Organization of the book

The eleven chapters of the book are organized into four parts: Part I deals with the theoretical and contextual background; Part II, the major part of the work, considers tourism development and national policy-making in China from 1949 to the present; Part III looks at tourism policy issues in four particular regions; Part IV concludes the book with a consideration of the theoretical and practical implications. Within these four parts the two introductory chapters provide a background perspective to national policy-making and tourism development in China; they also introduce the book's aims, conceptual and methodological considerations and theoretical and practical implications with Chapter 3 setting out the theoretical framework for the study. Chapter 4 starts the second part by considering China's national development models since 1949 with particular attention being paid to the transition from the planned economy to the market economy. The information in this chapter is from both primary data and existing literature. Though this chapter is about China in general, its interpretations are particularly relevant in understanding national policy-making in tourism. Chapter 5 reviews tourism politics and development in Mao Zedong's era, and explores its links with those in Deng Xiaoping's era. The subsequent chapters in this part all focus on China post 1978. Policy-makers are considered here as a key explanatory variable (e.g. Lindblom, 1980; Lindblom and Woodhouse, 1993; Howlett and Ramesh, 2003). Chapter 6 therefore investigates the key policy players and the associated institutional processes involved in China's tourism development by applying the concepts of 'policy-oriented learning' and 'coordination'. Chapters 7 and 8 examine the historical evolution of China's national policy-making and tourism development over four separate periods (1978–85; 1986–91; 1992–7) and the Collective Leadership era (1997–present). This considers how various factors have interrelated in shaping national tourism policy-making. Chapter 9 in Part III turns to four particular regions to examine tourism policy issues in Hong Kong, Macau, Taiwan (especially in the context of cross-Taiwan Strait relations) and Tibet. The theoretical and practical implications are set out in the final part, with the tenth chapter dealing with the theoretical implications centring on the specific relationships and influences on policy-making in the context of tourism. The final chapter, Chapter 11, reflects on China's tourism development from the perspective of policy-making.

2 Context, history and overview

China is poised to have more impact on the world over the next 20 years than any other country.

(United States National Intelligence Council,
2008: p.vi)

[F]or over twenty-five years, I have been a witness to not only the accelerated growth of the tourism industry worldwide but also to the spectacular development of China's tourism industry. . . . During the past decade, China surpassed all possible forecasts with its high and constant growth in international and domestic tourism activity.

(Dr Harsh Varma, Regional Representative for Asia and the
Pacific, United Nations World Tourism Organization,
cited in Lew et al., 2003: p.xvii)

Introduction

The development of tourism in China has taken place in the context of the country, its history and its politics. This chapter aims to provide this contextual background. It opens with a very brief outline of the country itself and the scale of Chinese tourism. It then turns to an historical background with a review of the way in which travel and tourism have figured in China's long history up to the formation of the People's Republic of China (PR China or PRC) in 1949. Next it considers key tourism developments and policy since 1949, during years of tumultuous change, providing a background for a more detailed examination in Chapter 4 of the changing political environment for tourism since 1949. The chapter concludes with an overview of national policy-making in China and an outline of the country's political and administrative system.

Some key features

With a land area of 9.6 million square kilometers, the People's Republic of China is roughly the same size as the United States of America and the world's third-largest country. With approximately 1.4 billion inhabitants it has by far the biggest population, accounting for roughly one-fifth of the world's people.

Its territory stretches from tropical climates in the south to the sub-arctic in the north and from the mountains and deserts in the west to the fertile plains of the east coast where the majority of the population live, and where the major cities, including the capital Beijing and Shanghai are located. The overwhelming majority (90 per cent) of the Chinese people are of the ethnic Hans group and the official language is Putonghua (Mandarin) but China also contains many other ethnic groups and many other dialects. Apart from the Chinese Mainland, which is the main concern of this book, China has two Special Administrative Regions (SARs) in Hong Kong and Macao, both of which were former colonies of Western countries and formally rejoined China in the 1990s. The island of Taiwan, 120 kilometres off the southeast China coast, has been separated politically from the mainland since 1949. Since the 1990s and especially after 2005, more economic and social integration has taken place between the Mainland and Taiwan (United Kingdom Foreign and Commonwealth Office, 2009a; United States Department of State, 2009; Xinhua Publishing House, 2009).

Politically China is a unitary state and since 1949 it has been ruled by the Communist Party of China (CPC). Apart from the CPC, the major political organs are the National People's Congress which is the highest state body and the only legislative assembly in China. The chief administrative authority, or government, is the State Council. This is chaired by the Premier and includes the heads of each government department and agency. Regionally China is divided into thirty-four province-equivalent regions, which include the two SARs, and below these, other levels of local government include prefectures, counties and districts and townships. The political structure of China is set out later in this chapter.

Economically, China now has the second-largest GNP in the world and is the fastest-growing major economy. Agriculture represents a relatively small proportion of the total economic output of the country, approximately 12 per cent of GDP, with mining, manufacturing and construction accounting for about 50 per cent and services about 40 per cent (United Nations Statistics Division, National Accounts Main Aggregates Database http://unstats.un.org/unsd/snaama/resCountry.asp).

As far as tourism is concerned, Table 2.1 sets out the development of inbound, outbound and domestic tourism since 1995. This points both to the

Table 2.1 China's tourism movements 1995–2009

Year	Inbound tourists (million)	Outbound tourists (million)	Domestic tourists (million)
1995	46.3	4.5	620
2000	83.4	10.5	744
2005	120.2	31.0	1,212
2009	126.4	47.6	1,902

Source: World Tourism Organization (UNWTO), 2001, 2006b, 2007; China National Tourism Administration (CNTA), 1996a–2009a; 2010b.

growth and to the sheer scale of tourism which has come to contribute to about 4 per cent of China's GDP.

Travel and tourism in China before 1949

While tourism as a separately recognized activity only really dates from 1949, this is not to say that it was absent before this date. Indeed, there is evidence of tourism taking place during the earliest stages in China's history. This section traces some of these early developments and briefly examines the world in which they were taking place as a background to considering the more recent experience.

China's five-thousand-year history can be divided into a number of different periods: 'ancient' (around 2500 BC–AD 1840[1]); 'modern'[2] (1840[3]–1911); and 'contemporary' (1911[4] to present) (Jian[5] *et al.*, 1981). As a further division, the ancient period includes the 'antique era' (about 2500 BC–221 BC) which was characterized by a decentralized system in which sovereigns ruled over various vassal states, and the 'imperial era' (221 BC[6]–AD 1911)[7] which featured a highly centralized monarchy. The latter part of this period (1840–1911) overlaps with the modern period during which China was increasingly subject to foreign influence. These classifications provide a broad background to this brief historical review of China's travel and tourism. For ease of reference the dynasties and periods are set out in Table 2.2.

Imperial China up to 1662

Tourist activities in China can be traced back to the antique and imperial eras. The Chinese character 'tour' ('*you*' in Chinese Romanization '*Pinyin*') emerged in the oracle bone scripts ('*Jiaguwen*') in the Shang Dynasty (about seventeenth to eleventh century BC) (Peng, 2006). As an agrarian nation, travel was not seen as an economic sector but rather was linked to political and social activities. Despite this, travel played an important part in, and contributed to, China's ancient civilization. Notable activities included Zhang Qian's overseas missions during the Western Han Dynasty (206 BC–AD 24), the publication of Li Shizhen's (AD 1518–93) *Compendium of Materia Medica* ('*Ben Cao Gang Mu*') and Zheng He's ocean expeditions in the Ming Dynasty (1368–1644). A number of works of the period took their inspiration from travel, such as Sima Qian's first account of China's general history '*Shi Ji*' in the Western Han dynasty, and Li Bai's poems in the Tang Dynasty (618–907). Based on official work (China National Tourism Administration (CNTA), 1993b, 1999b; Han Kehua, 1994) and the literature about communications in China (e.g. J R Chen, 1987; Bai, 1993; Qiu, 1994; Fang, 2008), some six types of travel by the 'state' (i.e. the imperial court) and the people of ancient China can be identified.

Context, history and overview

Table 2.2 China before 1949: dynasties and periods

Dynasty		Period
Xia		About 21st to 17th century BC
Shang		About 17th to 11th century BC
Zhou	Western Zhou	About 11th century to 771 BC
	Eastern Zhou	Spring and Autumn (770–476 BC)
		Warring States (475–221 BC)
Qin		221–207 BC
Han	Western Han	206 BC–AD 24
	Eastern Han	25–220
Three Kingdoms		220–265
Jin	Western Jin	265–316
	Eastern Jin	317–420
Southern and Northern dynasties		420–589
Sui		581–618
Tang		618–907
Five Dynasties and Ten Kingdoms		907–960
Song	Northern Song	960–1127
	Southern Song	1127–1279
Yuan		1271–1368
Ming		1368–1644
Qing		1644–1911
Republic of China (Early Republican)		1911–49

Source: Jian *et al.*, 1981, 2008.

Royal visits

At the state level, many Chinese emperors made royal visits, both formal and informal, for a range of ceremonial and supervisory purposes. Some rulers also took the opportunity to establish contact with locals and pursued sightseeing and recreational activities. Though Emperor Mu of the Western Zhou Dynasty (around eleventh century to 771 BC) in the antique era was believed to be the first traveller in the historical record, the formal royal tour started from the first Chinese emperor, Qin Shinhuang (259 BC–210 BC), who unified the divided nation and established the first centralized dynasty, Qin (221 BC–207 BC). During his reign, the Emperor undertook five imperial tours. Emperor Wudi (156 BC–87 BC) in the Western Han Dynasty made more than ten royal tours. On one trip he was reported to have covered over ten thousand miles (Han Kehua, 1994). China's imperial strength culminated in the Tang Dynasty. Emperor Gaozong (AD 628–83), the Empress Consort (later the Empress Regnant) Wu Zetian (AD 624–705) and their grandson Emperor Xuanzong (AD 685–762) all convened ceremonies for the Fengshan Sacrifices at Mount Tai in today's Shandong Province. This was the highest ritual in the imperial order to demonstrate the monarch's orthodoxy and contribution. In the last dynasty, Qing (1644–1911), ruled by the minority Manchu, Emperor Kangxi (1654–1722) and his grandson Emperor Qianlong (1711–99) paid six formal visits to the Eastern regions in their efforts to consolidate national unity and cultivate popularity.

Official travel

Travel at the state level also took the form of duty visits by imperial officials. Imperial China had, from the Qin Dynasty, established a well-structured and relatively advanced bureaucratic system (Lieberthal, 2004: p.5). Imperial officials, such as the secretaries for supervisions (*'yu shi'*) and inspectors for education and examinations (*'xue zheng'*), were frequently sent out by the imperial courts. Even though imperial China thought herself to be the centre of the world, the country increasingly assumed an open stance toward other countries (Ogden, 1995). This was before the reign of Emperor Qianlong, who fully implemented the 'Forbidden Ocean' measure (*'Hai Jin'*) that prohibited the Chinese from foreign links, thus marking the beginning of China's closed-door policy (Jian *et al.*, 1981). Over centuries, imperial officials undertook diplomatic missions overseas. For example, in 139 BC, facing border threats, Zhang Qian (unknown–114 BC) was appointed as envoy by Emperor Wudi of the Western Han Dynasty to visit neighbouring countries to establish military alliances. In two visits, Zhang's routes covered the whole of Central Asia, the beginnings of what was later to be called the 'Silk Route'. Zhang Qian's exploratory journeys stimulated subsequent East–West contact. Another example, a thousand years later, took place in the Ming Dynasty when Zheng He (AD 1371–1433) was sent by the Emperor Yongle (1360–1424) to conduct naval expeditions designed to expand the country's influence. During his seven expeditions (1405–33), Zheng He and his fleet further developed the 'Silk Route of the Sea' (Han Kehua, 1994). Official tours also included incoming visits, especially from China's immediate neighbours. In the Tang Dynasty, Japan sent her emissaries (*'qian tang shi'*) to study Tang's developments. Chang'An ('Perpetual Peace') city (today's Xi'An), as Tang's capital, was one of the largest cities in the world (J.R. Chen, 1987: p.136). In order to facilitate state travel, regional palaces (*'xing gong'*) for royal residences and government guest houses (*'ying bin guai'*) and hostels (*'yi zhan'*) for officials were constructed throughout the country.

Business travel

At the non-state level travel was undertaken for business, scholarly and scientific reasons, religious exchange and recreation. Though China was fundamentally an agricultural society, commerce and trade also began as early as the Shang Dynasty and blossomed from the Song Dynasty (960–1279) onwards. This brought a long history of business travel as well as considerable development in land and water transport. The Chinese character 'business' ('*shang*') originally meant 'the selling of goods by travel' (Han Kehua, 1994). A number of notable business tycoons, such as Fan Li in the Spring and Autumn Period (770–476 BC), Lu Buwei in the Warring States Period (475–221 BC), Shen Wansan in the Yuan Dynasty (AD 1271–1368), and Hu Xueyan and Shen Xuanhuai in the Qing Dynasty frequently led trade missions. Externally, Italian merchant Marco Polo arrived in 1275, during the Yuan Dynasty. Taking the opportunity of serving the imperial court, he visited widely throughout China. After his return home in 1295, he completed *The Travels of Marco Polo* introducing China to the West (J.R. Chen, 1987). Though the 'Silk Route' and the 'Silk Route of the Sea' were explored by imperial officials, their formation and frequent use relied on businessmen. By land, the Chinese monarchs constructed postal roads ('*Yi Dao*') that also facilitated commercial travel and the transport of goods. The so-called plank roads ('*Zhan Dao*') in the mountains were also developed, such as the Hui Road from Anhui to Zhejiang province. By water, the Beijing-Hangzhou Canal, also called the Grand Canal ('*Da Yun He*'), was started during the Sui Dynasty (AD 581–618). When completed, this ran for 2,000 km between Beijing and Hangzhou, the longest canal in the ancient world (Han Kehua, 1994). The development of the Grand Canal greatly contributed to commercial transport and travel in imperial China.

Scholarly and scientific travel

China's ancient scientists and scholars travelled a great deal. Travel provided them with inspiration as well as opportunities for social observations and collecting material. For example, before writing his magnum opus – *The Records of the Grand Historian* ('*Shi Ji*'), Sima Qian (135–87 BC) journeyed throughout the country to gather primary material. His visits included ancient monuments, such as the graves of sages like Yao, Yu and Shun. Li Daoyuan (AD 466–527) in the Northern Wei Dynasty (AD 386–534) was recognized by foreign scholars as one of the greatest geographers of the Middle Ages (AD 476–1453). In his capacity as a local governor, Li travelled throughout China's northern territories using the waterways. Based on his scientific observations, he annotated and compiled the *Commentary on the Waterways* ('*Shui Jing Zhu*'). Similarly the poets and writers of the Tang Dynasty, such as Li Bai (AD 701–62), Du Fu (AD 712–70) and Bai Juyi (AD 772–846) travelled extensively. Li Bai started his travels in Eastern China at the age of 26. This gave him opportunities to meet celebrities and to visit famous attractions that inspired his creative work, including his poems about China's mountains and rivers. Xu Xiake (AD 1587–1641) in the Ming Dynasty was a life-long traveller and geographer. Starting at the age of 20 he spent almost thirty years touring China before writing his geographical, topographical and literary work *The Travel Diaries of Xu Xiake* ('*Xu Xiake Youji*') (Han Kehua, 1994). Another prominent traveller in the Ming Dynasty was Li Shizhen, one of the greatest physicians and pharmacologists (in Chinese herbal medicine) in Chinese history. In order to prepare his work *Compendium of Materia Medica*, Li travelled extensively. In total he spent forty years completing this epic manuscript that is still recognized today. The US Library of Congress and Japan house copies of the original editions printed in 1596 (S.Y. Tan, 2003).

Religious travel

Travel was also an important medium for the spread of religion. Apart from the indigenous faith – Taoism – other faiths were introduced. After the arrival of Buddhism in the Western Han period, Chinese monks went abroad for pilgrimage, study and exchange. In the Eastern Jin Dynasty (AD 317–420), Monk Fa Xian (about AD 337–422) at the age of 60 travelled to Nepal, India and Sri Lanka to acquire Buddhist scriptures from which he wrote his famous manuscript *A Record of the Buddhist Kingdoms* ('*Fouguo Ji*'). This became an important source of information about the customs, history and geography of Central and South Asia. In the Tang Dynasty, another monk, Xuan Zhuang (AD 602–64), made trips to India (then called *Tianzhu* by the Chinese). He stayed for about fifteen years to learn the Buddhist sutras and also visited around 110 smaller or vassal states there (Han Kehua, 1994). On his return to China, he brought back over 600 Buddhism classics. Later, he also wrote his travel book *The Great Tang's Records on the Western Regions* ('*Da Tang Xiyu Ji*'). Western clerics also conducted missionary tours to China. These included Reverend Matteo Ricci (AD 1552–1610) of Italy and Minister Robert Morrison (AD 1782–1834) of Scotland. As a Jesuit missionary, Rev Ricci introduced Western science and technology, such as the chiming clock, the world map and geometry, to Chinese intellectuals and to the imperial court. This opened up the process of Chinese scholars studying Western knowledge. Because Matteo Ricci arrived in Guangdong in 1583 and Beijing in 1601, the year AD 1600 has been regarded by Chinese historians as the beginning of the influence of modern Western civilization (J.R. Chen, 1987; Fang, 2008). Sent by the London Missionary Society, Minister Robert Morrison reached China in 1807. Following the practice of Matteo Ricci, Morrison also spread the latest Western knowledge (e.g. medicine and astronomy) and established voluntary organizations including schools. These forerunners were followed by many other missionaries during the Qing Dynasty.

Festivals and holidays

The last of the six types of travel relate to festivals and holidays. China's long-standing culture has been formed through a blend of Confucianism, Taoism, Buddhism, regional diversities, ethnic distinctions, traditions and folklore as well as elements of Christianity introduced by the Assyrian Church of the East ('*Jingjiao*' in Chinese) in the Tang Dynasty (J.R. Chen, 1987). This diverse blend provided the basis for a range of festivals as well as multiple impacts on the daily lives of the ancient Chinese which found expression in etiquette, customs and in travel. The important events were the Qingming Festival for the worship of ancestors, the Chongyang Festival for mountain climbing, the Moon Festival for family union, the Spring Festival for the lunar New Year, the Buddha's Birthday, the Guanyin Bodhisattva's Birthday and the Temple Fair ('*Miao Hui*') for both Buddhism and Taoism. Travel in connection with these festivals for worship, recreation and family gatherings are reflected in the archives as well as in the prose, poems and travel writing of classical writers such as Han Yu (AD 768–824), Liu Zongyuan (AD 773–819), Fan Zhongyan (AD 989–1052), Ouyang Xiu (AD 1007–72) and Su Shi (AD 1037–1101). For instance, Liu Zongyuan's *Eight Records of Excursions in Yongzhou* ('*Yongzhou Baji*'), Fan Zhongyan's *Commemoration of the Yueyang Tower* ('*Yueyang Lou Ji*'), and Ouyang Xiu's *Regarding the Pavilion of the Old Drunkard* ('*Zuweng Tingj*') describe festival, holiday and leisure travel by the imperial Chinese population.

From empire to republic

The closure of China

Notwithstanding psychological and transport limitations, China before the Qing Dynasty was generally open to the West and to the rest of Asia. China in the Tang Dynasty welcomed foreigners and though the 'Forbidden Ocean' policy (also called the 'Sea Ban'), originated in the Ming Dynasty, at this time it was primarily intended to fight pirates and suppress revolts. The ban was effectively abolished for trade purposes when the unrest was curbed. The imperial courts before the Qing Dynasty had almost never restricted connections with the outside world. This situation was reversed following the establishment of the Qing Dynasty. Qing's 'Forbidden Ocean' policy, resumed from the reign of Emperor Kangxi in 1662, effectively started to close the door of China. It was fully implemented by Emperor Qianlong in 1757, strictly followed by the Emperor Jiaqing (AD 1760–1820), and continued until 1840 (Whiting, 1992: p.249). The reactivation of the policy mainly arose from the 'Chinese Rites Controversy' with the Vatican (T.G. Li, 1998). The Controversy led Emperor Kangxi to have doubts about Western technology and culture which were thought to pose a threat to the rule of the minority Manchu. Emperor Kangxi himself sought to learn Western science and technology from the Catholic missionaries, but prohibited others from doing so (Xi, 2002). Such a closed-door policy, in the views of Qing's rulers, would prevent contact with the West and thereby minimize the risk to governance (Jian *et al.*, 1981; J.R. Chen, 1987; Fang, 2008).

For their part the Western world did not give up their attempts to pursue links with China in trade and diplomacy. Appointed by King George III of England, Lord George Macartney (AD 1737–1806) led the first British diplomatic mission, arriving in Beijing in 1793 in an attempt to establish bilateral relationships and trade ties. Emperor Qianlong refused the trade request in 1793, marking China's full isolation from the outside world, except for Guangzhou where foreign businessmen were permitted to trade through designated Chinese firms (Jian *et al.*, 1981; Lieberthal, 1995). This closure became a fundamental reason for China lagging behind Western countries in modernization and development in the nineteenth century (Whiting, 1992).

The reopening of China

When China reopened its doors this was under the imposed force of the Western powers after the First Opium War in 1840. At this point Western tourism also entered China along with politicians, embassies, businesses, missionaries and scholarships. At the beginning of the 1900s, American Express and Thomas Cook and Sons began their services in China (CNTA, 1993b). In the meantime, the Chinese themselves once more had opportunities to travel overseas, as diplomats, officials, students, merchants and workers. The revolutionaries against the Qing Dynasty also frequently travelled overseas in preparation for uprisings (Han Kehua, 1994). The Qing Dynasty collapsed under external pressure and internal rebellions. The regime was replaced by the Republic of China between 1911 and 1949, which was mainly founded by Dr Sun Yat-San. At this time China again fell into a period of internal conflict between warlords covertly supported by various foreign powers.

In 1927, China entered a short period of peace and stability after the success of the Northern Expeditions ('*Bei Fa*') against the warlords, accomplished through an alliance between the Guomindang (GMD) (the Nationalist Party of China) originally formed in 1894 and the Communist Party of China (CPC) established in 1921. The divided territories seemed to be more unified. It was not until that time that Chinese indigenous tourism had a chance to emerge, albeit briefly. Even though China was soon plunged into civil war between the ruling GMD and the CPC, the conflicts were mainly in rural, mountainous and remote regions (Lieberthal, 2004). Eastern China felt few effects. Hence at this time Cheng Guangfu established China's first travel agency – the China Travel Services in Shanghai in 1927, originally based on a travel department within the Shanghai Commercial Bank (CNTA, 1993b; Han Kehua, 1994). Shanghai of the 1930s could be compared with other international cities like London, Paris and Tokyo. China's hotel sector developed in Shanghai, Beijing and elsewhere. Constructed in 1929 by a British tycoon, the Shanghai Peace Hotel was called 'the number one building in the Far East'. The Shanghai Park Hotel built in the 1930s, was the first 'skyscraper' tower financed by the Chinese and was seen as the most advanced hotel in decades. These two hotels are still operating today and are among the city's historical landmarks. This brief period was brought to a close with the Japanese invasion (1937–45) and the subsequent civil wars between the GMD and the CPC (1946–9) which effectively stopped the newly born tourism.

Implications for policy and development

From this brief account it is clear that tourist activity in ancient and imperial China had political, economic, social and cultural features. But in the context of China's agriculture-based peasant society, travelling and touring did not become an identifiable economic activity although interestingly some economic establishments, such as inns and restaurants, served the needs of travellers. At the state level, royal and official travel was primarily driven by political motives, though some emperors also pursued their leisure via tours. Travel among the civil population generally was for commercial, religious, scholarly and recreational purposes. There were few if any official measures specifically restricting inbound and outbound travel before the Qing Dynasty. However, this was overturned completely in the mid-Qing period when China closed her doors between 1662 and 1840. It was not until the Qing dynasty reluctantly opened its borders that Western tourism businesses began to offer services for their clients. China's native travel services emerged between the late 1920s and late 1930s, but the continuing turmoil, revolts, wars and strong foreign competition throughout the late Qing and early republican eras all made Chinese indigenous tourism unsustainable.

Given its nature and type before 1949 there was no national policy for tourism or any attempts to foster its development. Further, a combination of backwardness, internal conflict as well as external threats meant governments in the early republican period also had little interest in tourism. The development of tourism in its own right appeared only after 1949. Notwithstanding this limited development, the tourism that had taken place before 1949 laid some foundations for tourism development by the 1949 socialist regime, especially in political terms. For example, it was quickly realized that travel could be used to foster international awareness and showcase the country and the new regime as well as help to establish and deal with international contact. Hence after 1949 travel and tourism began to establish a presence for itself in the vision of the new leadership.

Tourism after 1949

Since the founding of the People's Republic of China in 1949 tourism has become an important part of state activities, political life and national development. In summary it experienced a slow start between 1949 and 1966, discouragement and stagnation between 1966 and 1976, and unprecedented development since 1978. However, notwithstanding the ups and downs in its fortunes, the political dimension of tourism has remained fairly constant throughout. In Mao Zedong's era (1949–78), tourism served solely as a political-diplomatic tool operating regardless of any cost or economic rationale. In Deng Xiaoping's era (1978–97), tourism shifted to be an economic industry within which its political role was generally concealed. From the Collective Leadership era (1997 onwards), tourism has emerged as a multifunctional strategic industry with economic, political–ideological, diplomatic and socio-cultural goals. These remarkable changes have all taken place within China's changing national development models and the dynamic international circumstances.

The national development models in China have moved from 'revolutionary and enthusiastic socialism' in Mao's era, through 'evolutionary and pragmatic socialism' in Deng's era, to 'Public and Harmonious Socialism' in the Collective Leadership era headed by Jiang Zemin and then Hu Jintao. The term 'national development model', as used here, specifically refers to a kind of ideological–political–economic–social framework, characterized by 'alteration' and 'evolution', with 'alteration' meaning a fundamental break with the past, such as Deng's entire departure from Mao's model, and 'evolution' signifying succession, adjustment and enrichment. The eras of Deng and the Collective Leadership can therefore be seen as a continuum. The dynamics in world politics run through the cold war, post cold war unilateralism (or unipolarism), the emergence of the potential great powers (India, China and some South American countries), multilateralism (Cheng, 2001; Wu and Lansdowne, 2008) to the financial problems of the first decade of the twenty-first century.

The change in the national development models over this period is dealt with in detail in Chapter 4. The purpose here is to examine the main strands of tourism development and policy that have taken place since 1949.

Mao Zedong's era (1949–78): revolutionary and enthusiastic socialism

After struggling with the Guomindang-led regime for over two decades, the Communist Party of China (CPC) eventually took power on 1 October 1949 when it founded a socialist republic, led by Chairman Mao Zedong (1893–1976). In Mao's era, China adopted his revolutionary and enthusiastic model adhering to 'politics-in-command', 'class struggle' and 'voluntarism' and implemented the centrally planned economy model. Externally, China confronted the containment by the US-led Western world from the early 1950s and the subsequent isolation from the Soviet Union from the mid-1950s. In this context tourism between 1949 and 1978 was used as a tactic of 'civil diplomacy' – i.e. 'tourist diplomacy' to promote China's socialist achievements and to enhance understanding, rapprochement and friendship through receiving international tourists – invited guests and permitted self-financed visitors. For example, through the visit in 1960 of Field Marshal Montgomery (1887–1976) from the United Kingdom, Mao conveyed that his communist China wished to establish friendly relationships with capitalist Western Europe. By arranging, in 1970, for the pro-communist American journalist Edgar Snow (1905–72) to stand on Tiananmen Square with Chairman Mao Zedong and Premier Zhou Enlai (1898–1976) the signal was given that China was ready to welcome the historic visit by President Richard Nixon from the United States (Han Nianlong, 1988). Entry permission granted to self-financed tourists was based entirely on political considerations. Prior to the improved relations with the United States in the early 1970s, tourists, especially from the West, were required to be politically friendly to socialist China. Strict scrutiny was applied to visitors from Western and capitalist nations who needed to provide in their visa applications information such as their political beliefs, party affiliations and religion. Through the government travel agency, the activities of international tourists were under the tight control of the Chinese authorities. The ideological background and the economic emphasis on industry and agriculture meant that domestic travel was basically confined to business and officially organized trips. During the Cultural Revolution (1966–76), tourist activities were viewed as part of the 'bourgeois lifestyle' and denounced (CNTA, 1996b: p.250). In short, throughout Mao's era, tourism meant inbound travel and then not as an independent economic activity but only as a part of China's foreign affairs and ideological politics. From this perspective, there was no tourism development in any real sense.

Since tourism was not considered a separate policy area, there was no tourism policy as such. Its role was primarily as an instrument of diplomacy and fostering recognition of socialist China. In this it only operated on a very limited scale. For example, as of 1978, China only had two travel agencies – China International Travel Services (CITS) and China Travel Services (CTS) and 137 hotels providing a total of 15,500 guest rooms (Han Kehua, 1994: p.291).

Deng Xiaoping's era (1978–97): evolutionary and pragmatic socialism

The Third Plenum of the Eleventh National Congress of the CPC held in 1978 marked the end of Mao's national development model and the beginning of Deng Xiaoping's era. Under Deng's rule, Maoist socialism was replaced by pragmatic and evolutionary socialism that still adhered to communist leadership, but now focused on economic modernization. Deng's model is called 'Socialism with Chinese Characteristics' in China or 'Dengism' in Western discourse. This began China's Economic Reform and Open-door Policy which represents one of the most significant events in the history of the twentieth century (Huang, 1999).

At the outset tourism fell into Deng's strategic consideration with the support of other veteran leaders. First, China should be opened to all travellers regardless of political inclination or religion. Tourism was seen as a window linking China with the world, especially for the inflow of new ideas. Second, tourism was envisaged by Deng as an experimental field for his reform programmes including the introduction of foreign investment. Interestingly, as a legacy of the Mao era, since tourism had never been a part of China's planned economy it was considered to be better suited to such experimentation. It was less hampered by institutional and bureaucratic burdens and also experiments with tourism did not need to conflict with the existing national plan. Third, China had an acute shortage of foreign exchange with which to fund her economic modernization. Tourism was thus considered as a strategic component of China's Economic Reform and Open-door Policy. Deng Xiaoping delivered a total of six speeches between late 1978 and 1979 to encourage the shift of tourism from a purely political tool to an economic activity. As a result, a series of specific policy decisions were implemented by the central government to achieve this, such as the adoption of foreign capital and expertise, decentralization as well as enterprise transformation. This marked the start of China's national tourism policy-making. Tourism was in fact the first sector to incorporate foreign funds and management. China's first three joint ventures were all with tourism corporations. The successful experience in utilizing foreign management in the first joint-venture hotel – Beijing Jianguo Hotel – was later promoted by the State Council for other enterprises.

In Deng's era, the key decision was about the construction of the socialist market-economy model in 1992 to supersede the planned-economy model of the previous forty years. In this, the market mechanism, which hardly existed before 1978, was allowed to play a fundamental function in the allocation of resources under state macro management. Tourism was in fact China's pioneer sector in applying market rationales. This was partly because, as noted, it was considered a safe area for experimentation as it had not been part of the national plan but also because international tourist markets were in any case outside the control of China's central plan. Market practices such as segmentation, positioning and price differentiation all started in the foreign-invested tourism businesses. Under the market economy, tourism, especially domestic tourism, demonstrated enormous growth. Between 1992 and 1996, the number of domestic tourists increased from 330 million to 640 million and associated expenditure rose six-fold from RMB¥25 billion to RMB¥163.8 billion (CNTA, 1993a–1997a).[8]

Externally, the collapse of the USSR in 1991 not only brought US-driven unilateralism, but also altered the balance of world power from the 'US–China–Soviet' strategic triangle (Lieberthal, 1995). In order to mitigate the pressures from the US, China adopted the strategy of maintaining a low profile, rarely challenging the US-led Western world while firmly safeguarding her national interests, by aiming to attract more investment from the developed countries and maintaining a relatively stable environment. Deng's China increasingly came under the expanding influence of Western ideologies, values and practices which triggered calls for westernization. As a primary contact point with the outside world, the Chinese leadership never considered weakening the political role of tourism but rather continued to use it, albeit inconspicuously, to promote the Chinese socialist model. For example television in hotels was utilized to publicize China's socialist achievements. Tour guides were instructed to protect China's interests and dignity when working with foreign tourists (CNTA, 1995b).

During Deng's era, tourism developed from a new economic activity to an important industry contributing to the growth of the Chinese economy. By the end of 1996, China had 4,418 hotels and 4,252 travel agencies, together with other related establishments and infrastructure which served over 51.1 million international tourists and 640 million domestic tourists. With total incomes of RMB¥248.6 billion, tourism accounted for approximately 3.7 per cent of China's GDP in 1996. This made a sharp contrast with 1978 when it only received 1.8 million international tourists and earned foreign exchange of US$262.9 million[9] (CNTA, 1997a; State Statistics Bureau of PR China (SSB), 2008).

The Collective Leadership era (1997–present): 'Public and Harmonious Socialism'

After the death of Deng Xiaoping in February 1997, China entered an era of collective leadership. After three decades of development, China had gained prosperity and had also emerged as one of the world's major powers (United States National Intelligence Council (USNIC), 2008). Internally, the country had undergone tremendous change. In terms of state ideology and governance, the dogmatic doctrines of the past were abandoned to be replaced by a relatively loose ideological framework. As for the political–economic system, China had basically built up a Chinese-style market economy firmly embedded within the state's regulatory and administrative framework. The outcome of the changes have included a rapidly developing economy, the expansion of the private sector and private wealth as well as significant socio-economic issues and problems including multiple social layers, disparities in wealth, regional imbalance, ethical downgrade, environmental degradation, civil rights and inadequate social welfare systems. These circumstances have led to the further shift in China's national model that places greater emphasis on all-round and coordinated development and being more public-based and people-oriented, so-called 'Public and Harmonious Socialism'.

This model provided tourism with a brand-new development mode. It has increasingly been seen as a multifunctional sector not only built on economic and market driven characteristics but also with political–ideological, diplomatic and socio-cultural roles. The key change is that the dominant role of the government in the planned economy, with the emphasis on micro management, has shifted to the role of guiding and regulating market forces, i.e. macro management. At the same time tourism's diplomatic and political–ideological and other wider functions have re-emerged.

As far as market and economic contributions are concerned tourism has continued to expand. In 2008, there were 14,099 hotels and 20,110 travel agencies providing services for 130 million international tourist arrivals, 1.7 billion domestic tourists and 45.8 million outbound tourists. China's domestic and international tourism generated incomes of RMB¥874.9 billion and US$40.8 billion respectively, together amounting in 2008 to RMB¥1.1 trillion,[10] or 3.84 per cent of GDP (a slight decrease from 4.4 per cent in 2007) (CNTA, 2008a; SSB, 2009).[11] With apparent impact from the worldwide economic downturn, tourism incomes in 2009 still totalled RMB¥1.2 trillion or 3.85 per cent of GPD (CNTA, 2009a, 2010b; SSB, 2010). Because of its growing economic significance, in 2008 the Chinese government officially affirmed tourism 'as a key industry in the national economy' (CNTA, 2008b). It is viewed as one of the five 'consumption hotspots' for stimulating weakened consumer demand (Xinhua News Agency (Xinhua), 2008e). Globally, the United Nations World Tourism Organization (UNWTO) (1997) has forecast that China will be the top tourist destination by 2020. In 2009, the country was ranked fourth and fifth for international tourist arrivals and tourism receipts (UNWTO, 2010b). The World Travel and Tourism Council (WTTC) estimated that among 181 countries in 2010, China's tourism economy ranked second in absolute size and 81st in terms of its relative contribution to the national economy, with the fastest rate of growth (WTTC, 2010).

Turning to the other implications of tourism, remarkably, its political-ideological and diplomatic roles have reappeared more strongly since 2000. One example relates to officially-called 'Red Tourism' – promotion of ideological values through tourism. Since 1949 efforts have been made deliberately to preserve the heritage of the communist revolution. With increasing diversity in Chinese society, rising social divisions and increasing Western impact, heritage sites for domestic tourism have become key vehicles to help maintain the legitimacy of the ruling socialist values as well as promoting nationalism and patriotism. At present, the development of state ideology is directed by a Standing Committee Member of the CPC's Politburo, who remarked in 2004 that such 'Red Tourism' belongs to 'political engineering in consolidating the ruling stature of the Communist Party' (Xinhua, 2004a). In contrast with Mao's era, however, when the key political role of tourism was diplomatic-oriented towards the international tourists, 'Red Tourism' focuses on Chinese domestic tourists, especially the younger generations.

In a similar fashion, the diplomatic role of tourism has also been significantly re-established. International tourism is now used as a means to promote the appeal and national image of China (CNTA, 2007b), so as to establish 'soft power'. The concept of 'soft power' originating from Nye (2004), is defined as 'the ability to attract' (p.6) based on the 'attractiveness of a country's culture, political ideals and policies' (p.x). This is in contrast to the 'hard power' of 'military or economic might' (p.5). At the same time, outbound tourism also has an increasing role to play in China's foreign affairs. The Chairman of the China National Tourism Administration (CNTA) acknowledges that the opening of outbound markets is to serve China's diplomatic strategies and international relations (CNTA, 2008c). Expenditure by Chinese outbound travellers brings economic impacts for host countries. For instance, according to the statistics from the Japanese Tourist Office in Shanghai (*Hong Kong Wenweipo Daily* (Wenweipo), 23 August 2009) Chinese tourists are now the highest spending group in Japan (Xinhua, 2009b), with average expenditures of RMB¥14,000. This then becomes linked to the pursuit of national interests through developing foreign relations – from cross-Taiwan Straits relations, the Tibet question or the recognition of China's full market-economy status. For example, it was not until the end of 2009 that the Chinese government opened the outbound market to Canada due to the Dalai Lama's visit there in 2008 and other political considerations (*Hong Kong Wenweipo Daily* (Wenweipo), 19 June 2008a) (Xinhua, 2009c). In the same vein, protests in Paris in June 2008, in connection with the Olympic torch parade, led to boycotts of tourism to France (*Hong Kong Wenweipo Daily* (Wenweipo), 19 June 2008b). In a more positive direction African countries are traditionally friendly and supportive of China. They previously supported the resumption of China's membership of the UN in the early 1970s. Aid to Africa includes not only financial, technical and human resources but also the opening of outbound travel. In return, the African nations provide unwavering support for the 'One-China' stance and other initiatives such as the 2008 Beijing Olympics, the Shanghai World Expo 2010 and the candidate nomination for executive director for the World Heath Organization (WHO) (Xinhua, 2006d, 2006e; CNTA, 2006b). In short, outbound tourism has been incorporated into the agendas of China's bilateral negotiations with foreign governments (CNTA, 2004b).

Domestic and outbound travel, especially holidays, are also seen as a part of the quality of life. Aspects of this are seen in the creation of three one-week-long holidays, the so-called 'Golden Weeks'.[12] The social aspects of tourism have not only been recognized, but also given a rather higher profile on the ideological grounds of 'fulfillment of the continuously increasing needs of people'. This was conveyed by Chinese President Hu Jintao who indicated 'we should enforce more competition in the traditional service industries like trade, commerce, catering and tourism etc. which . . . are closely related to the daily lives of people' (CNTA, 2004b: p.6). This sort of thinking is reflected in the official Xinhua News Agency, which in 2006 promoted the leisure economy and leisure travel through a theme article entitled 'the leisure society is coming to you' (Xinhua, 2006f). Similarly in 2009 the CNTA prepared the 'National Leisure Scheme' intending to boost leisure entitlement (Xinhua, 2009d).

National policy-making and tourism development

Strictly speaking, tourism in Mao's China was not seen as a separate entity or as an industry or economic activity. Its purposes were solely political and diplomatic. So-called 'tourist diplomacy' was embedded in China's ideological politics and foreign affairs and operated regardless of economic rationale. Policy decisions regarding tourism were confined to foreign affairs. Thus in a real sense, there was no genuine tourism or tourism policy-making as such in Mao's era. It was not until 1978 when tourism began to be seen as a distinct economic activity that central policy decisions began to be made specifically to foster and promote its development. From this point on China's national tourism policy-making has served as an overarching umbrella for its development. Given China's socialist political system, unitary state, the long history of the planned economy and the present state-governed market economy it is not surprising that central policy-making has had an overwhelming influence on tourism, notwithstanding the shift to a market orientation. As a socialist nation, China adopts the basic polity of 'Party-Lead-State' and 'State-Dominate-Society' (Lieberthal, 1995, 2004; Saich, 2004). Regardless of the economic boom, social diversification and political loosening, political power in China is ultimately vested in the sole rule of the Communist Party of China (CPC). The CPC determines all the major issues and enforces policy. It not only controls the state organs – legislature, executive, judiciary, military and security apparatuses – but also leads and monitors the satellite political parties, state-owned enterprises, public institutions, social organizations and community units. In brief, society is placed under the state and the state is overseen by the CPC.

China's unitary and centralized policy can be traced back to imperial times (Jian *et al.*, 1981). In many senses socialist China has simply continued this political and administrative legacy. Theoretically, a unitary nation means that the country operates as a single unit. Political power may well be transferred to regional and local governments but ultimately any such devolved governments can be created or abolished and have their powers varied by central government. Under the unitary and centralized state, China's state power originates from and is concentrated at the centre. The centre devolves power to local government in more than thirty administrative regions; these are ultimately responsible to the Chinese central government – the State Council. The Chinese Constitution empowers the State Council to lead and direct local government (National People's Congress (NPC), 2004). The integration of a unitary and socialist system gives decisions on national directions and strategies to the central authority.

China's centrally planned economy has a long history and even though market-orientated institutions have been established, state planning continues in the Socialist Market Economy Model. 'Socialist' is defined here by the CPC as being based on socialist principles such as 'social justice' and 'common prosperity' (CPC, 2007). The 'socialist' structure means that public ownership (state and collective sectors) occupies the predominant position in the national economy through the ownership of vital or strategic industries and significant investment in other major businesses. While private ownership (domestic and foreign) is officially recognized as important it is also directed and monitored by the state (CPC, 1992, 1993 and 1997). The key change after 1992 is that under the state's regulatory and administrative control the market mechanism has taken over from the central master plan as the fundamental implement for resource allocation and socio-economic development. But even so the state and hence public policy remains paramount. As empowered by the state constitution, the Chinese government now engages in the macro management of the national economy, operating and controlling strategic industries as well as regulating prices of designated products and services.

Unlike in the West where government intervention, to a large extent, took place after the creation of market institutions, in China market forces hardly existed between 1949 and 1978. As a result, in contrast with the West the functioning of the market in China is in fact granted by the state and limited on the basis that the state assumes that people can act primarily according to their interests (Lieberthal, 2004). One aspect of this is the way in which the government supervises pricing and seeks to direct market forces. A recent example from tourism is the role of the National Development and Reform Commission (NDRC) and the CNTA in taking regulatory action in the public interest to lower admission fees for popular visitor attractions. At a more fundamental level the state retains ownership of key industries and sectors for China's national and public interest, such as energy, utilities, civil aviation, banking and insurance. Similarly, over 80 per cent of China's industry associations are in fact created by the government. Though assumed to be professionally independent, they are still politically accountable. The Chinese-style market economy therefore operates within restricted market forces overseen by the government. Because of such distinctions from the West, it is interesting to note that there are only about ninety members of the World Trade Organization that recognize China as a market economy; her major trade partners – the US, the European Union and Japan – all hesitate to accept her as a full market economy (*Hong Kong Mingpao Daily* (Mingpao), 30 July 2009). *Newsweek* (America), as an example of Western views, comments 'there is no truly free market in China', as 'the state still exerts a strong and stabilizing hand' (19 January 2009). The market-economy model in China can perhaps be better described as a 'state-centric market economy'. If anything this model may become more widespread given the interventionist response by governments worldwide to the economic and financial crisis (USNIC, 2008: p.8).

To sum up, China's socialist polity, centralized political system and the commanding position of the state in the economy all point to the crucial, pivotal and irreplaceable role played by national policy-making in China's development, including that for tourism. Notwithstanding the shift from 'dominant status' in the planned economy to 'driving status' in the limited market economy, the position of the state remains of key importance. This was, of course, a prerequisite when tourism began to develop as an economic activity in 1978. It was simply impossible for China to follow the experience of capitalist developing countries where the private sector took the lead in investment and operation, such as in Thailand and Malaysia (Elliot, 1983, 1987; Woon, 1989). The development of tourism in China has had to rely on the actions of the state and hence on national policy-making. This is in addition to any policy-making to achieve political, ideological and diplomatic goals.

Political and administrative system in China

The basic political structure in China is the party-state or party-government (Cheng and Law, 1997). The ruling Communist Party of China (CPC) governs the nation. Under this structure, the influence of the CPC is dominant and pervasive, as the CPC leads not only central and local government, but also the National People's Congress (NPC), local people's congresses, satellite political parties, state-owned enterprises and public-social organizations (e.g. welfare, youth and women associations, education institutions). The national leaders of China consist of both the party and state leaders, including the General Secretary of the CPC Central Committee, Members of the Politburo and its Standing Committee, the Chairman and Vice-Chairmen of the Standing Committee of the National People's Congress, State President, Premier, Vice-Premiers, State Councillors, Chairman and Vice-Chairmen of the Chinese People's Political Consultative Conference (CPPCC). The key state positions (e.g. president, premier, vice-premiers) are concurrently held by the party leaders.

The state organs at the centre

This section briefly reviews the structure and function of the state organs at the centre – the Communist Party of China, the National People's Congress and the State Council.

The Communist Party of China – China's sole ruling party

The Communist Party of China (CPC) has governed the country ever since it came to power in 1949. The one-party ruling status of the CPC has been historically shaped and confirmed by the Chinese Constitution (The National People's Congress (NPC), 2004). Thus the status of the CPC is more than a ruling party; it is a state organ. The delegates of the CPC attend the National Party Congress which in theory is the most powerful body in the party, normally convened every five years (Lieberthal, 2004; CPC, 2010d). The most important decisions and resolutions are endorsed and passed in the National Congress. For example, the Party's shift from political struggle to economic modernization and to the open-door policy and economic reform was formally endorsed by the 12th National Party Congress held in 1982. The decision to establish the 'Planned Commodity Economy Model' was confirmed by the 13th Congress held in 1987. The 14th Congress proclaimed the establishment of the 'Socialist Market Economy Model' to replace the planned-economy model (e.g. CPC, 1987, 1992).

The National Congress selects the Central Committee of the CPC, usually referred as the 'Party Centre'. The Central Committee usually meets at least once a year and exercises the authority of National Congress when it is not in session. The leadership of the CPC is vested in the Politburo and its Standing Committee, which are selected by the Central Committee. When the Central Committee is not in session, the Politburo carries out its functions and exercises its authority. Described by Lieberthal (1995, 2004) as the command headquarters, the Politburo and its Standing Committee lie at the core of Chinese politics. Discussion, consensus building and decisions on major issues are carried out through the Politburo. As Huang (1999: p.35) comments, the Politburo 'is actually in charge of making the most important decisions of both the party and the country'. According to the official Xinhua News Agency, the Politburo normally meets monthly.

The most powerful layer of the Politburo is its Standing Committee (Lieberthal, 2004), currently with nine members, who are China's top nine national leaders. Among the Standing Committee members, one is selected by the Central Committee as its General Secretary who convenes the meetings of the Politburo and its Standing Committee and presides over the work of the Secretariat – the executive arm of the Politburo. Ranked first in the Politburo and its Standing Committee, the General Secretary is usually assumed to hold the final decision-making authority, described in Chinese as 'making the final determinations and holding the ultimate responsibilities'. Under current practice, the General Secretary of the CPC concurrently holds the positions of State President and Chairman of the Central Military Commission. The members of the Politburo and its Standing Committee are the leaders of the party; or strictly speaking, they are the institutional leaders. The term 'institutional leaders' here is used to distinguish them from 'pre-eminent leaders', such as Deng Xiaoping, Chen Yun and other party veterans, who gained their political power from their contribution to the communist revolution and the founding of socialist China, and possessed life-long political influence whether or not they occupied an official position (Shirk, 1993). Lieberthal and Oksenberg (1988) describe the core tasks of the pre-eminent leaders as including appointments at the highest levels, the enunciation of ideological principles and the identification of the nation's primary tasks. Since the death of Deng Xiaoping and Chen Yun, it is assumed that the collective leadership of the Politburo and its Standing Committee, as a whole, has replaced the roles of pre-eminent leaders. But under China's long-standing political culture, the retired leaders usually have an irreplaceable influence over their successors.

The National People's Congress – the organ of state power

The Chinese state constitution (NPC, 2004) confirms that the PRC is a socialist and unitary nation. According to the state constitution, the National People's Congress (NPC) – China's parliament – is the highest organ of state power. Subordinate to the ruling CPC, the NPC is mainly responsible for law-making, election and removal of state leaders and in theory overseeing the work of the government (NPC, 2004; Saich, 2004). Any rule or regulation with the title of 'law' must be legislated by the NPC. The State Council and provincial people's congresses can only enact 'ordinances' which have lower legal status than laws. The rules with the lowest legal status are 'provisional methods' or 'administrative methods' issued by the central agencies under their administrative functions (source: interviews). Parallel to the NPC, there is another state-level political assembly called the Chinese People's Political

Consultative Conference (CPPCC). This acted as the highest organ of state power prior to the establishment of the NPC in 1954. Designated by the CPC, the CPPCC still functions as the principal organization for the 'united (political) front' since its members are all prominent figures from satellite political parties, various socio-economic sectors, Hong Kong and Macau, and the overseas Chinese. In addition to its role in political unity, the CPPCC currently acts as the top advisory organ to provide a forum for nation-wide discussion and proposals, and provides the NPC and government with access to different views and expert support in decision-making (Saich, 2004). In recent years both the NPC and the CPPCC have gained a higher profile and become more influential in China's political and public life.

The State Council – the Central Government of China

Executive power in China's political system is vested in the State Council. This is roughly equivalent to the cabinet of Western democracies (Shirk, 1993). The Chinese State Constitution empowers the State Council, i.e. the Central Government, as the highest executive organ of state power and highest administrative organ of the state. The State Council is authorized by the constitution to submit bills to the NPC, to formulate administrative measures in accordance with the law, to exercise overall leadership and direction in state administration and to oversee local government. In theory, the State Council is accountable to the NPC and its Standing Committee. In practice, it is responsible to both the CPC Central Committee (i.e. the Politburo) and the NPC, and it implements decisions made by the CPC and laws enacted by the NPC (Lieberthal, 2004; NPC, 2004; Saich, 2004). In this sense, the Politburo is seen as the 'political cabinet' whereas the State Council is more like an 'executive or administrative cabinet'.

The leadership of the State Council consists of the Premier, Vice-Premiers, State Councillors (equivalent to Vice-Premier) and Secretary-General. Its establishment comprises this leadership plus commissions, ministries, the central bank, the state auditing office, offices of designated affairs, state administrations, non-administrative organizations and the non-permanent coordinating committee for all government agencies. The Premier assumes overall leadership. The central government agencies in the State Council and local government are all responsible and accountable to the State Council. Policy directions, significant decisions and rules made by the central agencies need the approval of the State Council. Normally, each vice-premier or state councillor is assigned a supervision portfolio covering related agencies (State Council, 1997; NPC, 1982, 2004). For example, currently the supervision portfolio of Vice-Premier Wang Qishan covers tourism.

By their role, there are three kinds of government agencies under the State Council – comprehensive or macro-management agencies, sector or functional agencies and non-administrative institutions. The comprehensive or macro-management agencies have policy and administrative responsibilities across the entire economy and society. Since the administrative restructuring in 1998 and 2003, there have been some four to five such agencies, including the National Development and Reform Commission (NDRC), the Ministry of Finance (MoF), the State Ethnic Affairs Commission and the National Population and Family Planning Commission. The sector or functional agencies are responsible for policy-making and administration for a socio-economic sector (e.g. education, agriculture) or functional area (e.g. foreign relations, culture, social security) of state affairs. The restructuring in response to the market economy has brought a significant reduction in the number of economic administration agencies. The newly established (e.g. Ministry of Industry and Information Industry) or long-standing agencies (e.g. Ministry of Railways, Civil Aviation Administration of China) reflect their current significance or role in the administration. In addition to the macro and sector agencies the State Council also has a series of non-administrative organizations directly under its jurisdiction. These are of two types. The first are concerned with public sector management in a designated area, such as bank regulation. The second are the so-called think tanks, responsible for conducting studies and providing advice. These include, for example, The Research Office, The Development Research Centre, The Chinese Academy of Sciences, The Chinese Academy of Social Sciences and The Chinese Academy of Engineering. The Research Office coordinates the preparation of the annual government report submitted to the NPC, while the Development Research Centre also provides policy proposals to government (State Council, 1997; Yu *et al.*, 2005).

In relation to their hierarchical or bureaucratic rank, the agencies under the State Council can be classified into four levels. At the top are the supraministerial agencies responsible for macro or comprehensive management. With the exception of the Ministry of Finance these are referred to as Commissions ('*Weiyuanhui*') (Lieberthal and Oksenberg, 1988). The Commissions enjoy a higher bureaucratic level than the ministries and have monitoring and coordination responsibilities over them, albeit such decisions are not final and the ministries can bring controversial and unresolved issues to the state councillor or vice-premier for judgement. For their part, the ministries also can bargain with the Commissions (Shirk, 1993). Below the comprehensive agencies are the line ministries ('*Bu*'), central bank and national auditing office, which are all at ministry rank. The government agencies at these two bureaucratic levels are cabinet-rank agencies, officially called the 'constituent organizations' *('zucheng bumen')* of the State Council. The establishment, restructuring or removal of these agencies together with the ministerial appointments needs to be approved by the NPC or its Standing Committee. The leadership, commissions, ministries, central bank and national auditing office form the plenary meeting of the State Council to discuss significant issues and take decisions. The third-tier government agencies are the offices responsible for designated affairs, state administrations and nonadministrative institutions. These are all directly under the State Council and their bureaucratic ranks normally range from ministry to vice-ministry grades.

The fourth-tier agencies are the state administrations supervised by the commissions or ministries. The creation, reorganization and abolition of the latter two tiers of agencies are at the sole discretion of the State Council. They are not statutory members of the plenum but they are invited to attend when appropriate (NPC, 1982; Shirk, 1993; Lieberthal, 1995, 2004; State Council, 1997, 2008).

In China, every organization and official in the state sector is assigned a bureaucratic rank. The state sector of China comprises the CPC apparatuses, government agencies, non-administrative institutions, government-sponsored public and social organizations (including universities), state-owned enterprises, residential communities and even the religious parties (e.g. the monks in the temples). The bureaucratic ranks (or levels) consist of leaders (with different grades, such as top-tier leader and second-tier leader), supra-ministry, ministry, vice-ministry, bureau, division and section (the lowest rank), which cover both the centre and the local level. For example, central ministries have the same bureaucratic rank as the provinces – the ministry rank; the minister in the central government is equivalent to the party chief or governor of a province-equivalent region. The rank of bureaus or departments within the ministries is equivalent to the departments of a provincial government, and so on. 'Where you stand is where you sit' is an apparent feature of Chinese bureaucratic politics (Shirk, 1993: p.99). The higher the hierarchical level or bureaucratic rank of a government agency, the higher will be their stature and the more will be their leverage and bargaining power in the policy-making process. Agencies with equal rank and at the same hierarchical level normally possess equal bargaining power (Shirk, 1993; Airey and Chong, 2010), unless they or their leaders have other political resources. For example, a minister rank official can take charge of a vice-ministry agency; this implies additional political, administrative or personal resources held by such an incumbent.

Local state power and governments

China is a unitary state without constitutional separation of political power between centre and provinces. Local political power is delegated from the state. The local administrative structure covers twenty-three provinces (including Taiwan), five ethnic autonomous regions, four municipalities (Beijing, Tianjin, Shanghai and Chongqing) and two special administrative regions (Hong Kong and Macao). These are all at the same bureaucratic rank equivalent to a ministry of central government. Under these province-equivalent administrative regions, there are three levels of political and administrative power – prefectures (commonly called the cities), counties and districts and townships. The most complicated level is the cities, whose bureaucratic rank varies in accordance with their size and importance (Lieberthal, 1995, 2004). Normally, the capital city of a province (e.g. Hangzhou City of Zhejiang Province in Eastern China) is graded at the vice-ministry rank; cities with high strategic and economic importance (e.g. Shenzhen, Xianmen, Dalian) enjoy a higher bureaucratic rank than other cities, which could be same as their capital cities. These cities are officially called 'sub-provincial cities' (*'fu shengji chengshi'*) and hold a higher degree of autonomy in economic and social development, though they are still administratively under the provinces.

Local people's congresses are the organs of state power at the different administrative levels. Those at the provincial level are authorized by the NPC to formulate local regulations or ordinances with a legal status equal to those promulgated by the State Council. The local government, elected by the local people's congresses, are responsible both to the congresses at the same level and to the next higher level of local government, and ultimately to the State Council (NPC, 2004). For example, Shenzhen is a sub-provincial city under the jurisdiction of Guangdong Province. Shenzhen People's Government is responsible both to the Shenzhen People's Congress and the Guangdong Provincial Government. In turn, Guangdong Provincial Government is responsible to the Guangdong Provincial People's Congress and to the State Council – the ultimate source of China's executive and administrative authority.

In fact, the centre and local authorities are in a matrix of supervisory and reporting lines. Local government departments follow the rules and receive instructions from the respective central government agencies but are responsible and accountable to their local government. Local government is then in theory responsible to the local people's congress where they are elected; but they are also accountable to the next highest level of local government (e.g. provincial governments) since the state power is delegated from central government. More importantly, all local government and local people's congresses are ultimately responsible to the local party committees which report to the higher level party committees. The local party secretary (i.e. local party chief) is the first-in-charge in a region, while its executive head (e.g. governor or mayor) normally appointed as the deputy party secretary is the second-in-charge. The provincial party committees, the highest local party organization, report to the party centre (i.e. the CPC's central committee). In fact, the provincial party secretaries are usually a member of the CPC's central committee; the party secretaries of four municipalities and some important regions such as Guangdong are concurrently appointed as the members of the Politburo (i.e. at the party leader level). Under such complex central-local relationships, neither the provincial leaders (party secretaries) nor the central ministers (concurrently serving as the head of party group in their ministries) have the final say on key or controversial issues. These issues are ultimately brought to the apex of China's political power – the Politburo and its Standing Committee of the CPC (Holbig, 2004; Lieberthal, 2004).

3   The conceptual framework

> Policy analysis is one activity for which there can be no fixed program, for policy analysis is synonymous with creativity, which may be stimulated by theory and sharpened by practice, which can be learned but not taught.
>
> (Wildavsky, 1979: p.3)

This chapter presents the conceptual framework for the book. It starts with a brief account of two overarching concepts, political economy and policy, before turning to an explanation and elaboration of the conceptual framework. This draws on different theories and models of public policy-making, such as public choice theory, group theory, elite theory, institutional theory, incrementalism and game theory (Howlett and Ramesh, 1995, 2003; Huang, 1999; Dye, 2008). The framework is presented digrammatically in Figure 3.1 and summarized in the conclusions to the chapter.

Political economy

'Political economy' is used here to provide a broad conception of the policy-making process. It is a term that has been in use for nearly three hundred years to express the relationship between political and economic affairs (Caporaso and Levine, 2003; Roskin *et al.*, 2006). As Lindblom says, 'in all the political systems of the world, much of politics is economics, and most of economics is politics' (cited in B.S. Clark, 1991, 1998: p.3). Friedman also suggests that 'there is no such thing as a purely economic issue' (also cited in B.S. Clark, 1998: p.3). Economy is understood here in its broad sense as social economy, or the way of life found in production. Social production is not regarded as a neutral act by neutral agents but as a political act carried out by members of classes and other social groupings (Peet and Thrift, 1989: p.3). Different schools view the political economy from different perspectives. The Liberal school focuses attention on the interconnections between a dynamic market system and an evolving set of social institutions and political decision-making structures, while the Marxist school emphasizes the relationships existing between the mode of production and the superstructure (Stone and Harpham,

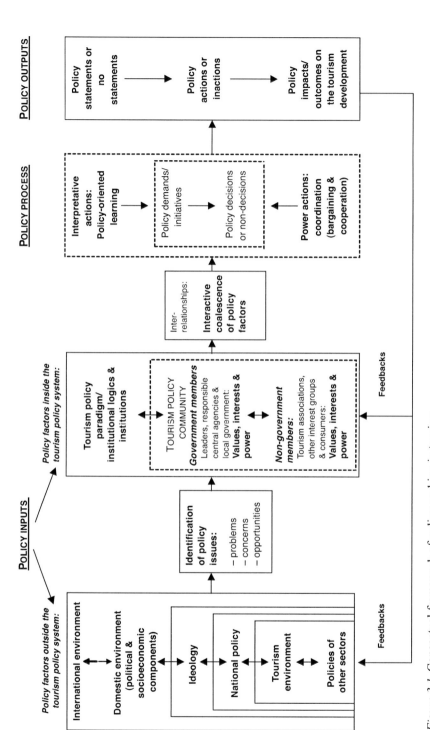

Figure 3.1 Conceptual framework of policy-making in tourism

1982). Roskin *et al* (2006: p.339) indicate that currently everyone, including conservatives, expects government to take a lead in economic prosperity; virtually all government actions and activities have economic ramifications. Hence the scope of political economy could be refined into the management of the economic affairs of the state (Caporaso and Levine, 2003: p.1). This conception does not merely focus on the interaction between the state and the economy, but takes a more holistic perspective to integrate ideology, economy, social stratification and the state into a coherent whole (Stone and Harpham, 1982). As Todaro puts it:

> Political economy goes beyond traditional (or simple economics) to study, among other things, the social and institutional processes through which certain groups of economic and political elites influence the allocation of scarce productive resources now and in the future, either exclusively for their own benefit or for that of the larger population as well. Political economy is therefore concerned with the relationships between politics and economics, with a special emphasis on the role of power in economic decision making.
>
> (Todaro, 1989, 1997, 2000: all p.8)

Policy and tourism policy

There is no universally accepted definition of public policy or of tourism policy. As C.L. Jenkins (1991: p.62) puts it, 'there is no simple consensus on what is meant by the term policy'. Generally policy can be defined as a set of interrelated decisions (or non-decisions) and actions (or inactions) formulated and implemented by government and public authorities to deal with public problems, concerns and opportunities (Simmons *et al.*, 1974; W.I. Jenkins, 1978; J.E. Anderson, 1979, 1990; Lindblom, 1980; Dye, 1987, 2008; Howlett and Ramesh, 1995, 2003; C.M. Hall and Jenkins, 1995; Howlett *et al.*, 2009). These decisions and actions are usually goal-oriented, and are formulated and implemented by a set of policy actors (W.I. Jenkins, 1978; J.E. Anderson, 1990). Thus, policy is the result of multiple decisions taken by multiple decision-makers (Howlett and Ramesh, 1995). Policies deal with a wide range of problems, concerns and opportunities. Some are as broad as the general orientation of a country, while others are as narrow as a specific issue, like environmental protection or the development of tourism. Policies can generally be classified into two categories – national policy and sector policy (Dror, 1971a, 1971b; Wu, 1989; J.M. Zhang, 1991; Sabatier and Jenkins-Smith, 1993; Howlett and Ramesh 1995, 2003).

National policy

Dror (1971a, 1972b) and Wu (1989) indicate that national policy or mega-policy deals with overall goals, assumptions, risk evaluation, degrees of innovation and provides guides for the substantive policy in a country. As Dror suggests:

> Megapolicies involve determination of the postures, assumptions, and main guidelines to be followed by specific policies. They are a kind of master policy, clearly distinct from detailed discrete policies, though these two pure types are on a continuum with many in-between cases.
>
> (Dror, 1971b: p.63)

Generally speaking, national policy determines the broad and general direction for a nation and applies to the whole of society. The national policy of a country is often stated and manifested in its constitution. Examples of national policy include the democratic politics and federalism adopted in the United States and the socialist-styled market economy adopted in China. In Singapore, the national policy shifted from inward foreign investment and the presence of TNCs (transnational corporations) to a new outward investment strategy in the 1990s. This 'outward turn' of Singapore aimed to spread its regional influence as a way of transforming 'Singapore Limited' into 'Singapore Unlimited'. In its turn this new national policy had significant impact on the making of sector policies, such as tourism policy, as explained below (T.C. Chang, 1998: pp.75–9).

Sector policy

Unlike national policy, sector[1] policy is concerned with a societal sector which W.R. Scott and Meyer (1991) define as all organizations within a society supplying a given type of product or service together with their associated suppliers, financiers and regulators. Examples may include sectors such as energy, tourism and transportation. Actually, there is no clear boundary between national policy and sector policy as a sector policy can in fact become national policy. In China, when the focus of government shifted from political struggle to economic development in 1978, the economic policy – 'Economic Reform' – became the national policy of China. As Dror (1971b: p.63) remarks, they are 'on a continuum with many in-between cases'.

Tourism policy

Tourism policy covers the interrelated decisions (or non-decisions) and actions (or inactions) adopted by government and public authorities to deal with the problems, concerns and opportunities in the tourism sector generally under the broad umbrella of national policy. Dieke (1993a: p.280) refers to tourism policy in the Gambia, which took into account the major concerns for the country, consistent with national policy objectives of economic growth, balance of payments and of narrowing the rural–urban economic development gap. Similarly, after examining Singapore's tourism policy in the 1990s,

T.C. Chang (1998: p.81) found that it was 'a reflection of national policy' – 'Singapore Unlimited'. In 1995, the Singapore Tourist Promotion Board unveiled its new mission statement 'Tourism Unlimited: Bringing the World to Singapore, Bringing Singapore to the World', aiming, according to T.C. Chang (1998), to develop Singapore not only as a memorable tourist destination, but also a tourism business centre and a tourism hub.

Nearly all governments are involved in the development of tourism. This involvement runs from providing political and social stability, without which tourism could not survive, to the provision of services such as immigration procedures, and bilateral aviation agreements, as well as infrastructure such as transportation. Kosters, in 1984, noted that 'the involvement of governments with tourism is a fact' (p.612). Williams and Shaw (1988: p.230) similarly argue 'the very nature of tourism – with its heavy spatial and seasonal polarization – usually requires some form of interventionism' and C.M. Hall (1994: p.30) further comments that there is inevitably some extent of government intervention in tourism regardless of political structure. However, such government involvement itself does not constitute a tourism policy (C.L. Jenkins and Henry, 1982; C.L. Jenkins, 1991; C.M. Hall, 1994). This requires involvement that is specifically intended to influence the way in which tourism is developed (C.L. Jenkins and Henry, 1982; C.L. Jenkins, 1991). According to C.L. Jenkins (2000: p.63), tourism policy is 'essentially a strategic declaration within which tourism is expected to develop' and offers 'a reference framework to guide the tourism development actions'. It not only reflects government's recognition of its specific needs, but also the necessity for its involvement (C.L. Jenkins, 1991; Wilkinson, 1997). From a theoretical point of view, tourism policy can be negative, restraining the development, although actually, most tourism policies seem to be positive, facilitating and promoting rather than hindering development. As C.M. Hall (1994: p.28) suggests, it appears to be universally accepted by governments around the world that tourism is a 'good thing', no matter which national ideology it follows. Richter (1989: p.19) argues that the political leadership does not ask if it is wise to develop tourism, but rather consults on how to develop tourism quickly to showcase the nation's attractions and bring big yields.

Types of tourism policy

Tourism policy comprises a wide range of decisions and actions because rarely do government or public authorities address a problem with a single decision and action (Howlett and Ramesh, 1995). Based on the work of Wu (1989), J.M. Zhang (1991), P. Hall (1993) and Howlett and Ramesh (1995), tourism policy is classified here into two interrelated types: basic policy decisions and concrete policy decisions. A basic tourism policy is a set of guidelines and statements that determine the general goals and development strategies and direct the planning for tourism. For example, the basic tourism policy in Canada has been to enhance growth and efficiency and to maximize the contribution from tourism, while in Britain, it has been to maximize the contribution of tourism to employment and income (Gee *et al.*, 1989, 1997). Basic policy decisions direct the making of concrete decisions, which deal with a wide range of concerns and opportunities such as stagnation in the growth of tourist demand or unsatisfactory service quality.

A conceptual framework

The term 'framework' 'sets the boundaries – a set of principles and guidelines which provide a philosophical base and an organizational structure – for construction' (South African Qualifications Authority, 2007). Miles and Huberman (1994: p.18) indicate that a 'conceptual framework' aims to explain the main things to be studied (i.e. the key factors, constructs or variables and the presumed relationships among them). A conceptual framework can be rudimentary or elaborate, theory driven or commonsensical, descriptive or causal. Miles and Huberman's view has provided a heuristic guide for this study. Its development is based on the following five premises:

1 Policy is determined by a set of factors ranging from the broad political and socio-economic conditions, to the institutional and organizational elements, and to the values, interests and power of individual policy players. This study considers the forces or elements that shape the policy or policy decisions as the 'policy factors'.
2 Any single policy factor, such as ideology and socio-economic conditions, cannot determine policy alone. Policy is shaped by multiple policy factors.
3 Interrelationships occur among policy factors.
4 The policy actors stand at the core of the policy-making process, as policy is formulated and implemented by them.
5 The policy factors can be viewed as a 'relational whole'.

Roles

The conceptual framework for this study, based on the literature, is set out in Figure 3.1. This shows policy-making for tourism at a national level. The interrelationships of the policy factors are described as bilateral and multilateral and the conceptual framework has two roles: to bring together the factors that affect policy-making in an organized and systematic way; and to provide a basis for understanding the policy-making process through the interrelationships of these policy factors.

Fundamental constructs

Miles and Huberman (1994: p.18) indicate that theory building relies on a few general constructs that subsume a mountain of particulars. In general, four fundamental constructs underpin this conceptual framework: (1) the origins of the policy factors; (2) levels of the policy factors; (3) systems theory; and (4) interrelationships.

Origins

Generally speaking, the policy-making process involves numerous forces. However, different scholars derive different overviews or conceptualizations in accordance with their own study aims and settings. For example, Simeon (1976) summarizes that policy is a consequence of the political environment, values, ideologies, the distribution of power, institutional framework, etc. Barrett and Fudge (1981) indicate that policy-making involves the economic, physical and social/political environments in a process of action and reaction over time. Self (1985) points out that public policy is influenced by the economic, social and cultural characteristics of society, as well as by the formal structure of government and other features of the political system. By reviewing studies of the 1970s and 1980s, Sabatier (1991: p.148) and Jenkins-Smith and Sabatier (1993a: p.5) suggest that public policy-making is influenced by the preference, interests and resources of policy actors involved, institutional rules and background socio-economic conditions. Sabatier (2007b) concludes that the policy-making process involves 'an extremely complex set of interacting elements over time' (p.3) and suggests that 'given the staggering complexity of the policy process, the analyst must find some way of simplifying the situation in order to have any chance of understanding it' (p.4).

According to Busch and Braun (1999) and Howlett and Ramesh (1995; 2003), the policy actors' subjective views (e.g. ideology, ideas, values and interests) have an influence on the objective reality – the surrounding environment. The subjective views serve as the interpretive prism or filtering mechanism for the policy actors to understand the objective reality. Stone (1988: p.106) also argues that there is no objective description of a situation and there can only be portrayals of people's experience and interpretations. The objective reality after the interpretation or filtering by subjective views becomes the perceived reality that determines the choices of strategy and the direction of actions. Elster comments:

> It would be naïve to think, for instance, that public policy can be explained by the goals of government and the opportunities that, objectively speaking, are open to it. Rather, goals interact with beliefs – in fact highly controversial theories – about what are feasible economic theories.
>
> (Elster, 1989: pp.20–1)

Therefore, the origins of policy factors affecting tourism policy-making can be identified as: (a) the objective realities (i.e. the environmental stimulus); (b) the subjective views (e.g. values, belief, ideas, ideology); (c) prescriptive mechanism – institutions (enabling and restraining); and (d) resources – power (Simeon, 1976).

Levels

The policy factors vary from the broad socio-economic conditions to the values and power of individual policy actors. From earlier works (W.R. Scott, 2001: p.83; Howlett and Ramesh, 2003: p.15), these can be classified into three levels – macro; sector or meso; and micro (organizational and individual).

Macro-level policy factors mainly include the environment and ideology. As far as tourism is concerned the environment can be divided into the international environment, the domestic political and socio-economic environment, the national policy environment, the tourism environment and policies from other sectors. At the second, sector or meso level (Howlett and Ramesh, 2003), are the organizations that constitute a recognized area of institutional life including key suppliers, resource and product consumers, regulatory agencies, and other organizations that produce similar services or products (DiMaggio and Powell, 1983: p.148; W.R. Scott and Meyer, 1991: p.108; W.R. Scott, 2001) in this case, related to tourism. The concept of sector here is built on the conventional conception of industry (W.R. Scott, 2001: p.83) and the policy factors comprise the sectoral view – tourism policy paradigm (Braun, 1999) and the sectoral mechanisms, such as tourism institutions. The micro-level policy factors are the tourism policy actors, their beliefs, values, interests and power. These can be organizations such as national tourism administrations, tourism associations or individuals (government ministers, industry leaders). A more detailed explanation of these will be provided later in this chapter.

Systems theory

According to Bertalanffy, the term 'system' is used to encompass:

> A set of elements standing in interrelation among themselves and with the environment . . . [and systems theory is] a way of seeing things which were previously overlooked or by-passed and in this sense is a methodological maxim.
>
> (Bertalanffy, 1972 cited in Leiper, 1979: p.395)

Generally, the policy-making process can be viewed as an input–output model of the political system. Drawing on the work of system theorists including Easton (1965a; 1965b) and Powell and Almond (W.I. Jenkins, 1978) the political system can be seen as a group of interrelated structures and processes functioning authoritatively to allocate values for a society (J.E. Anderson, 1979, 1990, 2003; Dye, 2008). It can be differentiated into various policy sectors or fields with each engaged in one or multiple state actions under the guidance of a sectoral worldview or paradigm (Braun, 1999: p.17). Howlett and Ramesh (2003: p.15) point out that rather than attempt to explain all government policy-making within a 'political system', many previous studies have focused instead on policy sectors or fields or domains. The framework presented here considers the part of the political system, which functions to process tourism policy decisions as the tourism policy system (Goeldner and Ritchie, 2006: p.416). The tourism policy system encompasses the tourism policy paradigm, tourism institutions and tourism policy actors. In other words, the tourism policy system covers the policy factors ranging from sector to micro levels.

In brief, the framework suggests all of the policy factors, from both inside and outside the tourism policy system, to be its inputs. It is conceived that the forces in the environment are kinds of inputs. Values, interests and the power of policy actors together with institutions are also considered as inputs, which influence tourism policy-making as well as the environment. All of these factors interrelate to generate demands for tourism policy. When demands are generated, the tourism policy system processes and transforms them into policy decisions and actions, which represents its output. The impacts of policy decisions may subsequently affect and modify the policy factors and the demands generated, which in turn provides a feedback mechanism in the model (Dye, 1987, 2002; J.E. Anderson, 1990, 2003). W.I. Jenkins (1978) developed a four-stage framework of policy-making, which has been incorporated into Figure 3.1. These four stages are the policy demands, decisions, outputs and outcomes.

Interrelationships

The study of the interrelationships of policy factors affecting tourism policy-making is a difficult and challenging area because of their dynamic, complicated and organic natures. There is also limited literature related to this. An attempt is made here to explore the setting and scope of the interrelationships, and to develop some propositions about their nature.

In terms of their setting, the various policy factors do not operate in isolation. The conceptual framework here is based on the view that they exist within a funnel of causality, in which each policy factor is nested within another (Hofferbert, 1974; Simeon, 1976; Howlett and Ramesh, 1995). This is the setting of the relationships between them. From the tourism (or sector) perspective (shown in Figure 3.1), the tourism policy actors face the tourism environment as well as the broad international, domestic political and socio-economic environments. This sector environment is assumed to influence the sector policy-making both directly and indirectly. For example, the tourism environment includes the structure of the tourism market, the activities and entities constituting the tourism industry and the issues arising from these activities and entities (Dieke, 2000b: p.7).

The policy decisions of other sectors and the tourism environment affect each other. An expansive policy for the transportation sector, for example, benefits the development of tourism; in the same way a large influx of tourists will trigger subsequent adjustments and changes in transportation policy.

In the meantime the tourism environment and the policies of other sectors operate within national policies. A national policy on, for example, foreign ownership and tax incentives will have implications for tourism, even though it is not specifically aimed at it (C.L. Jenkins and Henry, 1982; Wilkinson, 1997). Development in tourism will also affect its position in the national policy. According to Clancy (1999: pp.11–12), tourism in Mexico by the end of the 1990s was largely the outcome of deliberate state actions since the 1960s; in consequence, tourism became the leading sector within Mexico's national development strategy focusing on export-oriented growth.

National policy and all sector policies, in their turn, are set within an ideology. This is the political thought that defines the orientation of all kinds of policy decisions in all policy sectors. Hettne (1995) indicates that development strategy is the means of implementing the development process guided by a specific ideology. The implementation of national policy and sector policies can also serve to strengthen and intensify the position of the ruling ideology. Finally, the ideology will affect political and socio-economic development, and changes in these environments, such as an economic crisis, may lead to changes in ideology (P. Hall, 1990, 1993; Howlett and Ramesh, 1995). Sherman (1987: p.49) summarizes this by suggesting that the social structure (including ideologies and institutions) is a function of the economic structure (economic forces and relations) and vice versa.

As far as their scope is concerned, generally speaking, there are two categories of interrelationships: interaction and coalescence, which combine to determine both national policies and sector policies. For interaction, the various policy factors are not independent of and isolated from each other, but rather they interact. As Elliot (1987: p.223) comments: 'The role of government in the development of tourism in any country is crucial, but governments must operate within the given environment and with established factors which continually change and react with each other.' Such interactions are assumed to be 'bilateral' or 'multilateral'. For bilateral interaction, change in the political and socio-economic environments, such as a crisis, may result in a change in ideology, while ideology also affects the political and socio-economic development. This is shown by the double-headed arrows in Figure 3.1. With multilateral interaction, socio-economic development can affect the development of a sector, which in turn affects the position of this sector in national policy, such as Clancy's Mexican example cited above. Ultimately policy is jointly shaped by the coalescence of multiple policy factors with each assumed to have its own role in the policy-making process. Sherman argues:

> Never assume that a particular social phenomenon is accidental or isolated . . . although one may analytically separate a single phenomenon from the whole for study, no valid policy conclusion can be drawn until the possible relations to the rest of the social system are also studied.
>
> (Sherman, 1987: p.14)

For example, once the issues from the environment are transmitted to government for a policy response, the examination of environment alone cannot explain how the issues will be perceived or what policy responses will be made. Ideas are especially important in setting the assumptions to define the policy problems and limit the range of policy alternatives, but they do not provide the full explanation since they tend to be general and only account for broad orientation rather than the specific details of policy (Simeon, 1976). For example, Indian tourism policy is a peculiar blend of ideals about traditional hospitality, and ideas of contemporary capitalist development, but such 'ideational' factors do not provide sufficient explanation as to why the current national tourism policy is relatively underdeveloped. Singh (2001: p.143) suggests that perhaps the institutional element of the democratic framework can account for the several revisions and modifications in the policy outputs.

Policy-making involves the exercise of authority and power and the distribution of power among the policy actors affects the policy outputs. Wilson (2000: p.253) summarizes the position by suggesting that the major changes in public policies can be partially explained by ideological shifts resulting from political struggles in which subordinate classes attack the governing ideology with an alternative ideology underpinning a set of different arrangements and policy packages. With this in mind, the respective roles of policy factors need to be examined in terms of relative importance, specific relationships and significant causalities.

Exploring the conceptual framework

The exploration of the conceptual framework here is organized into three sections, as set out in Figure 3.1 – policy inputs, process and outputs.

Policy inputs

The policy inputs are the policy factors from the macro, sector/meso and micro levels.

Macro-level policy factors

INTERNATIONAL, DOMESTIC AND SECTOR

As noted, the macro-level policy factors cover every facet of society, including the tourism sector and the tourism policy-making process. Based on systems theory, the environment refers to any condition or circumstance defined as external to the boundaries of the tourism policy system. Public policy is seen as a response of government to challenges and pressure from the environment (Hofferbert, 1974: p.6). Generally, it can be assumed that there are two layers of environment – structures and anomalies. According to Giddens (1984: p.377), structure comprises rules and resources, implicated in the production and reproduction of social systems. The rules refer to the generalized procedures although it also needs to be noted that a concept of structure that ignores asymmetries of power is radically incomplete (Giddens, 1984: p.21; Sewell, 1992: p.9). The resources, according to Giddens (1979: p.92), are the 'media whereby transformative capacity is employed as power in the routine course of social interaction'. What the structure produces are the persistent and patterned social practices made by and transformed through collective human activities (Cox, 1987: p.4; Sewell, 1992: p.6). These persistent social practices can be anticipated or explained by the social members. The other layer of the environment is the anomalies. The anomalies in the environment mean the 'real world developments' that cannot be anticipated or explicated by the social actors. Policy-making cannot be adequately studied apart from the environment in which it occurs (J.E. Anderson, 2003: p.38). Environments that the tourism policy actors confront at the macro level comprise the international, the domestic political and socio-economic, the sector (i.e. tourism), the national policy and policies from other sectors. These are shown in Figure 3.1.

Governments around the world have certain responsibilities or principles to run a country. These responsibilities vary. But providing stability and security, and raising the standard of living are commonly and widely accepted responsibilities (Elliot, 1997). In the *International Environment*, the political, economic and cultural values of tourism may enable governments to fulfil these responsibilities. Politically, tourism can be used to improve foreign relations with other countries, enhance international recognition and promote positive and desirable images of the host country and international peace. What is noteworthy about tourism is its economic values, such as earning foreign exchange, generating income, providing employment, contributing to regional development and stimulating other industries. In terms of social and cultural values, tourism can promote mutual understanding and friendship with other countries (Lickorish, 1991; C.M. Hall, 1994; Elliot, 1997). Which values of tourism are utilized by government, relies largely on the environment that the government confronts. For example, in Japan the economic value of tourism to earn foreign exchange was rapidly eclipsed by other export industries and by a strong domestic economy in the 1980s and 1990s. Inbound tourism was used by the government to facilitate the understanding of tourists towards Japan, rather than to earn revenue. Meanwhile, outbound tourism was encouraged by the Japanese government as a means of reducing the trade imbalance and to serve broader educative, diplomatic and political goals. So the function of the Japan National Tourism Organization (JNTO) shifted from attracting foreign tourists and the promotion of domestic tourism, to facilitating the overseas travel of the Japanese (C.M. Hall, 1994).

The environment generates problems, concerns and opportunities that are transmitted by policy actors to the tourism policy system. Changes in the environment provide a base for development and change in tourism policy through attracting the attention of government to a set of problems, which need to be dealt with (Heclo, 1974). In the international environment it is undoubtedly the case that states are increasingly constrained and shaped by

global forces including supranational institutions. The international environment not only influences policy sectors that are apparently internationally
oriented such as trade, but also sectors with no immediate international
connection such as health care and old age pensions (Howlett and Ramesh,
2003). Since tourism, especially international tourism, is an international
market-driven sector, the international environment must always be recognized
by government as an important influence on its actions; albeit that national
governments can do little to alter it (Elliot, 1983: p.379). During the 1960s,
international tourism saw growing demand from the United States, Europe,
Japan and Australia for vacations. As a result international tourism was
perceived by the government of many developing countries as the catalyst for
economic development (H.G. Matthews, 1978). Security issues and crisis also
affect government's public policy-making for tourism. Terrorist attacks on the
West, the Iraq War, the outbreak of SARS (Severe Acute Respiratory
Syndrome) and the threat of bird flu all restrained people's desire and ability
to travel, and thus the well-being of tourism destinations around the world
and as such had to be taken into account in the public sector management of
tourism destinations (Goeldner and Ritchie, 2006).

International institutions can influence and even determine the political and
economic activities in a nation (Mowforth and Munt, 1998: p.289). The World
Trade Organization (WTO) requires its members to work towards lowering
trade barriers by according 'national treatment' to imports and not subsidizing
exports (Howlett and Ramesh, 2003). Due to the huge impact of crisis on global
tourism, the United Nations World Tourism Organization (UNWTO) established its Recovery Committee which formulated their Crisis Guidelines for
the Tourism Industry, a step-by-step working document to guide governments
in helping to get tourists to return to a destination as soon as possible (Goeldner
and Ritchie, 2006: p.426).

Turning to the *domestic political environment* there are not many studies
concerned with the relationship between this political environment and
formulation of tourism policy, and few elements in the political environment
related to tourism policy-making have been effectively identified. The two
obvious ones are political stability and international relations. The Marcos'
Philippines and Taiwan provide two notable examples. In the Philippines, due
to the increasing unpopularity of President Marcos and an increasing crime
rate, martial law was imposed in 1972 and, since tourism was a high priority,
the President looked to use it to maintain the legitimacy of his regime by
creating a favourable image of the country both for international tourists and
for foreign governments. International tourist visitation was held up by the
regime to be an endorsement of its activities and of martial law. The resulting
tourism development programme included the hosting of the Miss Universe
contest, a World Bank Conference and the mass construction of luxury hotels
(Richter, 1989; C.M. Hall, 1994). A second example is Taiwan, where,
because of its separation from mainland China, it is restricted in its formal
relations with other countries. This, along with its massive accumulation of

foreign exchange reserves, prompted an emphasis on outbound tourism to improve its image, to strengthen substantive external relations (C.M. Hall, 1994), as well as to take pressure off its strengthening currency.

Japan and Taiwan, as described above, provide examples of how the *domestic socio-economic environment*, notably their economic conditions, weakened the economic importance of tourism and hence changed their respective tourism policy objectives. These examples contrast with most other cases where the socio-economic environment has led governments to formulate economic-oriented policy decisions to strengthen tourism to create employment, earn foreign exchange, help address economic recession and support regional development (C.L. Jenkins and Henry, 1982; Airey, 1983; Williams and Shaw, 1991; C.M. Hall, 1994; Clancy, 1999, etc.). For example, the balance of payments crisis during 1967, which had an impact on the domestic economy, motivated the British government to enact the Development of Tourism Act in 1969 (Airey, 1983; Elliot, 1997). In Thailand, there was no real support for tourism from government before 1985. This attitude changed radically when tourism became the top foreign currency earner in 1985. Since then, the Thai government has taken the lead to develop tourism by significantly increasing the budget of the Tourism Authority of Thailand and cutting the hotel room tax (Elliot, 1987). Similarly Woon (1989) links Malaysian tourism policy to changes in oil prices. As a leading export, after 1980, oil eclipsed the importance of tourism development. The collapse of oil prices in 1985 and 1986 forced the Malaysian government seriously to rethink its tourism planning and development strategy and as a result, top priority was given to tourism.

The *tourism environment* contains the issues that are closest to the tourism policy-maker. Elliot (1997) explains how tourism problems and negative tourism impacts, which are part of the tourism environment, often result in direct government involvement. Problems such as increases in air traffic, caused by mass tourism in the peak season, demand direct action, while negative impacts of tourism such as environmental degradation may also lead to government intervention. There appears to be little understanding of the relationship between the stages of tourism development and the formation of tourism policy. According to the UNWTO (1994), the Organization for Economic Cooperation and Development (OECD) identified its member governments playing different roles at the different stages of tourism development. For example, in what is referred to as the second stage of tourism development (the late 1960s), tourism underwent a democratization with the development of tour operators, charter flights and major tourist destinations. These developments caused governments to become involved in infrastructure projects and work-force development. In stage three (the early 1970s), the rapid growth in tourist demand led to a deterioration in standards, which caused governments to implement control measures in, for example, tourist protection, price control and regulation of travel agencies.

According to Dror (1971b: p.63), the macro policy or 'mega policy' of a nation guides 'the determination of the postures, assumptions and main guidelines to be followed by specific policies'. Based on this rationale, tourism policy-making takes place under the broad umbrella of National Policy. D.G. Pearce (1992: p.6) acknowledges that the scope of government intervention in tourism largely reflects 'broader political philosophies and policies'. Goeldner and Ritchie (2006: p.416) view tourism policy as 'being directly based upon and derived from the policies that direct the total socioeconomic system of the nation or region in which the tourism subsystem is located'. As made for a particular sector, tourism policy-making should stick to the principles of and integrate harmoniously with national development policy (Wu, 1989; Wilkinson, 1997). The British Tourist Authority in 1988 also stated that a successful tourist industry relies on effectively undertaking essential national tasks within a framework of national policy.

After examining the political economy of tourism development in Mexico, Clancy (1999) concluded that 'state action toward tourism is better understood in the context of the larger development strategies pursued by the state itself' (p.11). He identified that in Mexico's case national policy and tourism policy interacted in a mutually supportive manner. According to Clancy (1999), by the 1960s, in common with many Latin American countries, Mexico had maintained an import substitution strategy for over thirty years to encourage industrialization at home, viewed as a more secure and orderly basis for sustained growth (J. Broham, 1996). However, along with the resulting enviable growth rates of the so-called 'Mexican Miracle', economic and social pressures also arose in the form of balance of payments deficits and uncontrolled growth of urban areas. Tourism's foreign exchange and regional development potential was considered by the government as a means to ameliorate these difficulties and as such the Mexico government began a programme of planning tourist resorts, providing infrastructure, investing and operating the tourist facilities and introducing investment incentives for the private sector. This successful development of tourism also contributed to the continued import substitution strategy (Clancy, 1999).

Finally, in this overview of the macro-level inputs, according to Sabatier (1993), a sector's policies are impacted by *policies from other sectors*. An obvious example is the restrictive effect that a conservative aviation policy may have on an expansive tourism policy. Given the broad nature of tourism and its links with other sectors such policies play an important part in its development.

INTERPRETATION FRAMEWORK: IDEATIONAL FACTORS AND INTERESTS

The environmental conditions as identified here represent objective realities. However, the issues, concerns and opportunities provided by the environment do not have an 'objective existence' waiting to be recognized by the government. To be converted into a problem they must also be seen to represent appropriate topics for governmental action (J.E. Anderson, 2003: p.82). This means that the identification of environmental stimuli is not a mechanical process, but rather a socially constructed one that involves the definition of normalcy and what constitutes an undesirable deviation from that status (Howlett and Ramesh, 2003). J.E. Anderson (2003: p.82) argues that 'there is no single correct way to assess a condition and define a problem, although many people will have strong views and preferences on some matters. Problem definitions compete for acceptance.' Policy problems are constructed in the realm of public and private discourse (e.g. Spector and Kitsuse, 1987; Rochefort and Cobb, 1993). Problem definition, according to Stone (1988: p.106) is strategic as government, interest groups and individuals deliberately and consciously offer 'portrayals' to promote their favoured course of action. The policy decisions and actions are the outcomes of the understanding and interpretation made by the policy players toward the objective realities (Braun, 1999: p.12).

Ideas versus interests　Ideas and interests serve as an interpretation framework or filtering mechanism for the policy actors to perceive the environmental stimulus. Ideas differ from interests (Braun, 1999; Nahrath, 1999). In the policy-making process, interests refer to the self-interests guiding the policy actors to pursue their best advantage (Howlett and Ramesh, 1995, 2003). Ideas, such as traditions, knowledge, beliefs and values, affect how individuals consider, derive and defend their interests. Habermas (1972) heavily emphasizes the notion of knowledge, constituting interests. Hamilton (1987: p.20) indicates that one role of ideology is to promote, serve or reflect interests.

According to Dijk (1998: p.15), ideas are objects or processes in and/or of the mind; they are the products of thinking. Ideas can be new, original, interesting thoughts and about important issues. They can be personal or socially shared. Ideas enable the policy actors to generate meanings about the environment that help to engender the policy decisions (Braun, 1999: p.12). Meaning stands at the heart of all social lives. Without a framework of meaning, neither collective nor individual life is possible (Berger, 1976; Stunkel and Sarsar, 1994). Phillips (1994: p.57) suggests that at the heart of politics is a struggle over meaning.

The ideational dimension　C.W. Anderson (1978: p.23) argues that 'policies are made within some system of ideas and standards which is comprehensible and plausible to the actors involved'. Sabatier (1999b: p.3) points out that 'the process of public policymaking includes the manner in which problems get conceptualized and brought to government for solution'. Likewise, Busch and Braun (1999: p.1) consider 'for, like any other human action, public policy is only possible within a cognitive framework that relates the goals to be achieved to the available means and other data relevant for a particular decision'. Howlett and Ramesh (2003: p.121) conclude that how the environmental conditions come to be interpreted as a public problem, demanding a policy response, pertains to the nature of human knowledge and the social construction of that knowledge. These views all support that notion that the ideational and cognitive dimension of policy issues stands at the focal point of policy-making and confirms the explanatory value of this dimension. This conceptual development of the ideational dimension of policy-making, in many ways, is at the exploratory stage; it has emerged recently in the analysis of politics and public policy with growing dissatisfaction with 'interests' as the key causal variable in explaining the policy process. Up to now interests have been regarded as the driving force of decisions and actions of policy actors (e.g. voters and elected politicians in Western democracies) (Busch and Braun, 1999; Braun, 1999).

The ideational approach makes the point that the enduring ideas such as ideologies, traditions, culture and worldviews have a significant impact on policy-making. These ideas act as prisms for policy actors to conceive the problems of the real world, inspiring their demand for government action. The policy process is permeated by ideas about what is the best course of action, and by beliefs about how to achieve goals (Howlett and Ramesh, 1995; Kerr, 2003). Howlett and Ramesh argue that problems, issues or concerns arising from the environment are not considered to have an objective base in society, but rather they are constructed in the discourses interpreted by the enduring ideas of policy actors. Tourism is not an exception to this. Kerr (2003) observes that among many lobbyists participating in the development of Scottish tourism, some preached for radical measures such as compulsory registration and tourism tax, whereas others initiated more conservative ideas such as maintaining the membership of the national tourism organization.

From ideas to beliefs   Dijk (1998: p.18) conceives that the notion of 'idea' is too general or too vague; more importantly, ideas are often seen as new or original thoughts. 'Beliefs' are therefore used as a central conception in the study of the ideational dimension (Dijk, 1998; Braun, 1999). Akin to ideas, beliefs are the products of thinking and the building blocks of human minds (Dijk, 1998). Both Dijk (1998) and Braun (1999) indicate that beliefs have cognitive and evaluative properties. Cognition tells the policy actors 'what it is' about the environment and 'what is feasible'. These beliefs are taken to be 'true beliefs' through universally accepted criteria that are valid, correct, certified and generally held; knowledge plays such a cognitive role. Knowledge is the justified true belief or factual belief (Dijk, 1998) including know-what, know-how, know-why and care-why (Malecki, 1999). Phillips (1994: p.57) argues that science and social science are both creative forces in the construction of meaning. Knowledge generated by academics has been widely utilized in policy-making (P. Hall, 1990). Scientific knowledge is not only a creative force in the construction of meaning, but is also an integral aspect of political control since it is via the opportunity to create and impose intellectual ways of seeing the world that governments and other actors gain and maintain political dominance (Phillips, 1994: p.57) The cumulative effect of findings from different studies and from ordinary knowledge has, according to Lindblom and Cohen (1979), the greatest influence on policy. For example, in the

United States, air pollution was scarcely a subject of policy debate in the mid-1950s. By the mid-1970s, under the fundamental influence of research reports that indicated that air quality posed significant health risks to many urban people, the principal responsibility for pollution control was elevated from local and state government to the federal government (Sabatier, 1993: p.13).

Beliefs are not just the thoughts about 'what exists' or 'what is', they also belong to evaluation (Rokeach, 1973: p.6). As Rokeach (1979: p.16) explains, our judgements of what should be are always related to our judgements of what is. Upon comprehending 'what is' by cognitive attribute, the evaluative attribute of beliefs enables the policy actors to make the judgement on 'what is good or bad', 'what is acceptable or unacceptable', 'what one ought to do', 'what is permitted or prohibited' based on values and norms (Dijk, 1998; Braun, 1999: pp.12–13). In fact, the cognitive and evaluative attributes are not independent of each other. Goldsworthy (1988: p.508) points out that all development theories consciously or unconsciously express the preferred notions of what development is, which in turn reflects values. As a simple example, the term 'developed countries' is virtually interchangeable with the 'good' society.

When applying values in studying tourism policy-making, Henning's concept (1974: p.15) was employed at an early stage. This defined values as 'ends, goals, interests, beliefs, ethics, bias, attitudes, traditions, morals and objectives that change with human perception and with time, and have significant influence on power conflicts relating to policy'. However, this definition just reflects the many manifestations of 'value' (Rokeach, 1973: p.22). According to Rokeach (1973: p.13; 1979: pp.16 and 48) and J.E. Anderson (2003: p.126), the core essence of value (e.g. truth, happiness, equity, etc.) is the presence of criteria or standards of preference. A value is 'an enduring belief that a specific mode of conduct or end-state of existence is personally or socially preferable to an alternative' (Rokeach, 1972: pp.159–60; 1973: p.25; 1979: p.15). W.R. Scott (2001: p.54) summarizes the argument that 'values are the conceptions of the preferred or the desirable, together with the construction of standards to which existing structures or behaviour can be compared and assessed'. Therefore, 'all values have cognitive, affective and directional aspects' (Rokeach, 1973; 1979: p.16). Some values pertain to desirable terminal or end-states of affairs that are worth pursuing (e.g. wisdom, liberal, pleasure, etc.), while others belong to desirable modes of actions that are instrumental or competitive to the attainment of ideal end-states (e.g. honesty, trust or accountable, logical, etc.) (Rokeach, 1973: pp.7–8; 1979: p.48). Generally speaking, value is a desirable thing (e.g. Rokeach, 1973: p.7; 1979: p.15), it is simply 'a broad tendency to prefer certain states of affairs over others' (Hofstede, 2001: p.5).

Value and norm are the two instruments for the evaluative function of beliefs. W.R. Scott (2001: p.55) emphasizes that norms specify how things should be done and define the legitimate means for valued ends, such as rules and procedures of how to carry out the works and fair business practices. Norms are obligatory demands, claims, expectations and rules (Rokeach, 1973: p.19; 1979: pp.15 and 21).

A goal, objective, attitude or interest can be used to observe value. But value is not identical and synonymous with these terms per se (Rokeach, 1973: p.17). For example, value differs from attitude. According to Rokeach (1972: pp.109–24; 1973: pp.17–18) and Borden (1991), an attitude refers to an organization of several beliefs around a specific object or situation, but a value refers to a single belief of a very specific kind concerning a desirable mode of behaviour or end-state. Attitude results from the application of general value to concrete objects or situations. A value, unlike attitude, is a standard or yardstick to guide actions, attitudes, comparisons, evaluations and justifications of self and others. Values help shape attitudes and attitudes function to express values. Likewise, interest is apparently a narrower concept than value; it cannot be classified as an idealized mode of behaviour or end-state of existence (Rokeach, 1973: p.22). Furthermore, values are not the concrete rules of conduct, so values cannot be merged together with other factors affecting policy-making institutions, although institutions must be conceived either as complex sets of rules or as value-embraced (Rokeach, 1973; 1979: p.16).

Stunkel and Sarsar (1994: p.48) assert all social and political action is rooted in actors' values; they comment that it is individual people, acting on their personal or traditional values, their normative maps of reality, who are involved in the formulation and implementation of social values in the form of public policy. This is why Easton (1965a) views public policy as the authoritative allocations of values (decisions) that are binding on society. Simmons *et al.* (1974: p.475) recognize that 'it is value choice, implicit and explicit, which orders the priorities of government and determines the commitment of resources within the public jurisdiction'. Therefore, values lie at the core of public policy (Henning, 1974; Wu, 1989; J.E. Anderson, 1990, 2003; Sabatier, 1991; Sabatier and Jenkins-Smith, 1993; Howlett and Ramesh, 1995), as with tourism policy (C.M. Hall and Jenkins, 1995). C.M. Hall and Jenkins (1995) stress that when considering different tourism policy alternatives, decision-makers are also judging between different sets of values. For example, emphasizing deriving economic returns rather than on promoting foreign relations from tourism obviously represents the dominance of the economic value of tourism over its political value. Value changes towards tourism will lead to changes in tourism policy.

To sum up, the cognitive and evaluative attributes constitute the beliefs – the subjective mental models to represent the world and to learn from that world in order to improve the resulting decisions and actions (North, 1996 cited in Braun, 1999). Dijk (1998: p.26) indicates that beliefs are not only personally rooted, many of them are socially acquired, constructed and changed through social practices and interaction. Braun (1999: pp.13–14) also conceives that the policy actors 'generally have a set of beliefs that are related to other social actors in a relatively coherent fashion'. Such a set of beliefs was defined by Braun as a belief system, that is, 'a set of generalized, unified and abstract mental models shared by a specific community'. For Braun (1999: p.14), the belief system is the pivotal point of most ideational approaches to studying politics and public policy-making, since 'a society without some consensus on values would not be a society at all' (Stunkel and Sarsar, 1994: p.48). The social belief systems largely take the forms of ideology at society-wide level and policy paradigm at the sector or policy field level.

IDEOLOGY

> Some writers argue that in the last decades of the twentieth century ideology has receded as a force in human affairs, that economic and social problems are technical rather than political or ideological for 'post-industrial' peoples and nations . . . but ideology remains a potent force in shaping the conduct of politics in the 1990s, as resurgent nationalism in eastern Europe and militant Islamic fundamentalism in North Africa illustrate.
>
> (Stunkel and Sarsar, 1994: p.2)

Dijk (1998) asserts that there is no such thing as a purely individual or personal ideology; ideology is a social and general belief system shared by social groups. The term 'ideology' was first initiated by the French philosopher Antoine Destutt de Tracy in the late eighteenth century to describe the 'science of ideas' (Roskin *et al.*, 1997: p.99). Generally, ideology is a body of more or less coherent ideas that has the power to focus perceptions of the world and society and to mobilize groups for political and social actions (Stunkel and Sarsar, 1994: p.2). Young (1989: p.28) argues 'the most powerful form which ideology can take is to be taken-for-granted, to be not only natural but also unquestioned or even unarticulated'. The study of politics has also been an examination of the power of ideology, the conflicts among different ideologies, and the impact of ideology on nations (H.G. Matthews and Richter, 1991).

Basically all ideologies (e.g. liberalism, conservatism, capitalism, socialism and communism) possess the cognitive and evaluative essentials about human beings, society and the world. Knowledge and values are inseparable constituents in forming an ideology. Dijk (1998) concludes that knowledge is the basis of ideologies and that all knowledge is ideologically based. This is because 'the way knowledge develops shapes our perceptions of the world around us and in turn those perceptions shape the search for knowledge' (North, 2004: p.76). Like knowledge, values also play a central role in the construction of ideology (Dijk, 1998). Ideology is a systematic representation of values leading to a preferred or obligatory state for a social system (Rokeach, 1972: p.124; 1979: p.21; C.M. Hall and Jenkins, 1995). On the basis of knowledge and values, ideologies define the truth and right. Many of them have 'definite views on the big questions of human nature, knowledge and truth, political and social organization, sources of authority, uses of power, the status of property, and the forms of economic life' (Stunkel and Sarsar, 1994: p.3).

According to Hamilton (1987) ideology is a complex concept involving over twenty elements. It is thus hard to give a single and all-inclusive definition (W.W. Zhang, 1996: p.4). But, all political discourse and actions are either overtly ideological or have ideological overtones; many ideologies define for millions of people their political loyalties and social commitments (Stunkel and Sarsar, 1994). More specifically, ideology is a system of politically focused ideas to explain the political world, provide an interpretation framework for particular events and to offer recommendations and prescriptions for future actions (Simeon, 1976: p.570). It usually advocates 'how government should be organized, what roles it should play, and how a nation's economy should be managed, the distribution of resources among groups making up the populace, etc' (Ladd, 1989: p.56). The most obvious aspect is the left–right dimension that is closely related to the scope and distribution of government intervention (Simeon, 1976). In summary ideology is essentially a set of ideas or beliefs with a discursive framework for guiding and justifying public policies derived from certain values and assumptions (W.W. Zhang, 1996). Edelman (1988: pp.12–13) argues that problems come into existence as 'reinforcements of ideologies, not simply because they are there or because they are important for well-being'. Furthermore, ideology is not merely a kind of political thought in a metaphysical form, but rather a system of behavioral beliefs for political actions, as ideology emphasizes the action rather than critical thought and understanding (Stunkel and Sarsar, 1994: p.2).

Ideology ideally aims to reform society. In the real world, creating, adopting and sustaining ideology are closely related to pursuing and maintaining power and interests. Mowforth and Munt (1998: p.38) argue that 'ideology is about the ways relationships of power are inexorably interwoven in the production and representation of meaning which serves the interests of a particular social group'; they further comment that ideology not only refers to sustaining relationships of domination in the interest of a dominant political power or social thought but also to interests opposing the dominant power. Likewise, Stunkel and Sarsar (1994) also point out that ideologies are used to form, defend, strengthen and enhance group interests.

There are many contending and complementary ideologies. According to Stunkel and Sarsar (1994), the more traditional ideologies include conservatism, liberalism, socialism, communism, nationalism, positivism, totalitarianism, anarchism and social Darwinism; more recently emerging are feminism and liberal theology and movements. Tourism policy-making cannot be exempted from the remarkable and pervasive influence of ideologies. Elliot (1997: p.56) summarizes that ideology can determine whether tourism development will be supported, how much financial support is given; it can set the style of tourism and the nature and extent of government involvement. J. Henderson (2003) remarks that political ideologies have helped to determine the prominence given to tourism in planning, resource allocation and decision-making; in consequence, tourism fulfils a role in supporting the reigning ideologies.

During the 1980s, the United Kingdom and the United States saw the rise of Thatcherism and Reaganism, named after their political leaders. These strictly adhered to the market-economy ideology, retreating from active government intervention. As a result, deregulation, privatization, tax incentive elimination and withdrawal of discretionary government intervention led to 'smaller government'. In this context governments withdrew support from tourism as far as possible. In the US, the United States Travel and Tourism Administration (USTTA) was abolished and in the UK funding for similar organizations was reduced. In other examples, British Labour governments have stressed the role of tourism in assisting less-developed regions and in the early 1970s, the Australian Labor government allowed the Australian Tourist Commission to become involved in domestic tourism to improve people's life quality (C.M. Hall and Jenkins, 1995; Elliot, 1997).

In the era of the former socialist countries in Eastern Europe, tourism played an important ideological role in promoting model communist achievements to foreign tourists especially from Western countries. The sites and areas selected for tourist visits together with the routes, accommodation and transportation were all used by the government to project positive images of socialist systems. At the same time, for domestic tourism, for the privileged groups, mainly the party, military and bureaucratic elites, tourism was used to strengthen their power base and enhance relationships while for the non-privileged it was adopted for ideological (i.e. consolidating the socialist ethics) and political goals (solidifying the ruling power) (D.R. Hall, 1991; C.M. Hall, 1994; C.M. Hall and Jenkins, 1995). Mellor (1991) examined domestic tourism in the former Eastern Germany – German Democratic Republic. Here there was 'considerable emphasis on group recreation and holidays in accommodation provided by the workplace or trade union . . . designated to build social coherence and an *esprit-de-corps*, besides allowing recreation time to be mixed with political indoctrination' (p.149). In this connection, domestic travel was subsidized by government-supported trade unions and state-owned enterprises in the form of cheap accommodation and transportation (D.R. Hall, 2001). In the meantime, restrictions were imposed on travel by citizens to the Western world for fear of ideological contamination or moral pollution (C.M. Hall, 1994; Elliot, 1997). As D.R. Hall (2001: p.94) puts it, until 1989, it was easier for Czechs and Slovaks to travel several thousand kilometres to holiday in Cuba or Vietnam than to cross the Czechoslovakian border into West Germany. D.R. Hall (2001: pp.93–4) further finds that 'this appeared to suggest that a centralized command economy and successful international tourism were incompatible'. Likewise, socialist countries like China, North Korea, Albania and Cuba followed, to varying degrees, socialist principles in the determination of their tourism policies (C.M. Hall, 1994).

Chambers and Airey (2001) examined public policy-making in Jamaica in the socialist and capitalist periods and concluded that 'tourism public policies are strongly influenced by the ideological thrust of the governing political parties' (p.117). In the socialist period between 1972 and 1980, democratic socialism was upheld by Jamaica's new government led by Michael Manley. According to their work, democratic socialism placed 'the people of Jamaica at the centre of all its new policies and programme'. Under this political ideology, tourism was seen as a development engine for building a 'new society' (p.98). Tourism was designated to maximize the economic benefits (i.e. foreign exchange earnings and employment) and to achieve the Jamaicanization of the tourism industry (integration of tourism into Jamaican life through domestic travel, indigenous participation and promotion of indigenous values). The government showed strong intervention in the tourism industry through nationalization. By 1980, seventeen of the largest hotels were owned by the government, representing around 60 per cent of first-class hotel rooms. In the capitalism period from 1980 to 1989, democratic socialism was replaced by 'dependent capitalism' advocated by the new government and dependent on the United States. Nationalization gave away to privatization; by 1982, fifteen previously state-owned hotels were leased to the private sector.

Sector-level (tourism) policy factors

The macro-level policy factors refer to those policy factors outside the tourism policy system, whereas the sector-level policy factors are those that occur inside a sector, in this case the 'tourism policy system'. The policy factors at the sector level mainly include the tourism policy paradigm and tourism institutions. Although ideologies enable the policy actors to make sense of complex realities, they tend to be very diffuse and do not necessarily translate easily into specific views on specific policy problems. The sectoral views or beliefs can exercise a much more direct influence in policy-making for a sector (Howlett and Ramesh, 2003).

POLICY PARADIGM

According to the Oxford English Dictionary (1999: p.1063), the word 'paradigm' means the 'type of something or pattern or model'. The concept of 'paradigm' originated from the American philosopher Thomas Kuhn, who defined the 'paradigm' and used this concept to describe progress in natural sciences. Kuhn (1970: p.175), asserted that a 'paradigm' is 'the entire constellation of beliefs, values, techniques and so on shared by members of a given community'. It refers to a common epistemological vision in terms of approach, a general theory and some important conclusions at the hardcore of a science shared and taken for granted by the members of a science community such as physics, chemistry or economics. Change in paradigm was termed a 'punctuated equilibrium model', that goes through alterations between long periods of stability involving incremental adaptations and brief periods of revolutionary shift. The underlying reason for this pattern might be that the members in any epistemic community adhere to a deep structure of basic values and beliefs prohibiting anything but marginal changes. Kuhn suggests that the observation of anomalies, which cannot adequately be explained by the existing paradigm, eventually leads to replacement by a new paradigm. During the course of events, the members initially try to adapt the existing paradigm to anomalies, but eventually they fail. The new paradigm represents a new way of understanding the phenomenon, therefore, it represents a fundamental break from the past that could be considered as a 'revolution' (Sherman, 1987; P. Hall, 1990, 1993; Howlett and Ramesh, 1995). Later, the concept of paradigm was applied to studies in social sciences. Jenson designed the concept of 'societal paradigm' for this, describing it as follows:

> A societal paradigm is a shared set of interconnected premises which make sense of many social relations. Every paradigm contains a view of human nature, a definition of basic and proper forms of social relations among equals and among those in relationships of hierarchy, and specification of relations among institutions as well as a stipulation of the role of such institutions. Thus, a societal paradigm is a meaning system as well as a set of practices.
>
> (Jenson, 1989: pp. 238–9)

Guba (1990: p.17) defines the 'paradigm' as 'A basic set of beliefs that guides action, whether of everyday garden variety or action taken in connection with a disciplined inquiry.'

The application of paradigm to studies of public policy-making can be thought to begin with the work of Peter Hall (1990, 1993), who initiated the concept of 'policy paradigm' to inquire into British macroeconomic policy-making between 1970 and 1989. Howlett and Ramesh (1995: p.190) suggest that Hall 'has perhaps done the most to develop the concept in recent times'. Menahem (1998: p.283) remarked 'the widening use of the concept of policy paradigm for understanding policy process has significant implications for research agendas'. Hall's initiative arose from the growing importance of knowledge utilization in public policy-making. Hall remarks that state policies were 'deeply conditioned by the findings and presumptions of contemporary social sciences' (1990: p.53) and 'economic policy-making is a knowledge-intensive process' (1993: p.277). He conceived that a policy paradigm occurred in a policy field, rather than applied to the whole society. According to him, a policy paradigm is an 'overarching system of ideas' that 'connects certain conceptions of the relevant policy problems to a particular set of instruments commonly associated with policy in that sphere' (1990: p.59). He further describes the role of a policy paradigm as:

> It defines the broad goals behind policy, the related problems or puzzles that policy-makers have to solve to get there, and, in a large measure, the

kind of instruments that can be used to attain these goals. Like a gestalt, this framework is all the more powerful because it is largely taken for granted and rarely subject to scrutiny as a whole.

(P. Hall, 1990: p.59)

P. Hall (1990, 1993) indicates that British macroeconomic policy-making hinged on the shift from Keynesianism to Monetarism between 1970 and 1989, which, in his view, were two distinct and contending policy paradigms. Keynesianism took a view that the private economy was unstable and government intervention was necessary whereas Monetarism saw the private economy as stable with government intervention causing barriers to economic efficiency.

Hall ascribed the shift in British economic policy paradigms to both cognitive (i.e. scientific or intellectual) and political processes (1990: p.67). Cognitive processes in this case refer to the problems and anomalies of the real world such as high inflation, economic stagnation and unemployment which were not envisaged under Keynesianism. The political processes in their turn meant that Margaret Thatcher's Conservative Party, advocating Monetarism, won the election in 1979. Subsequently, Monetarism replaced Keynesianism as the paradigm for British macroeconomic policy. Hall (1990: p.68) illustrates how the implementation of the paradigm started with institutionalization, including the rearrangement of organizations and standard operating procedures as well as the appointment of supporters to key positions. He provides a description as follows:

> Once in office, Thatcher played a key role in institutionalizing the new policy paradigm. She packed the influential economic committees of the cabinet with its supporters, appointed the outside monetarist to be chief economic advisor at the Treasury ... The locus of authority over policymaking in this period again shifted dramatically towards the prime minister. Over time, an aggressive policy of promoting civil servants who were highly pliable or sympathetic to monetarist views implanted the new paradigm even more firmly. By 1982, the operating routines at the Treasury and the Bank of England as well as the terms of policy discourse had shifted decisively toward Monetarism.
>
> (P. Hall, 1993: p.287)

Howlett and Ramesh (1995: p.190) provide a refinement to Hall's work. They summarize the concept of the policy paradigm as 'an intellectual construct intimately linked to policy subsystem' adopted to form the broad goals, the ways of perceiving the policy problems and kinds of solutions. They (1995: p.189) also perceived a close relationship between ideology and policy paradigm but without further elaboration. Braun (1999) envisages that the policy paradigm defines the place of a sector within the overall structure of the state by providing the enduring principles, basic values and causal assumptions driving feasible approaches and practical actions.

In another example, Menahem (1998) examines the evolution of the water sector policy paradigm in Israel since 1948 and identifies that Israel's Zionist state ideology was the 'important component' between 1948 and 1990 (p.290). Menahem points out that 'within the Zionist ideological framework, agriculture held symbolic importance in the movement to rebuild the social structure of a people gathering from the Diaspora and inhabit the territories and ultimately to achieve statehood' and 'for a long period in the history of resettlement of Jews, agriculture settlements in Palestine were considered to be of primary national importance' (p.290). Menahem then goes on to illustrate how the water policy paradigm was ideology-dominated as it 'originated from the dominant ideology that both connected agriculture to nation building and viewed water policy as part of the agriculture endeavor' (p.306). This was reflected in the water policy paradigm of a 'state supported expansion of agriculture [that] was a major cornerstone of both nation building and state building' and 'in order to enable the expansion of agriculture, both the regulating of water consumption by the state and the subsidizing of water for agriculture was considered to be essential' (p.292). Later, the policy paradigm evolved into 'the priority of expansion of agriculture over preserving scarce water resources' (p.296). Like Hall's studies, Menahem also found that institutionalization was an inseparable stage in pursuing a policy paradigm. Israel's water policy paradigm was formally institutionalized into the Water Law enacted in 1959 making water policy the responsibility of the Water Commissioner and Water Council with supreme authority resting with the Minister of Agriculture. In this way the essence of the water policy paradigm, 'priority of agriculture over water', was institutionalized into the legal framework.

In summary, the policy paradigm is very similar in nature to ideology. Both are intellectual constructs – knowledge as well as belief – which point out that society and policy-making can be better than they are. They are basically plans to improve society. Their differences lie in their scope. Ideology is designed for the whole of society; whereas the policy paradigm is for a specific sector, such as economic policy and tourism policy. So the policy paradigm serves as a 'mini-ideology' or 'policy ideology' (Wilson, 2000: p.254).

POLICY PARADIGM AND TOURISM

P. Hall (1990: p.59) remarks that 'it seems likely that policy-makers in all fields are guided by some such paradigm, even though the complexity and coherence of the paradigm may vary considerably across fields'. Braun (1999) also indicates that each policy sector or field is guided by a sectoral worldview or paradigm. Goeldner and Ritchie (2006) adapt the concept 'philosophy' to tourism policy-making and argue that tourism philosophy is 'an essential foundation on which to develop a coherent policy' (p.416). According to them:

A tourism philosophy may be defined as a general principle or set of principles that indicates the beliefs and values of members of a society concerning how tourism shall serve the population of a country or region, and that acts as a guide for evaluating the utility of tourism-related activities.

(Goeldner and Ritchie, 2006: p.416).

Here the term 'tourism philosophy' has remarkable similarity to 'policy paradigm' and although, in this case, it is not derived from empirical work, Goeldner and Ritchie's heuristic work nevertheless envisages the significance of an ideational dimension to tourism policy-making of a type that was not well explored or understood in the existing tourism policy literature.

The examination of the policy paradigm shift in British macroeconomic policy-making led P. Hall to discern that the influence of policy paradigms was closely related to the extent of their establishment, development and rigour in academic terms. He (1990: p.59) suggests that 'in the sphere of contemporary macroeconomic policy-making, of course, policy paradigms of this sort are obvious and highly developed', because 'policy is made by reference to a complex set of economic theories developed with increasing sophistication over a hundred years'. Against this background, Hall (1990: p.59) acknowledges that the extent to which policy paradigms are established and the extent of their rigour might vary from field to field. He further adds that 'not all fields of policy will possess policy paradigms as elaborate or forceful as the ones associated with macroeconomic policymaking'; such 'forceful' and 'elaborate' paradigms most likely exist in fields where 'some highly technical issues' and 'a body of specialized knowledge' are required for policy-making, such as arms control, environmental regulation and energy policy (1993: p.291). Notwithstanding this, he still suggests that the degree of coherence and complexity does not matter for the existence of a policy paradigm in a field of public policy-making; as he puts it 'even in non-technical fields, policymakers are generally guided by an implicit set of assumptions and images that impart meaning to their work and direction to their endeavors' (1990: p.60). Hall is not the only proponent of these views. Howlett and Ramesh (1995: p.190) also argue that the policy paradigm 'is not always coherent, reflecting the limitation innate to the study of public problems and the complex compromises public policy-makers must contend with'. The last point has particular relevance in a consideration of the applicability of the policy paradigm for tourism which is not at the same stage of development as long-standing academic disciplines such as economics, political science or sociology.

Compared to other economic sectors such as agriculture, heavy industry and banking, tourism is a relatively young sector, which developed rapidly after World War Two (Gee *et al.*, 1989, 1997). According to C.L. Jenkins and Lickorish (1997: p.2), 1945 was the year that development of the major growth in the tourism industry began. Since then, its economic, social and political impacts have started to draw the attention of government and academics, although for government, all too often it has been seen as a 'candy-floss' activity (Elliot, 1997: p.83) while the academic community has seen it as 'frivolous' and 'inappropriate for mature scholars' (Richter, 1983a; H.G. Matthews and Richter, 1991: p.122). Echtner and Jamal (1997: p.868) comment 'the study of the tourism phenomenon is a relatively recent addition to academic endeavor'. Its multi-faceted nature has only gradually been reflected in the academic literature. Previous studies observe that the spectrum of tourism studies has expanded from an economic imperative before the mid-1970s, to socio-economic-cultural impacts from the mid-1970s, to environmental concern from the early 1980s, and to political and administrative perspectives in the 1990s. Nevertheless its youthfulness and incremental development has laid tourism open to criticism as lacking intellectual credibility (Tribe, 1997: p.638) and P.L. Pearce (1993) and Echtner and Jamal (1997: p.875) indicate that tourism studies is in the pre-paradigmatic or pre-science phase, that is, according to Kuhn (1970), 'characterized by total disagreement and constant debate over fundamentals . . . there will be almost as many theories as there are workers in the field and each theoretician will be obliged to start afresh and justify his own particular approach'.

With this background tourism policy paradigms cannot be expected to be as solid and rigorous as British macroeconomic policy-making resting on academic disciplines like economics with a history dating back to the eighteenth century. However, the academic limitations of tourism appear not to affect the existence of a tourism policy paradigm, and its role in directing the thought of government in deciding tourism policy. Pursuing and maximizing the economic contribution of tourism development is perhaps the most explicit, widely implemented or even leading tenet in many developed and developing countries. Elliot (1997: p.29) concludes 'governments became involved in tourism historically, and are still involved in the management of tourism today, mainly for economic reasons'. Sharpley (2002: p.14) also points out 'throughout the world, the most compelling reason for pursuing tourism as a development strategy is its alleged positive contribution to the local or national economy'. The Manila Declaration made by UNWTO in 1980 demonstrates that the broad economic orientation of tourism policy was widely accepted at an early stage:

> World tourism can contribute to the establishment of a new international economic order that will help to eliminate the widening economic gap between developed and developing countries and ensure the steady acceleration of economic and social development and progress, in particular in developing countries.
>
> (UNWTO, 1980: p.1)

However, the economic focus is only one strand of tourism policy thinking. According to a study conducted by the Commission of the European Communities (CEC), government intervention in tourism is based not purely on an economic rationale, but also on the 'impracticability or inability of the enterprises representing organizations and individuals to undertake certain necessary functions' (C.L. Jenkins and Lickorish, 1997: p.187). The idea, in which government is primarily responsible for marketing and promotion, and the development of infrastructure and product is left to the private sector, is another belief in tourism policy-making, held by the Australia and New Zealand governments (C.M. Hall and Jenkins, 1995: p.28). Further, this does not mean that all countries or regions take a consistent direction in tourism policies. Not all tourism policy paradigms are economic oriented. As already noted, in Taiwan, the tourism policy paradigm became diplomatic or politically oriented when massive foreign exchange reserves had been accumulated (C.M. Hall, 1994).

In summary, the policy paradigm acts as a lens that filters information and focuses attention; it shapes the way that the problems are defined, the types of solutions offered and the kinds of policies proposed (Wilson, 2000: p.257). It is generally assumed that the policy paradigm exists and functions in the tourism context and guides tourism policy-making, considering that each policy sector or field is directed by a sectoral worldview or philosophy.

TOURISM INSTITUTIONS

Institutions represent the rules of society (Simeon, 1976; P. Hall, 1986; W.R. Scott, 2001; Lowndes, 2002; North, 2004), which are strongly held and supported by entrenched resources (W.R. Scott, 2001), to prescribe political and social behaviour. As an integrated concept (W.R. Scott, 2001), they embody values and norms, as well as power and authority which are manifest in the form of regulations, routines, standard operating procedures and organizational forms (Rokeach, 1979; March and Olsen, 1989; Lowndes, 2002). They shape political and social actors' conception of reality and constrain and empower their activities so as to achieve stable patterns of behaviour (Howlett and Ramesh, 1995; Goodin, 1996; W.R. Scott, 2001). In this sense institutionalization denotes a process for attaining such patterns (Jepperson, 1991: p.144).

W.R. Scott (2001: pp.49–58) describes institutions as being composed of coercive or regulatory, normative and cultural-cognitive pillars. It is through these three pillars, which are the building blocks of institutions, with their associated activities and resources that institutions provide stability and meaning to social life. The regulatory aspect involves the capacity to enact rules, monitor conformance and manipulate sanctions. The normative pillar institutionalizes the ends and means into structures and rules such as standard operating procedures and routines (March and Olsen, 1989: pp.21–2). The cultural-cognitive pillar is built on the shared conceptions that constitute the nature of social reality and the frame through which meaning is created. Hoffman (1997: p.36) indicates that these three pillars function in a continuum moving 'from the conscious to the unconscious, from the legally enforced to the taken for granted'.

Tourism institutions exist at government and industry levels (Simeon, 1976; March and Olsen, 1983; C.M. Hall and Jenkins, 1995; Howlett and Ramesh, 1995; Rhodes, 1995). Tourism public policy is forged and shaped principally in the political and public institutions (C.M. Hall and Jenkins, 1995: p.26; C.M. Hall, 1998: p.205). As early as the 1970s, Sessa (1976: pp.240–1) indicated that the type of tourism policy was directly dependent on the institutional framework of a nation; different institutional arrangements led to obligatory planning of tourism development in a collectivist system and mainly indicative planning in a mixed economy. Tourism institutions provide a set of rules and procedures to regulate how and where demands for policy initiatives can be made and who has the authority to make and implement policy decisions (Simeon, 1976; C.M. Hall and Jenkins, 1995). Simeon (1976: p.575) further argues that 'institutions may themselves be seen as policies, which, by building into the decision process the need to consult particular groups and follow particular procedures, increase the likelihood of some kinds of decisions and reduces that of others'.

According to Brunsson and Jacobsson (2002) tourism institutions are an integrated or broad policy factor. They embody a set of other policy factors including ideology, power, values and interests as well as a policy paradigm, all of which are institutionalized into strongly held rules (P. Hall, 1993; Rhodes, 1995). In line with the market-economy ideology, the idea that government should be responsible for tourism marketing and promotion became popular in much of the Western world and the institutional arrange-ments for tourism evolved accordingly. For an example, in New Zealand this led to a split between promotion and policy in the 1990s with the abolition of The New Zealand Tourism Department (NZTD) and the creation of two government organizations – The New Zealand Tourism Board (NZTB) and Tourism Group under the Ministry of Commerce. The NZTB was responsible for international marketing and promotion; the Tourism Group responsible for policy advice. This restructuring reflected the philosophy that government involvement in tourism is primarily oriented towards marketing and pro-motion with the development of the product increasingly left in the hands of the private sector. This was considered by the government to be the effective way to build a relationship with industry in marketing New Zealand as a visitor destination (C.M. Hall and Jenkins, 1995; C.M. Hall, 1998).

Coleman and Skogstad (1990), cited in C.M. Hall and Jenkins (1995), suggest that political institutions promote certain ideologies and constrain choices, while March and Olsen (1983: pp.738–9) argue that institutions have an autonomous and coherent role in defining and defending interests, being political actors and decision-makers in their own right. They claim that 'the organization of political life makes a difference'. In the long run, institutions will change if political pressures are sufficiently strong (Simeon, 1976), so institutions can be viewed as both an 'independent factor' in the short run and a 'dependent factor' in the long run. As a dependent variable, institutions represent policies themselves (Simeon, 1976; Huang, 1999: p.17) so when policy-makers begin to understand the inadequacies of existing institutions in the context of new policies, new sector institutions will replace the old ones.

Friedland and Alford (1991: p.248) conclude that each of the most important Western institutions has a central logic – a set of material practices and a symbolic construction, which help to forge the organizing principles and are available for individual and collective elaboration. Capitalist institutional logic is an accumulation and the commodification of human activity. The logic of the state is to rationalize and regulate individual and collective behaviour through a coercive and bureaucratic framework. Friedland and Alford's explication of institutional logic offers an ideological perspective. W.R. Scott (2001: p.139) defines the institutional logic in a sector as a set of guidelines to sector participants as to how they are to carry out their work.

In summary, the tourism policy paradigm and tourism institutions are considered in this study as two policy factors affecting the policy-making process at the sector level. Generally speaking, the policy paradigm provides sectoral beliefs, or a mini-ideology or policy ideology that shapes the policy-making in a particular sector. Although the policy paradigm is rarely referred to formally in a tourism context it is nevertheless assumed to exist and function, in that every policy sector is directed by a sectoral view or philosophy. Tourism institutions are the institutions at government and industry levels. They provide sets of rules to forge and shape the tourism policy. The policy paradigm and sector institutions do not exist independently, with the latter an inseparable partner of the former through institutionalization.

Micro-level policy factors

Micro-level policy factors are the tourism policy actors themselves, including their beliefs, values, interests and power. They may be organizations, such as national tourism administrations, tourism associations or individuals such as government ministers, industry leaders.

PROFILE OF POLICY PLAYERS IN TOURISM

The policy actors stand at the core of the policy-making process, because policy is formulated and implemented by them identifying and transmitting problems and opportunities in the environment, interpreting ideology and values, expressing and protecting their interests, and exercising their authority and power. Lindblom (1980: p.2) highlights the role of policy participants as follows: 'To understand who or what makes policy, one must understand the characteristics of the participants, what parts or roles they play, what authority and other powers they hold, and how they deal with and control each other'. Their importance has recently been acknowledged in tourism policy studies (Dredge, 2006; Pforr, 2006; Bramwell and Meyer, 2007; Stevenson *et al.*, 2008; Airey and Chong, 2010).

The policy actors comprise the official policy-makers and unofficial participants (J.E. Anderson, 1990, 2003). Sector policy-making usually involves a set of policy actors, including the leaders, responsible government agencies for a sector, local government and interests groups. Tourism is a sector that covers a wide variety of economic activities; it is typified by great diversity and a great number of organizations and issues (Elliot, 1997). This means that the tourism policy-making process will involve a wide range of both government agencies, non-government organizations (NGOs) and businesses, but the actual participation will vary according to the policy issue. Some policy issues, like regulating tour guides, will involve a small number of participants while development of a theme park will involve not only government and business groups but also environmental and local community groups.

TOURISM POLICY COMMUNITY

The concept 'policy community' refers to all those actors involved in the policy-making process for a sector, who share a common idea set or outlook (Howlett and Ramesh, 2003). In this connection, Elliot (1997: p.71) indicates that tourism policy-making proceeds through a policy community which he defines as 'the key organizations and actors who participate in policy and who are continually in touch with and talking to each other about tourism issues'. Some organizations, such as a sponsoring government ministry and national tourism organization (NTO), in the tourism policy community will be involved in almost all issues, while others will participate if an issue is relevant to them. For example, the formulation of a national tourism plan or strategy will involve all or at least most members of the policy community, but regulating travel agencies will usually involve only those directly affected. The members of the tourism policy community and their roles are described as follows.

Leaders   The leaders like the president, prime minister or leader of a ruling political party are especially important in the formulation of both national policy and sector policies. There can be no tourism policy or no progress in tourism policy unless there is at least passive support at this level, because leaders have the authority or influence to place a policy initiative on the agenda, make a policy decision, enforce its implementation, assure the provision of resources and monitor the outcome. For example, the strong support of Field Marshal Sarit of Thailand in the late 1960s boosted business and tourism development. Tourism Minister John Brown in the Australian Labor Government of 1983 contributed to putting Australian tourism into the major league (Elliot, 1997).

National tourism organizations or administration (NTO or NTA)   NTA and NTO are two terms frequently used in the tourism context, with the former involved in policy and administration and the latter primarily for marketing and development. Organizationally they may be separate entities or combined.

This section mainly deals with the NTAs (UNWTO, 1979). Although top political leaders have the power to decide policy, they lack time and information to formulate tourism policy itself. So there is often a need for a specific government department or public organization to hold responsibility for tourism policy-making and tourism development. The NTA in many countries plays a leading role in the initiation, formulation and implementation of tourism policy decisions (Elliot, 1997). For example, Dieke (1993a: p.281) describes how the Ministry of Information and Tourism in Gambia determined the overall tourism policy at home and abroad. Established in 1964, the Singapore Tourist Promotion Board (STPB) is tasked with developing Singapore as a tourist destination (T.C. Chang, 1998: p.73). The forms of NTA vary from country to country. The different forms include (D.G. Pearce, 1992):

- A separate and independent cabinet ministry as in the Philippines;
- A combined ministry, like the Department of Resources, Energy and Tourism in Australia;
- A department or agency under a ministry like the former United States Travel and Tourism Administration, which was under the Department of Commerce;
- A non-ministry government or statutory organization, such as the Tourism Authority of Thailand.

In many countries, the NTAs actually play a significant role in the development of tourism through the initiation and implementation of policy decisions. For example, the tourism ministry in Mexico – SECTUR – took the lead in planning and implementing a multi-year master plan that covered the planning and construction of five resorts, infrastructure and hotels during the 1960s (Clancy, 1999). The Tourism Authority of Thailand (TAT) is also a key body in formulating the National Plan of Tourism Development for that country (Elliot, 1997).

One important feature of NTAs is that, to a large extent, they cannot determine tourism policy independently. Tourism covers a wide range of economic, social and cultural activities, and many other government ministries and agencies are actually involved in tourism. During the tourism policy-making process, the NTAs typically need to seek coordination and cooperation with other government agencies, and this is the reason why Elliot (1987: p.226) comments that the role of TAT was as a pressure group on government and industry.

Other responsible government agencies for tourism   According to Elliot (1997), there are two kinds of government ministries related to tourism policy-making. The first are the 'service ministries' including finance, planning or development ministries. Elliot indicates that these ministries perform a control and overview function. For the finance ministry, it decides what finance should be available for infrastructure or administration. Planning or development ministries, such as the National Development and Reform Commission of China and the National Economic and Social Development Board of Thailand, are common in developing countries. These are usually responsible for long-term planning and development. Elliot argues that such ministries are usually long-standing and powerful. They have their own responsibility and objectives, and they have to be convinced that the tourism policy objectives are not contrary to their own objectives. The second kind of ministry are the 'sector ministries'. These typically control one activity, like transport, immigration, education, which can be crucial for the development of tourism. For example, the actions of the immigration agency will greatly affect the growth of international tourism in a country.

Local government   Local government is not only responsible for implementing tourism policy decisions formulated by the central government, but also often has authority to develop local tourism. The effectiveness of tourism policy formulated at the centre cannot be taken for granted because local interests may diverge from those of central government. Actually it is the local level that experiences tourism impacts directly and has to live with them permanently (Williams and Shaw, 1991; Elliot, 1997). Thus, the importance of local government in their role as representing the interests of local people, cannot be disregarded.

Interest groups   The unofficial members of the tourism policy community are the interest groups, which can be interchangeably used with the term 'pressure groups', 'lobby groups' or more recently 'special interest groups' (C.M. Hall and Jenkins, 1995: p.49) or 'stakeholders'. C.M. Hall (1999: p.281) claims that the 'role of interest groups is crucial to any discussion of collaboration in tourism'. According to T. Matthews (1980), interest groups refer to any association or organization which makes a claim, either directly or indirectly, on government to influence public policy without itself exercising the formal powers of government. The most important interest group in tourism policy-making is the business community. According to Lindblom (1980), the position of business in policy-making is privileged. Business performance affects employment, prices, inflation, production, growth and living standards, which are items utilized by governments to measure success. The tourism industry has knowledge of markets, customers and products and has the skills and dynamism necessary to operate in highly competitive markets. So, the relationship between government and industry is particularly important. A good relationship can enhance the provision of information for tourism policy-making (Elliot, 1997).

Liaison of government with industry is through the tourism industry leadership, especially industry organizations such as hotel associations and travel agencies associations. Elliot (1997) identifies the roles of industry associations to include the collection of information and communication with government; lobbying government to support the industry and monitoring, controlling and securing compliance. So they can significantly influence tourism policy-making. Besides tourism businesses, other interest groups such as labour unions, environmental protection groups and the local community also play an increasingly important role in tourism policy-making. Sabatier and Jenkins-Smith (1993) and Howlett and Ramesh (1995) argue that participants in the policy community might not hold the same values or interests towards a policy problem. According to Sabatier (1993), those participants holding the same set of value priorities will form an 'advocacy coalition' in relation to a particular policy. Examples are industry associations that emphasize the economic value of tourism and the environmental protection groups that focus on the preservation and protection of natural resources.

VALUES, INTERESTS AND POWER OF POLICY PLAYERS

The fragmented structure of the tourism sector means that its policy community is typified by a diversity and complexity of values, interests and power relationships. As far as fragmentation is concerned tourism comprises a number of different economic sectors. Some are directly related to tourism like travel agencies, hotels and airlines while others have a more indirect relationship such as transport, leisure, catering and retailing, not all of whose customers are tourists. These sectors are interdependent and contribute to the success of tourism. This fragmented nature has two implications. First, different sectors have different values and interests, leading to different objectives when they demand tourism policy; second, because of their mutual interdependence, their power to influence government is constrained (Elliot, 1997). Therefore, it may be difficult for players in the tourism sector to form a coherent position to lobby government. Wanhill (1987) for example suggests that its fragmented nature may make it harder for tourism in Britain to form a strong lobby to encourage government policy-making in favour of the industry. Likewise, this nature may also weaken the ability of government to mobilize the industry towards the resolution of tourism problems (Howlett and Ramesh, 1995).

The structure of government agencies responsible for and related to tourism is also fragmented. Although the NTAs may play a leading role, tourism policy in fact touches on many government agencies responsible, for example, for civil aviation, immigration and environmental protection, and it is impossible to group all of these into one ministry or agency (Airey, 1983; Elliot, 1997). Again the values and interests among the different agencies differ, and the authority to determine tourism policy is similarly fragmented, yet NTAs cannot formulate and implement a coherent and detailed tourism policy independently of these agencies.

Turning to conflicts of values and interests, these exist at the organizational as well as at the individual level. At government level, previous studies (Elliot, 1987, 1997; Gee *et al.*, 1989, 1997) have found that different government agencies have different formal and informal values. The formal values can be observed through organizational missions, goals and objectives. For example, an environmental protection agency is more concerned with the protection and conservation of natural resources while the NTA aims to speed up the development of tourism and to maximize its economic contribution. The informal values refer to the self-interests of the organization, for example the bureaucratic need for maintenance and expansion (Simeon, 1976). These formal and informal values may conflict with formal tourism development objectives.

Elliot's (1987: p.227) study of Thailand's tourism policy found conflicting objectives among different government agencies. For example, the main objective of the government-owned Thai Airways International was the expansion of its share of the market and increased profit. This led the Thai government to oppose the entry of other scheduled and charter airlines into Thailand, thus acting contrary to the government policy of encouraging more tourists. In terms of informal values, Gee *et al.* (1989: p.103) observe some long-standing agencies, like economic development or public works ministries that predate the NTA but whose programmes for infrastructure impact on tourism, tend to be jealous and protective of their functional 'turf' and resist redistribution or reassignment of their functions to the NTA.

Similar conflicts of values and interests exist at the industry level. Protection of natural resources by an environmental group may be against the interests of the tourism business, which favour tourism development. Elliot (1987: p.228) describes the circumstance in Thailand where 'every manager wants to do their own thing and build up their own organization. Even when a sector can agree to have a peak industry association, such as the Thai Hotels Association (THA), to represent it, there can still be conflict.' But, it is also possible for the industry members to achieve consensus on certain policy issues such as government funding of research and marketing and deregulation of the industry.

Richter (1989) identifies that in the initial stage of tourism development, there is often little apparent conflict over policy, and that developing tourism is a policy with apparently substantial rewards and with few interests to placate or offend. Tourism tends to become a subject of political debate later when major social costs become apparent. However, not every government official related to tourism holds positive and supportive attitudes towards tourism development. Some are suspicious of tourism from the start. They do not regard it as a serious industry but a 'candy-floss' activity, unreliable, menial, destructive, and tainted with the seediness and corruption of sex tourism (Elliot, 1997). In Thailand, Elliot (1987: pp.227–8) found that some bureaucrats saw tourism as a luxury industry for foreigners and not of benefit to the mass of the people. Hence, scarce resources should not therefore be used for tourism. He also points to both nationalism and morality in the condemnation of the sexual aspects of tourism and its damage to the overseas image of Thailand.

Individual policy actors may also have their own interests, such as personal gain and promotion. This may contradict the goals and objectives set for the development of tourism. The operation of values, interests and power of the individual players is the same as at the organizational level, where contradiction and conflict of values and interests results in power struggle, albeit, it is often hard to observe.

In terms of power, according to Dahl (cited in Ham and Hill, 1993), where there are differences or preferences between policy actors, power must be studied. Power is defined in terms of capacity to overcome resistance or to affect or modify the behaviour of another group or individual. This can be described as 'all forms of successful control by A over B – that is, of A securing the compliance of B' (Lukes, 1974: p.17; P.H. Chang, 1975; Ham and Hill, 1993; C.M. Hall and Jenkins, 1995; Elliot, 1997), in the form of authority, coercion, force, influence and manipulation. Sources of power include rules, wealth, expertise and knowledge (Foucault, 1980: pp.61–62; Hill, 2005: p.30). Generally power can be exercised in three dimensions. First, there is the exercise of power that occurs in observable, overt conflicts between policy participants over key issues. Second, there is the exercise of power that occurs in covert conflicts between actors. Third, power is exercised to shape the preferences of people so that neither overt nor covert conflicts exist (Lukes, 1974; Ham and Hill, 1993; C.M. Hall and Jenkins, 1995; Hill, 2005: pp.33–4). Hall and Jenkins (1995) suggest that tourism policy-making is a political process involving the values and interests of policy actors in a struggle for power relative to this process. The exercise of power by tourism policy actors is value-laden, or as Lukes (1974: p.26) argues, power is ineradicably value-dependent. Tourism policy actors whose preferences prevail in conflicts over key political issues are those who exercise power in the tourism policy system (Ham and Hill, 1993; Hill, 2005).

Policy process

Having considered the policy inputs, particularly in relation to the factors that influence and create policy, this next section turns to the policy process itself, considering how policy is made. Based on the work of Howlett and Ramesh (2003) the policy process can be considered from the perspective of the ideal, which suggests how the process should proceed or the real, which describes the actual process in the real world.

The ideal: the rational model

The rational model of policy-making aims to maximize the solutions to complex problems in which the required information is gathered and then focused in a scientific fashion on the assessment of policy options (Howlett and Ramesh, 2003). Such a process is usually called 'policy analysis' and involves relevant professionals and experts (Lindblom and Woodhouse, 1993). The rational model suggests that the choice of the most efficient possible alternatives for achieving the policy goal can be sought by following a series of activities: establishing goals, identifying alternatives, and evaluating and selecting choices (Dye, 2002; Howlett and Ramesh, 2003). Lindblom and Woodhouse (1993) suggest that real world constraints of human fallibility, poorly defined problems, conflicts of values and interests and resource restrictions severely limit the rational model. Despite these, the importance of an intellectual component in policy-making has been widely acknowledged. P. Hall (1990: p.53) indicates that state policies are 'deeply conditioned by the findings and presumptions of contemporary social science'. Lindblom and Woodhouse (1993: p.6) also point out that 'the study of policy-making has paid special attention to the roles of information and analysis, with some books and courses focusing almost entirely on these intellectual components of political life'. On the basis of acknowledging the utilization of knowledge and analysis, they (1993: p.24) nevertheless assert that 'there is no possibility of replacing politics by analysis'. This is because:

> To reach a solution without any exercise of power, sheer information and reasoning alone would have to be sufficient to bring all relevant parties into agreement. For unless they all are persuaded by the facts to accept the same policy outcome, their differences will have to be reconciled by power, by some political process such as voting.
>
> (Lindblom and Woodhouse, 1993: p.16)

Lindblom and Woodhouse (1993: p.7) conclude that 'all government policy making can be considered political, since it involves the use of authority'; public policy-making is the authoritative allocation of values by government that are binding on society (Easton, 1965a; J.E. Anderson, 2003). The role of policy analysis is rather to adapt to the political process; it can serve as an instrument of persuasion to move the policy actors closer to reasoned and voluntary agreement, so that the quality of the political process of policy-making can be improved (Lindblom, 1980: pp.28 and 30; Lindblom and Woodhouse, 1993: p.127 and 129).

The real: policy-oriented learning and coordination

The policy-making process might be better conceptualized as a process of policy-oriented learning (or policy learning) and coordination (see Figure 3.1). As far as tourism is concerned, with its diverse beliefs, values and interests, policy-oriented learning will lead to distinct or even conflicting outcomes. Coordination will then be needed among the policy actors, often with the exercise of power.

POLICY-ORIENTED LEARNING

As the policy actor stands at the core of policy-making, the relationship between the policy actors and all policy factors can be conceptualized as 'policy-oriented learning'. This concept was pioneered by Heclo (1974) and developed by P. Hall (1993). Learning is usually said to proceed when individuals assimilate new information, including that based on past experience, and apply it to their subsequent actions (P. Hall, 1993: p.278). Public policy-making can be conceived as an iterative process of active learning on the part of the policy actors about the nature of policy problems and the solutions to them (Howlett and Ramesh, 1995).

The conceptualization of politics as learning started from the application of cybernetics, organization and psychology theories in foreign policy-making (P. Hall, 1993: p.275). A wider application of learning to the thinking about policy-making started with Heclo (1974) who from his studies of social policy-making in the United Kingdom and Sweden (P. Hall, 1990, 1993) envisaged policy-making as a process of social learning. Heclo's work provided an alternative to the traditional conception of politics as power struggle and of policy as the outcome of conflict over scarce resources (P. Hall, 1990: p.55). In Heclo's words:

> Tradition teaches us that politics is about conflict and power . . . Governments reconcile conflict and through public policy give authoritative expression to the resulting courses of action . . . This is a blinkered view of politics and particularly blinding when applied to social policy. Politics finds its sources not only in power but also in uncertainty – men collectively wondering what to do . . . Government not only "power" . . .; they also puzzle. Policy-making is a form of collective puzzlement on society's behalf . . . Much political interaction has constituted a process of social learning expressed through policy.
>
> (Heclo, 1974: pp.304–5)

According to Hall, social learning in policy-making initiated by Heclo and developed by others (e.g. P. Hall, 1990, 1993; Jenkins-Smith and Sabatier, 1993b; Howlett and Ramesh, 1995, 2003; Sabatier and Jenkins-Smith, 1999; Busenberg, 2001; Sabatier and Weible, 2007; Howlett *et al.*, 2009) emphasizes the role of ideas in policy-making (P. Hall, 1993: p.279). Policy actors undertake learning because of the cognitive limitations identified by behavioural scientists such as Simon (1957) and Lindblom (1980). Simon (1957: p.198) concludes that 'the capacity of the human mind for formulating and solving complex problems is very small compared to the size of the problems whose solution is required for objectively rational behavior in the real world'. According to Lindblom and Woodhouse (1993: p.17) economists do not know enough to deal well with simultaneous inflation and unemployment; sociologists have a grossly incomplete understanding of social problems like drug abuse or criminal rehabilitation. Similarly tourism analysts cannot entirely understand the impact of crises such as 'the 9/11 tragedy' and 'SARS'. The policy actors cannot know what will happen in the environment in advance, nor can they fully grasp what has happened as their knowledge is limited. Hence, individual and collective policy-oriented learning is necessary.

For instance, Singh (2001: p.143) described India's national tourism policy-making as a 'long process of learning through trial and error'. Busenberg (2001) suggests, however, that at present, although the significance of learning is widely acknowledged in studies of public policy, the literature lacks sufficient empirical work.

Heclo (1974) views policy-oriented learning as what government does in response to a new situation, leading to a relatively enduring alteration in behaviour. P. Hall (1993: p.278) views policy-oriented learning as a deliberate attempt to 'adjust the goals or techniques of policy in response to past experience and new information. Learning is indicated when policy changes as the result of such a process.' Hall concludes that the fundamental and ultimate change in policy as a result of policy-oriented learning is a shift of policy paradigm, which will change, rather than adjust, the policy goals and instruments. Howlett and Ramesh (1995, 2003) comment that both Heclo and Hall see policy-oriented learning as a response to external environments; policy actors must adapt to enable their decisions to succeed when environments change.

Jenkins-Smith and Sabatier (1993b: p.42) and Sabatier and Jenkins-Smith (1999: p.123) consider policy-oriented learning as the relatively enduring alterations of thought or behavioural intentions that result from experience and new information and that are concerned with the attainment or revision of policy objectives. Jenkins-Smith and Sabatier (1993b: pp.42–3) view the most important topics of policy-oriented learning as the improvement in actors' understanding of the status of goals and other variables and the identification and response to challenges to actors' belief systems, including exogenous events and opponents' activities. In other words, the target of policy-oriented learning has expanded from the environment stimulus to a series of factors considered to be related to policy-making (Jenkins-Smith and Sabatier, 1993b: p.43).

Based on Sabatier's work, policy-oriented learning could be further refined as the cognitive process undertaken by policy players to comprehend a set of policy factors in relation to policy-making. It is argued that policy actors conduct policy-oriented learning not only on environmental forces, but also on ideology, values, interests and power. The ideology, values and interests will be incorporated into policy-oriented learning when the policy actors explore the environmental stimulus. They serve as an interpretation framework for the actors to generate meanings about the environmental circumstances for the initiatives. As each policy actor or each group of policy actors has their own values, interests and power, they are viewed as different 'partisans' with each pursuing 'some combination of private purposes and their own vision of the public interest' (Lindblom, 1980: p.31; Lindblom and Woodhouse, 1993: pp.24–5).

'Policy analysis' is a policy-oriented learning method. The Australian Bureau of Tourism Research provides an example of policy analysis in a tourism context, with its mission 'to enhance (measure) the contribution of tourism to the well-being of the Australian community, through the provision of accurate, timely and strategically relevant statistics and analysis to the tourism industry, government and the community at large' (Elliot, 1997: p.68). According to Lindblom (1980: p.13), and Lindblom and Woodhouse (1993: 13 and 15), policy analysis refers to the collection and interpretation of facts and the subsequent debates and informed discussions undertaken by the policy actors. Since the values and interests are diverse or even in conflict, the analysis conducted by each partisan is called 'partisan analysis' by Lindblom (1980: p.31) and Lindblom and Woodhouse (1993: pp.24–5) with each using the analysis to buttress their own arguments (Lindblom and Woodhouse, 1993: pp.127–8). Thus, the outcomes of policy analysis, to a large extent, are fragmented. Analysis rarely can find policies unequivocally beneficial for all (Lindblom, 1980: p.22). For any given policy problem, different policy actors will attend to different aspects of the problem and produce different kinds of information (Lindblom and Woodhouse, 1993: p.19 and 30).

To sum up, policy-oriented learning refers to a cognitive and epistemic process through which the policy actors apply ideas and information to decisions (Busenberg, 2001). Policy actors undertake policy-oriented learning to formulate and implement policy. The differences in their beliefs and interests produce different results. Under this condition, 'power' will inevitably have to be exercised.

COORDINATION

As early as the 1970s, the International Union of Offical Travel Organizations (IUOTO) (the forerunner of the World Tourism Organization) stated: 'Since tourism is a manifold activity consisting of numerous units with divergent and often conflicting interests . . . The coordinating role of the state is expanding with the complex problems arising from the fast growth of tourism' (IUOTO, 1974: p.68).

Jansen-Verbeke (1989: p.240) argues that the greater the number of policy actors involved, the greater the risks in consensus building and establishment of a community of interests as a result of divisions of views and prevalence of departmentalism. D.G. Pearce (1992) comments that given the multi-faceted nature of tourism and the many activities involved, the question of coordination and inter-organizational interaction is likely to be critical. C.M. Hall (1994: p.32) further remarks that among all the roles of government in tourism, coordination is probably the most important since 'the successful implementation of all the other roles will, to a large extent, be dependent on the ability of government to coordinate and balance their various roles in the tourism development process'.

R.H. Hall *et al.* (1977: p.459) define coordination as the 'extent to which organizations attempt to ensure that their activities take into account those of other organizations'. They further point out that the form and degree of coordination vary from the minimal and informal to comprehensive and formal. According to C.M. Hall and Jenkins (1995) and C.M. Hall (1998), numerous individuals and organizations seek control or influence over tourism policy-making, since these actors and stakeholders have views on what tourism development and planning paths best meet their interests. Therefore, coordination in tourism policy-making is about power and politics. Hogwood and Gunn (1984: pp.205–6) acknowledge that 'coordination is not, of course, simply a matter of communicating information or setting up suitable administrative structures, but involves the exercise of power'. In fact, power distribution in the tourism policy community determines who gets what, when and how (Elliot, 1997). Although the exact power distribution in the tourism policy community varies from case to case the two extremes can be considered as the presence and absence of a dominant power holder.

Where there is a dominant power holder, Hill (2005) argues that any consideration of how the policy process proceeds will tend to involve propositions about who dominates. If one group of policy actors holds dominant power, their values or interests will prevail. For example, the Australian Industries Assistance Commission (IAC) conducted an inquiry into travel and tourism in Australia. The draft report, questioning government funding of tourist promotion through the Australian Tourist Commission (ATC), advocated the 'user pays' principle by the tourism industry. Following the release of the draft report, the tourism industry and the Australian Tourism Industry Association, which is a peak industry body with substantial influence over government, undertook intensive lobbying and was able to ensure that significant revisions of draft recommendations were included in the final report. As a result, the final report recommended that funding be continued for five years, at which time the role of ATC would be reviewed (C.M. Hall and Jenkins, 1995).

If no policy actor possesses dominant power, coordination occurs to build up consensus. In fact, coordination is commonly and frequently conducted in tourism policy-making because of the fragmented power structure at government and industry level. The need for a coordinated tourism strategy has become one of the great truisms of tourism policy-making (see for example Jansen-Verbeke, 1989; C.M. Hall, 1994). Authority and power in deciding tourism policy is shared by a number of policy actors (Jansen-Verbeke, 1989; Elliot, 1997) and it appears that, except for the top leaders, no other agency possesses dominant power. NTAs lack power to make decisions independently of other government agencies, and the industry members may fail to form a coherent view to influence government. As Lickorish *et al.* argue:

> There is a serious weakness in the machinery of government dealing with tourism in its coordination, and cooperation with operators whether state or privately owned. Government policies or lack of them suggest an obsolescence in public administration devoted to tourism . . . political will is lacking.
>
> (Lickorish *et al.*, 1991: p.vi)

In consequence, the NTA has continuously to coordinate with relevant policy actors to build consensus using coordination that comprises communication, negotiation, bargaining and cooperation. This pattern resembles the 'incrementalism' advocated by Lindblom (Dye, 1987; Ham and Hill, 1993; Howlett and Ramesh, 1995; Elliot, 1997) indicating that policy changes occur in marginal increments. Elliot (1997: p.77) further argues: 'In this process there are no strong, clear or long-term objectives or plans, and policy appears to drift or react to market or other forces. This process, in practice, is common in countries such as Britain and United States, and in Australia even with its national tourism strategy.' In Thailand, the Tourism Authority of Thailand had considerable freedom on the marketing side, but in the development of tourism, its role was severely restricted by lack of power and resources, and also by outside opposition. Consequently, only limited success has been achieved in development control, plan implementation, environmental protection and resolving long-standing problems (Elliot, 1987).

In many ways policy-oriented learning and coordination can be seen to form a theoretical continuum. The policy players proceed with their cognitive behaviour through policy learning, and pursue their power actions through coordination when different outcomes arise. This continuum really makes sense in the tourism context typified by its late academic development as well as the diverse values and interests within a fragmented structure of power, and helps the understanding of real policy process.

Policy outputs

The outputs of the tourism policy system are the sector policy statements and actions. In some cases these may take the form of written policy statements specifically devoted to tourism or even legislative acts, but more typically the policies are conveyed in the form of ministerial or other speeches, statements or press releases or are simply conveyed by the actions themselves. And sometimes there may be no statement. Sometimes there may be a conscious decision not to formulate a policy and this, by default, may represent a decision for the status quo to remain. After a policy decision is implemented, it will have impacts on the policy factors and the subsequent policy demands (J.E. Anderson, 1990, 2003; Dye, 1987; 2002). Some of these impacts are intended, such as a growth in tourist arrivals, tourism receipts and employment, while others, like environmental deterioration, are not intended (W.I. Jenkins, 1978; Elliot, 1997). Both intended and unintended impacts on the policy factors may generate new problems, concerns and opportunities, and hence foster new demands for policy, and so on (J.E. Anderson, 1979, 1990).

Conclusion

The theoretical inquiry explored in this book partly arises from gaps in the tourism policy literature. Policy-making in tourism generally has not been well conceptualized; the factors affecting tourism policy-making are not sufficiently incorporated into existing models and frameworks. More importantly, the interrelationships of policy factors influencing tourism policy-making have not been well explored. Furthermore, the ideational dimension of tourism policy-making, which is considered as pivotal among the factors, has also not been well addressed. Based on the literature primarily from political science, public policy studies and tourism policy cases, a conceptual framework has been designed. This is based on policy factors which are seen to provide the starting point, environmental stimulus or origin of the policy. These fall into: (i) objective realities (i.e. the environmental conditions); (ii) subjective views (i.e. beliefs and interests); (iii) prescribing mechanism – institutions; and (iv) resources – power. The policy factors are distributed over the three levels – macro, sector and organizational, and micro levels. Based on systems theory, the tourism policy-making process can be viewed as an input–output model. The policy factors at all three levels are considered as its inputs; they interrelate together in shaping the policy decisions and actions, or the output of the tourism policy system. It is generally suggested that the funnel of causality provides the setting of the interrelationships. The policy actors themselves stand at the core of policy-making, since the policy is formulated and implemented by them through identifying and transmitting problems and opportunities arising from the environment, interpreting ideology and values, protecting their interests, and exercising their power. The interaction and coalescence of the policy factors are manifest through policy-oriented learning and coordination undertaken by them. Policy-oriented learning broadly refers to the cognitive process of the policy actors to interpret the environmental conditions based on their beliefs and interests. This involves using both knowledge and values that enable them to generate meanings about the environmental stimulus for initiating the proposals. The beliefs come together as 'ideology' for society and what is called here the 'tourism policy paradigm' for the tourism sector. Within the ideology and paradigm, each policy actor has their own beliefs, values and interests; therefore the policy initiatives engendered from the policy-oriented learning reflect these and hence coordination is needed among the actors in which power is unavoidably wielded. This conceptual framework provides the basis for the investigation of the relationships and causalities in China's national policy-making in tourism.

Part II

Tourism development and policy-making in China from 1949

4   Changing national models of China since 1949

When China wakes, it will shake the world.

(Napoleon Bonaparte cited in Y. Wang
and Sheldon, 1995: p.41)

Planning and market forces are the means of economic development. The essence of socialism is the liberation and development of the productive forces, the elimination of exploitation and polarization, and the ultimate achievement of common prosperity.

(Deng Xiaoping (conveyed in 1992)
cited in Deng, 1992b)

National policy-making and tourism development in China have neither proceeded smoothly nor in a vacuum. They have developed in the context of tremendous change, especially after the implementation of the Economic Reform and Open-door Policy in 1978. This chapter examines China's evolution since 1949 through three national development models, which have mainly taken the country from a planned economy to a market economy. The chapter aims to provide a contextual background to China's national tourism policy-making.

The evolution of the People's Republic of China: a brief review

Perhaps the most important event in China's recent history is the establishment of the People's Republic of China by the Communist Party in 1949. This marked a clear break with the imperial past and although there have been many changes over the following sixty years its impact is still evident today. The period since 1949 can broadly be divided into three. The first is the revolutionary and enthusiastic socialism in Mao Zedong's era (1949–78). This became a more evolutionary and pragmatic socialism focusing on economic modernization in Deng Xiaoping's era (1978–97). This then transformed into the so-called 'Public and Harmonious Socialism' emphasizing comprehensive and coordinated development in the collective leadership era (1997–present). Over this period there have been four generations of leadership commencing with Mao Zedong himself, followed by Deng Xiaoping, who took power in 1978 with the veteran leaders' support and who in turn was followed by his designated leaders (Lieberthal, 2004), Jiang Zemin (1989–2002) and Hu Jintao (2002–present).

Mao Zedong's era (1949–78): revolutionary and enthusiastic socialism

Understanding the impact of Mao's national development model is crucial to an understanding of the national tourism policy-making process and tourism development post 1978. It was within the setting of Mao's development model and his tourism landscape that the national policy-making and tourism development of Deng Xiaoping's reforms began. Mao's period started after twenty-two years of armed struggle with the Guomindang-led nationalist government, when the Communist Party of China (CPC) eventually took control and founded a new republic based on socialist and communist ideologies.

On 1 October 1949 Mao Zedong proclaimed the establishment of the People's Republic of China. Until his death in 1976, the history of the PRC, to a large extent, was the history of Mao in driving and shaping China in a socialist development model. Mao's model was marked by the nationalization and collectivization of urban and rural economies and the elimination of private ownership; a revolutionary approach that entailed rapid, violent and mass changes (Ogden, 1995: p.87). The momentum rested on the utopian ideals of ideological correctness and politics-in-command with the model originating from Maoism or Mao Zedong Thought (C.F.J. Wang, 2002).

The visions of Maoism: contradictions and revolution

Maoism is characterized by contradiction, struggle and revolution. Mao viewed that society had always been full of the contradictions from class conflict. Among these contradictions, some were considered to be more important than others and the role of an effective leader was to identify them and formulate strategies to solve them. In Mao's view, the most important class contradiction was between proletarian and bourgeois thinking and behaviour that would continue even though society had advanced into a higher level of socialism; the implication being that class struggle would continue for an indefinite period. In order to eliminate bourgeois influences, the revolutionary environment had to be maintained in the form of political campaigns that meant the mass mobilization of the people with concentrated attacks on specific issues. The momentum for the political campaign was 'politics-in-command' to ensure ideological correctness, instead of material rewards. Two other important elements of Maoism were 'egalitarianism' and 'self-reliance'. In Mao's view, 'egalitarianism' meant frugal living, levelling average incomes down to those of the poor regions and prohibition of conspicuous consumption. 'Self-reliance' did not mean that China should rely only on her own efforts, but rather should keep the initiative in her own hands (CPC, 1951–77; Lieberthal, 1995, 2004; Ogden, 1995; C.F.J. Wang, 2002). Shirk's comment provides a succinct summary of Mao's approach:

> In China, Mao Zedong attempted to sustain his revolutionary charisma and stem the trend of institutionalization (disparagingly called 'revisionism' by Mao) by launching mass campaigns such as the Great Leap Forward (1957–58) and the Cultural Revolution (1966–69).
>
> (Shirk, 1993: p.8)

The early road to socialism

According to Kornai (1992), the main determining features of the socialist system are a centrally planned economy with predominant social ownership as the means of production. Such a structure was overseen by a highly centralized political regime under one-party rule with a relatively weak or ineffective society. This provides an accurate description of Socialist China before 1978. In the period immediately after 1949 the Chinese government placed foremost priority on reviving and modernizing the war-ruined economy, industries and agriculture. In face of confrontation, diplomatic isolation and trade embargos by the Western world, the CPC took the so-called policy of 'leaning to one side' (Whiting, 1992: pp.233–4) in order to transplant into China the Soviet Union's command economy which at the time was the sole successful model in socialist development. The Soviet model generally assumed that socialist transformation should be based on industrialization. The Chinese leadership took the view that modernization was to be achieved through rapid and expansive industrialization and urbanization; that was, 'bigger was better', 'fast pace took priority over quality' (Saich, 2004: p.33), and 'heavy industry (e.g. steel and military equipment) was preferred to light industry' (Ogden, 1995: p.86). During this period the main role of agriculture was to feed industrialization and urbanization although it also had a strategic role of its own in relation to national survival and political stability. Grain production not only satisfied the basic needs of people but rural areas also contained the majority of the population which was the constituent base for the communist regime (Saich, 2004; Yu *et al.*, 2005).

Under China's centrally planned economy, the central master plan and state enterprises served as the main avenue and vehicle respectively to achieve industrialization. During the 1950s, nearly 90 per cent of state capital funds were injected into heavy industry to build over 640 major industrial enterprises (Saich, 2004). Initially, between 1949 and 1958, the Chinese government undertook a gradual approach to nationalize and collectivize the national economy. By the end of 1956, there were two major ownership forms in the urban economy: state-private ownership and sole state ownership with the latter being dominant (Ogden, 1995). In the rural areas, the land confiscated from the landlords was redistributed to peasants. Agricultural production was characterized by the household-based farming system.

The Great Leap Forward and the Cultural Revolution

Motivated by the success of the first national plan, in 1958, the Chinese government started a more radical development based on the vision of Maoism. This took the view that economic development was a step-by-step resolution of contradictions with each resolution progressing to a higher mode of production (i.e. ever-larger production units) until attaining communism (i.e. with the people owning everything) (Ogden, 1995: p.86). Under this vision, The Great Leap Forward programme (GLF) was launched in 1958 to speed up the collectivization (Saich, 2004). The GLF aimed to achieve great economies of scale through the high level of collectivization. The incentive for greater productivity was based on Mao's ideological orthodoxies – 'politics-in-command', 'redness', 'egalitarianism', rather than on an economic rationale or materialism. In the rural areas, around 750,000 collective farms were amalgamated into around 24,000 communes where the peasants were not permitted to own the means of production (private land or farm animals) or run businesses on the side. In both the urban and rural areas, priority was given to ever-larger production quotas, rather than efficiency and quality. Many production outputs were of very low quality. Combined with the withdrawal of Soviet aid and natural disasters, China's Gross National Product fell by around 35 per cent. The most serious decline was in agriculture with an annual fall of around 10 per cent. The GLF provided almost no flexibility and the only adjustments were implemented by a few pragmatic leaders – the State President Liu Shaoqi, Premier Zhou Enlai and General Secretary of the CPC, Deng Xiaoping, between 1962 and 1965 (Lieberthal, 1995; Ogden, 1995; W.W. Zhang, 1996; Saich, 2004).

For Mao, the failure of the GLF was due to the existence of 'the representatives of the bourgeoisie who have infiltrated the party, government and army' who wanted to 'overthrow the dictatorship of the proletariat and replace it with that of the bourgeoisie'. After the economic recovery, Mao launched the Cultural Revolution (1966–76) to purge 'those persons within the party in authority taking the capitalist road' and the 'capitalist class' through endless political struggle (Ogden, 1995; Saich, 2004: p.48). During the ten-year Cultural Revolution, 'class struggle', 'politics-in-command' and 'continued revolution' were extended to the whole of society (C.F.J. Wang, 2002). Political struggle took precedence over economic development as reflected by a slogan 'upholding the revolution to boost the production' (Gao, 2003). As a result economic and technological progress stagnated. Commodities, differential wages and bonuses were all seen as the 'persistence of capitalist factors' and condemned as the 'reproduction of capitalism' and the 'emergence of new bourgeoisie'. In the rural areas, private activities and production outside the plan were criticized as the 'tails of capitalism'. As a consequence the private economy and market mechanism were virtually non-existent. Sticking to 'self-reliance', foreign trade was seen negatively, playing only a residual role. Aiming to purify Mao's socialist system, efforts were made to restrict the import of bourgeois ideas; the utilization of foreign technology and expertise was thus condemned as the 'appendage of imperialism' (Tsou, 1986; Yan and Gao, 1987; Gao, 2003; Saich, 2004). The Cultural Revolution ended in 1976 with Mao's death. A key informant shared his views as follows:

> The Cultural Revolution itself was a radical phenomenon. The 'politics' highlighted specifically refers to the 'political struggle'. Under such ideology, economic development became subordinate to politics. Everything needed to be justified by political reasons. After this ten year disturbance, China's economy became very difficult.

Dominated by 'politics-in-command', during Mao's period the Chinese state became coterminous with her society. The state knew the best interests of society and played the role of national educator in setting the ethical model for the people (Lieberthal, 1995, 2004). Almost all parts of people's lives were administered by the state, covering for example, education choices, career selection, marriage, mobility. The political vulnerability of the Chinese people culminated in the Cultural Revolution.

As for Chinese foreign policy in Mao's era, this aimed to assist the pursuit of an independent, strong and unified China with worldwide influence and respect through the development of foreign relations and the maintenance of international peace (Han Nianlong, 1988). To this end, China's national interests, especially the integrity of sovereignty and territories, were placed among the top ideological issues. When confronted by Western blockades from 1949, China turned to the USSR-led Eastern Bloc for diplomatic recognition and economic aid, and actively engaged in developing bilateral and multilateral relationships with the Asian and African countries under the banners of 'anti-imperialism' and 'anti-colonialism'. These ideological links ultimately served China's national interests both for external support and for differentiating the new regime from its predecessor. In the meantime, China still kept contact with the US and tried to unfreeze relations with Western Europe. Following the Sino-Soviet split formally in the 1960s, China started to develop closer ties with Western Europe including full diplomatic relationships with France in 1964. After the military clashes with the USSR in 1969, China had been plunged into a crisis of challenging both superpowers. This was resolved through reconciliation with the US in the 1970s. The official visit of President Richard Nixon to Beijing in 1972 started the normalization of relations between China and the West. Between 1970 and 1978, China established full diplomatic relations with the majority of the Western Bloc nations (Han Nianlong, 1988; Lieberthal, 1995, 2004; Gao, 2003; Saich, 2004).

The prototype of China's planned-economy model

As already noted, China's centralized planned-economy model was trans-planted from the Soviet Union (USSR) (e.g. Saich, 2004; Yu *et al.*, 2005). A key informant indicated:

> [s]ince the founding of new China [i.e. PR China], the only model that could be taken was that of the Soviet Union, which had already adopted the planned economy. Therefore, China completely copied the government and economic model from the Soviet Union.

China's centralized planned-economy model dictated that the central master plan instead of market forces was adopted by the state to manage and control both the supply and demand sides of the national economy. The supply side was managed by the government through formulating various plans or issuing administrative commands for products to be produced, while the demand side was restrained by the government through rationing. The prices of consumer and producer goods were also set by the government. The supply side of the Chinese planned economy, however, did not aim to satisfy the demand. There was no role here for the market mechanism in which supply and demand interacted to determine prices (B.S. Clark, 1991). The government, replacing the market, became the sole mechanism for resource allocation. As of 1978 over 600 items were controlled by the central master plan (Lieberthal, 2004). Under the planned economy, public ownership was the dominant form of enterprise. A key informant offered a summary:

> The concept of the planned economy was that the government developed and controlled the economy through the central plan. Under this concept, everything should be placed under the plan. On the supply side, the government was responsible for production and distribution; the demand side was also controlled by the government through issuing various kinds of coupons like grain coupons, clothes coupons. The enterprises produced goods in accordance with the government plan in terms of varieties and quantity; and the prices of products were fixed by the government. The sale and distribution of products were not the concern of enterprise managers; the distribution agencies were responsible for sales and distribution in accordance with the plan. Production and distribution were two separate lines. There was no linkage between demand and supply.

The planned-economy ideology formed the core of the economic institutions, in terms of structures, organizational forms and rules. Central government established a number of professional ministries by economic sector to implement national production, to construct capital projects and to distribute the major commodities, with supra-ministerial agencies providing planning and coordination (Lieberthal and Oksenberg, 1988). A set of state-owned enterprises came directly under these government agencies that directly supervised the operation, management, personnel, finance and other resources. Supervision was provided through administrative measures – the common form of standard operating procedure in the planned-economy era. The enterprises were not granted management autonomy and revenues were to be handed over to the government. This institutional arrangement was called 'integration of government function with enterprise function'. Strictly speaking, the enterprises merely acted as production units (*'shengchan danwei'*) (Saich, 2004). The key informant further remarked:

> Under the planned economy, all state-owned enterprises and their supervisory government agencies fell into the various 'systems' [*'xitongs'*]. The 'systems' consisted of the professional economic ministries at the centre and their subordinate enterprises. Raw materials, personnel and finance of enterprises were under the control of the government.

The government agencies shielded the interests of their subordinate enterprises. When the interests of one enterprise came into conflict with another enterprise, the supervising government agencies would unavoidably be involved. Within the enterprise, the CPC's party committee headed by a party-secretary took overall leadership based on 'politics-in-command' orthodoxy. Public ownership under the socialist system offered a permanent and secure career to its employees, known as the 'iron rice bowl'; employees could not be dismissed regardless of their performance. Along with the 'iron rice bowl' notion, an effective appraisal system was absent. Generally speaking, the whole of China under the planned-economy model resembled a big factory (Shirk, 1993). The central plan and bureaucratic controls restrained and then annihilated market forces as well as the economic incentives of enterprises and employees.

In China, there was another kind of organization roughly translated as 'non-administrative organizations' (*'shiye danwei'*). These are non-profit-making units established to accomplish the goals and tasks designated by the state. Like the state-owned enterprise, they were also assigned a bureaucratic rank by the government and were supervised by relevant government agencies. Funding for such bodies came directly from the state budget and surpluses could be retained for some purposes such as staff welfare. Travel agencies before 1978 belonged to this category of organization. The relationship among government agencies, enterprises and non-administrative organizations was institutionalized into an administrative structure delineated by the state as the *'xitong'* ('system'). As a self-closed structure, the responsible government agency was in charge of managing its own 'system' and could not intervene in other 'systems'.

Deng Xiaoping's era (1978–97): evolutionary and pragmatic socialism

After Mao's death in 1976, China entered a period of reform that formally commenced in 1978. This period can be further divided into that led by Deng

Xiaoping between 1978 and 1997 and by the Collective Leadership from 1997 to the present. In Deng's period, Mao's revolutionary and enthusiastic socialism was superseded by Deng's evolutionary and pragmatic socialism focusing on economic modernization through the Economic Reform and Open-door Policy. The centrality of political power shifted from 'Mao-in-command' in all spheres to 'Deng-in-dominance' on key issues and at key moments (Whiting, 1992; W.W. Zhang, 1996).

Brabant (1998) considers that transition and transformation in former or present socialist states is generally characterized by stabilization, privatization, liberalization, institution building and maintaining a sociopolitical consensus. The impetus for Deng's reform originated from the failure of Mao's model and overall weaknesses in the Soviet-style planned economy that became increasingly apparent in the 1970s. As a result, China had lagged behind other developed and developing countries. At the end of the Cultural Revolution, China's economy was on the verge of collapse with living standards stagnating (Yu *et al.*, 2005: p.1). Internal studies conducted in 1977 and 1978 shocked the new Chinese Leadership. More than 70 million peasants suffered from severe deprivation. On average, peasants fared no better in 1978 than in 1952 (Lieberthal, 1995: p.147). GDP per capita as of 1978 was only RMB¥379 per annum (Yu *et al.*, 2005: p.1). The average wages of state employees and industrial workers were 5.5 per cent and 8.4 per cent lower than 1957. The supply of commodities or economic goods all fell short of demand; rationing and queuing were part of the daily life for most urban residents (Saich, 2004: pp.56 and 241). The political chaos during the Cultural Revolution and deteriorating socio-economic conditions all challenged the credibility of Maoism. The new Chinese leadership was faced with a considerable decline in confidence in the party. Deng Xiaoping and his supporters recognized that the crisis provided the CPC with a catalyst for change in ideological orthodoxies and national policies. Deng clearly saw that the improvement in people's livelihoods mattered for the legitimacy of the Communist Party itself. A new ideological orthodoxy was deemed necessary to recapture the allegiance of the Chinese and to underpin new national policies, leading to the rise of Dengism or Deng's socialism, officially called 'Deng Xiaoping Theories' (W.W. Zhang, 1996; C.F.J. Wang, 2002; Lieberthal, 2004; Yu *et al.*, 2005).

The political logic of Dengism: carrying on economic reform by adhering to communist institutions

Unlike the former Soviet Union leader Mikhail Gorbachev who launched political reform ahead of economic reform, the overarching logic of Dengism was to carry out economic reform by sticking to one-party governance and existing communist institutions (Shirk, 1993: pp.11–14; Saich, 2004: p.57). Dengism was not simply an ideological repackaging of Mao's orthodoxies for capturing, garnering and wielding political power, but rather had its own attributes significantly different from Maoism. As a career revolutionary and political leader holding the values of socialism and communism, Deng found it hard to launch China's economic reform in a way that deviated from the path of socialism. Considering that China's communist revolution had only triumphed at the expense of enormous loss of life and uncountable human endeavour, Deng took the view that the ruling status of the Communist Party should be safeguarded while allowing some level of criticism. In Deng's vision, China's socialist practices during the previous three decades had narrowed the gap with the developed countries, despite the 'mistakes' made by the party between 1957 and 1976 (W.W. Zhang, 1996). According to Ogden (1995), by 1978, China under socialism generally had maintained national unity, sustained agriculture and industrial growth, and ensured the requisite provision of food, housing and medical care for most Chinese. With these achievements Deng supported the 'superiority' of socialism over capitalism and insisted on China adhering to the road of socialism. Deng's revolutionary experiences and the political chaos in the early republican era led him to equate liberalization with political disorder. He also agreed with the deep-rooted values of most Chinese about the importance of harmony and stability. Accordingly he disagreed with the adoption of the Western-styled multi-party system and asserted that China needed a unified ideology for national coherence. To Deng, the abolition of the CPC leadership would be tantamount to the failure of China's socialist modernization, ideological muddle and anarchy (Deng, 1986; W.W. Zhang, 1996).

By contrast to Mao's socialism, Deng's socialism was pragmatic and evolutionary with emphasis on economic modernization and on the reality of China. Deng never intended to put Maoism aside, but was committed to reducing radicalization, turning back to the pre-Cultural Revolution tracks and making Maoism more pragmatic in dealing with existing conditions. Actually Deng was a keen defender of Mao's philosophical base, since he shared the values and basics of Marxism. To Deng and other veteran leaders, downplaying Maoism would eventually weaken the identity and legitimacy of the CPC (Deng, 1980). What Deng intended to do was to revive those parts of Marxism and Maoism that he considered useful for present-day China; on this the continuity from Mao's era to the reform era could be maintained (W.W. Zhang, 1996). He was particularly inspired by Mao's revolutionary experience of working within China's own circumstances and highlighting the importance of exploring a Chinese path towards modernization. The pragmatic discourses frequently advocated by Deng and his supporters were 'seeking truth from facts' and 'practice is the sole criterion of truth' (Deng, 1984). Considering the deficiencies of the Soviet command economy and China's uniqueness and identity, it was generally accepted by Deng that China should search for its own development model, not simply copy foreign experience, even those from the socialist countries in Eastern Europe (Deng, 1982; W.W. Zhang, 1996).

Deng put forward his ideological concept of 'building Socialism with Chinese Characteristics' in 1982:

> In carrying out our modernization, we must commence from the Chinese realities ... We must integrate the universal truth of Marxism with the concrete realities of China, go on our own road and construct Socialism with Chinese characteristics.
>
> (Deng, 1982)

Deng elaborated the 'Chinese realities' in a meeting with North Korean President Kim Il Sung in 1982:

> We must concentrate on economic development. In a country as big and as poor as ours, if we don't try to increase production, how can we survive? How is socialism superior, when our people have so many difficulties in their lives?
>
> (cited in W.W. Zhang, 1996: p.52)

According to Deng, there should be 'no socialism with pauperism, so to get rich was not a sin' (Jiang, 1993). He entirely rejected the 'impoverished socialism' (Deng, 1984) canonized in the Cultural Revolution and placed economic modernization as the foremost priority of the party to remove poverty. Recognizing China's poorly developed socio-economic conditions, Deng acknowledged that the country was in the 'primary stage of socialism' and should evolve to the 'higher stage' of socialism when it became wealthier (CPC, 1987). As he said:

> At the first stage of communism ... we must do all we can to develop the productive forces and gradually eliminate poverty, constantly raising the people's living standards. Otherwise, how will socialism be able to triumph over capitalism? ... When the economy is highly developed and there is overwhelming material abundance, we shall be able to apply the principle of, from each according to his ability, to each according to his needs.
>
> (cited in W.W. Zhang, 1996: p.52)

Under his slogan 'getting rich is glorious', Deng gave up Mao's 'political and ideological correctness' and egalitarianism as the main incentives for economic development and replaced them by material rewards in stimulating people to work harder (CPC, 1978; Shirk, 1993). Deng viewed that egalitarianism was abused in Mao's era. Instead he encouraged some people and some regions to get rich first, so that other people could follow them as exemplars. In terms of the emerging inequality, Deng justified that this should be a temporary phenomenon (Deng, 1986; W.W. Zhang, 1996).

Having recognized the large gap between China and advanced countries, Deng urged that relevant experiences from capitalist countries should be used and as such was determined to introduce foreign capital, technology and management expertise (Deng, 1984). Similar to Mao, Deng insisted that the existing world institutions and power relations favoured the developed countries (W.W. Zhang, 1996), given that they were both the game makers and players in the international political economy. Deng understood the emotions of the Chinese people in relation to self-esteem, having previously been humiliated by Western interference and Japanese invasion, and stressed the importance of 'self-reliance' (Jiang, 1993). Deng warned:

> It isn't easy to get funds and advanced technology from the developed countries. There are still some people around who are wedded to the ideas of the old-line colonialists; they are reluctant to see the poor countries develop, and attempt to throttle them. Therefore, while pursuing the policy of opening to the outside world, we must stick to the principle of relying mainly on our own efforts.
>
> (cited in W.W. Zhang, 1996: p.50)

Deng defined that foreign investment constituted an indispensable supplement to China's socialist economy as follows:

> At the current stage, foreign-funded enterprises in China are allowed to make some profits under (our) existing laws and policies. But the state levies taxes on those enterprises, workers earn wages from them, and we learn technology and management. In addition, we can get information and open markets. Therefore, subject to the constraints of China's overall political and economic conditions, foreign-funded enterprises are useful supplements to the socialist economy and ultimately they are conducive to our socialism.
>
> (Deng, 1992a, 1992b)

Meanwhile, Deng and other veterans foresaw that Western ideologies, values and cultures would increasingly influence China, accompanying the inflow of Western technology and management expertise. In their view, these Western ideologies and values would shake the vulnerable socialist values and alter China's socialist constituents. Deng criticized the inclination to the Westernization of China as 'bourgeois liberalization' (W.W. Zhang, 1996; Saich, 2004) that included the worship of multi-party systems, doing everything solely for profit, seeking advantage at the expense of others and always putting money first. Deng found it necessary to define 'socialism with Chinese characteristics', rather than leave it as a vague notion. In Deng's view, 'socialism with Chinese characteristics' should maintain the one-party rule and public ownership, and promote the socialist spiritual and material civilization. Placing communist values at the core, the notion of 'socialist civilization' was used by Deng and other veterans to withstand Western influences and to direct the materialization and commercialization of society (Deng, 1980, 1986; CPC, 1986).

The political orthodoxy of Dengism provided a loosening ideological framework that paved the way for advocating and implementing his economic orthodoxy – marketization. The marketization advocated by Dengism entirely deviated from the Soviet Stalinist model that considered marketization as the antithesis of socialism. Deng concluded that China's command economy model was the ultimate reason for the stagnation of economic development. Deng took the view that the market economy should be ideologically acceptable to China's socialism, since public ownership should not naturally conflict with market forces (W.W. Zhang, 1996; Yu *et al.*, 2005). As Deng expressed it in 1979:

> It is surely not correct to say that the market economy is only confined to capitalist society. Why cannot socialism engage the market economy? . . . A market economy existed in the feudal society. Socialism may also engage in market economy.
>
> (cited in W.W. Zhang, 1996: p.60; Yu *et al.*, 2005: p.5)

Deng's ideas of marketization were formed very early in the reform era. Nevertheless, China's evolution to a market economy was contested on a nationwide basis and it was not until 1992 that the Communist Party proclaimed the establishment of the socialist market-economy model.

For diplomatic orthodoxy, Deng assumed that China's economic modernization required a peaceful international environment. With this background it was appropriate for China not to take the lead in international affairs, nor directly to defy the United States, and to play the US-Soviet-China triangle (Lieberthal, 1995). By safeguarding China's national interests, the strategy of 'not challenging the US-led Western Bloc' became a main theme in China's foreign affairs after the collapse of the USSR-led Eastern Bloc in 1991 (Cheng, 2001; Saich, 2004). To detail this strategy, which was pursued until the 2000s, Deng Xiaoping himself outlined the '28-Characters Tactic':

> Observe Calmly; Secure Our Position; Cope with Affairs Calmly; Hide our Capacities and Bide our Time; Be Good at Maintaining a Low Profile; and Never Claim the Leadership; Make Some Contributions (The 28 Characters Strategy)
>
> (cited in United States Department of Defense, 2007: p.14)

Transition and transformation from the planned-economy model to the market-economy model: three cycles

Initially in Deng's reform camp, formed in 1978, there was no disagreement in ending radical socialism. However, when the reform deepened, the reform camp was split into two factions: pro-market economy and pro-central planned economy. The former advocated marketization, decentralization of decision-making, depoliticization of social and individual behaviour, and faster opening-up to the outside world. The pro-central planned-economy faction, which was usually referred to in the West as 'conservative forces', insisted on the central planned model supplemented by market forces. They also supported adherence to the dominance of public ownership with a limited private sector and foreign investment, the tightening of ideological control, the slowing down in the process of depoliticization and only limited opening to the world (Lieberthal, 1995, 2004; Yu *et al.*, 2005). The sticking point between the two factions was whether the planned economy or the market economy should be the primary mechanism in economic development and the allocation of resources. The market-economy model was criticized as turning the direction of reform from socialism to capitalism (W.W. Zhang, 1996). China ultimately transformed to a market economy through three cycles.

The first cycle 1978–86: dominance of the planned economy supplemented by market forces

The first cycle from 1978 to 1986 was characterized by the dominance of the planned-economy model supplemented by market forces. The political logic of carrying the economic reform through the existing communist institutions was affirmed. Despite the fact that the planned-economy model remained as the dominant mechanism, its weaknesses had been acknowledged by the whole reform camp and a sense of marketization emerged. Utilization of market forces started through experiments in rural areas, Special Economic Zones (SEZs) (Yu *et al.*, 2005), new economic sectors such as tourism and in selected state-owned enterprises on a small scale.

The starting point was decided in the Third Plenum of the CPC's Eleventh National Congress held in December 1978 when the central thrust of the Party's work shifted from political struggle to economic modernization. The political orthodoxies of the Cultural Revolution – 'political struggle', 'politics-in-command', 'grasping revolution and promoting production' were replaced by 'material rewards', 'law of value' and 'law of economic efficiency and rationale' as incentives to boost economic development. The Communiqué of the Third Plenum stated 'the centrality of the whole party should shift to the construction of socialist modernization from 1979' and to emphasize the material wants of the people. The Communiqué stressed the need to 'work in accordance with the laws of economics' (CPC, 1978). In 1979, Deng advanced the 'four cardinal principles': a commitment to Marxism-Leninism-Mao Zedong Thought; Party Leadership; the Socialist Road (i.e. undertaking economic reform by sticking to communist institutions); and Dictatorship of the Proletariat (Deng, 1979).

Under the banner of 'pragmatism', the function of market forces in China's economy was discussed among the leaders, senior officials and intellectuals. Pro-marketization reformers ascribed the underlying cause of China's stagnant economy to the command economy model based on public ownership.

Their marketization initiative met with strong opposition which asserted that China's socialism should be based primarily on the planned economy. Although at the same time acknowledging the limitations and inefficiencies in the planned economy the opposition also allowed a supplementary role for market forces (Yu *et al.*, 2005). Chen Yun remarked:

> A socialist economy should still adhere to the principle of planned and proportionate development . . . Taking the country as whole, the statement about the primacy of the planned economy supplemented by market regulation is still valid.
>
> (Chen Yun, 1985)

The pro-planned-economy faction asserted that the state sector operated on behalf of the 'whole people' and therefore did not need exchange through the market. They criticized the full play of market forces which in their view would cause anarchy and condemned the marketization of China's economy as an attempt to reform according to the capitalist model. Although Deng Xiaoping found no contradiction between socialism and the market economy, he did not have full confidence in the effective functioning of the market, which had never operated in Socialist China. Therefore, he only supported market-oriented reform on an experimental basis (W.W. Zhang, 1996).

Based on the new ruling orthodoxy, the previous self-imposed isolationist stance was replaced by an open-door policy and economic reform, designed to invigorate the stagnant national economy and to reform overcentralized administrative and economic institutions. One of the key national decisions was the 'decentralization of power' incrementally and in stages (CPC, 1978). Deng Xiaoping recognized that China had dramatically lagged behind the Western world, Japan and Southeast Asia. As Deng himself put it 'today's world is an open world' and 'it is impossible to build our nation behind a closed door' (Deng, 1984). The leadership envisaged that China's economic growth in the short term could only rely on the advantage of relatively low labour costs, but in the long term, technological and management advances would be needed to sustain economic growth. Deng Xiaoping said 'the absorption of capital from abroad is an important supplement to our country's social construction. Looking forward from today it is an indispensable supplement' (Deng, 1986; Yabuki, 1995: pp.245–6). Thus Deng opened China's door to introduce foreign capital and expertise to reform China's economic institutions and to transform China's backward economy.

The market-driven economic reform first took place in the rural areas. Mao's collective-based 'people's communes' were gradually abolished and replaced by the household-based 'production responsibility system' through contracting the output to the households. The farmers were allowed to undertake sideline production and sell their surpluses in the private market. In the urban industrial sector, the reform was conducted on selected state enterprises through the decentralization of decision-making and profit retention. In 1982, the newly revised Chinese Constitution confirmed the existence of the private economy as a complementary sector to the socialist public ownership system. More importantly, Special Economic Zones (SEZs) were established in Shenzhen, Zhuhai, Shantou, Xiamen and Hainan to attract foreign investment (W.W. Zhang, 1996; Yu *et al.*, 2005). Furthermore, tourism started to be seen as an economic activity.

The second cycle 1987–91: the market mechanism in the planned economy

On the basis of the initial success of the limited market-oriented reform in rural areas and selected state-owned enterprises in the urban sector, further marketization reform was launched in 1986 and 1987 with the aim to break away from the mandatory instructions of the planned economy. The degree of marketization deepened as its scope expanded. At the Thirteenth National Congress of the CPC held in 1987, the market mechanism was given a more salient position but alongside the planned economy. It was acknowledged at the Congress that the roles of the market mechanism and the central master plan overlaid the whole of the economy and therefore the 'state should adjust the market, and in turn, the market guide the enterprises'. The Plenum proclaimed the establishment in stages of the 'Planned Commodity Economy based on Public Ownership' (CPC, 1987). This meant that the market mechanism was allowed to function incrementally in the domain of the planned economy.

The establishment of the 'planned socialist commodity economy' entirely deviated from the classic Marxist view and Stalinist model that the commodity market and money exchange ultimately came to an end under socialism. Under the assumption of the planned commodity market, the state, collective and private sectors should all engage in the exchange of commodities (W.W. Zhang, 1996). The essence of the 'market economy' was pragmatically and politically interpreted as the 'commodity economy' to satisfy the people, conservative leaders and bureaucrats. Before 1978, the state's entire emphasis on industrial production and accumulation of national wealth had sacrificed the rise in living standards of the Chinese people (Saich, 2004). When China opened its doors to the world, the large gap in living standards with those enjoyed in the developed world was revealed. Political commitments to the development of the commodity economy enabled the CPC to regain the allegiance of the Chinese people. However, this decision could also be viewed as a political compromise between pro-marketization reformers and the proplanning camp. Some views remained opposed to market forces, equating marketization with capitalism as illustrated in the following: 'We are the communist party, and the communist party engages in building socialism . . . [Socialism] should continue to practise planned and proportionate development' (cited in W.W. Zhang, 1996: p.136).

Marketization was criticized by the conservatives as the seedbed of liberalization. Without proper control under socialism, marketization would trigger 'bourgeois contamination', which would eventually alter China's socialist nature. Some conservative views worried that a rapid market-oriented programme would make the national economy uncontrollable (Yu *et al.*, 2005). Furthermore, bureaucrats of the central planning and economic apparatus were also afraid that a fast pace of marketization would quickly reduce their long-standing role in making socio-economic policy. The term 'establishment of the planned commodity economy', to a large extent, moderated the degree of passive resistance.

On the basis of the SEZs, the Chinese government quickened the pace and undertook its 'Coastal Development Strategy' to attract foreign manufacturing industry. At the same time the reform in urban areas was formally implemented in state-owned enterprises and in the introduction of the pricing mechanism. Enterprise reform aimed to enable them to be economically responsible entities through decentralizing more economic decision-making powers and retaining more profits. In the pricing mechanism, a dual price system was adopted under which for a transitional period a product could bear both the state-fixed price and the market price. Gradually, the scope of state-set prices reduced and the share of market prices expanded (W.W. Zhang, 1996; Saich, 2004; Yu *et al.*, 2005).

Increased marketization unfortunately caused economic problems in the mid-1980s. A shortage of economic goods, greater autonomy for enterprises and the relaxation of administrative price setting led to aggregate demand outstripping aggregate supply. As a result the economy overheated and, in the absence of effective macro-control instruments, inflation took off. This led to the decision in 1988 to restore the central master plan and to slow down the process of marketization (Yu *et al.*, 2005). Widespread anger about inflation contributed to the unrest that came to the fore in June 1989 in what is known in China as the June 4th Incident and in the West as the Tiananmen Square Protests. The conservatives condemned the Incident as 'bourgeois liberalization' and blamed the rapid marketization. Deng Xiaoping took a strategic retreat from his firm stance on market-oriented reform and, as a result, a more austere retrenchment policy was launched to contract the economy and to downplay market forces. At the cost of the lowest GNP growth since 1978, the retrenched economic policy led to reduced inflation and cooled the overheated economy. With fears of an economic downturn and likely political instability, the trend to centralization was suspended (Saich, 2004). In the Seventh Plenum of the Central Committee of the Thirteenth National Congress of the CPC held in 1990, it was viewed that the state should turn from micro control to macro control in formulating the national development plan and industrial policies, and in counterbalancing economic sectors (CPC, 1990; Yu *et al.*, 2005).

Throughout the period from 1978, the planned-economy model still dominated but it was declining. For example, the scope of the central master plan contracted from over 600 items in 1978 to around twenty-five items by the late 1980s. Some of the planning authority shifted to the local levels of government but much of it was released to market forces (Lieberthal, 1995; Saich, 2004; Yu *et al.*, 2005). Similarly the proportion of government set prices declined from 97 per cent in 1978 to 20 per cent in 1991 (W.W. Zhang, 1996).

The third cycle 1992–7: the establishment of the socialist market-economy model

After 1992, the CPC's ideological orthodoxies underwent a major change, politically, socio-economically and diplomatically such that they represented a brand-new approach. The change started from Deng Xiaoping's southern inspection tour ('*nan xun*') in early 1992 launched ahead of the inauguration of the Fourteenth CPC National Congress. After the June 4th Incident in 1989 and subsequent collapse of communist regimes in the Soviet Union and Eastern Europe, China muddled through the political and economic ideological debates with the former dominating the latter. It was reaffirmed that 'class struggle' would continue for a considerable period within 'certain parts' of China, which contrasted apparently with the basic line affirmed in 1978 of the centrality that CPC gave to economic development (Saich, 2004). The trend of political radicalization emerged again and the tough view of equating marketization and liberalization with capitalism rose on the political agenda. Even though further centralization ceased, market forces to replace the central master plan as the main economic mechanism could not be accepted. This tested the acceptance of Deng and the pro-market reformers. Actually before Deng's Southern tour, localities had been pushing the reform ahead without consent from the central government (W.W. Zhang, 1996). For example, in Shanghai, the municipal government had begun a key infrastructure project, a new bridge to link two parts of the city, without the approval of central government (Saich, 2004; Yu *et al.*, 2005).

The speeches delivered on Deng's tour were deliberately planned with other reform leaders and their 'think tanks'. Deng first concluded that the continuing reform mattered to the party's legitimacy and the nation's survival. He claimed that the communist regime could be at risk if the Economic Reform and Open-door Policy were reversed. Second, he labelled the radicalization of communist doctrines as 'leftistism', which was identified as the obstacle to further reform and the greatest problem for China at that time. Deng then attacked the ideological impasse in the economic sphere. He tactfully advocated that economic reform 'should not proceed slowly like a woman with bound feet'; he then went on to assert that the planned economy did not infer socialism, and that the market economy would not drive China to capitalism; both the planned economy and the market economy were described by Deng as vehicles to serve China's socialist development (Deng, 1992a, 1992b; Saich, 2004). In his words:

A planned economy is not equivalent to socialism, since capitalism has also adopted planning; a market economy is not equivalent to capitalism, because socialism also should adopt the market economy. Planning and market forces are the means of economic development. The essence of socialism is the liberation and development of the productive forces, the elimination of exploitation and polarization, and the ultimate achievement of common prosperity.

(Deng, 1992b)

Deng's Southern tour allowed him finally to triumph in the long battle against political radicalization. At the CPC's Fourteenth National Congress held in October 1992, Deng was venerated as 'the chief architect of our socialist reform, of the open-door policy and of the modernization programme' and was praised as 'founder for developing the theory of building socialism with Chinese characteristics' (CPC, 1992). In response to Deng's call, the Congress proclaimed the replacement of the centrally planned economy by the socialist market economy (CPC, 1992, 1993). In his report submitted to the Congress, General Secretary Jiang Zemin commended the utilization of market forces in the previous reform practices as follows: 'In China, practice has proved that where market forces are given fuller play, the economies are vigorous and have developed in a sound way' (CPC, 1992). Jiang further described the prototype of China's socialist market-economy model in this report:

The Socialist Market Economy Model that we aim to establish is to allow the market the fundamental role in resource allocation under the macro adjustment and control of the state. Thereupon, economic activities can follow the law of values to meet the changes in demand and supply; and, resources can be allocated more efficiently through the pricing and competition mechanism.

(CPC, 1992)

The CPC and the Chinese government have, since 1992, been constructing the market-economy model in phases as one of their major tasks. China's socialist market economy, however, is clearly distinguished from the Western liberal market economies. The CPC defines socialist principles as 'social justice and equity' and 'common prosperity' (CPC, 1992, 2007). These principles are manifested in a structure in which public ownership (state and collective sectors) occupies the predominant status in the national economy. The CPC's understanding and policy actions in relation to public predominance have moved from 'quantity' to 'quality'. In this context 'quantity' means that the public sector exceeds the private sector, in terms of size and share in the GDP; whereas 'quality' indicates that the public sector dominates vital or strategic industries and holds an influential level of investment in important businesses (CPC, 1993, 1997). As a key informant said, 'our understanding regarding the predominance of the state sector also changed. Previously we emphasized quantity, but now we highlight its role.' From hardly existing at all before 1978, private ownership (both domestic and foreign investment) was officially recognized as a contributory component in the national economy, albeit, directed and monitored by the state (CPC, 1993, 1997, 2002). All enterprises were assumed to enter fairly and compete in the market (CPC, 1992). Based on these premises, the market mechanism under the state's regulatory and administrative control has superseded the central master plan as the fundamental institutions in resource allocation and socio-economic development.

As empowered by the state constitution (National People's Congress (NPC), 2004), the Chinese government exercises macro management of the national economy, operates and controls the strategic industries identified by the state (e.g. energy, civil aviation, banking, insurance), regulates prices of designated products and monitors the general pricing level (State Development Planning Commission (SDPC), 2000; CNTA, 2003b; Airey and Chong, 2010). In this way the functioning of the market mechanism in China is both granted and restricted by the state (Lieberthal, 2004). The industries and sectors which are of national and public significance, do not fall into the scope of market forces. The Chinese-styled market economy only runs under restricted market forces overseen by the state and also entails intervention by the state whenever deemed necessary in order to turn the market forces back onto the desirable or pre-set track. It is more appropriate to describe the market economy in China as the 'state-centric market-economy model'.

Under the market-economy model, the demand side of the economy was substantially freed from the control of government. The planned-economy concept that economic growth fully depends on state investment shifted; the supply side should meet and satisfy demand under the guidance of the state. The roles and functions of government transformed from micro-controlling enterprises through administrative orders to the macro management and control of the economy (CPC, 1992, 1993). China's domestic market was further geared to the international market through increasing openness to the outside world. Pricing liberalization also went ahead. The categories of commodities and services fixed by the state reduced from 141 in 1992 to thirty-three in 1994, the latter including energy products, chemical industry products, metallurgical products and transportation charges. There was a further reduction to thirteen in 2001 (Lieberthal, 1995: p.248; 2004: p.262). The structural reform of the state-owned enterprises also continued. They were separated from their supervisory government agencies thus enabling them to become independent business entities and ensuring more fair market competition (CPC, 1992, 1993; Yu *et al.*, 2005).

In the later years of Deng's life, it appeared that he had found the future direction for China's reform, namely 'development'. As he put it, 'development is the absolute tenet' (Deng, 1992b), but he also noticed the inequalities and imbalances that went along with rapid development. Ultimately however the interpretation of his 'development' notion was left to Deng's successors. As Deng put it, 'we trust that our new generations have more wisdom than us and they could have the issues solved wisely'.

Under Deng's depoliticalization, a non-political realm was created and incrementally became enlarged, which made society separate from the state. The Chinese leaders in this era basically accepted that people could act initially according to their own interests. Their careers, marriages, personal thoughts and even their lifestyles no longer fell within the areas of political importance. The state also gradually gave up its role in providing the 'hard' moral model that people were obliged to obey (Lieberthal, 2004), but rather left the ethical building to the 'softer' means of education, the official mass media and even revived religious forces.

Collective Leadership era (1997–present): 'Public and Harmonious Socialism'

After Deng Xiaoping's death in February 1997, China entered a period of collective leadership in which political power shifted from 'Deng-in-dominance' on key issues to the core leader exercising a convening role in agenda setting and decision-making. There was also an evolution toward 'Public and Harmonious Socialism' advocating people-oriented, comprehensive and coordinated development. The result of three decades of development since 1978 is a China which has not only gained in prosperity and strength, but has become one of the emergent great powers in a multilateral world. Internally, China has undergone enormous changes. In state ideology and governance, China entirely abandoned its dogmatic doctrines and in their place it has maintained a relatively loose ideological framework with China's national interests as the top priority. In its political–economic system, China has basically built up a Chinese-style market economy placed firmly within the state's regulatory and administrative framework, with nearly 400 laws and regulations enacted to build up the market mechanism and make it function (Xinhua News Agency (Xinhua), 2008a). The government structure for the economy has been streamlined with economic regulation as the primary role, rather than the previous economic administration. The private sector is now acknowledged by the government as an 'important component' in the economy (CPC, 1997). Together these changes were influenced by and were important to China's accession to membership of the World Trade Organization in 2001. They also played an important part in enabling China to become the second-largest economy in the world in 2009 (*Hong Kong Mingpao Daily* (Mingpao), 22 January 2010) and rank second in terms of purchasing power parity (United Kingdom Foreign and Commonwealth Office, 2009a).

The development of the market economy and the loose ideological framework have not been without concerns. China has seen significant social changes and socio-economic difficulties, contributing to the third shift in the national development model. Notably decentralization, marketization and foreign investment have not only brought about incentives for high economic growth, but also created greater diversity of ownership (i.e. state, collective, private, foreign and mixed). China's state-centric market economy has driven domestic and foreign businesses to establish formal and informal ties with government agencies out of which numerous interest groups have been formed. These groups in their turn have posed difficulties for the implementation of deepened reforms, since government agencies have worked to protect their respective sectors (Xinhua, 2006g) and at the same time local government has pursued its own territorial goals (Saich, 2004). The substantial depoliticization since Deng's era has meant that career selection is no longer the concern of government; individuals can pursue their own career choices according to their interests and the availability of jobs and China's social structure has been completely altered from the simple layers of Mao's era (workers, peasants, soldiers and cadres) to a far more diverse structure, including but not limited to entrepreneurs, professionals, managers and executives, party cadres, government officials. The middle class has grown rapidly from 15 per cent in 2001 to 23 per cent of total population in 2010 (Xinhua, 2010a).

These changes have obviously brought changes to the traditional constituents underpinning the communist ruling power. Under China's political relaxation the government no longer has a monopoly on the provision of information and also has much less control over its flow. Vivid images of the outside world are now provided to the Chinese through Western media, as well as through the many foreign visitors. Many Chinese now also have experience overseas and nearly free access to the internet (Lieberthal, 1995, 2004). These have brought new lifestyles and have created new social and personal values. Some typical alterations include 'enterprise' prevailing over 'personal stability', 'respect for civil rights' replacing 'adherence to authority', 'pursuit of wealth' instead of the 'denunciation of wealth', 'ability to earn and to spend' replacing 'pure saving', 'life quality' instead of 'plain living', and 'religion' coexisting with 'atheism'. Society in the reform era has been increasingly characterized by a prosperous consumer culture.

China's state sector has also shrunk in relative size. Though state and collective enterprises still represent the mainstay, the private sector in 2007 contributed not less than one-third of GDP (Xinhua, 2008b). Non-government organizations (NGOs) have also seen a growing role in China's political, economic and social arenas, some prompted by government initiative. The NGOs include religious organizations, environmental groups and other voluntary bodies such as professional and personnel associations, and affinity and leisure groups. But whether or not they were set up in response to government initiative all are subject to government registration, approval and audit (Lieberthal, 2004). Recent estimates put the number of NGOs at more than 260,000 (Xinhua, 2004b).

In summary, China now has a differentiated and diversified society instead of Mao's mono-society. As a result state–society relations have changed remarkably. Although the state is still authoritarian and maintains dominance, the authorities have tried to adopt a more open mind in understanding civil interests and demands. For example, people in many cities such Beijing and Shanghai now have official channels to express their views or even lodge complaints against government services (Lieberthal, 2004; *Newsweek* (America), 19 January 2009). The authorities have also endeavoured to influence society through publicity, persuasion and guidance rather than by mandatory measures.

The focus on economic development, described in the Western media as 'pragmatic radicalism' (*Newsweek* (America), 19 January 2009), has brought its own problems in overshadowing such concerns as common prosperity, enhancing justice, social conciliation and moral rebuilding. This has caused a series of pressures associated, for example, with wealth disparity, regional imbalance, ethical issues, corruption and environmental degradation at the same time as there has been a lack of a comprehensive social protection system. In China there is now a large gap between the rich and the poor. For example, annual incomes range from RMB¥630,000 for senior officers in businesses with foreign investment and ¥550,000 for top executives in state-owned enterprises, to ¥12,000 for the population at large (*Hong Kong Wenweipo Daily* (Wenweipo), 10 February 2009a). At the end of March 2009, around 320,000 multimillionaires in China together accounted for RMB¥8,000 billion – i.e. one-third of China's GPD (*Hong Kong Mingpao Daily* (Mingpao), 1 April 2009) but at the same time the senior economist of the World Bank indicated that China ranked second in terms of people living in poverty (*Hong Kong Wenweipo Daily* (Wenweipo), 9 April 2009). With job insecurity and an immature social welfare system, the Chinese are commonly under pressure. According to the Chinese Ministry of Health, in 2009 around 100 million people in China suffered from psychological stress or mental illness (*Hong Kong Mingpao Daily* (Mingpao), 8 March 2009).

The ten-year Cultural Revolution effectively destroyed traditional cultures and values and in the following periods there have been plenty of individuals seeking to exploit get-rich-quick ideas, too often by deception and fraud. This sort of activity has led to a deterioration in ethical behaviour. Reported incidents include 'slave labour' in 2007 and 2008, and the 'milk scandal' in 2008. In the former thousands of people including children were forced to work and were tortured by their owners in illegal brickyards in Shanxi Province. The latter concerned milk, infant formula and other food materials being adulterated with melamine. Corruption in China has reached an alarming level with senior officials being implicated. For example, a former Politburo member and party chief of Shanghai was imprisoned for bribery and more recently over fifteen officials at the level equivalent to minister have faced penalties for inappropriate behaviour (*Hong Kong Wenweipo Daily* (Wenweipo), 11 March 2010). Furthermore over 4,000 suspected officials escaped abroad, taking with them some US$50 billion (Xinhua, 2005b). Such tensions have inevitably prompted social dissatisfaction. For example, in 2008 a Beijing resident attacked a Shanghai police station and killed six police officers and in February 2009, immediately before the session of the National People's Congress (NPC), three people set fire to themselves near Tiananmen Square (*Hong Kong Mingpao Daily* (Mingpao), 26 February 2009). As a multi-ethnic country, the Chinese authorities also face ethnic conflict as reflected in the riots in Tibet in 2008 and Xinjiang in 2009. Faced with these disturbances, it was confessed in the 6th Plenum of the 16th CPC Central Committee held in 2006 that 'there are many conflicts and problems affecting social harmony. . . . We must always remain clear-headed and be vigilant even in tranquil times' (CPC, 2006b).

In the international arena, China in the collective leadership era generally faces three dimensions of foreign relations. First, China is being increasingly impacted by Western ideologies and fierce global competition resulting from her increased openness. Second, China's development has greatly increased her importance in international politics and the global economy generally (Lieberthal, 2004), especially within current multilateral world politics. *Global Trends 2025: A Transformed World* forecasts that China will be one of three major powers in the world by 2025 (United States National Intelligence Council (USNIC), 2008: p.iv) and in 2009, in his first such policy paper entitled *The UK and China: A Framework for Engagement*, the British Prime Minister emphasized that 'the emergence of China as a global economic and political force is one of the most significant developments of our time' (The UK Foreign and Commonwealth Office, 2009b: p.2). Third, the Western world has also expected China to take an active and constructive role during the economic downturn from 2008. For example, shortly after the inauguration of President Obama's administration, the US Secretary of State paid an official visit to Beijing to get support for US state bonds and China has actively made similar purchases in Western Europe (*Hong Kong Wenweipo Daily* (Wenweipo), 25 February 2009).

Divergences in ideologies, political systems, cultures and values also means that the rise of China has posed challenges to the existing 'rules of the game' mainly made by the Western world. China's state-driven development model is regarded as a challenge to the Western liberal model (USNIC, 2008: p.iv). Alongside cooperation, it is also recognized that China–Western relationships will also experience what is called 'controlled friction'. Recent incidents include the tensions in 2009 between Chinese vessels and the American naval ships, 'Impeccable' and 'Victorious'. There is also continued tension in relation to human rights, trade, intellectual property, exchange rates, energy depletion, environmental protection and stimulation of the global economy.

From class-based to public-based constituencies

As already discussed, the move to 'Public and Harmonious Socialism' was in response to internal pressures as well as external dynamics. In order to safeguard and enhance the position of the CPC it was recognized that its ideological representation needed to be broadened (Lin, 2003; Saich, 2004). General Secretary Jiang Zemin, designated by Deng Xiaoping as the 'core of the third generation of leadership', put forward in 2000 the idea of the party giving triple representation: to production; to culture; to the people.

As the CPC put it, the party should 'always represent the development trend of China's advanced productive forces, represent the orientation of China's advanced culture, and represent the fundamental interests of the overwhelming majority of the Chinese people' (CPC, 2006a), officially translated as 'Three-Represents' (CPC, 2002, 2006a, 2010a). The essence of this triple representation aimed to demonstrate that the CPC is a self-innovating ruling party advancing ahead of China's socio-economic and cultural transformation and expanding its constituencies from the proletariat (industrial workers, rural peasants, intellectuals, managerial cadres of state-owned enterprises and officials of government and party apparatuses) of Deng's era to the diversified general public at present.

Recognizing the imbalances in development, rising social tension, diverse public opinion and enlarged societal gaps, General Secretary Hu Jintao, who succeeded Jiang, took this further and from 2004 initiated the idea of 'Scientific Development' and a 'Socialist Harmonious Society' (CPC, 2004a, 2007, 2010b). Intending to turn back from an overconcentration on economic growth, 'Scientific Development' preached the pursuit of 'comprehensive, coordinated and sustainable development' in economic, political, social, environmental, regional and urban–rural affairs 'with the starting point on the people'. The term 'people-based' in this context means the 'fulfillment of the continuously increasing needs of the people' and 'enhancement of the all-round development of the people' (CPC, 2007). By way of 'Scientific Development' the CPC endeavoured to establish a 'socialist harmonious society' (CPC, 2006b; Xinhua, 2006a) underpinned by political, economic, social, cultural and ethical appeals (CPC, 2006b; Xinhua, 2006b, 2007a). These overall mean 'Public and Harmonious Socialism'. The enhancement of life quality became an indispensable part in the construction of a harmonious Chinese society (CPC, 2007). Actually, the term 'harmony' here represents not only a formal response to existing tensions in society but also refers back to traditional Confucian values. The vision was that a more harmonious society would be established after socio-economic pressures were eased. This focus on 'harmony' signifies the CPC formally abandoning the 'class struggle' of Marxism as a governance tool to deal with social contradictions and conflicts.

While the 'Three-Represents' and the 'Scientific Development Concept' provide an orientation for the CPC toward national development they are both fairly general in approach. In order to substantiate political faith in the CPC, strengthen the national union and rebuild moral standards, the CPC also brought together past and present socialist values into a new ideological base called the 'Socialist Core Values System' (CPC, 2006b). According to the official interpretation this 'system' consists of five layers, namely (1) Marxist doctrines and the Thoughts of Mao Zedong; (2) Socialism with Chinese Characteristics (i.e. officially also called 'Deng Xiaoping Theories'); (3) nationalism and patriotism; (4) reform initiatives and (5) socialist ethical values (the officially-called 'Eight Virtues and Eight Shames' promoted by Hu Jintao) that articulate with traditional culture and values (Xinhua, 2006b, 2007a;

CPC, 2007). This 'system' gives two important messages. First, that the CPC no longer uses communist values to establish the whole ethical model as in Mao's time. Second, that traditional Chinese culture and values have been reaccepted and reincorporated into the formal value system. By the time the Cultural Revolution failed in the 1970s, not only had the economy virtually collapsed but traditions had been substantially destroyed. In this context many Chinese simply lost their moral direction. The changes of the early 2000s began to re-establish traditional values and to provide some behavioural norms. The collective leadership period therefore is characterized as one which is 'people-based' in order to maintain and consolidate the legitimacy and dominance of the socialist system and the ruling CPC in China's differentiated society with diverse values, interests and public opinions.

The Chinese Vice-Premier then in charge of foreign affairs, Qian Qichen,[1] proclaimed in the 1990s that China's foreign policy was an extension of home affairs (Kim, 1998: p.15). The dramatic changes in China's domestic circumstances have led to adjustments in foreign policy supported by rising economic power. China not only recognizes but also promotes multilateralism and diversified development patterns (Xinhua, 2003). Recognizing that world order and globalization are still driven by the West, China has gradually moved away from the strategy of not challenging the US-led Western world. Chinese leaders have stressed openly that China's rise does not pose a threat and they have tried to project an image as an important stakeholder and fair player. But at the same time China is now utilizing its resources to defend its national interests and actively taking the initiating role in international affairs (Cheng, 2001; Saich, 2004; Xinhua, 2006c; 2006i; 2007b; 2008g).

While the communist and socialist doctrines remain important, since Deng Xiaoping's time and under his influence, they have been placed almost as items of spiritual worship only to come to the fore during periods of political pressure. The doctrines are less involved in directly shaping people's daily lives such as in the Cultural Revolution, but rather they are part of the softer influences provided by education, culture and organizational learning. For example, the political campaign 'Talk more about politics, justice and learning' was launched by the CPC in 1995 to fight against the trend of neglecting official duties for money-making activities (Saich, 2004). On the whole, the government does not interfere in individuals' lives politically, provided they do not engage in organized activity against the CPC or the state (Lieberthal, 2004).

Under Deng, national policy decisions and development strategies were mainly concerned with the establishment of the market economy focusing on setting up rules and fostering decentralization and enterprise reform. These have now been joined by attempts to deal with the imbalances created by development, government reorganization, weaknesses in demand, integration with the world economy and provision of social welfare. For example, between 2000 and 2006 state-level rejuvenation programmes were launched for the western, central and northeastern regions to narrow down the developmental gap with more advanced regions (Holbig, 2004). Similarly, faced with weaknesses in aggregate demand from the late 1990s, a decade-long programme of measures to stimulate the economy was implemented. In the economic crisis of 2008 particular attention was focused on boosting domestic consumption (e.g. the State Council, 2009a, 2010a). Within government itself the State Council introduced administrative reforms in 1998 and 2003 to streamline the structure of government and make it more fitting for a market economy. Cabinet-rank agencies were reduced from forty in 1998 to twenty-eight by 2003 and more than fifteen economic ministries for the planned economy were removed or reorganized (Yu *et al.*, 2005). Under this new administrative structure, the state withdrew from direct intervention in the operation of enterprises and shifted toward strengthening macro-control and industry-wide administration.

In 2008, a new round of government reorganization began to simplify further the processes and reduce the coordination burdens; for this purpose central agencies with similar functions were integrated. As a result, there are now twenty-seven cabinet-rank agencies. Internationally, in December 2001, after lengthy multilateral negotiations, China was admitted to the World Trade Organization thus signifying its formal integration with the world economy. At the same time marketization also intensified with more than 90 per cent of goods and services being priced within the state-regulated market economy (Lieberthal, 2004; Xinhua, 2009e, 2009f). State-owned enterprises were similarly reformed. Except for strategic sectors of national or public import-ance other state-owned enterprises have been opened to privatization in the form of multiple ownership (CPC, 1992, 1993, 1997, 2002, 2007). As for social welfare, central government has now embarked on a programme of medical services reform costing the state RMB¥850 billion with the goal of establish-ing an effective public health service system within three years (*Hong Kong Mingpao Daily* (Mingpao), 7 April 2009). In terms of governance the new generations of Chinese leadership remain committed to the political logic of Dengism that continues the reform by maintaining the CPC-led political system. Recognizing the emergence of greater social diversity and conflict, the CPC in 2004 took the decision further to strengthen its position. The offi-cial view was that the ruling effectiveness of the CPC itself depended on the ways in which it handled these tensions (CPC, 2004b). Learning from the Western world, professional consultants were hired to equip the officials with public relations skills and politically reliable market research firms were com-missioned to carry out public opinion surveys.

In foreign relations, China now claims a more leading role and international respect in world affairs. During the financial and monetary crisis of 2008 China has been active in setting the agenda and proposing new directions. For example, prior to the meeting of the G20 group of nations held in 2009, the Governor of the People's Bank of China Zhou Xiaochuan called for the development of a kind of supra-national currency (Xinhua, 2009a). Similarly, Vice-Premier Wang Qishan wrote in the *London Times* that developing countries should have more say in the international financial system (*Hong*

Kong Mingpao Daily (Mingpao), 28 March 2009). Accepting the term 'soft power', China also stresses the importance of developing a favourable image with other countries in addition to establishing links through 'hard' resources such as financial aid. Since 2006 the official Xinhua News Agency has published a series of articles on China's 'soft power' and the originator of the concept, Nye (2004) himself visited China and accepted an interview with Xinhua in 2006 (Xinhua, 2006h). In order to enhance its 'soft power', China is now undertaking a series of state-level image-building and propaganda projects. For example, in order to promote Chinese culture, it has established a number of Confucian colleges across Asia, Africa, North and South America. The government also developed a RMB¥42.5 billion publicity strategy and a second English language newspaper *Global Daily* (English Edition) joined the original *China Daily* in April 2009. These both aim to provide an alternative to the Western media in presenting a Chinese perspective on events.

Conclusion

This chapter reviews and examines the evolution of China since 1949, with a focus on the transition from a planned economy to a market economy. The chapter sets out how China's national development models have changed from revolutionary and enthusiastic socialism in Mao Zedong's era (1949–78), to pragmatic and evolutionary socialism with economic modernization in Deng Xiaoping's era (1978–97), and then to 'Public and Harmonious Socialism' under the current collective leadership (1997–present). Among these three eras, Deng Xiaoping marked the real turning point. His work effectively ended a two-centuries-long period of a closed and stagnant China and started a new era of openness with the outside world on an equal basis (Huang, 1999). Under Deng Xiaoping's reform logic, China's socialist, party-leading-state political structure remains intact while administratively, particularly in relation to the operation of the market, there have been remarkable changes. In general, the role of state in development has shifted from 'dominant' in the planned economy to 'driving' in China's market economy. It is against this historical and contextual background that China's national tourism policy-making process has developed as presented in the following four chapters.

5   Tourism politics in Mao Zedong's era

The founding of the People's Republic of China in 1949 provided tourism with a relatively stable environment for development. But as noted in the previous chapter this long term view disguises the fact that in reality there were two very distinct periods after 1949: the Mao era (1949–78), when interest and indeed activities related to tourism were mainly limited to its political and diplomatic dimensions; and the Deng Xiaoping era (1978–97) when tourism began to be recognized as an economic force. Previous work (e.g. H.R. Li, 1987; Tisdell and Wen, 1991) has tended to treat these two eras in isolation from each other. The approach taken here also recognizes that Mao's tourism has important implications and linkages to subsequent developments. This chapter deals with what is called here *Period One*. Subsequent periods are dealt with in later chapters.

Period One 1949–78: tourism as a political and diplomatic vehicle

Tourism in Mao's era was predominantly limited to international inbound activities by foreigners, overseas Chinese[1] and compatriots from Hong Kong,[2] Macau[3] and Taiwan.[4] Domestic tourism as such did not exist and even domestic travel was essentially restricted to business and officially organized activities. Outbound travel was confined to that organized by the government for officially approved purposes, such as links with other socialist nations and support to African countries.

Mao's tourism was overwhelmingly political; it was both a part and an extension of China's foreign affairs. Tourism served as a tactic of 'civil diplomacy'[5] or 'people-to-people diplomacy' through receiving foreign tourists and 'external relations and friendship' through receiving Hong Kong, Macau and overseas Chinese. It did not aim to provide economic returns. The policy of isolation from the Western world meant that the reception of foreign tourists was inevitably the key focus of China's tourism politics. For this reason the data available and used here are mainly restricted to foreign tourists. The first part of the chapter deals with the complexities of tourism politics in Mao's era. It commences with an examination of related international and domestic circumstances, followed by an overview of the political nature of tourism. The subsequent part provides an account of the three development stages: start-up (1949–66[6]), stagnation (1966–71) and restoration (1971–8).

International and domestic circumstances

Both international and domestic factors shaped the political nature of tourism in this period providing encouragement for international arrivals and restriction for domestic tourism. As far as the international context is concerned, an important driver was that externally, China did not formally join the inter-national community, having been isolated from 1949 by the US-led Western Bloc. With international recognition and understanding seen as prerequisites for the survival and development of the newly born republic and with official barriers to diplomatic contact in place the Chinese government turned its attention to making contacts at the civil and individual levels. In this context tourism was seen as a vehicle to nurture understanding between China and other nations. By contrast, on the domestic front, with China's focus on recovery from the war and pursuit of Soviet-styled development, tourism, seen as a kind of 'advanced consumption', was not accepted as a 'productive force'. Accordingly it was not included in any development plans. More importantly, China's national development model gave priority to politics in terms of 'ideological correctness' and 'class struggle' and in these terms tourists and their behaviour were condemned as a display of a bourgeois lifestyle.

International environment

Internationally Mao's era was characterized initially by isolation and contain-ment by the Western world with a slow thaw in the 1960s and with anything like normal relations not beginning until the 1970s. The background and explan-ation for this lies in the cold war (1945–91) and in Chinese foreign policy. In the cold war, essentially between the Western (capitalist) Bloc headed by the United States and the Eastern (socialist) Bloc led by the USSR, China was effectively forced to choose sides (Lieberthal, 1995, 2004). For the Chinese people and CPC leaders, the period of China's domination by the Western powers from the nineteenth century had been a 'century of shame and humili-ation' and 'semi-colonialism'. In their view the Western powers represented imperialism and although the US was not centrally involved in this history, her aid to the nationalist government during the Chinese civil war meant that she was viewed with mistrust. Right up almost to the end of the civil war the communist armies clashed with the Western powers. Thus suspicion of foreign powers, rejection of any inferior status and maintenance of sovereignty dominated the foreign policy-making of the new republic. Mao Zedong's article '*Farewell (Ambassador) Leighton Stuart*'[7] in August 1949 provides a good illustration of this new diplomacy of combining full independence with alliance with the Soviet Union (Han Nianlong, 1988).

The Soviet Union was supportive of the Chinese communist revolution from the start. Recognizing a common ideology and security threats, and an opportunity to consolidate power and strengthen economic development, Mao declared that China had no choice but to 'lean to one side' (i.e. the Soviet Union). He declared 'all Chinese without exception must lean either to the side of imperialism or to the side of socialism. . . . Internationally, we belong to the side of the anti-imperialist front headed by the Soviet Union' (Whiting, 1992: pp.233–4). The USSR was the first nation to recognize China's new regime; and in 1950 the two countries signed the 'Sino-Soviet Treaty of Friendship, Alliance and Mutual Assistance'. The Soviet Union offered not only military support and weapons but also economic and technical aid including advisors and access to technological and engineering advances (Lieberthal, 2004). Following the USSR, the socialist nations in Eastern Europe (e.g. Poland, Hungary, Romania) and Asia (Vietnam and North Korea) also established diplomatic relationships with China (Ministry of Foreign Affairs (MoFA), 2009).

By contrast, China took a much more negative view of the Western powers, not acknowledging their privileges gained from the unequal treaties signed with the Qing Dynasty and re-examining all treaties made by the former Nationalist Government. This decision was fully in line with Mao's report in March 1949 to the Second Plenum of the Central Committee of the Seventh National Congress of the CPC that prepared for the establishment of the new regime:

> We did not recognize the legitimate status of the foreign diplomatic apparatuses and personnel in the Guomindang Era, we also did not acknowledge the continuance of all the betrayed treaties in the Guomindang Era. We will abrogate all the propagandistic organizations established by the imperialists.
>
> (CPC, 1949)

In the 1950s, just four Scandinavian nations and Switzerland established full diplomatic relations with China; the UK and Netherlands had representation only at *chargé d'affaires* level, though they acknowledged the new republic in 1954 (Han Nianlong, 1988; MoFA, 2009). The outbreak of the Korean War in 1950 turned Sino-American relationships from opposition to enmity. Besides the military attacks, the US also deployed its naval fleet in Taiwan to prevent military unification. The mutual hostility had not eased by the end of the war. With this background the US launched a trade embargo against the PRC and rejected her access to all non-communist international organs (Lieberthal, 2004). The US Secretary of State John Dulles even refused to shake hands with Premier Zhou Enlai[8] at the Geneva Conference held in 1954 on Korean and Indo-China issues. The US also did not issue passports to American citizens wishing to visit China (Han Nianlong, 1988: p.96). These scenarios further strengthened China's solidarity with the Socialist Bloc.

The Western blockage at the official level gave birth to China's 'civil diplomacy' for non-governmental ties with Western and other non-socialist countries. This started with the 'Asia-Pacific Peace Conference' held in 1952; a total of 378 delegates from thirty-seven countries including the United States, Japan, Australia and Chile attended (Han Kehua, 1994; CNTA, 1995b). This 'civil diplomacy' initiative proved effective, as it helped to clarify concerns of delegates and provided them with a new understanding of socialist China. As a result, the country's international recognition and status began to develop. This achievement was helped by her effective resistance to the US in Korea as well as the roles she had played in the Geneva Conference and in the first Asian-African Conference held in 1955 in Bandung, Indonesia. At the Bandung Conference, Zhou Enlai responded that China did not intend to 'export' communism and revolution and encouraged more people to visit China to draw their own conclusions (Han Nianlong, 1988: p.86). After this conference, China established diplomatic relationships with a number of Asian and African nations, especially the Arab states. Established in 1954, the main official organization for civil diplomacy was the Chinese People's Association for Friendship with Foreign Countries (CPAFFC) (Chen Haosu, 2004).

In the meantime, Sino-Western relationships also saw some degree of quiet unfreezing particularly with Europe. In the late 1950s, the UK was the first Western country substantially to lift its trade embargo (H.X. Wang, 1999). During and after the Bandung Conference, Zhou Enlai repeatedly expressed the view that China was ready to negotiate with the US and allowed pro-China Americans to visit. Subsequently, between the mid-1950s and late 1960s, the US and China undertook over 130 ambassadorial-level talks in Geneva and Warsaw (Han Nianlong, 1988). Despite the failure to solve fundamental issues such as the trade embargo and the question of Taiwan, these meetings served as important lines of communication. In this improved atmosphere, more and more people became interested in coming to China and the scope of civil diplomacy was extended. Besides CPAFFC, media, youth and women's organizations and educational and cultural institutions also participated in the promotion of people-to-people communications.

The Sino-Soviet alliance lasted until the death of Stalin in 1953. After the mid-1950s, tensions between the two nations emerged over issues of ideology, sovereignty and economic development. These finally caused the Sino-Soviet split in the 1960s (Han Nianlong, 1988). Ideologically, Mao was severely dissatisfied with Khrushchev's 'de-stalinization' in 1956 as well his peaceful coexistence policy with the Western Bloc (Waller, 1981; Saich, 2004). More important, however, was the Soviet Union's approach to sovereignty and independence, which the Chinese leaders regarded as of paramount import-ance. Notably the Soviet side were thought to make China subordinate to their global strategy for collaboration with the US, they provided only weak support for China's unification with Taiwan and for the 'joint naval' proposal and also they seemed to attempt to manipulate China. Further, during the Sino-India border conflicts in 1959, the Soviet Union did not provide support

(Han Nianlong, 1988: pp.112–16). In terms of economic development, the Soviet Union criticized Mao's Great Leap Forward (GLF) of the late 1950s, warning China not to 'skip the socialist stage' (Ogden, 1995: p.50). The division between the two sides worsened in the 1960s. The Soviets suddenly withdrew all experts and advisers in 1960 creating economic difficulty for China. The Sino-Soviet ideological disputes deepened and became public from 1960 to 1965. These struggles finally culminated in armed clashes on the border in 1969 (Han Nianlong, 1988; Saich, 2004). Not surprisingly, contacts and exchange with the Eastern Bloc countries subsequently declined significantly (Xinhua, 2008h).

China's simultaneous challenge to the two superpowers obviously potentially put her in a difficult situation. As a result she began to shift her position to pursue understanding, friendship and support with the developing world and with the Western nations. Premier Zhou Enlai undertook goodwill visits to China's six neighbouring nations including India in 1960. Between 1963 and 1964, Zhou visited a further thirteen Asian and African countries with a view to reaching a consensus on 'anti-colonialism' and 'anti-imperialism'. Also recognizing that Western Europe was not a coherent whole, China made a breakthrough with the establishment of full diplomatic relations with France. As Mao told a delegation from the French Congress in 1964 'let's make friends, make good friends; you are not the communist party; we are also not your party; we disagree with capitalism, you also oppose communism; but we still can cooperate' (Han Nianlong, 1988: pp.187–8). In 1964, China established non-official trade offices in Italy and Austria but because of the influence of the US, neither the Federal Republic of Germany nor the UK was able to explore further relationships with China. Notwithstanding such setbacks, however, with this diplomatic progress China connected air routes with Pakistan, Burma and Afghanistan, with the air route with Pakistan becoming the link with the Western world. France and Japan also approached China for air connections (Han Nianlong, 1988; Han Kehua, 1994).

By the 1970s, the landscape of world politics had changed and rapprochement had become a common need for both China and the United States. Against the background of the Vietnam war, and in a weakened position against the USSR, the United States needed to establish links with China. For China, the threat from the USSR became clear following the military clashes of 1969, the building up of ground forces on its long border as well as concerns about the USSR sounding out the US on using nuclear weapons. In this context cooperation between China and the United States was in the interests of both countries. As early as 1969, US President Richard Nixon relaxed restrictions on visits and trade with China and in 1970 openly expressed his willingness to visit red China (Han Nianlong, 1988). At this stage, however, China still had some scruples. 'Anti-imperialism' had been a key message in the communists' rise to power and at this time, the height of the Cultural Revolution in which the US was seen as the 'No. 1 Imperialist Nation', Mao doubted whether the Chinese people, especially hard-liners, could accept China's reconciliation. Also, for the Third World, which looked to China as the leader against imperialism and on this basis had supported China in, for example, gaining membership of the United Nations in 1971, such a move would not easily be understood. For Mao, therefore, it was important to give the message that it was the US who was seeking reconciliation (Lieberthal, 1995; Gao, 2003; Xinhua, 2006j).

Civil diplomacy was used to take this forward. Arranged by Zhou Enlai, on 1 October 1970 (China's National Day), a photograph taken in Beijing's Tiananmen Square of Mao Zedong and Edgar Snow (1905–72), the American journalist,[9] appeared in the *People's Daily*[10] (Gao, 2003; Xinhua, 2005a). This was followed by Mao telling Snow that 'if President Nixon would like to come, I am willing to talk with him' (Han Nianlong, 1988: p.220). These messages and signals were well received by the US. Later, during that same month President Nixon for the first time used the name of 'People's Republic of China'[11] in the official welcome for the Romanian President Nicolae Ceauşescu. Such civil diplomacy was taken further when Mao Zedong gave permission to admit American politicians to China in 1971, including those who opposed the communist system (i.e. 'rightists') (Han Kehua, 1994). Further, with Mao's approval, China invited the American Table Tennis Delegation to visit on 6 April 1971, the first such tour group since 1949. The hospitality they received helped Nixon to overcome the resistance from the American pro-Taiwan politicians. On 14 April, when Zhou Enlai met the American players, Nixon also announced the substantial lift of a trade embargo against China that had lasted for over two decades. This was the co-called 'Table-Tennis Diplomacy' which Zhou Enlai called the 'Little Ball (pingpong) running the Giant Ball (the world)'. Subsequently between July and October 1971, the US National Security Advisor, Henry Kissinger, paid two visits to Beijing, paving the way for direct talks between the two leaders. On 21 February 1972, President Nixon began his historic trip to China.

The 'China-United States Joint Communiqué' ('The Shanghai Communiqué') signed during the trip set out the path to the normalization of relations. To this end, the two countries agreed to increase civil and cultural exchanges, including the admission of American self-sponsored tourists. After having cleared all obstacles, China and the United States ultimately established full diplomatic relations in 1979 when Deng Xiaoping was leading China into the Reform Era. The improved US–China relations were followed by links with other countries. Between 1970 and 1978, China established full diplomatic relations with the majority of Western Bloc nations (Han Nianlong, 1988; Lieberthal, 1995, 2004; Gao, 2003; *People's Daily*, 2003a, 2003b; Saich, 2004).

Domestic factors

If the international environment prompted the political and diplomatic nature of tourism for China, the domestic environment was inherently simply negative to its development. The background to this lay partly in China's pursuit of the path taken by Soviet communism which suggested that tourism should at best be accorded the lowest priority in economic development. In China's case it went even further and tourism essentially occupied no position at all, with negative comments precluding it from forming a part of the economy. Mao Zedong's 'politics-in-command' orthodoxy was undoubtedly the determining factor here. This was not just his worldview but also the CPC's response to political realities. Mao made this doctrine even more extreme in his later years. From the very beginning, the top priorities of the new socialist republic were survival, development and consolidation of power; all challenging tasks in themselves. An important part of the background to this was provided by the Guomindang (or Nationalist Party of China) (GMD) forces. After their retreat to Taiwan, the GMD authorities never gave up political and military action, especially in front line regions. This essentially continued right up to 1979. In the early years, the GMD was strongly antagonistic toward the new regime and in this, in the eyes of the CPC, they were supported by 'exploitative' land-lords and unsympathetic, unsupportive and critical industrialists who usually had foreign interests and links with the former regime. The CPC quickly launched the 'Suppression of Counter-Revolutionaries' campaign in 1951 (Saich, 2004).

Mao at the same time gave rather more attention to being vigilant about what he called 'bourgeois thoughts'. In the absence of any clear definitions and boundaries for this term it came to encompass all practices, behaviour, lifestyles, attitudes, notions and values, real or imaginary, which could be considered as posing threats to the communist regime. In the 1950s it initially included the GMD forces in Taiwan and their associated foreign influences. Later, in the 1960s, it was extended to include 'Khrushchev's revisionism' and 'socialist imperialism' (Lieberthal, 1995). Mao absolutely feared that bourgeois ideologies, having seeped into the CPC, would corrupt the whole regime and eventually change the colour of red China. He repeatedly reminded his comrades of what he had said in 1942 in Yan-an[12] that 'unarmed enemies still exist even when the armed ones have been annihilated' (CPC, 1949). In March 1949, seven months before the formal establishment of the PRC he had put it:

> Because of our victory, people appreciate us; the bourgeoisie also adulate us. We have proved that the military forces of our enemies failed to defeat us. However, the capitalists' adulation may conquer some weak-willed ones in our forces. There may be some communists who have never been defeated by armed enemies, they are deemed to have the honour of a hero in front of these (i.e. armed) enemies. But they may be incapable of resisting the 'sugar-coated bullets of the bourgeoisie'; they will lose the battle faced with 'sugar-coated bullets and bombs'.
>
> (CPC, 1949)

Mao's concern indeed warranted the attention of the ruling communists. When they had taken power, the CPC's membership was overwhelmingly made up of peasants who had had little contact with urban life. Indeed some were even anti-urban (Lieberthal, 1995). The risk was that these peasant members might easily be tempted by the appeal of urban life. Therefore Mao waged a series of political campaigns in his attempts to stem any such developments and to purify the party. These ranged from the 'Three-Anti and Five-Anti'[13] between 1951 and 1952, the 'Thought Reform of Intellectuals' from 1951 to 1952, the 'Hundred Flowers' and the 'Anti-Rightists Campaign' in 1957, to the 'Socialist Education Campaign' between 1962 and 1965 (Ogden, 1995; Saich, 2004). When Mao finally came to the view that what ultimately hindered his purification efforts were the tremendous party-state-administrative apparatuses founded by him and his revolutionary partners but now steered by 'China's Khrushchev and revisionists' who had 'changed' from 'revolutionaries' to 'reactionaries', he, in an extraordinary dare, launched The Great Proletariat Cultural Revolution. The challenge was to shake and even rebuild these socialist institutions.

Tourism undoubtedly fell into the category of the 'sugar-coated bullets of the bourgeoisie'. It most certainly was not seen as part of the lives of the proletariat classes, workers and peasants living in poverty or of the leftist intellectuals (Lieberthal, 1995) who were the focus of the Chinese communists' efforts. By way of background it is noteworthy that except for China Travel Services founded by Chen Guangfu in 1927, almost all travel agencies in China in the GMD era were set up by foreign businesses (CNTA, 1993b) primarily to serve foreign nationals. Tourist activities for leisure and recreation were naturally viewed as a part of a 'lavish and luxury lifestyle' (Han Kehua, 1994; CNTA, 1996b). Tourism as a part of the economy or an industry for the Chinese had no room to develop under Mao's national development model focusing on 'politics-in-command'. Of course, travel at the individual level, for holidays, family gatherings and meetings of friends, was not forbidden but it was not encouraged either. The only other significant form of domestic travel was for official purposes, such as for group activities or for rewards and incentives. It was really only when it became a part of 'tourist diplomacy', that tourism gained official recognition: not as a 'villainous bourgeois activity' but rather as a political and diplomatic task assigned by the state to exhibit socialist China. The tourism officials who operated under this foreign affairs banner were highly trained political and professional cadres with a focus on their ideological loyalty. Thus tourism as a part of foreign affairs was seen as being isolated from the 'seedbed of a bourgeois ethos'.

Prior to the Cultural Revolution, the power arrangements and the rather freer environment at the top provided some latitude for alternative views including those related to an economic consideration of tourism. While politics after 1945 began with 'The Thoughts of Mao Zedong' as the ruling doctrine, over time, while Mao retained a firm grip on key decisions, ideology and military and security control, he tended to leave policy implementation and the daily running of the state machine to his partner leaders. Between 1949 and 1966, the CPC also practiced 'democratic centralism' quite effectively. Built up in the revolutionary era, this not only required individual party members to obey the organization, but also enabled them either to hold different views or to put them forward for discussion at party meetings (Saich, 2004). This came to an end at the start of the Cultural Revolution, when there was little latitude for alternative views but it provides the political background in which in 1957 Chen Yun put forward his economic ideas about tourism. These are considered further in a later section (p.129) (Xinhua, 2008j, 2009h).

In summary, tourism as a political tool served both external and internal needs in Mao's era. The international and domestic environments did not provide the necessary conditions for 'normal' tourism development, especially in relation to its economic and social dimensions. The international factors were explicit and overt whereas the domestic conditions were implicit and covert. A key informant generalized the explicit and apparent impacts of the international environment as follows:

> Because of the international politics at that time, we did not have the conditions to develop tourism as an economic activity. China and the Western world were hostile to each other. We were also highly alert toward visitor flows from Hong Kong, Macau and Taiwan.

The internal ideological orthodoxy of 'politics-in-command' and its associated national development model were the basis for the political use of tourism. Under this orthodoxy international tourism could never become a business activity, even though China–Western relationships began to normalize and tourist demand increased markedly in the 1970s. Above all this was because international tourism as a business activity would lead to the promotion of 'leisure', 'recreation' and 'enjoyment'. This would not only contradict the reigning orthodoxy which prioritized 'plain living' but also prompt the emergence of domestic tourism, and the associated spread of 'bourgeois lives'.

Overview of tourism politics in Mao's era

Goals of tourism politics

As noted, its isolation by the Western world, the subsequent Sino-Soviet split and China's internal circumstances, meant that tourism in Mao's era solely served as a political and diplomatic tool focusing on 'civil diplomacy' and 'external relations and friendship'. Overtly, tourism was adopted as a means to promote the superiority of socialist China, to expand China's international influence, to consolidate the union between the socialist nations, to win the sympathy and understanding of international society broadly and to nurture friendship through overseas tourists. In 1964 the policy document 'Report on the Development of Tourism' prepared by the Foreign Affairs Leadership Group of the CPC Central Committee stated:

[The goals of tourism development are] to propagandize the socialist achievements of China, to expand China's international political influence and to enhance mutual understanding and friendship between the Chinese people and the people of the rest of world. Besides, tourism also can absorb some foreign exchange.

(CNTA, 1995b: p.10)

Covertly, tourism was utilized as a channel to gather information in relation to China's security and development. Premier Zhou Enlai conveyed this message to the officials of the China International Travel Services (CITS) in relation to a delegation of rural youth from Japan: 'there are so many people [in this delegation]. They came to visit us on their own initiative. Why don't you undertake some investigations and studies about them?' (Han Kehua, 1994: p.214). Zhou later directly asked the guests about agricultural development in Japan. Zhou formally called this the wish to 'publicize ourselves [socialist China] and understand others [other nations]' (CNTA, 1995b: p.14). Tourists initially only included invited guests of political and social importance but the scope quickly expanded to permitted self-financing travellers; they were known as China's 'foreign friends and guests'. It is worth noting that there were two categories of self-financed tourists: independent (e.g. students and businessmen) and group. Both were required to make their arrangements through travel agencies recognized by China in their respective countries, especially Western and non-socialist nations. In this sense all these self-sponsored tourists to China were organized rather than fully independent.

Interestingly, the economic function of tourism also emerged in this period with respect to self-financed tourists. This idea first found expression in the desire that they should cover their costs. Subsequently consideration was given to earning foreign exchange to help fund China's mass construction programme. This economic aspect of tourism was nevertheless entirely subordinate to its political and diplomatic nature. All self-financed tourists still had to obtain entry permission which was granted on political considerations. Tourists, especially those from the Western world, needed to be politically friendly toward socialist China. One key informant who joined China's travel services in the early 1970s remarked:

It was not a matter of whether Western people were willing to spend money on visiting China, but rather we should undertake scrutiny of their political inclinations. When filling up their application forms to visit China, tourists were required to provide information including their political beliefs, political party affiliations and religion.

It was not until the early 1970s that some Western 'rightists' were allowed to enter, at the time when China was preparing for dialogue with the United States.

In fact, for the most part tourism operated at a loss, especially at its outset and during the period of the Cultural Revolution. It was not until 1973 that

Premier Zhou Enlai instructed that: 'tourism should earn some surpluses but we are still running at loss. Fees should be based on the principle that self-financing visitors should pay for their travel' (CNTA, 1995b: p.16). In 1965, the Central Committee of the CPC and the State Council reiterated and reaffirmed the political nature of tourism: 'Tourism should adopt politics-in-command, proceed steadily and develop gradually' (CNTA, 1995b: p.11).

Actually an annual quota, approved by the State Council and even by the top leaders, was set to limit the number of self-financed tourists. For example, in 1956 they were restricted to a maximum of 3,000. In order to attract such self-financed tourists, a favourable package of privileges was offered. Tourists could enjoy a 50 per cent discount on the railways and ships and a 25 per cent discount on airfares with Chinese carriers; tourists were also able to purchase quality products at discounted prices in designated stores (CNTA, 1995b: pp.6 and 10). A key informant said:

> As tourism served politics and diplomacy, if a commercial purpose was pursued, it would be found difficult to attain political and diplomatic purposes [i.e. profit-making would discourage visits of some people on the basis that they could not afford it]

and

> In that era, Western people who were friendly . . . to China might not be able to afford trips to China. They did not want to spend money or only wanted to spend a little on visiting China. This was why we kept the fees at the minimum or even did not charge. Our fee-charging was not based on economic principles. This was why we reduced fees for compatriots to half of those charged to Western visitors for the same package. At that time, there were far fewer Western people and compatriots coming to China . . . ; we hoped that more of them would come.

The reception of the compatriots (i.e. ethnic Chinese) from Hong Kong, Macau and overseas Chinese was also within this same goal of tourism politics. In a strict sense, the compatriots did not belong within the scope of 'civil diplomacy'. For instance, the Chinese government rejected the British request for China to establish a diplomatic agency in Hong Kong to match that of the nationalist government before 1949, but rather they set up the Xinhua News Agency, Hong Kong Branch. However, Hong Kong, Macau and the overseas Chinese, who were under foreign jurisdiction and continued to aid China, held a unique position for the new republic, in terms of funds, material, information and understanding. Dating back to China's republican revolution, Dr Sun Yat-Sen appraised the overseas Chinese as 'the mother of revolution' who gave all-round support to the uprising against the Qing Dynasty. Hong Kong was one of Sun's revolutionary bases. In the communist regime, He Xiangning and Liao Chengzhi, who were the widow and son of the GMD leftist leader Liao Zhongkai[14] respectively, were in charge of overseas Chinese affairs. These two plus Song Qingling (Madame Sun Yat-Sen) were able to organize support from the overseas Chinese for socialist China.

Against a background of Western isolation and embargo, Hong Kong was almost the sole contact point between China and the Western world as well as the sole place to raise external capital, and acquire material and information. Prior to rejoining the UN, only about sixty countries maintained full diplomatic relations with China (Xinhua, 2006j). As an international city adjacent to the Mainland, the 'bridging role' of Hong Kong was seen as unique. Furthermore, since the GMD authorities in Taiwan claimed themselves as the sole legitimate regime, the recognition and support from the Chinese in Hong Kong, Macau and overseas was able to provide special assistance to socialist China. Hence within the overall goal of tourism politics, the reception of compatriots from Hong Kong, Macau and overseas aimed to enhance the understanding and support from the ethnic Chinese under foreign rule. Although not formally falling into diplomacy, it was regarded as its extension or a part of China's foreign affairs in a broad sense. From another perspective, this kind of visitor movement also supported a major political thrust of the CPC, the 'United Front', which according to Mao meant to mobilize all possible forces to solve major contradictions (Lieberthal, 1995; C.F.J. Wang, 2002). All of these efforts paved the way for a tremendous amount of investment and aid from Hong Kong, Macau and overseas Chinese in the reform era.

The institutions and structure of tourism politics

In serving political and diplomatic goals, tourism was a part of China's external affairs and operated in a highly centralized structure in terms of decision-making, administration and operation. The ultimate decision-makers were the two top leaders Mao Zedong and Zhou Enlai: the heads of the ruling CPC and the government respectively. In reality many instructions for tourism came directly from Zhou. As an inter-agencies committee under the CPC Politburo, the Foreign Affairs Leadership Group exercised leadership over China's foreign and external relations at the party, state and civil levels. Regarding the relevant agencies, the Ministry of Foreign Affairs (MoFA) was and remains the central government agency responsible for foreign policy implementation and foreign affairs administration. At the level of the political party, the International Department of the CPC was in charge of the Party's external affairs; in Mao's era it mainly promoted international communist exchange. Directly under the jurisdiction of MoFA, the Bureau of Travel and Tourism of China (BTTC), founded in 1964, was responsible for the administration of tourism affairs. The BTTC and China International Travel Services (CITS) established in 1954 actually formed one entity in terms of goals and staffing, with the former responsible for supervision and the latter for travel services (CNTA, 1995b: pp.10 and 14). The Overseas Chinese Affairs Commission (OCAC)[15] took charge of policy-making, administration and liaison in relation to the overseas Chinese. As supervised by the OCAC, the Overseas Chinese Travel Services (OCTS) established in 1949 (renamed China Travel Services (CTS) in 1974) served Hong Kong, Macau and the overseas Chinese. In view of the political role assigned to tourism, agencies concerned with security and ideology were also involved. The security agencies included the Ministry of Public Security (MoPS) and the Department of Investigation of the CPC. The ideological agencies encompassed the Central Publicity Department of the CPC, Xinhua News Agency, the Foreign Languages Press and Broadcasting Administration Bureau among others. Within local government, the foreign affairs offices and the overseas Chinese affairs offices were responsible for tourist activities in their respective regions. All staff directly involved in tourism (BTTC, CITS, OCTS/CTS, local officials, etc.) fell within the foreign and external affairs establishment; they were required to obey the general disciplines of this establishment and the specific codes for receiving tourists.

At the operational level, the CITS directly managed and operated guest houses, tour buses and other relevant facilities. Though the local branches of CITS were under the leadership of local government, its head office exercised professional supervision over them. The head office undertook tourist planning, liaison with foreign partners, work deployment, staff training and oversight of local branches. More importantly, local branches were not allowed to make foreign contacts. In other words, the local branches were just the ground operators and service providers. The CITS identified the tourists mainly through Chinese embassies and the foreign friendship organizations together with their associated travel agencies. Likewise, the OCTS (CTS) also adopted a centralized approach. Both the CITS and CTS were non-administrative government agencies; but they were allowed to portray themselves as business enterprises for the convenience of external liaison (Han Kehua, 1994; CNTA, 1995b, 1999b).

Activities in tourism politics

The tourist activities in Mao's era were under tight control of the government. Visa applications were strictly scrutinized and approved by the MoPS and MoFA. Foreign tourists were only permitted to visit forty-eight open cities in China, within which they were only allowed to tour the non-restricted areas. Approval was required if the tourists intended to visit restricted areas in these open cities. Once entry visas had been granted, tourists were prohibited from changing their travel arrangements or routes. All tourists had to be received, entertained and escorted by representatives of the CITS. In other words, foreign tourists were under close scrutiny of the authorities; there were no real contacts between the Chinese hosts and foreign guests. Regardless of the tourists' actual interests, all their programmes, which were designed and arranged by the government, concentrated on showcasing China's socialist achievements. Alongside any natural and cultural heritage attractions the visits invariably included socialist exemplars – model factories, rural communes, work units and social establishments (for example, the Beijing Capital Steel Corporation, the Beijing National Agricultural Exhibition Hall). As illustrated in the cases of Edgar Snow and Anne Louise Strong[16] arrangements were made for important guests to meet senior officials and leaders, accompanied with official presentations and banquets. Like inbound travel, outbound travel was similarly limited, only being permitted for officially approved purposes and to socialist countries (Han Kehua, 1994; CNTA, 1995b, 1999b).

In short Mao's China was neither a tourist destination nor a tourist-generating nation in the normal sense. Tourism was subordinate to and embedded within China's ideological politics and foreign affairs. It was not an independent phenomenon and was neither an industry nor an economic activity. The incoming tourists were required to follow officially arranged itineraries highlighting China's socialist achievements and there were no genuine communications between hosts and guests. Though the economic consideration of tourism as an auxiliary function was proposed, it was not really implemented. In a Western sense, there was no true 'tourism' or 'tourism development'. 'Tourism development' in essence was about a specific political development as designated by the party-state. Also and importantly, in light of later developments, because of its political and diplomatic purpose, tourism never became a part of China's planned economy. As for domestic tourism, as an activity that contradicted the reigning socialist ideology, this hardly existed. Domestic travel was really confined to individual activity and certainly not supported or encouraged by the state.

Three development stages

Within the broad framework of 'tourist diplomacy', three stages can be identified in the development of tourism politics in Mao's era, each with its own characteristics. This section examines how tourism politics operated in these three phases.

Start-up (1949–66)

This was an important stage during which the political-diplomatic nature of tourism was affirmed and its structure and operation were built up. In general, tourism politics actually commenced from practice and was then consolidated by policy responses.

Although the Overseas Chinese Services (OCS) (Overseas Chinese Travel Services (OCTS) from 1957) was first established in October 1949 to provide travel arrangements and hospitality for compatriots and overseas Chinese, it was not until the end of the Korean War in 1953 that tourism was fully operated as an element in China's civil diplomacy. After tourism had effectively functioned as a tool for 'civil diplomacy' in the first 'Asia Pacific Peace

Conference' held in 1952, Premier Zhou Enlai approved the 'Report on the Establishment of the China International Travel Services' submitted by the International Activities Committee of the CPC; the Report drew on the experience of the Soviet Union. In April 1954, China's first country-wide international travel agency – China International Travel Services – was established on the Fifth Anniversary of the establishment of the new republic; it had its headquarters in Beijing and planned to set up branches in the major cities. During 1954 and 1955 CITS started its work in a very limited way. As of 1955, the facilities directly used by the CITS only comprised one guest house and some eight automobiles. These limitations posed challenges for its performance. For example in 1955, Vice-Premier Deng Xiaoping designated the CITS to entertain a civil delegation from Japan, a rare and important event. However, in the end the delegation could only stay in the guest house because the CITS did not have the cars to transport them elsewhere (Han Kehua, 1994: p.198). Local branches were also only just being set up and so the country-wide network was not yet effective (Han Kehua, 1994; CNTA, 1995b).

THE PERIOD 1956–60

Following its slow start, in 1956 and for the next four years, the CITS was increasingly tasked with the provision of hospitality and travel arrangements for foreign delegations, experts and invited guests, primarily from the USSR and Eastern Europe. These services were all to serve the needs of central and local government. To respond, a centralized management system was established. In 1957, the State Council transferred the operation of guest houses and cars to the CITS. Subsequently in 1958, the supervision of the branches of the CITS was divided between the head office and local government, with the former being responsible for professional leadership and the latter for political and administrative leadership. All external contacts and job assignments were centralized at head office.

In addition to visitors from Eastern Bloc countries, the slight thaw in relationships with the Western world meant that a small quota of self-financed Western tourists was also received. The tourists from the USSR included academics, journalists, recipients of socialist honours, engineers, artists, peasants and students. This profile of tourists not only served to demonstrate the success of the socialist model, hence justifying and supporting China's own choice, but also facilitated the publicity of socialist progress in China. Western tourists were made up of political activists, scholars, and businessmen. It was thought that such a profile would enable different groups in these nations to understand socialist China. Regardless of their background all tourist groups were entertained and escorted by CITS staff. The CITS itself also directly played its own part in China's civil diplomacy. For example, CITS officials successfully clarified the concerns and doubts of a pioneer French travel agency making its exploratory trip to China in February 1957. This agency subsequently organized three groups of self-financed tourists to China in the same year, becoming the first batch of Western organized tourists (Han Kehua, 1994: p.200).

Along with China's growth, interest in visiting China developed. More and more foreign tourist organizations and Chinese embassies sought tourist information about China. As of 1957, over twenty-two tourist organizations of twelve socialist and non-socialist nations, including North Korea, Czecho-slovakia, the United States, France and Japan, sought to establish business relationships with the CITS (Han Kehua, 1994: p.201). These pointers showed that tourism, particularly through self-sponsored tourists, who were usually self-motivated, had become an active component in China's civil diplomacy. Furthermore, the introduction of self-financed tourists saved the state's entertainment and hospitality budget which in turn could be reallocated to other visitors deemed to be important or necessary. Some major measures were therefore taken to boost such visits. In 1958, the State Council decided to expand the number of self-financed tourists and instructed the CITS accord-ingly (CNTA, 1995b). For incentives, they were offered favourable discounts on air and land transportation. Their visa applications were scrutinized and approved by the MoPS and MoFA with the former taking the main role. As noted, the self-financed tourists were only allowed to visit forty-eight places during a maximum stay of two months in China.

In the meantime, in 1958 China also entered the period of the Second Five-Year State Plan for the National Economy and Social Development (Saich, 2004: p.37). The planned mass construction demanded more funds and foreign exchange. It was against this background that an economic consideration of tourism emerged. In political terms this was a relatively relaxed period even though it coincided with Mao's launch of the Anti-Rightists Campaign to crack down on criticisms of the CPC. The CPC itself was in debate about how to speed up China's socialist development which led to The Great Leap Forward of 1958. Under these circumstances, in 1957, as a key planner for China's planned economy, Vice-Premier Chen Yun suggested using tourism to earn more foreign exchange:

> We have a plan to allow more self-financed tourists to visit China for recreation. We also have a plan to open more cities for touring and recre-ation. At present, our high-class guesthouses are vacant. So, we can earn an amount of foreign exchange.
>
> (CNTA, 1995b: pp.5–6)

In March 1958, the role of CITS was further designated by the State Council:

> Through its own tasks, to promote friendly intercourse between the Chinese people and the people of other nations, to enhance mutual understanding among the people of different nations and to carry out an

independent foreign policy of peace; also to earn some foreign exchange for accumulating development funds.

(CNTA, 1995b: pp.6–7)

The measures identified earlier were effective in attracting more self-financed tourists. As of 1958, the number of such tourists, at 6,000, for the first time exceeded the 4,800 invited guests, supported by state funds (Han Kehua, 1994: p.208). The majority came from the Socialist Bloc. The numbers continued to increase in 1959 and 1960. The CITS accordingly expanded its staff establishment and increased its branches to thirty-five. It also formulated three codes of conduct in 1959, namely 'Notices to Escorting Interpreters', 'Eight Requirements for Interpreters and Tour Guides' and 'Service Provision at Borders and First Stops'. These three codes not only highlighted the political-diplomatic nature of travel services, but also aimed to enhance the political and professional competencies of the front-line staff. One interesting change was that in 1960 CITS was permitted to describe itself externally as a business enterprise (CNTA, 1995b: p.8). Notwithstanding its formal position as a non-administrative government agency, this was allowed in recognition of the fact that similar agencies in overseas countries, with which it was engaged, were typically classed as business firms.

Although the numbers of self-financed arrivals from Western countries grew during this period, over 80 per cent still came from the Eastern Bloc and other socialist nations. China's aim remained to establish ever closer links with the Eastern Bloc, despite the emerging divisions in Sino-Soviet relations. The representative of the Soviet Union's International Travel Services to China conveyed his thoughts in writing 'my heart is always with China; the impressions that China gives me are tremendous' (Han Kehua, 1994: p.208). The General Manager of East Germany's Travel Services remarked: 'Our government has reviewed the previous experience of the travel services, and affirmed that the organization of tours to the USSR and China are regarded as a measure of socialism education for our people' (Han Kehua, 1994: p.208).

THE PERIOD 1961–6

Tourism politics underwent a period of change and consolidation between 1961 and 1965 – the eve of the Cultural Revolution – influenced particularly by a marked increase in Western tourists and internal political tightening.

With the attention of the leaders focused on the failure of The Great Leap Forward, tourism as a political-diplomatic showcase seemed to have little role to play at the start of this period. It temporarily left the state agenda in 1961 while a series of adjustment measures were being adopted, although it quickly returned after these measures were found to be effective. The Sino-Soviet split now prompted China to emphasize relationships with Western Europe, alongside Asian and African countries. Attracting more Western European tourists became the major task of China's civil diplomacy. In fact, the improved political situation, including the development of air routes and the creation of business links, meant a marked increase in demand for travel to China from the West. In the meantime, the Japanese government had freed travel overseas, and the Nippon–China Friendship Association in Japan immediately set up the Nippon–China Travel Agency to organize visits to China. Demand from Japan was enhanced by the mutual understanding that had been achieved through civil diplomacy and trade links. In 1964, the CITS received eight groups with a total of 172 Japanese tourists; this rose to ninety-two groups and 1,656 tourists in 1965. Under these circumstances, in 1964 the MoFA and MoPS jointly relaxed the restrictions on tourist entry from the capitalist nations. The number of self-financed tourists increased sharply to 12,800 in 1965. Of these, the self-financed tourists from Western and non-socialist countries totalled 3,915 accounting for 86 per cent of all group self-sponsored tourists; a three-fold growth over 1964.[17] This figure equals the sum of all tourist arrivals from non-socialist nations between 1958 and 1964. On the other hand, self-financed tourists from the USSR and Eastern European nations dropped significantly to become almost insignificant. In order to cope with the rising trend in arrivals, the local branches of CITS increased to forty-six as of 1966 (Han Kehua, 1994; CNTA, 1995b, 1999b).

The sharp increase in tourist arrivals created policy pressures with which the operationally oriented CITS was not well placed to cope. In 1964, the State Council established the Bureau of Travel and Tourism of China (BTTC) as a superior body to the CITS. Though in theory, as created by the National People's Congress, it was intended that the BTTC should function as a separate central agency, it was in fact placed under the jurisdiction of the MoFA, effectively as its bureau for tourist diplomacy. The BTTC's main task was to exercise an administrative role in tourism politics, including the management of CITS, external liaison and propaganda, monitoring the local CITS branches and the organization of outbound travel for official exchanges.

The years from 1961 to 1965 were the eve of the Cultural Revolution, characterized by a re-emphasis on 'politics-in-command', increasing inter-party tensions and a tightening in the political atmosphere (e.g. Lieberthal, 1995; Ogden, 1995). Though China's economy had revived from disaster after 1962, Mao Zedong and his supporters remained strongly dissatisfied with the rejuvenation measures adopted by Liu Shaoqi and Deng Xiaoping with support from Zhou Enlai and Chen Yun. In Mao's views, their practices were steering China away from the revolution and would eventually fall into the 'Soviet Revisionism' as seen under Khrushchev (Lieberthal, 1995; Saich, 2004). In these years, Mao continuously deployed his forces to prepare for the launch of the Cultural Revolution.

Chen Yun was criticized by Mao Zedong on his de-collective proposal in 1962. He was not purged but subsequently left the centre of power until the end of the Cultural Revolution. His ideas about the economic value of tourism were naturally discarded. Under these political circumstances, Premier Zhou Enlai not only became very cautious, but also tried his best to keep up with

Mao's thinking. At a national conference held in 1963, Zhou required all front-line officials of tourism to be competent in the areas of ideological orthodoxy, foreign languages and professionalism with priority given to ideological orthodoxy specifically in relation to 'Marxism', 'Leninism' and 'the Thoughts of Mao Zedong'. Zhou required the front-line staff to play five roles as 'propagandist', 'investigator', 'services provider', 'security officer' and 'interpreter'. They were required to design propaganda material about China's socialist development and ethics for different types of tourists on the basis of policy guidelines (Han Kehua, 1994; CNTA, 1995b). The idea of tourism as an economic force completely disappeared. In 1965, 'politics-in-command' was reiterated and highlighted by the CPC and the State Council as the sole philosophy for tourism politics. Thus, the goals and institutions of tourism politics were firmly consolidated. This structure of tourism politics remained in place until the end of 1978.

Throughout this stage, the OCTS also expanded rapidly and established a nation-wide network. For example, the OCTS had over forty branches in Guangdong Province as a major gateway and destination for the Hong Kong, Macau and overseas Chinese. Likewise, the OCTS operated guest houses (called 'Overseas Chinese Tower') and automobiles (Han Kehua, 1994). During the delivery of travel services the OCTS consistently provided 'socialist education' to the tourists in order to nurture the compatriotic union.

Stagnation (1966–71)

The Cultural Revolution was the most turbulent period in the history of the PRC. It was an ultra-radicalization of 'politics' that expanded from the inner CPC to the whole of society. It was accompanied by widespread political struggle and rebellion manifested in violence which in turn created difficulties for the functioning of the party-state apparatuses. The disorder culminated between 1966 and 1969, and then declined following the death of Lin Biao in September 1971. Chinese foreign affairs, including Chinese and foreign missions, were not immune from the disturbance. In 1967, the Red Guard broke into the British Legation in Beijing and assaulted the staff; British officials in Shanghai were also attacked in a separate incident in the same year. A radical leader Kang Sheng preached that 'the world has entered the era of the "Thoughts of Mao Zedong"' (Han Nianlong, 1988). In response to his call, some Chinese diplomats circulated promotional material about the Cultural Revolution, causing unrest abroad. Tourism and tourist activities were denounced as 'giving our splendid mountains and rivers for the enjoyment of the bourgeoisie', 'selling feudal, capitalist and revisionist products' and 'serving the bourgeoisie' (Han Kehua, 1994). A number of heritage sites and relics were destroyed; and many historical and natural attractions were closed. Incoming tourists were not allowed to stay in guest houses or to take part in sightseeing and recreation; but were required to participate in Chinese political life, including elements such as 'frugal living', 'military training' and 'political struggle assemblies'. Many local offices of the CITS were either disrupted or forced to stop operation. The resulting insecurity meant that many tourists cancelled their trips. CITS ceased to receive tourists from Western nations and only accepted group visitors from friendship associations in socialist and third world nations; costs were not taken into consideration in the provision of services to such visitors. As a result international tourist arrivals dropped massively to 4,551 in 1966, 866 in 1967 and 303 in 1968 (Han Kehua, 1994; CNTA, 1995b). The reception of tourists had effectively become a special kind of 'political hospitality'. In 1969 Mao Zedong made a point of emphasizing the need to 'not impose ourselves on others' (Han Kehua, 1994: p.213). The OCTS was also compelled to stop operation in 1969.

Restoration (1971–8)

Lin Biao, as Mao's designated successor, was the main radical leader in the Cultural Revolution followed by the 'Gang of Four'.[18] However, Mao was cautious about Lin after the state president Liu Shaoqi and the general secretary of the CPC Deng Xiaoping were purged and exiled in 1969. Lin lost Mao's trust in 1970 when he attempted to take the state president position. After this the split between them became overt. Between August and September 1971, Mao used his inspection visits in Southern China to severely criticize Lin, who escaped from China with his wife and son on 13 September 1971; subsequently, on the same day, they were all killed in an air accident in the Republic of Mongolia – the '9.13 Incident'. The downfall of Lin's clique marked the decline of political extremism and the failure of the Cultural Revolution, though Mao and his supporters tried to safeguard what they called the 'revolutionary fruit' in the following years. Actually China started to resume its activities in foreign affairs at the end of 1970, preparing for negotiations with the United States and improving relations with Western Europe. In early 1970, Mao Zedong advised China 'to pin our hopes on the people' (Han Kehua, 1994: p.35) in activating civil diplomacy. As one of its components, tourism politics started to function again under the guiding hand of Zhou Enlai. The plan for tourist arrivals prepared by the BTTC, received instruction from Mao in 1971 that 'numbers can be more' and 'different kinds of persons can come' (Han Kehua, 1994: pp.35 and 214), including 'rightists' from the Western Bloc. At the same time the constraints on tourist diplomacy were relaxed. The CITS took the initiative to resume contact with travel agencies in Albania, Romania and Yugoslavia. Mao and Zhou certainly recognized the importance of developing mutual understanding in nurturing the relationships with the Western world. In order to avoid the negative effects of radical politics on tourism, Zhou Enlai further interpreted Mao's instruction 'not imposing ourselves on others' as 'propagandizing ourselves and understanding others' (CNTA, 1995b: p.14). Zhou also put a lot of effort into making preparations including, for example, the instruction to BTTC to research the reopening of China to America and the West.

The year 1971 was the turning point in China's diplomacy in terms of her return to UN membership and Sino-US negotiations. As far as tourist diplomacy was concerned the high point was Zhou Enlai's meetings with tourist groups (Han Kehua, 1994). In all, as part of an effort to demonstrate goodwill, he met over ten out of the eighty groups visiting China. The first batch of self-financed tourists from the United States included two American scientists who had come to China in advance of the visit by American Secretary of State, Henry Kissinger. After President Nixon's official visit, self-sponsored travel to China developed further. In the meantime, more and more Western political figures visited China, including parliamentary members from the UK, Ministers from Sweden, members of the Royal Families of the Netherlands and Spain. The British Prime Minister Edward Heath normalized his country's relations with China. In his 1974 visit, he met and established a friendship with Deng Xiaoping during Deng's second rise to power. Later, Heath played an important role in the Sino-British negotiations regarding the handover of Hong Kong. China's tourist diplomacy at this stage helped allay some of the worries of the Western world. This then paved the way for the effective implementation of China's Open-door Policy after 1978 and its associated tourism development.

Tourist arrivals were quickly restored and climbed to over 50,000 in 1976, with Japan and America as the two major markets. At the same time, over thirty branches of CITS also reopened (Han Kehua, 1994: pp.37 and 216). In 1972 the State Council had also restored the OCTS and its local branches. In 1974, reflecting the view that the term 'overseas Chinese' no longer suited those Chinese who had become foreign nationals, the OCTS was renamed China Travel Services (CTS). The increase in tourists also demanded an expansion of accommodation capacity. A total of nine hotels were opened in the major tourist cities although in the after-effects of the Cultural Revolution it was notable that costs and economic rationale were totally ignored in this development. Tourism simply operated at a loss, which had led to Zhou Enlai's instruction in 1973 that 'tourism should earn surpluses', an instruction that, for the time being, was largely ignored (Han Kehua, 1994; CNTA, 1995b, 1999b).

The Cultural Revolution ended in 1976, along with Mao's death and the fall of the 'Gang of Four'. The years between 1976 and 1978 were transitional. During this period, in 1977, Deng Xiaoping rose to power for the third time. He allied himself with other veteran leaders, like Chen Yun and Ye Jianying, to defeat political radicalism and prepare for the launch of his reform programme. In these two years, the revolutionary model and 'politics-in-command' softened and tourists were allowed to visit China's natural attractions and cultural relics. The plenum held by the CPC Central Committee in late 1978 formally marked the end of Mao's revolutionary and utopian socialism and started Deng's pragmatic and evolutionary socialism, centering on economic modernization. China's tourism after 1978 entered a new era.

Conclusion

In summary, tourism in Mao's China was, above all, a part of foreign affairs and served as a political and diplomatic tool of 'civil diplomacy' and 'external relations and friendship'. It was certainly not considered as an industry or as an economic activity. There was no tourism policy as such, in the sense that there was no series of decisions specifically for the development of tourism. This had to await Deng's era.

Although Mao's tourism was significantly different from what followed in the reform era there are nevertheless some important links to Deng Xiaoping's tourism. This point has generally been overlooked in earlier studies which have tended to see the two eras as almost totally isolated from each other. One example of the links can be seen in the ways in which Chen Yun's suggestions in 1957 provide a precursor to Deng's economic initiative on tourism after 1978. But perhaps more interesting is the way in which the earlier manifestation of tourism, treated as an activity completely separate from the planned economy of China, provided an activity for Deng to use as an experimental field for the introduction of foreign investment and expertise. Also of course, the tourist facilities established in Mao's era formed the initial capacity for tourism development in Deng's era. When China moved away from Mao's model in 1978, her tourism also stepped on an unprecedented path towards rapid development.

6   The national policy-makers

> Policies (in China) are shaped by the bargaining arena within which they are deliberated.
> Where you stand is where you sit.
>
> (Shirk, 1993: pp.92 and 99)

As discussed in the analytical framework, policy-makers represent a key explanatory factor in public policy-making; they stand at the core as policy is formulated and implemented. In advance of the more detailed account of the development of tourism policy in China after 1978, covered in Chapters 7 and 8, the purpose of this chapter is to identify the key players and institutional processes involved in national policy-making for China's tourism. It examines, from the policy-makers' perspective, the ways in which tourism policy-making has proceeded. Using the concepts of 'policy-oriented learning' (or 'policy learning') with 'coordination', as explained in Chapter 3, it considers how the policy-makers have developed and implemented policy during a period of change in ideologies, organizational values and interests. In doing so it reveals how the fragmented nature of tourism and the fragmented power structure have meant that policy-making has been conducted by a variety of policy-makers, with a diversity of values and interests. It also shows how policy-oriented learning has allowed the policy-makers to succeed in a number of key areas, often with support from the national leaders. These themes are also developed further in Chapters 7 and 8.

Overview

As discussed in earlier chapters, since 1949 China has operated on the basis that the ruling Communist Party of China (CPC) governs the nation. The Central Government, the State Council, is constitutionally accountable to the National People's Congress (NPC) (China's Parliament), but in fact it is politically responsible to the Politburo of the CPC (Lieberthal, 2004; Saich, 2004). The State Council consists of both cabinet rank and non-cabinet rank agencies, with grades ranging from 'supra-ministry', 'ministry', 'sub- or vice-ministry' to 'bureau' grades. One particular feature is that although cabinet-rank and non-cabinet-rank agencies can be at the same 'ministry' grade, only cabinet agencies are present at the plenary meetings of the State Council (i.e. cabinet sessions) and have voting rights. Different grades have different degrees of decision-making, bargaining and administrative power in policy formulation and implementation. China's national policy-makers operate within this political structure with policy-making shaped by both official and unofficial actors. More than twenty years ago Lampton (1987a, 1987b), Lieberthal and Oksenberg (1988) and Lieberthal and Lampton (1992) referred to Chinese policy-making as fragmented, with authority in shaping decisions being vested in so many different central agencies all engaged in bargaining and consensus building. This remains a feature and it is further exacerbated by tourism's multi-faceted nature. Different government agencies deal with different aspects. A key informant suggested: 'We [China National Tourism Administration – the NTA] have working relationships with over thirty government agencies in the State Council, different opinions usually occur and the degree of difficulty in coordination is very high.' As a recent example, in December 2009, a State Council directive to upgrade tourism to 'a strategic pillar industry in the national economy' needed the joint efforts of thirty-nine central agencies (State Council, 2009b).

There are two kinds of policy players among the community, the core and the functional. Core players are concerned strategically with tourism. Functional players are involved because tourism has an influence on, or is influenced by them. The CNTA is an obvious example of the former, while resources management agencies like the State Administration of Cultural Heritage are among the latter.

Core policy-makers

In summary the core policy-makers include:

- The China National Tourism Administration (CNTA) – the specialized agency for tourism;
- The National Development and Reform Commission (NDRC) – a supra-ministerial agency (or comprehensive or macro-management agency) responsible for national planning and macro management of the economy;[1]
- The Ministry of Foreign Affairs (MoFA) – responsible for visas and the development of outbound destinations;
- The Central Publicity Department of the CPC – responsible for ideological monitoring;
- The Ministry of Finance (MoF) – a supra-ministerial agency responsible for budget and finance;
- Deputies of the National People's Congress and Members of the Chinese People's Political Consultative Conference (CPPCC);

- The State General Administration for Quality Supervision, Inspection and Quarantine (SGAQSIQ) – responsible for the quality of products and services;
- Regional Development and Local Government agencies;
- The Chinese Academy of Social Sciences (CASS), the Development Research Centre of the State Council and the Research Office of the State Council – all policy think tanks.

However, it is really China's political leaders who have led the development since 1978. Only they have had sufficient power to launch major initiatives, often in response to proposals or requests from the subordinate agencies. A key informant acknowledged: 'In China, the instructions, speeches and talks from the national leaders are considerably powerful and effective.'

Among the leaders, the vice-premier or state councillor whose supervision portfolio covers tourism has immediate oversight. As a specialized agency, CNTA is responsible for overall policy and development. Of the supra-ministerial agencies NDRC exercises macro management of the national economy and integrates tourism development with other sectors. CNTA and NDRC, particularly the former, are the main sources of proposals. The MoF provides financial support. The SGAQSIQ has responsibility for establishing quality standards; it collaborates with CNTA in setting up quality assurance measures. The think tanks provide consultancy advice to government and suggest policy proposals.

Almost inevitably, given the wide range of responsibilities covered by these different bodies and the wide scope of tourism, disagreements occur between them. Where this happens, and CNTA as the primary agency is unable to resolve or coordinate them, it turns to the General Office of State Council for assistance, which in turn may seek the views of the vice-premier or state councillor with immediate responsibility. Other vice-premiers or state councillors may also be involved as appropriate. Consensus building is provided by the National Tourism Works Conference, which is held annually and acts as a nation-wide forum. It is in this institutional landscape that China's national policy-making for tourism takes place.

Ultimately it is a continuous process of policy learning and coordination. On the one hand, it can be seen as a cognitive process of policy learning. On the other hand, the state ideologies, values and interests that have formed the distinct organizational goals and responsibilities of each agency, provide an interpretation framework to understand the environmental circumstances. Coordination in the form of bargaining and negotiation occur ubiquitously. Except for marketing strategies and quality standards at the industry level (national-level quality issues are agreed jointly with the SQAQSIQ), almost all initiatives from CNTA have a bearing on other central agencies and need to be coordinated with them. In this way, China's national policy-making proceeds through this combined process of policy-oriented learning and coordination.

Leaders

Since the Economic Reform in 1978, all national leaders have supported the development of tourism and recognized its role in the state. With this support tourism has evolved from an economic to a more multifunctional activity. Perhaps the leaders' most important influences have been to plant tourism into the mindsets of the bureaucrats and to prompt tourism initiatives. They have also determined tourism's position in the state structure, established the organizational arrangements and responsibilities and encouraged popular support.

Initial recognition after 1978 began with leaders Deng Xiaoping and Chen Yun. With the shift in ideology from 'political struggle' to 'economic modernization', the shortage of foreign exchange led them to consider international tourism as a foreign exchange earner. Between late 1978 and early 1979, Deng delivered six consecutive speeches on tourism as an economic activity, with support from other senior leaders. As a result, officials, who since 1949 had seen it purely in political and diplomatic terms, began to accept its commercial development. Subsequently revenue generation became a goal of the Bureau of Travel and Tourism of China (the forerunner to the CNTA). Deng also saw tourism as playing an experimental role to bring in foreign investment and expertise. For example, at Deng's insistence, the first project with foreign investment was the development of the 'Jianguo Hotel' in Beijing. The degree of political controversy and hence coordination involved in this is shown by the fact that its approval required the consent of all twelve vice-premiers plus some vice-chairs of the NPC's Standing Committee. Since then foreign capital has played a key role in China's economic transformation.

Tourism development before the late 1980s took place in the context of a national imperative plan in which only the CNTA and its subordinate enterprises could run tourism businesses. This was changed in the mid-1980s when the General Secretary of the Communist Party of China agreed to the decentralization of investment and operations to other central government departments, local government and the emerging private sector. More recently the new generation of Chinese leadership has elevated tourism's status. In the late 1990s, in recognition of its strong growth and size, tourism was given a boost by the State Council identifying it as a new economic growth pole. This was reflected in comments by Premier Zhu Rongji who in 1998, during a visit to Xinjiang in less developed western China, urged local government to take full advantage of its resources and speed up its development. As a result the MoF granted Xinjiang RMB¥50 million and the General Administration of Customs permitted the import of 300 tour buses on a tariff-free basis. Zhu emphasized the importance of tourism more than ten times in his inspection visits. A key informant commented: 'Premier Zhu even designed a tourist route for Xinjiang, called the *Zhu Rongji Tourist Route*'.

China is currently facing a number of issues, from the decline in the relative size of the state sector, to a greater diversification of society, tensions among different interest groups and social unrest as well as terrorism and perceived threats from abroad. Against this background, tourism is seen by the leaders as having multifunctional roles in economic, political–ideological, socio-cultural and diplomatic spheres. Politically and ideologically, it is seen to support nationalism, patriotism, and socialist values and to strengthen the union of the country. In foreign relations, it is involved in strengthening the country's national image and promoting its achievements through both inbound and outbound travel; outbound tourism is further used as a diplomatic resource in winning international support. Socially and culturally tourism can enhance quality of life and social harmony. But perhaps most importantly it is its economic role that supports these other functions. The National Tourism Works Conference 2004 summarized this as follows:

> We should emphasize the function of tourism as an economic industry; we also should emphasize more the comprehensive functions of tourism in providing employment, promoting Chinese culture and building a socialist spiritual civilization.
>
> (CNTA, 2004b: p.7)

In bringing together both the political and economic attributes of tourism, this draws on legacies of both Mao and Deng. In some ways this continues in the current leadership. As from 2002, reflecting its economic role, tourism has been assigned to a vice-premier with economic responsibilities but since vice-premiers are also usually appointed as a Politburo member of the CPC, this also allows it to link to China's political, ideological, socio-cultural and diplomatic goals.

China National Tourism Administration

The CNTA is the central government agency directly responsible to the State Council for policy-making, development and administration. However, in common with National Tourism Administrations (NTAs) elsewhere, and for similar reasons, its powers are limited. Notably policy-making authority for tourism is widely distributed with, for example, resources and attractions being under the jurisdiction of a number of different agencies: the Ministry of Housing and Urban–Rural Development, the Ministry of Culture, the Ministry of Agriculture, the State Forestry Administration, the State Administration for Religious Affairs, the State Administration of Cultural Heritage, to name just a few. Also like other NTAs the CNTA has a relatively low administrative status. Tourism is a latecomer to policy-making. Though directly under the State Council, CNTA is not a cabinet-rank agency being graded at the 'sub- or vice-ministry' rank. In this position it cannot directly raise issues at cabinet meetings and nor can it launch major initiatives. In reality, political–ideological, socio-cultural and diplomatic dimensions of tourism are dealt with at higher political levels. For example, state ideology is the responsibility of a Standing Committee Member of the Politburo and it was in this context, in 2004, that the instruction was given for tourism to be a means to promote socialist and communist values. CNTA's policy-making authority is effectively limited to marketing and setting non-mandatory quality standards. Beyond these it cannot independently decide on initiatives. Instead it coordinates with related agencies, including, as will be seen later, the NDRC. In this position, through a process of policy learning and coordination with other agencies, CNTA has achieved a certain degree of success in introducing initiatives. These typically stem from the identification of solutions by learning from international norms and practices. One interviewee suggested:

> Our [CNTA] primary task is to study the circumstances in our industry. Our policy initiatives (or proposals) basically arise from two origins. First, we need to learn the realities; we need to understand the real needs of our industry. Second, we will make reference to international practices.

Inside the CNTA, the policy-oriented learning typically begins with the Policy and Legal Affairs, and the Quality Standardization and Administration Departments whose officials work with the regions and industry to identify issues demanding a policy response. They then draw upon international practice in forming an initiative. A good example of this, as explained in more detail in Chapters 7 and 8, relates to the problem of unsatisfactory levels of service quality in luxury hotels, which was identified in the mid-1980s. CNTA used international experience, with professional support from the United Nations World Tourism Organization (UNWTO) to develop the 'Regulation on Star-Standards and Star-Rating of Tourist Hotels of the PRC'.

Since 2000 the policy learning of CNTA has seen growing participation by the academic community and professional policy research. Annually it launches a list of research areas and invites submissions. The approved projects fall into two categories: fundable and non-fundable but supported. Each fundable project attracts a total of RMB¥30,000 with a study period of one year. In 2009, the CNTA approved thirty-five out of 981 submissions (CNTA, 2009b). More importantly, in 2008, in order to enhance research capabilities, it established the first government research institution for tourism – the China Tourism Academy. Previously, policy research had been undertaken by CNTA officials or in collaboration with the CASS and the Development Research Centre of the State Council. It now has a team of full-time professional researchers, most with doctoral qualifications.

Once a proposal has been drafted it needs the approval of CNTA senior management before being processed for comment and coordination with other agencies. The process of coordination depends on the complexity of the issues, the number of agencies involved, as well as their attitudes and respective bargaining power. Clearly where there is complete agreement from all the agencies implementation can begin without delay. This was the case with the construction of twelve state-level resorts in the mid-1990s, It not only obtained the overall consensus from over ten central agencies but also had support from two vice-premiers. Where there is not complete agreement it may be able to negotiate an acceptable decision with the other agencies. For example, it took the CNTA almost four years with the State Planning Commission to gain permission for hotels to charge fees on local telephone calls. Regional support is often significant in achieving a mutually agreed arrangement with other central agencies. For example, CNTA's acquisition of the principal policy and administrative responsibility for outbound travel in the late 1990s resulted from the successful negotiation with the Ministry of Public Security supported by local party chiefs. In some cases intervention from the leadership (e.g. State Council) is required. For example, the MoF was opposed to the 'Regulation on Quality Service Guarantee Funds of Travel Agencies' because of the perceived excessive fees involved. Eventually this needed the support from two vice-premiers for its implementation. Finally, some situations result in no agreement or have a long lead time. This was the case with the proposed Tourism Law which the CNTA began drafting in the 1980s. After about twenty versions and many rounds of discussions with the Legislative Affairs Office of the State Council and the Financial and Economic Affairs Committee of the NPC, the bill only got into the legislative calendar at the end of 2009. The reasons for the delay were primarily that a higher priority was given to legislation relating to the establishment and consolidation of the market economy and the Tourism Law was not seen as a part of this. But also the multi-faceted nature of tourism and its early stage of development played a part in the delay. Although it regularly had the support of some NPC and CPPCC members (twenty CPPCC members in 2008 and thirty NPC members in 2009), tourism was not able to establish a sufficiently large or powerful lobby. It was only after the State Council's new strategic initiative and with the direct intervention from the Chairman of the NPC's Standing Committee (i.e. China's top legislator), and the Financial and Economic Affairs Committee of the NPC that the formal legislation process began in December 2009 (CNTA, 2008f, 2010c).

The effectiveness of central decisions rests with local implementation. In this connection the National Tourism Works Conference plays an important role. This annual conference normally takes place in January after the Central Economic Works Conference of the CPC Politburo and State Council in November or December. This timing allows for the incorporation of the latest central economic decisions. The tourism conference is usually convened by the CNTA, but sometimes, when necessary, by the State Council. The participants normally include the vice-premier in charge, all senior officials of CNTA, heads of local bureaus, consultants from the government think tanks, and representatives of state enterprises, government media and academics. Provincial party secretaries and governors of key tourist regions are also invited. It normally lasts for one or two days and has the role of briefing, consensus building and taking forward decisions already agreed by the vice-premier.

The move to a market economy has brought challenges to the CNTA but it has also provided it with important opportunities to break through some of the bureaucratic barriers. In many ways examples of work by the CNTA provide new models of policy-making and administration in China. For example, in the context of the shift away from government being directly involved in investment in attractions, to providing guidance to market forces, CNTA has managed to have significant influence on the flow of investment by working with the NDRC in preparing directories of government recommended projects. Similarly, following its success with hotel standards the CNTA pursued this further, recognizing it as an effective instrument to influence supply without involving compulsion. This was seen to fit well with macro management in a market economy and avoid significant controversy with the bureaucracy as well as being a common concern of the market including both industry and tourists. In this case the formulation of standards is not purely an administrative process but rather has prompted substantial involvement by the industry as well as academics. This can be seen in the membership of the 'Tourism Standardization Committee of China', established under the standardization law, which operates under CNTA leadership. Membership by government officials is, in fact, limited to one-eighth, with the remainder coming from industry and academia. The Committee mainly formulates standards according to the requirements of the SGAQSIQ (i.e. central quality agency) together with the CNTA (CNTA, 1998b). As a result, quality standards have become central to CNTA's work with some twenty-one quality specifications implemented (CNTA, 2010b).

This combination of policy learning in relation to quality standards, including making reference to the quality mechanisms in other countries, with coordination where necessary, together with an awareness of how to progress initiatives, has permitted the CNTA to develop into an effective agency even in the absence of real political power and administrative authority. Through the various administrative and regulatory measures made during the past three decades, the CNTA has effectively built up its professionalism in the eyes of industry. As a result some attractions seek the views and advice of the CNTA, even though they are not under its administration.

National Development and Reform Commission

The NDRC is a supra-ministerial cabinet agency in charge of the macro management of economic and social development. It works closely with the MoF and the People's Bank of China, both of which provide fiscal and monetary support. The forerunner of the NDRC, the State Planning Commission (SPC), established in 1952, had responsibility for managing China's command economy. This not only gave the SPC the most influential position in determining China's economic and social affairs, but also drove its thinking about policy formulation and resource allocation. The SPC was renamed the State Development Planning Commission in 1998 and became the NDRC in 2003, reflecting the fact that the central master plan was giving way to market forces. Under China's state-centric market economy, the Commission is mainly responsible for macro control of the national economy and major economic and social policies.

In contrast with the CNTA, which takes an insider's perspective, the NDRC has a more generalist approach. In fact, neither agency puts forward initiatives independently, but rather coordinates with each other, together with the MoF when fiscal support is required. The generalist and specialist angles usually complement each other with the former taking precedence. The NDRC occupies five areas of policy-making. First, it has the role of trying to achieve balance between inputs, for example, between planned tourist arrivals and the carrying capacity of civil aviation. It uses the national planning process as the main instrument for this, being the agency responsible for preparing and coordinating the implementation of China's 'Five-Year State Plan for the National Economy and Social Development'. For the work of CNTA to be integrated into the plan, it is essential for the NDRC to be involved from the outset and for it to provide agreement and support (CNTA, 2001b). Second, it links tourism with state development strategies, such as determining its position in the national economy. Third, it has responsibility for planning major domestic and foreign investment projects and scrutinizing the composition of total investment. Fourth, the NDRC, as the state's main pricing authority, either fixes the prices (or ranges) directly or provides oversight of pricing for a range of commodities and services; popular tourist attractions fall into this category. The NDRC requires the prices of these attractions to take public affordability and welfare into consideration as well as economic return. To this end, the NDRC, CNTA, MoF and other relevant central agencies are responsible for enforcing local compliance (CNTA, 2008e). Finally, the arrangement of national statutory holidays is under its policy purview. Considering the wide economic, social and cultural impacts of holidays, any revisions are usually made through a process of public consultation. For example, prior to the acceptance of the three traditional festivals, *Qingming* (ancestor worship), *Duanwu* (dragon boat racing) and *Chongyang* (ancestor worship and ascent) as the statutory holidays in 2008, the NDRC undertook extensive consultation with academia, industry and the public. Within the NDRC, the Social Development Department is the main working body for tourism. This will be examined in detail in Chapter 8.

As a supra-ministerial agency, the NDRC considers economic and social issues from a strategic perspective. Generally, since 1978 it has been supportive of tourism development. The degree of support, however, has varied with changes in ideological orthodoxies, organizational values, socio-economic conditions and performance. A relevant case is tourism's positioning in the national economy. Although recognized as an economic activity in 1986, tourism failed to obtain real status in the economy until 1998. Over this decade, both the NDRC and CNTA were actively studying and coordinating its economic role. As already explained in Chapters 4 and 5, in the planned-economy era, market-driven industry was generally considered insignificant and even frivolous. Economic growth was viewed as mainly a supply-side matter with state investment directly in industry and agriculture. Domestic tourism, with strong market growth, was not recognized as an effective vehicle, whereas the weak contribution of tourism to GDP certainly failed to convince the SPC and MoF of its economic significance. This was reversed in the market-economy era when the government began to attach importance to the demand side. The stimulation of consumption demand became regarded as a key source of economic growth. Issues facing China started to include insufficient aggregate demand, high unemployment and imbalanced regional development. Tourism development demonstrated its potential in generating income, creating employment and promoting regional development. As such, a series of policy studies and discussions took place among the State Planning Commission (NDRC), MoF, CNTA and other relevant agencies with the result that the view of tourism was revised and it became a significant industry. It was subsequently positioned by the State Council in 1998 as a 'new growth pole in the national economy' (CNTA, 1999c), and in 2008 was further upgraded to 'a key industry in the national economy' (CNTA, 2008b) and in the global downturn to 'one of five consumption hotspots' in 2009 (Xinhua, 2008e). These advances in recognition have led to substantial measures such as the inclusion, since 2000, on the recommendation of the NDRC, of investment funded from state bonds issued by the MoF. The NDRC also now takes the initiative in discussions with senior management of the CNTA. In 2006, during a study visit to the CNTA, the vice-minister expressed the NDRC's view of the comprehensive role of tourism as follows:

> During the current 11th Five-Year Plan, we need to exert great effort for the development of tourism. Tourism development can offer an industrial function, as well as a wide range of social effects. Tourism has also played significant roles in shifting the approaches to economic growth, promoting employment, expanding domestic demand, accelerating the construction of infrastructure, boosting the development of a new socialist countryside, as well as enhancing external relations.
>
> (NDRC, 2006a)

Ministry of Finance

Like the NDRC, this is also a cabinet-rank agency exercising a macro-management role through fiscal and public finance policy. In terms of overall fiscal policy, the main development has been a shift from expansion between 1998 and 2004 to more restraint from 2005. Under the economic crisis from 2008, it has reverted to 'active' direction supported by an 'adequately loose' monetary policy. With its overview of China's socio-economic circumstances, the MoF has been supportive of the enhancement of tourism in the national economy. It has direct responsibility for approving the CNTA budget and the inspection fees imposed on the industry. The CNTA derives its funds from two sources: state appropriation covering administrative expenses, and a portion of airport tax for marketing and development projects. For the former, based on information available, it is estimated that CNTA's expenditure has increased from RMB¥60 million in 1992 to ¥100–200 million. For the latter, a 'Tourism Development Foundation' was established in 2001 mainly to finance CNTA's promotional activities. The CNTA now administers the Foundation, with the MoF maintaining an inspection role in line with its ministerial obligations. The MoF also has responsibility for ensuring the reasonableness of fees levied by the CNTA on industry, such as quality guarantee charges for travel agencies and administrative fees for its services (e.g. charges on the tour guide examinations and certificates).

Central Publicity Department of the CPC

Unlike the agencies of the State Council, which are mainly concerned with administration of state affairs, the central party apparatuses of the CPC are more concerned with governance aspects, such as ideological direction. In this the Central Publicity Department (CPD) is responsible for ideological and propaganda matters. The Department has the authority to monitor relevant aspects of government agencies. The head of the CPD is normally a Politburo member of the CPC, who reports directly to the Standing Committee member of the Politburo in charge of state ideology. With the growing size and impact of tourism, the Department has increasingly overseen its ideological and cultural aspects in two ways. First, it has responsibility for policy relating to the promotion of socialist and patriotic values through domestic tourism; the NDRC and CNTA provide the infrastructure and professional support with funds arranged by the MoF. Second, the Department is concerned to ensure that tourist products, especially their non-physical aspects, such as those involved in religious tourism, are ideologically supportive of, or at least not detrimental to, China's socialist civilization. Senior officials from the Department carry out inspection visits to the regions. For example, two deputy directors paid visits to Sichuan and Hunan provinces in 2007 and 2008 to study cultural and heritage tourism. Although religion is an important part of Chinese life, religious activities take place within a context that is officially atheist so the authorities need to be convinced that religion will not lead people to what is officially called 'blind worship'. For example, some attractions have used 'ghosts' and the 'underworld' as selling points. In this connection, in 2000, the Department, together with the CNTA, the State Administration for Religious Affairs and the Ministry of Construction, issued the 'Notice to Firmly Prohibit Feudal Activities and Blind Worship in Tourist Attractions'. This notice was reiterated in 2010 (Central Publicity Department *et al.*, 2000).

Ministry of Foreign Affairs

Ranking first in the Chinese cabinet, the MoFA's responsibilities for diplomatic relations and foreign policy take it into two areas of tourism. It has responsibility for issuing visas to foreign visitors, including direct visas for those taking group tours organized by travel agencies on the approved CNTA list. It also has responsibility for negotiations with CNTA on opening the outbound market. Travel abroad by Chinese citizens for leisure purposes is still restricted to group tours organized by China's travel agencies to tourist destinations with what is officially called 'Approved Destination Status' (ADS). The initiative for ADS largely came from the leaders, with one informant suggesting that: 'leader(s) usually instruct the MoFA and the CNTA to study a particular country before it can become an ADS'. The consideration by MoFA takes into account China's national interest and foreign policy, with support for the 'One-China' stance and the recognition of China's full market-economy status being important elements in gaining approval. The negotiation is very much seen as an extension of China's foreign affairs. The CNTA has a complementary role in carrying out a destination feasibility study (CNTA, 1996b) for Chinese tourists. The ADS initiative is considered in more detail in Chapter 8.

The NPC deputies and CPPCC members

NPC deputies and CPPCC members play two roles in policy-making for tourism. First, both are top institutional forums for initiatives, brainstorming and discussion. As the highest organ of state power, the NPC has constitutional obligations. The deputies launch their initiatives in the form of bills (either motions or draft laws) and speeches. The former usually require the collective agreement of at least thirty deputies or a whole delegation (i.e. a region). Since the 1990s tourism has come in for considerable attention, with NPC bills covering a wide range of issues, such as visitor attraction management and service quality. For example, NPC deputies have regularly submitted motions urging the acceptance of the Tourism Law, referred to earlier (p.142); some 200 did so in 2002. Deputies also frequently deliver speeches about tourism in formal sessions. Recently in 2009 and 2010 these speeches were made from Hubei, Tibet, Sichuan, Shaanxi and Anhui provinces. This has helped to raise the profile of tourism and encourage thinking about development and policy. The second role of the NPC lies in its constitutional duties for monitoring the administration. This has become far more obvious since the 1990s. In the words of a key informant: 'Our NPC deputies nowadays differ from the past. Previously our media reported that our deputies "studied hard" the reports submitted by the government; but now the words have changed to "reviewing", "commenting" and "examining" government reports and documents.'

During the sessions of the NPC, ministers and senior officials need to be available in Beijing to respond to enquiries, critiques and suggestions. For example in the NPC session 2008, the Director-General of the CNTA joined the delegation meetings relating to the Taiwan and Xinjiang regions. The CNTA was not only there to answer questions but also to solicit support.

State General Administration of Quality Supervision, Inspection and Quarantine

This ministerial but non-cabinet agency is responsible for establishing quality standard frameworks for both products and services. With a background of concern about standards, the quality framework has become an essential constituent of China's market institutions. The agency has given its support to the CNTA, sometimes against other agencies, in its attempts to develop a quality assurance mechanism for tourism. For example, when the Ministry of Internal Trade, now merged into the Ministry of Commerce, issued its own set of grading criteria for guest houses (for domestic travellers) that also extended to hotels, the support from SGAQSIQ helped the CNTA's star rating system to prevail for hotels. In 1993, the agency incorporated tourism into the Master Catalogue of Standardization, with the CNTA as the sole authority for making quality specifications. CNTA subsequently designed the Catalogue for Tourism with six broad categories: tour operation, accommodation, catering, travel, shopping and amusement. Tourism is now formally recognized as a sector of China's quality standards framework.

Local government

Local government at province-equivalent level is directly accountable to central government in China although some politically important regions, such as Beijing, Tianjin, Shanghai, Chonqqing and Guangdong, also enjoy superior status, as their party chiefs are concurrently appointed as a Politburo member of the CPC. Generally, local government is responsible for tourism development in their areas with local bureaus as their main agent. The local tourism bureaus report to local government not the CNTA. A process of decentralization has provided increasing local autonomy for economic and social development, especially in strategically or economically important regions.

In fact local government has a degree of flexibility and is encouraged to formulate its own strategies. In the absence of a nation-wide Tourism Law, many localities, such as Sichuan, Liaoning, Fujian, Shandong and Yunnan, have enacted their own ordinances for tourism. A recent example is that when the central government reduced the number of the 'Golden Weeks' from three to two in 2008, the Guangdong Provincial Government attempted to maintain the status quo, although in the end this failed. The development of domestic tourism owes a lot to local government. Originally, from the 1980s, central government favoured international over domestic arrivals. This reflected tourism's foreign exchange earning potential as well as capacity constraints. The growing impact of tourism on regional economies led local government to seek a policy shift during the late 1980s and, in 1993, jointly with support of the CNTA, a decision was made to develop domestic tourism. Since 1995, tourism (especially domestic) has been acknowledged as a 'pillar industry' in 80 per cent of the provinces, including Beijing, Shanghai, Jiangsu, Yunnan, Guizhou, Shaanxi. As the main stakeholders representing local interests, local government is an active player in tourism policy-making. During the formulation of national tourism plans, the CNTA usually holds meetings with relevant provinces. Once policy proposals are drafted they are submitted to local government for views before finalization and submission (CNTA, 2001b).

Government think tanks

Among the official research organizations, the *Chinese Academy of Social Sciences* (CASS) has for a long time been a leader in policy studies for tourism. Formally established in 1978 and usually headed by a prominent figure,[2] the Academy is a government research institution with ministry rank directly under the State Council. It is the country's top academic and research institution in the social sciences and philosophy, and a premier think tank for central government. It plays an influential role in the State Council with its research findings underpinning central decisions. CASS pioneered tourism studies in China in the 1980s. Co-organized with the Development Research Centre of the State Council, China's first strategic study of tourism in 1987 concluded that it was a 'sunrise' and market-oriented industry and notably emphasized the potential importance of domestic tourism. This was particularly significant during the early stages and among other things motivated the CNTA and local bureaus to take a market-oriented approach. This same study also put forward a vision that the pace of tourism development should be ahead of overall economic growth. This was reiterated in 2008 by the vice-premier in charge. In 1999, the Academy established a research centre to provide tourism research and consultancy advice to central and local government. The Development Research Centre has also maintained an involvement in tourism studies and associated policy consultations. The Research Office of the State Council mainly serves government leaders through integrative policy research and the preparation of policy documents and speeches. Recently it has been directly involved in studies for the State Council's new direction in upgrading tourism as 'a strategic pillar industry' (The Research Office of the State Council, 2009).

Other policy players

Apart from the national organizations noted above and local government, tourism's multi-faceted nature means that there is a wide range of other public and non-public bodies that are influential in policy-making and implementation (Xinhua, 2000). Notable among these are:

- *The Ministry of Transport*: This oversees all transport (except for the railways for which there is a separate agency – the Ministry of Railways) with responsibility for transport capacity, including in aviation, ensuring that it can meet the demands of inbound, outbound and domestic tourists. To support this CNTA reports tourist flows to the Civil Aviation

Administration of China (CAAC), which is part of the Ministry of Transport, and they work closely in dealing with capacity issues; with the NDRC providing a macro view. The CAAC also provides support for tourism, such as complimentary air tickets to delegates to trade conferences hosted by the CNTA. The Ministry of Transport also works with the CNTA in the approval of cruise ships on inland waterways.

- *The Ministry of Education*: The academic status of tourism in the state education system and the approval of education programmes and institutions rests with the Ministry. Currently tourism is classified as a 'Second-Tier Discipline', located within one of the 'First-Tier Disciplines' (e.g. management, economics). This means that doctoral candidates are admitted to the major discipline rather than directly to tourism. CNTA have endeavoured to change this. A NPC deputy from Hunan Province raised this issue again in 2009 commenting that the current relatively low status of tourism might not be conducive to its academic and research development. While Ministry approval is required for institutions and programmes at degree level or above, the offer of sub-degree programmes and establishments is under the discretion of institutions or local government.

- *The Ministry of Health*: With recent experience of disease such as avian flu, SARS and swine flu the Ministry of Heath is now playing a more obvious role in tourism. The Ministry and its State Food and Drug Administration plays a role in the health, hygiene and food safety in the key tourist regions and attractions, including the preparation of emergency plans.

- *The Ministry of Commerce*: The Ministry has two main tasks in relation to tourism. First, it is responsible for ensuring that there is sufficient provision of services and commodities for tourists, especially during the peak season. Second, the Ministry, together with CNTA, approves tourism businesses with foreign investment. In addition, the Ministry is the main responsible agency for preparing and updating the Closer Economic Partnership Arrangements (CEPAs) that lower access barriers for eligible businesses in China's two special administrative regions (SARs) – Hong Kong and Macau. Tourism businesses benefit from this (Central Government and HKSARG, 2003).

- *The Ministry of Agriculture*: The growing urban–rural imbalance has brought the Ministry of Agriculture more prominently into tourism. The CNTA and the Ministry are currently exploring ways in which rural tourism can contribute to countryside development. To this end, in November 2008 the two agencies joined in an investigation and study trip in Anhui and Shandong provinces; concurrently their local bureaus in eight provinces were commissioned to undertake similar inquiries. The research results are being used to underpin a series of policy measures, such as the provision of infrastructure and facilities, development of rural tourism exemplars and the preparation of 'Guidelines on Rural Tourism Development 2009–2020' (Ministry of Agriculture and CNTA, 2009).

• *Other agencies*: Other agencies with a bearing on policy-making include those with an interest in its potential for income generation such as the forestry administration which has recently developed forestry tours. When CNTA proposes plans for the development of such attractions, the agencies concerned may raise objections if they perceive that their objectives are affected. The reforms in China have also promoted the development of non-governmental organizations (NGOs), estimated to number over 240,000 (Xinhua, 2004b). These include both government-sponsored and voluntary bodies representing stakeholders and interest groups. At present it is the state-owned enterprises, often with their own personal lobbying channels, and foreign investment organizations, such as the International Hoteliers of Shanghai, that are the most developed.

• *Foreign expertise*: Foreign organizations have both direct and indirect involvement in policy-making. Directly, for example, between 1997 and 2003 the UNWTO assisted in the compilation of regional master plans for seven provinces: Sichuan, Shandong, Yunnan, Hainan, Guizhou, Anhui and Helongjiang. These exercises were important in providing considerable experience as well as exposure to international practice. The cost in consultancy fees totaled US$2.4 million (CNTA, 2003c). The World Travel and Tourism Council (WTTC) has had a more indirect involvement, through lobbying and advice. Since 2003, the WTTC has produced a country report for China. In addition to the analysis of development, the reports also make recommendations to the policy-makers, such as that to upgrade CNTA to a full ministerial agency.

Conclusion

This chapter has drawn attention to three aspects of the policy-makers in China. First, in common with other countries, there is a diverse, somewhat fragmented, range of government and non-government agencies involved in tourism policy. The highly bureaucratic nature of China if anything exacerbates this fragmentation. Second, again in common with other countries, the body with nominal responsibility for tourism, the CNTA, has a relatively low administrative position with few powers of its own. The late development and recognition of tourism in China partly explains the extent to which CNTA has only recently begun to grow into its role as the lead agency for tourism. Finally, and perhaps most importantly for this study, the chapter has highlighted in a number of ways how the process of policy-learning and coordination between the agencies has taken place. The relatively recent emergence of tourism as a prominent policy issue, the rapid changes and developments in China, including in its ideological direction, as well as the fragmented nature of the policy environment in many ways makes China a fascinating context in which to observe this process. Most particularly, the ways in which the CNTA has used policy learning and coordination demonstrate how without any real authority the agency has been able to influence tourism. For example, by using policy learning, relating to the quality assurance framework, with coordination where required, the experience of CNTA shows how to operate effectively within the bureaucratic structure.

Acknowledgement

An early version of this chapter was published in *Annals of Tourism Research* – 'National Policy-Makers for Tourism in China' (Volume 37, Issue 2, pp.295–314) by the same authors.

7 Deng Xiaoping's era

A period of change

> In the course of political reform and greater openness . . . under the leadership of the CPC, the government of China has shifted its emphasis from endless ideological campaigns to concrete economic construction as a way to make the country more successful, prosperous, and powerful. As a component of the country's social and economic development, tourism policies have been adopted in line with the general orientation of the entire nation.
>
> (G.R. Zhang, 2003a: pp.23–4)

This chapter examines the evolution of national policy-making and tourism development under Deng Xiaoping from 1978 to 1997. Following Period One which is covered in Chapter 5, it divides Deng Xiaoping's era into three further periods. The period between 1978 and 1985 (referred to here as Period Two) was transitional, in which the economic function of tourism was slowly recognized and policy shifted accordingly. From 1986 to 1991 (Period Three), notwithstanding the widespread recognition of tourism as a market-driven activity, China's planned economy effectively prevented the emergence of a true market approach. As a result tourism policy only saw a partial evolution to market orientation. The final period covered in this chapter (Period Four) took shape from 1992 to 1997 when policy-making and tourism development started to be congruent with the market economy but still within a context in which administrative agencies sought to manage market forces. For each period an outline of the key developments and issues is presented before an outline of the basic and concrete policy decisions affecting tourism.

Period Two 1978–85: tourism as an economic activity

As explained in Chapters 2 and 5, tourism was not seen as an independent entity in Mao's era. As such there was no national tourism policy nor anything that resembled what is called here a 'tourism policy paradigm'. Economic-oriented tourism policy-making and its associated paradigm or set of behavioural beliefs held by the policy-makers only really began in Deng's era.

Background

Ideological orthodoxy and the environment

The economic orientation of the tourism policy paradigm was the result of shifts in the reigning ideological orthodoxy, in the socio-economic conditions, in China's foreign relations and in the implementation of the Economic Reform and Open-door Policy. Above all its origins lay with the two top leaders Deng Xiaoping and Chen Yun.

PRAGMATISM AND ECONOMIC MODERNIZATION

Ultimately the shift in the political consideration of tourism was prompted by a change in the reigning ideological orthodoxies. It is fair to say that only when 'economic development and modernization' became a part of the orthodoxy, could the economic function of tourism be recognized and the economic development of tourism be justified. A key informant shared their views on the shift in ideological orthodoxy as follows:

> Before 1978, China insisted on 'politics-in-command'; all affairs were to serve a political purpose. Tourism therefore was also to serve politics and did not aim to produce economic revenue. After 1978, the political circumstances reversed, the emphasis of government shifted to economic development. A change in many policies was to achieve economic development.

The Chinese leaders at this time started to take a more pragmatic approach to policy decisions. Notably, the specific political and socio-economic circumstances led them to consider using tourism for economic development, and especially to earn foreign exchange.

THE NEED FOR FOREIGN EXCHANGE

Limited foreign exchange reserves and the extent to which this hampered ambitions for economic modernization was a key issue. Above all China lacked advanced equipment and technology to support economic development and hence required foreign exchange. One key informant noted:

> At that time [i.e. the initial era of Economic Reform], the amount of foreign exchange was scarce, the demand for foreign currency nevertheless was huge. Almost all materials had to be imported. Therefore, the insufficiency of foreign exchange was very severe.

In 1978, the foreign exchange reserves of China totalled US$167 million (State Administration of Foreign Exchange (SAFE), 2010) (see Table 7.1). By 1980,

Table 7.1 Year-end foreign exchange reserves in China 1978–2010

Year	Foreign Exchange Reserve (US$bn)	Year	Foreign Exchange Reserve (US$bn)
1978	0.167	1995	73.597
1979	0.840	1996	105.049
1980	−1.296	1997	139.890
1981	2.708	1998	144.959
1982	6.986	1999	154.675
1983	8.901	2000	165.574
1984	8.220	2001	212.165
1985	2.644	2002	286.407
1986	2.072	2003	403.251
1987	2.923	2004	609.932
1988	3.372	2005	818.872
1989	5.550	2006	1,066.34
1990	11.093	2007	1,528.25
1991	21.712	2008	1,946.03
1992	19.443	2009	2,399.15
1993	21.199	2010	2,447.08 (March)
1994	51.620		

Source: SSB, 2009; SAFE, 2010.

there was a shortfall of US$1.3 billion. The petroleum and textile industries were the main generators of foreign exchange, but their earning capacities fell well short of the country's needs. With this background the Chinese leadership identified tourism as potentially the second-largest foreign exchange earner, after the energy sector (petroleum and coal), but ahead of the incomes from the Special Economic Zones (SEZs) in Guangdong (Shenzhen, Shekou) and Fujian provinces (Xiamen) and other light industries (CNTA, 1995b).

ABUNDANT TOURISM RESOURCES

As in many other developing countries, in the initial stage, tourism to some extent was perceived as a 'panacea' for economic development. China has abundant tourism resources, both physical and cultural. Its large territory contains areas of natural beauty and China boasts one of the greatest continuous civilizations in recorded history with extensive historic, cultural and religious relics and heritage. These tourism resources were seen to have significant appeal to international tourists, few of whom had been admitted to the country for at least thirty years. Also, in comparison with other sectors, tourism was considered to need less investment and to yield quicker returns, and therefore was viewed as a 'short-cut' and 'effortless development tool' for generating foreign exchange. As one Chinese leader put it, 'tourism was an industry characterized by less investment, quick rewards, low costs and high profits' (CNTA, 1995b).

Tourism development became a strategic component of China's Economic Reform and Open-door Policy. In order to convince foreigners of China's firm commitment to openness, travel permission was extended to all foreigners, rather than to invited guests and selected tourists only. Consideration was also given to opening restricted areas. In a meeting with delegates from Pan-America Airlines in October 1978, Deng Xiaoping indicated: 'we should open Lhasa [capital city of the Tibet Autonomous Region], foreigners will have an interest in Lhasa, tourists in Nepal also could come' (CNTA, 1995b: p.22). More importantly, tourism was envisaged by Deng as an experimental area for foreign capital and management expertise. On the same occasion Deng commented 'civil aviation and tourism are worth development, we shall utilize foreign capital to construct more guesthouses' (CNTA, 1995b: p.22). Since international tourists came mostly from the West, they demanded a level of quality that could not be satisfied by China's indigenous facilities, services and management. Consequently the use of foreign funds and expertise was deemed necessary. More importantly, unlike manufacturing industry that was highly centralized, tourism had never been a part of China's planned economy. Hence the introduction of foreign investment and management in tourism would not be viewed as an 'attack' on existing economic institutions in which public ownership predominated. Deng's vision of the role of tourism in China's Economic Reform and Open-door Policy was elaborated by Vice-Premier (later State Councillor) Gu Mu. He advised the CNTA in March 1983:

> Tourism development should go ahead of other industries, because industries have been a part of the old framework for several decades, whereas, tourism is a young industry. Tourism should have a new system at the outset. Your reform going ahead of others will affect and impel reform in other areas.
>
> (CNTA, 1995b: p.44)

A key informant commented: 'tourism was a pioneer sector in the Economic Reform and Open-door Policy'. Tourism was also seen as a window for information and ideas enhancing China's openness. The same informant summarized the general importance attached to tourism: 'The Economic Reform and Open-door Policy provided the fundamental conditions for the development of tourism. Tourism development became an important catalyst and further stimulated China's openness.'

The development of international tourism could not proceed smoothly without friendly foreign relations. Diplomatic relations between China and the rest of the world paved the way for the development of international tourism. As of 1978, China had basically returned to the international political arena.

Following the resumption of membership of the United Nations in 1971, China's foreign relations were quickly restored. In his memoirs, *China Today: Foreign Affairs*, former Vice-Foreign Minister Han Nianlong explains how between 1971 and 1978 China almost normalized diplomatic relationships with the major Asia Pacific, European and American nations (Han Nianlong, 1988; Ministry of Foreign Affairs, 2009). These countries were of course important source markets for international tourists.

The influence of the leaders

Given the fact that for almost thirty years tourism was seen solely as a political and diplomatic activity and that the Cultural Revolution had only just come to an end, it is not surprising that the change in views about the role of tourism was politically controversial. Notably, the political conception of tourism was deeply rooted in the mindset of the bureaucrats. Against this background it needed the top leaders to bring about change. With the pragmatic approach for which he was noted, Deng Xiaoping recognized China's socio-economic conditions and the international environment that it faced and, as already noted, he believed that the development of international tourism could contribute foreign exchange earnings. Between late 1978 and early 1979, he delivered six speeches on the economic development of tourism. These are summarized in Table 7.2. Generally, he considered that tourism was an economic activity that would contribute to foreign exchange and to the economy. As Deng put it: 'we should make a great effort to earn more revenue from tourism' (2 January 1979). He insisted that 'tourism is able to reap income quickly, why don't we develop tourism with major efforts . . .?' (6 January 1979).

Deng Xiaoping played the pivotal role in national policy-making and tourism development. His influence among the leaders and bureaucrats was pervasive. He not only shifted the focus of government officials from politics to economics, but was also able to put his initiatives into action. A key informant commented as follows: 'Deng Xiaoping's speeches were the foundation of China's tourism development. Other leaders had to accept the economic function of tourism although they might disagree or were unable to understand the implications.' Nevertheless, unlike Mao, Deng did not possess absolute power. Whiting (1992) indicates that Deng did not dictate decision-making to the same extent. He required support from other leaders on controversial matters particularly relating to ideological, political and socio-economic matters. The use of tourism as an economic activity fell into this category.

As the second most influential leader, Chen Yun was not only pragmatic but also a financial and economic expert, who played a key role in stabilizing the finance and the economy in the early period of the PRC. Thus his views on the direction of tourism were also seen as significant. Consistent with Deng, Chen's two speeches on 10 December 1978 and 18 September 1979 also

Table 7.2 Speeches delivered by Deng Xiaoping on the economic development
of tourism 1978–9

Date	Meeting with senior officials and/or foreign visitors/guests	Summary
January 1978	During the official visit to Burma: Vice-Minister of Foreign Affairs Ministry of Foreign Affairs Deputy Director, Department of Asia	'We should well develop our tourism by all means; with the vast territories, China boasts numerous attractions. We need to open some cities, to proceed with the construction of tourist attraction sites and open more tourism corporations.'
		In response to Lee Kuan Yew's vision that China's tourism once developed could earn about US$ 2 billion per year, Deng expected the figure to exceed Lee's estimation.
9 October 1978	Chief Executive Officer of Pan American Airlines, USA; accompanied by SGATT & CAAC senior officials	Civil aviation and tourism is worth development.
		Adoption of foreign capital for the development of hotels.
2 January 1979	SGATT senior officials	The development of tourism should aim at increasing revenue.
		Development of a pool of talent for tourism such as tour guides, interpreters and managerial staff.
		Developing tourism into a comprehensive industry.
6 January 1979	Leaders of the State Council	Tourism can generate income more quickly.
		Tourism also can provide employment.
		The development of tourism needs supporting facilities such as entertainment.
13 January 1979	Local leaders of Anhui Province (in Beijing)	Huangshan is a good place for the development of tourism (Huangshan is a mountain located in Anhui province; it is a renowned natural attraction in China).

continued . . .

Table 7.2 continued . . .

Date	Meeting with senior officials and/or foreign visitors/guests	Summary
15 July 1979	Local leaders of Anhui Province and Huizhou County (in Huangshan)	Huangshan is a good place for the development of tourism, also a good source of revenue generation. It is necessary to provide transportation, accommodation facilities for foreign tourists. Major efforts should be on service quality of tourism employees.

Source: CNTA, 1995b (interpreted by the authors); CNTA and Department of Literature Research of the CPC Central Committee, 2004.

attached considerable importance to the commercial role of tourism. It was Chen who described the development of tourism as an 'export of attractions'. This was seen as substantial support for the economic development of tourism. He remarked:

> We need to emphasize the development of tourism. In fact, tourism incomes resemble the 'export of attractions' that earn foreign exchange more quickly than foreign trade. The United Kingdom earns tourism receipts of US$5.4 billion annually. We, China, such a vast country, can generate more tourism incomes.
>
> (CNTA, 1995b: p.23)

Another supporter, as both a generalist and economic specialist, Vice-Premier Li Xian-nian, echoed Deng and Chen's remarks in agreeing that tourism was an economically beneficial activity. After the speeches by Deng and Chen, Li said in a meeting with SGATT held in September 1979: 'Tourism can generate revenues; it is the export of beauty spots. I concur that Comrade Deng's goal to earn US$5 billion could be accomplished' (CNTA, 1995b: p.28).

The emergence of an economic-driven tourism policy clearly owes a great deal to the collective efforts of the Chinese leadership, especially the two top leaders Deng and Chen. Over this period it was consistently agreed among the Chinese leadership that the development of tourism should adhere to Deng Xiaoping's 'Socialism with Chinese Characteristics'. This was the consensus of the meeting on 19 March 1981, jointly held by the Secretariat of the CPC and the State Council, which agreed that the development of tourism should follow a Chinese path. Later the same year, on 11–24 July, at the National Tourism Works Conference, Vice-Premier Wan Li gave instructions that tourism development should proceed on a path with Chinese characteristics (CNTA, 1995b). In 1982, Vice-Premier Gu Mu reinforced this:

> We must adhere to the socialist principles in the development of our tourism. Sex and erotic tourism must be prohibited. Nevertheless, we should welcome our foreign guests and also encourage them to stay for more days. So we need to do something to make them more enjoyable. We can broadcast films of Chinese culture, western classical culture and other healthy features.
>
> (CNTA, 1995b: p.41)

In 1983, Vice-Premier Wan Li put forward similar remarks at the Standing Meeting of the State Council: 'We need to demonstrate that we are a great socialist nation in every aspect' (CNTA, 1995b: p.45).

Politics or economics?

As already noted, the conception of tourism as political and diplomatic propaganda had been deeply institutionalized in China. This was reflected, for example, in arrangements for visa applications to ensure that only those with a favourable view of socialist China were admitted as well as in restictions on visitors as to the places they visited and the people they were able to meet. As far as the Bureau of Travel and Tourism of China (BTTC) was concerned, its plans to receive invited guests and tourists required the State Council's approval. Similarly its operational officers came under the foreign affairs establishment, and were obliged to abide by its working codes. With ideological orthodoxy (i.e. 'politics-in-command') and the political function of tourism deeply rooted in the mindsets of the officials, they found it hard to come to a new view of tourism. Some operating officials even felt frustrated in running travel and hospitality services as a business. According to a key informant:

> These officials had no idea about running travel businesses. They equated travel services with hospitality, which was funded by government. They felt uncomfortable about asking for money from guests. In the meantime, they were not used to business operations, services improvement, quality enhancement or bearing commercial risks. If tourism changed to a business activity, many of them could not adapt.

The debate about tourism as a political or as an economic activity continued during this period. For example, in December 1980, the State General Administration of Travel and Tourism (SGATT) (successor to the BTTC) and the Chinese Academy of Social Sciences (CASS) jointly organized the first Tourism Economy Conference. In this, the participants discussed the function of tourism as an economic activity and the approaches to development. Subsequently, a second conference was held in 1981 to discuss how to develop tourism in Chinese style (CNTA, 1995b: pp.34 and 39). In the meantime, the large amount of foreign exchange earned by tourism, increasing from US$262.9 million in 1978 to US$1.25 billion in 1985 (see Table 7.3), began to convince those who were doubtful about tourism as an economic activity.

Table 7.3 International and domestic tourism receipts in China 1978–2009

Year	International tourism receipts (US$m)	Growth rate (%)	Domestic tourism receipts (RMB¥bn)	Growth rate (%)
1978	262.90	–	–	–
1979	449.27	70.9	–	–
1980	616.65	37.3	–	–
1981	784.91	27.3	–	–
1982	843.17	7.4	–	–
1983	941.20	11.6	–	–
1984	1,131.34	20.2	–	–
1985	1,250.00	10.5	8	–
1986	1,530.85	22.5	10.6	32.5
1987	1,861.51	21.6	14	32.1
1988	2,246.83	20.7	18.7	33.6
1989	1,860.48	−17.2	15.0	−19.8
1990	2,217.58	19.2	18.0	20.0
1991	2,844.97	28.3	20.0	11.1
1992	3,946.87	38.7	25.0	25.0
1993	4,683.17	18.7	86.4	245.6
1994	7,322.81	56.4	102.4	18.5
1995	8,732.77	19.3	137.6	34.4
1996	10,200.46	16.8	163.8	19.0
1997	12,074.14	18.4	211.3	29.0
1998	12,602.00	4.4	239.1	13.2
1999	14,099.00	11.9	283.2	18.4
2000	16,224.00	15.1	317.6	12.1
2001	17,792.00	9.7	352.2	10.9
2002	20,385.00	14.6	387.8	10.1
2003	17,406.00	−14.6	344.2	−11.2
2004	25,739.00	47.9	471.1	36.9
2005	29,296.00	13.8	528.6	12.1
2006	33,950.00	15.9	623.0	17.9
2007	41,920.00	23.5	777.1	24.7
2008	40,800.00	−2.7	874.9	12.6
2009	39,680.00	−2.8	1,020.0	16.4

Note: The figures for domestic tourists before 1985 are not available.

Source: CNTA, 1985a–2010a; CNTA, 2010b; Wei, 1996.

International or domestic?

A combination of it being a closed country for three decades and the programme of economic reform raised the level of interest in visiting China. In just one year, from 1978 to 1979, international tourist arrivals jumped from 1.8 million to 4.2 million In fact, as shown in Table 7.4, except for 1989 (the year of the June 4th Incident), 2003 (the outbreak of SARS) and 2008 (global economic downturn), the growth rate of visitor arrivals after 1978 has remained positive every year (see Table 7.4).

Also in this period domestic tourism began to grow. There were three main reasons for this. First and foremost, the coastal and rural areas began to experience increases in disposable income. Second, having been condemned during the Cultural Revolution as the 'life style of landlords and the bourgeoisie' (CNTA, 1996b), the shift in ideological orthodoxies to 'economic development' gradually changed the views of the Chinese about tourist activity and sightseeing. This was all part of the changes in attitudes toward the pursuit of quality of life such as earning more income, acquiring consumer goods, wearing stylish clothes, taking leisure and recreational activities. The third reason was that incoming international tourism demonstrated to the Chinese that travel and touring was an attractive way of taking recreation and leisure. With these influences the number of domestic tourists totalled 200 million in 1984, rising to 240 million in 1985 (see Table 7.5).

However, the growth of tourism created problems, particularly because the supply of tourist facilities significantly fell short of demand. The shortage of hotels was the most serious problem. From 1978 to 1979, the hotel growth rate was 9.5 per cent, compared to a 132 per cent growth in visitor arrivals (see Tables 7.4 and 7.6). International tourists arriving in China found their room reservations had not been confirmed and they had to take their luggage with them during sightseeing visits. Some tourists even had to sleep in the lobby of their hotel. In some extreme cases, the vice-premier directly contacted the senior management of hotels with room requests. The additional pressure from domestic tourists made the problem particularly acute in the major tourist cities such as Beijing and Shanghai. More importantly, as the leaders had initiated only the foreign exchange earnings function, domestic tourism came to be regarded as an obstacle to the development of international tourism.

In summary, this period is characterized by the rise of the economic-oriented tourism policy paradigm in which socialist principles and Chinese charateristics remained central, tourism was seen as a strategic component of China's economic reform, the foreign exchange earning capacity of tourism was of paramount importance and international was prioritized over domestic tourism.

Basic tourism policy decisions

Since this was a transitional period in which the economic function of tourism was only just beginning to be recognized, both political and economic goals

Table 7.4 Inbound (or international) tourist arrivals to China 1978–2009

Year	Total visitor arrivals	Growth rate (%)	Foreigners	Growth rate (%)	Overseas Chinese	Growth rate (%)	HK, Macau and Taiwan compatriots	Growth rate (%)
1978	1,809,221	–	229,646	–	18,092	–	1,561,483	–
1979	4,203,901	132.4	362,389	57.8	20,910	15.6	3,820,602	144.7
1980	5,702,536	35.6	529,124	46.0	34,413	64.6	5,138,999	34.5
1981	7,767,096	36.2	675,153	27.6	38,856	12.9	7,053,087	37.2
1982	7,924,261	2.0	764,497	13.2	42,745	10.0	7,117,019	0.9
1983	9,477,005	19.6	872,511	14.1	40,352	–5.6	8,564,142	20.3
1984	12,852,185	35.6	1,134,267	30.0	47,498	17.7	11,670,420	36.3
1985	17,833,097	38.8	1,370,462	20.8	84,827	78.6	16,377,808	40.3
1986	22,819,450	28.0	1,482,276	8.2	68,133	–19.7	21,269,041	29.9
1987	26,902,267	17.9	1,727,821	16.6	87,031	27.7	25,087,415	18.0
1988	31,694,804	17.8	1,842,206	6.6	79,348	–8.8	29,773,250	18.7
1989	24,501,394	–22.7	1,460,970	–20.7	68,556	–13.6	22,971,868	–22.8
1990	27,461,821	12.1	1,747,315	19.6	91,090	32.9	25,623,416	11.5
1991	33,349,757	21.4	2,710,103	55.1	133,427	46.5	30,506,227	19.1
1992	38,114,945	14.3	4,006,427	47.8	165,077	23.7	33,943,441	11.31
1993	41,526,945	9.0	4,655,857	16.2	166,182	0.7	36,704,906	8.1
1994	43,684,456	5.2	5,182,060	11.3	115,245	–30.7	38,387,151	4.6

continued . . .

Table 7.4 continued . . .

Year	Total visitor arrivals	Growth rate (%)	Foreigners	Growth rate (%)	Overseas Chinese	Growth rate (%)	HK, Macau and Taiwan compatriots	Growth rate (%)
1995	46,386,511	6.2	5,886,716	13.6	115,818	0.5	40,383,977	5.2
1996	51,127,516	10.2	6,744,334	14.6	154,601	33.5	44,228,581	9.5
1997	57,587,923	12.6	7,428,006	10.1	99,004	−36.0	50,060,913	13.2
1998	63,478,401	10.2	7,107,747	−4.3	120,704	21.9	56,249,950	12.4
1999	72,795,594	14.7	8,432,296	18.6	108,141	−10.4	64,255,157	14.2
2000	83,443,881	14.6	10,160,432	20.5	75,487	−30.2	73,207,962	13.9
2001	89,012,924	6.7	11,226,384	10.5	–	–	77,786,540	6.3
2002	97,908,252	10.0	13,439,497	19.7	–	–	84,468,755	8.6
2003	91,662,082	−6.4	11,402,855	−15.2	–	–	80,259,227	−5.0
2004	109,038,218	19.0	16,932,506	48.5	–	–	92,105,712	14.8
2005	120,292,300	10.3	20,255,100	19.6	–	–	100,037,100	8.6
2006	124,942,096	3.9	22,210,266	9.7	–	–	102,731,830	2.7
2007	131,873,287	5.5	26,109,668	17.6	–	–	105,763,619	3.0
2008	130,027,400	−1.4	24,325,300	−6.8	–	–	105,702,000	−0.1
2009	126,475,900	−2.7	21,037,500	−9.8	–	–	105,438,500	1.1

Note: The total number of visitor arrivals to China includes (1) foreigners; (2) overseas Chinese (not provided from 2001); and (3) compatriots from Hong Kong SAR, Macau SAR and Taiwan (Chinese nationals residing in Hong Kong SAR, Macau SAR and Taiwan region).

Source: CNTA, 1985a–2010a; 2010b.

Table 7.5 Domestic tourists in China 1984–2009

Year	Number (m)	Growth rate (%)
1984	200	–
1985	240	20.0
1986	270	12.5
1987	290	7.4
1988	300	3.4
1989	240	−20.0
1990	280	16.6
1991	290	3.6
1992	330	13.8
1993	410	24.0
1994	520	27.8
1995	620	19.2
1996	640	3.0
1997	644	0.6
1998	694	7.8
1999	719	3.6
2000	744	3.5
2001	784	5.4
2002	878	12.0
2003	870	−0.9
2004	1,102	26.7
2005	1,212	10.0
2006	1,394	15.0
2007	1,610	15.5
2008	1,712	6.3
2009	1,902	11.1

Note: The figures for domestic tourists before 1984 are not available.
Source: Wei, 1996; CNTA, 1996a–2009a; CNTA, 2010b.

of tourism were pursued so as to achieve what leaders called a 'double harvest in both the political and economic spheres' (CNTA, 1995b: p.36). In a Secretariat meeting in March 1981, General Secretary Hu Yaobang remarked 'tourism should accomplish both economic and political tasks' (CNTA, 1995b: p.35). In October of the same year, Hu further encouraged the CNTA to:

> Instruct your subordinate units to accumulate new experience and to found new milestones in the course of tourism development. On the one hand, tourism development should increase revenues; on the other hand, it should expand our influence and enhance our spiritual civilization
> (CNTA, 1995b: p.38)

Table 7.6 Hotel capacity in China 1978–2008

Year	Hotels	Growth rate (%)	Hotel rooms	Growth rate (%)
1978	137	–	15,539	–
1979	150	9.5	17,149	10.4
1980	203	35.3	31,788	85.4
1981	296	45.8	43,251	36.1
1982	362	22.3	51,625	19.4
1983	371	2.5	59,588	15.4
1984	505	36.1	76,994	29.2
1985	710	40.6	107,513	39.6
1986	974	37.2	147,479	37.2
1987	1,283	31.7	184,710	25.2
1988	1,496	16.6	220,165	19.2
1989	1,788	19.5	267,505	21.5
1990	1,987	11.1	293,827	9.8
1991	2,130	7.2	321,116	9.3
1992	2,354	10.5	351,044	9.3
1993	2,552	8.4	386,401	10.1
1994	2,995	17.4	406,280	5.1
1995	3,720	24.2	486,114	19.6
1996	4,418	18.8	593,696	22.1
1997	5,201	17.7	701,736	18.2
1998	5,782	11.1	764,797	9.0
1999	7,035	21.7	889,430	16.3
2000	10,481	49.0	948,185	6.6
2001	7,358	−29.8	816,260	−13.9
2002	8,880	20.7	897,206	9.9
2003	9,751	9.8	992,800	10.7
2004	10,888	11.7	1,237,851	24.7
2005	11,828	8.6	1,332,000	7.6
2006	12,751	7.8	1,459,836	9.6
2007	13,583	6.5	1,573,784	7.8
2008	14,099	3.8	1,591,140	1.1

Note: since 2001, only the star-rated hotels have been included in CNTA's statistics.
Source: CNTA, 1985a–2009a; Han Kehua, 1994.

The political goal of tourism was to promote socialist China, to expand and strengthen the international influence of China; the economic goal was to earn foreign exchange. Owing to the limited capacity of tourist facilities, the Chinese government decided to develop international tourism in a prudent manner 'based on reality, developing actively, acting according to China's own capacities, progressing steadily and going on China's own path of tourism development' (Han Kehua, 1994: p.45; CNTA, 1995a: p.36). In light of the importance attached to international tourism and the negative view of domestic tourism, a passive policy for domestic tourism was formulated, known as the 'Three-No' policy – 'No Support, No Objection and No Promotion'. The Chinese government decided that all tourist facilities and transport should first satisfy the demand of international tourists. A key informant explained:

> The huge number of domestic tourists made the attractions extremely overcrowded and caused a shortage in the supply of transportation services. Thus, the State Council instructed the adoption of the 'No Support, No Objection and No Promotion Policy' towards domestic tourism.

Concrete tourism policy decisions

Weaknesses in capacity in this period meant that policy-making was dominated by supply-oriented decisions. When the new ideological orthodoxies ('economic development' and 'decentralization of power') and the new tourism paradigm ('tourism as an economic activity') emerged, they immediately conflicted with existing tourism institutions. The existing institutions still embodied the old ideological orthodoxies – 'politics-in-command' and the planned economy as well as the political conception of tourism. The institutionalization of the economic and market-oriented ideological orthodoxies and the tourism policy paradigm took place concurrently with their emergence, debate, formation and advancement. However, the institutionalization did not move ahead in a vacuum, but under the legacies of the central planned economy and the view of tourism as a political activity. The spontaneous resistance caused by these two legacies meant that adoption of the new approach proceeded fitfully. Ultimately the institutionalization had to compromise with these two legacies.

The initial institutional landscape

The institutional landscape for tourism development in 1978 reflected the model of the centrally planned economy. As discussed in Chapter 4, this period was characterized by a planned economy supplemented by market forces. In the initial years of economic reform, market forces were only introduced experimentally, most often confined to rural areas. In 1978, for the most part there was considered to be no alternative but to develop tourism as part of the familiar planned economy. Under the planned economy, state investment was the sole engine for development. Hence faced with insufficient accommodation, the policy response was for the state to make provision for investment and direct transfers. In early 1978, the State Council injected RMB¥360 million for hotel construction and the purchase of tour buses. At the same time central and local government allocated existing guest houses and tourist buses to the SGATT

(CNTA) and the local tourism bureaus (interviews; CNTA, 1995b: pp.19–27). In this way a 'tourism system (or '*xitong*') (see Chapter 4 for an explanation of '*xitong*') under the planned-economy model was formed.

This '*xitong*' was highly centralized and unified. SGATT (CNTA) and local tourism bureaus had a set of subordinate enterprises including travel agencies, hotels and tour bus companies. The enterprise functions were tied up with the government functions since the SGATT directly ran the tourism businesses. Sales and marketing were also highly centralized. Only the head offices of the three travel agencies, CITS, China Travel Services (CTS, established in 1974 by the Office of Overseas Chinese Affairs) and China Youth Travel Services (CYTS, established in 1980 by the Communist Youth League) had authority to make overseas contacts and sales, leaving ground services to their local offices. This institutional framework hindered the implementation of the new ideological orthodoxies and the new tourism policy paradigm, and hence restricted the development of tourism as an economic activity.

Institutional development

The policy paper 'Decision to Strengthen the Works for Tourism' issued by the State Council in October 1981, set out the institutional logic for tourism development as based on 'centralizing leadership and decentralizing operations'. 'Centralizing leadership' centralized policy decisions and plans, while 'decentralizing operations' delegated management to local tourism bureaus with responsibilities divided among travel agencies. Institutionally therefore a clear distinction was made between the policy and planning functions of central government and the operational functions of accountable enterprises at a more local level.

UPGRADED LEADERSHIP ARRANGEMENTS

The prime reason of the State Council for centralizing and elevating the leadership of tourism development was to reinforce the thrust of policy implementation. In 1978, a Tourism Leadership Group of commissions and ministries was set up to control overall policy direction and coordination. The group members comprised the State Planning Commission, the State Infrastructure Commission and the Ministry of Finance, functional ministries such as the Ministry of Foreign Affairs and line economic ministries such as the Ministry of Foreign Trade, Ministry of Light Industries and Ministry of Commerce, as well as some party organizations (CNTA, 1995b: p.20). The composition of the group membership reflected both the political and economic directions of tourism development.

In the same year, the main executive and administrative body for tourism development, the BTTC, was upgraded to the State General Administration for Travel and Tourism (SGATT) under the direct jurisdiction of the State Council. In 1982, with the approval of the Standing Committee of the National

People's Congress, SGATT was further upgraded to the China National Tourism Administration (CNTA, 1995b: p.42) with vice-ministry rank. CITS was also separated from the CNTA, which was no longer involved in business operation. Along with its organizational upgrade and transformation, generalists and economic specialists took over leadership positions in order to implement the economic-oriented policy. As an economic specialist, Vice-Premier Chen Muhua became the Deputy Head and then the Head of the Tourism Leadership Group. In 1981, Han Kehua, a generalist and diplomatic specialist, was appointed as Director-General of SGATT in order to counterbalance both the political-diplomatic and economic roles assigned to tourism. Han had held senior positions in the military, local administration and diplomatic affairs including a period as Vice-Governor of Hubei Province and Vice-Minister of Foreign Affairs. In the meantime, local government at province and municipality levels were required to establish subordinate agencies for tourism (Han Kehua, 1994; CNTA, 1995b).

RELAXATION OF MARKET ACCESS

Institution building and the opening up of the market played crucial roles in the development of tourism. As noted already, by 1979 state provision of hotels and guest houses was far from satisfying the huge growth in tourist arrivals. For example, in 1979 there were only 150 hotels and guest houses, a slight increase from 137 in 1978 (see Table 7.6). The large gap between demand and supply simply could not be filled through state investment and provision. In response, in 1979, Deng Xiaoping initiated the decision to attract foreign investment for hotels from the developed world. But at the same time he also pointed to the need for self-reliance: 'we need to construct guesthouses for tourism development. We can utilize investment from foreign countries and overseas Chinese for the first batch of guesthouses; afterwards, we should develop by ourselves' (CNTA, 1995b: p.24). As has been seen, tourism was, in fact, the first sector to be able to take advantage of foreign investment. As a key informant pointed out: 'The first three projects in introducing foreign investment were all tourism related. They were in air catering, the Beijing Jianguo Hotel and the Beijing Great Wall Hotel.'

The introduction of foreign investment represented a ground-breaking development, since it was considered a challenge both to the centrally planned economy and public ownership, and to the anti-imperialism and self-reliance that was a key element of Mao's thinking. Without public ownership the central plan simply could not be effective in allocating scarce resources. As for anti-imperialism, prior to Deng's era, the Chinese leadership insisted that the international economy was manipulated by capitalist powers and that foreign investment by capitalists would ultimately drain China's resources, exploit her labour and extract huge profits. The hostility between China and the West hardened this belief. Foreign investment, even from international financial institutions such as the World Bank and International Monetary Fund (IMF) was strictly forbidden during the Cultural Revolution. Self-reliance was widely advocated (Lieberthal, 1995; Ogden, 1995). Earlier, China had had bad experience with foreign aid from the Soviet Union. In the late Cultural Revolution, utilization of foreign capital had triggered a debate between pragmatic and leftist leaders but on 2 January 1977, the editorial of *People's Daily* proclaimed 'we never allow the adoption of foreign investment to develop our domestic resources' (*People's Daily*, 1977). Truly in the early reform era, the introduction of foreign investment was politically and ideologically highly sensitive. Therefore when the policy proposal was raised in relation to hotel investment, there were strong objections by government officials and society more generally.

Against this background the policy proposal was prepared cautiously in order to safeguard the public ownership and self-reliance orthodoxies. As a result only two types of foreign-invested hotels were permitted at the outset: joint venture and cooperative. Full foreign ownership was strictly prohibited. For the joint-venture type, the hotel was jointly financed by Chinese and foreign partners, with the Chinese capital accounting for at least 51 per cent. Both sides shared the profit and risk in accordance with the proportion of investment. For the cooperative type, the Chinese side provided the land and labour, while the foreign investor provided funds, resources and technology. Both sides shared the profit and risk in accordance with the contract. On expiry of the contract the ownership of both types would be transferred to the Chinese (Han Kehua, 1994; CNTA, 1995b). Given the sensitivities, the first foreign-invested hotel project, '*Jianguo Hotel*' in Beijing, still required the approval of many leaders including vice-premiers and vice-chairmen of Standing Committees of the NPC. A key informant disclosed:

> The approval body for the first foreign invested hotel project – Beijing Jianguo Hotel – was the State Council. This project required the consent of all twelve vice-premiers and some vice-chairmen of the Standing Committee of the National People's Congress. For a project requiring the consent of so many leaders, you can see how difficult and stressful the project was.

Later five further foreign-invested hotel projects were approved, located in four major tourist cities, Beijing, Shanghai, Guangzhou and Nanjing (CNTA, 1995b). The first hotel – Beijing Jianguo Hotel – proved to be successful in yielding a profit within two years (Han Kehua, 1994). Foreign investment not only introduced capital, but also a new management style, with management responsibility assigned to a general manager, rather than to a party secretary. Later, foreign investment and foreign management styles were widely applied in many economic sectors.

In many ways the introduction of foreign investment and management expertise in the hotel sector did not actually pose a frontal challenge to the planned economy as initially feared. The hotel sector was not in fact considered as a part of the planned economy in the same way as the industrial sector and its associated state-owned enterprises. Rather it was on the periphery and developments in this sector were not seen as being at the heart of the Chinese model.

Internal decentralization of operations and investment was a fundamental change to the planned economy. Except for the hotel sector, tourism operations and investment before 1984 were fundamentally part of the centralized system. There were two reasons for the State Council starting to decentralize operations and investment in 1979 and 1980. First, the centralized approach made it hard to cope with the enormous number of tourist arrivals and their diversity. Second, profit was as high as 80 per cent of the tour price in travel services and 30 per cent of the room rate in the hotel sector. This high profit rate stimulated other government agencies and enterprises outside the 'tourism system' to establish international tourism businesses. These included, for example, the All China Federation of Trade Unions, the All China Women's Federation, the State Sports Commission and the Ministry of Foreign Trade. These all had policy and administrative responsibilities in relation to foreign counterparts and therefore found advantages in running their own travel businesses (CNTA, 1992b, and interview).

In November 1979, tour marketing and sales were cautiously decentralized to regional branches of CITS. These were followed in September 1980 by operations and investment which were decentralized to other non-tourism government agencies and enterprises at the centre and in the regions. After a trial period of only one year tourism operations and investment were re-centralized. Further recentralization came with three policy documents. In the first, entitled 'On the Decision to Reinforce the Tourism Works', issued in October 1981, the State Council prescribed that sales and marketing should be confined solely to the head offices of CITS and CTS. The second document, issued by SGATT in November 1981, reinforced the first in the form of a regulation – and specified the date for implementation. Finally, in February 1982, the State Council distributed the third policy document which effectively prevented non-tourism agencies from running international tourism businesses (CNTA, 1995b).

This recentralization effectively called an automatic halt to the institutionalization of tourism. In effect tourism was brought back into the 'system' or '*xitong*' under the centrally planned economy model, as a kind of self-closed and self-entrenched institution. Professional government agencies were established to administer the relevant enterprises. Tourism businesses delivered by other government agencies were assumed to weaken the jurisdiction of SGATT (or CNTA) over the tourism sector and to infringe the interests of the enterprises embedded into the 'tourism system'. A key informant remarked:

> Actually, the policy decision of non-tourism government agencies or enterprises not being allowed to run international tourism businesses was initiated by CNTA. Under the planned economy era, government

functions were integrated with enterprise functions; we [CNTA] of course needed to protect our enterprises. Therefore, we naturally thought in monopolistic terms.

SGATT was of the view that only the 'tourism system' was capable of operating tourism businesses in a politically and professionally correct way. As a key informant suggested: 'we considered that non-tourism government agencies and enterprises would not handle tourism business appropriately'. Some incidents confirmed SGATT's views. For example, complaints were lodged against the tour guides, employed by travel agencies set up by other non-tourism departments, who asked for tips. This was considered politically and professionally inappropriate. This idea of a 'tourism system' providing a collection of standard operating procedures and structures is in line with work by March and Olsen (1983) who see such institutions as having a more autonomous role in defending interests. In this case, the real player was not SGATT itself, but rather the 'tourism system'.

Obviously, the ban on internal market access restrained the economic development of tourism and hindered the work of organizations outside the 'tourism system'. A key informant commented that 'the monopolistic operation by the "tourism *xitong*" could not meet the needs of tourism development'. Between 1979 and 1983, state and foreign investment expanded the number of hotels but the total bed-capacity still fell well short of demand. The number of hotels and hotel rooms increased from 17,000 rooms in 150 hotels in 1979 to 77,000 rooms in 505 hotels by 1984, by which time international tourist arrivals had soared to 12.9 million in 1984, (see Tables 7.4 and 7.6).

The underlying cause of this imbalance was that the growth in tourism development, consequent on economically oriented policy decisions, was not matched by institutional change. As a result of economic decisions, international tourism receipts rocketed from US$263 million in 1978 to US$941 million in 1983. There is no figure for domestic tourism receipts before 1985 but by that year they had reached RMB¥8 billion (see Table 7.3). The economic linkages between tourism and other related industries had also been substantially strengthened. For example in 1979, shopping, catering, transportation and postage amounted to US$152 million, US$51 million and US$104 million respectively. By 1983 they had increased sharply to US$348 million, US$118 million and US$186 million (State Planning Commission, 1990: p.421). At the local level, tourism had become either a new economic sector or an important foreign exchange earner. Furthermore, motivated by high growth and profit potential, both the domestic and foreign investors anticipated a prosperous prospect for China's international tourism and aspired to join (CNTA, 1992b). It was assumed that further institutional change would stabilize and legitimize the emerging structure and underpin its further development. Motivated by the centre, many local government agencies had established tourism bureaus to boost tourism development and some, such as Guangdong, Fujian, Tianjin Municipality and Inner Mongolia, had formulated tourism development plans with specific economic goals (CNTA, 1995b). Ultimately, in the face of these developments and especially the rapid growth of demand, the restriction which meant that tourism investment could only be channelled via the 'tourism system' proved unworkable, the imbalances that it created meant that it could not stand the pressure of development.

The restriction was eventually removed in 1984. Initiated by the General-Secretary of the CPC, Hu Yaobang, the Secretariat of Central Committee decided that tourism should be invested in and run by the state, together with local government, individual government agencies, collectives and individuals (i.e. the emerging private sector). This was the so-called 'Five (Parties)-Together' policy decision. The supply of hotels and travel agencies increased sharply during a short period after the implementation of this policy decision (see Tables 7.6 and 7.7).

Table 7.7 Travel agencies in China 1987–2008

Year	Number of travel agencies	Growth rate (%)
1987	1,245	–
1988	1,573	26.3
1989	1,617	2.8
1990	1,603	–0.9
1991	1,561	–2.6
1992	2,592	66.0
1993	3,238	24.9
1994	4,382	35.3
1995	3,826	–12.7
1996	4,252	11.1
1997	4,986	17.3
1998	6,222	24.8
1999	7,326	17.7
2000	8,993	22.8
2001	10,532	17.1
2002	11,552	9.7
2003	13,361	15.9
2004	14,927	11.7
2005	16,245	8.8
2006	17,957	10.5
2007	18,943	5.5
2008	20,110	6.2

Notes:
1 The figures for travel agencies before 1987 are not available.
2 CNTA adopted the quality gurarantee deposit measure for travel agencies in 1995. The licences of those who were unable to settle the amount were revoked, thus resulting in a reduction (CNTA, 1998b).

Source: CNTA, 1988a–2009a.

ENTERPRISE REFORM

Strictly speaking, China did not have tourism enterprises prior to 1978. Travel agencies and guest houses were the extended arm of government to provide travel and hospitality services for invited guests and approved self-financed tourists. As discussed in Chapter 4, the travel agencies and guest houses were non-administrative government bodies. The staff members of travel services were the same as the officials of government agencies – BTTC in central government and foreign affairs offices in local government. A number of guest houses were operated at a loss and subsidized by government (CNTA, 1992b; Han Kehua, 1994).

At the outset of transition to economic activity, the Chinese leadership had to acknowledge that travel services and guest houses should become business enterprises. For this, broad guidelines were proposed relating, for example, to profit-making as the organizational goal and the establishment of an independent accounting system. At the time neither government officials nor managers had any clear understanding about how to run tourism businesses or how to prepare to match international tourism practices in highly competitive and dynamic international tourist markets. Vice- Premier Gu Mu remarked in 1982:

> Tourism is a new industry in our country. We do not have much experience. We do not know how to manage a hotel well or how to offer front-line and counter services. We need to learn the experiences and practices from foreign countries.
>
> (CNTA, 1995b: p.41)

A key informant also talked about the initial ideas of policy-makers and practitioners: 'At that time, we actually did not know how to develop tourism. We assumed that we would earn revenues only if there were seaside guesthouses and attractions.'

The key issue for China's tourism sector at the time was to learn how to operate international tourism business in a socialist context. The success of Jianguo Hotel provided an example of the effective implementation of international management expertise (or what the Chinese called 'modern' hotel management) in a Chinese setting. It had established modern enterprise management that was comparable to international practice and, importantly, was distinguished from the inflexible system inside the state-owned enterprises. In essence it was operated in a comparatively non-political context in which business goals and business professionalism replaced 'politics-in-command' as the guide to management and operation. The main measures of performance, profit and service were based on market demand rather than on administrative orders. The general manager replaced the party secretary in holding overall responsibility for management and business performance, and department managers reported directly to the general manager. Each staff member was employed on a contract basis and was provided with a job description, performance criteria and work procedures. Staff appraisal was conducted on a daily basis. The employees were remunerated in accordance with their work performance. The enterprise could penalize staff for unsatisfactory performance or even terminate their contracts. All of these practices were unprecedented in China's enterprise system (Han Kehua, 1994; interviews).

The successful application of foreign management expertise in Jianguo Hotel rested on two important conditions. First, Jianguo Hotel was newly established without pre-existing systems and interests tied up with the administrative agencies. Second, the foreign management model needed to fit with the communist institutions. In the state-owned enterprises, the CPC party committee provided the core of enterprise leadership. In Jianguo Hotel, the party committee retreated from enterprise management to party and labour union affairs only. Jianguo's enterprise management model in fact not only broke down the 'egalitarianism' and 'iron rice bowl' of the state-owned enterprises, but also established an independent enterprise that was outside the direct administration of government agencies and acted in accordance with market demand. The Jianguo Hotel's management model coincided with the theme of China's enterprise reform and gained recognition by the Chinese leaders. In 1984, the State Council decided to promote Jianguo's management model through a nation-wide 'Learning Jianguo Campaign'. The modern enterprise management model represented by Jianguo was gradually diffused to the rest of the hotel sector (CNTA, 1995b; interviews).

By contrast enterprise reform did not proceed as smoothly in the travel agency sector. The separation of enterprise from government encountered opposition from government agencies and enterprises. Many enterprises and their supervisory government agencies were reluctant to implement change. With the integration of government with enterprise, government agencies could control the personnel, finance and resources of enterprises and hence gain advantage from them. For example, the supervisory government agencies could require tourism enterprises to provide funds to them. The government agencies also represented and protected the interests of enterprises, and used their political influence to seek advantages such as interest-free loans and tax exemptions. As a key informant indicated: 'such an arrangement was beneficial to both sides [government agencies and enterprises]' and:

> For example, China Youth Travel Services was under the Communist Youth League at that time; the revenues earned were not required to be handed over to government and were also exempted from taxes. The League could directly allocate the revenues. The foreign affairs offices of local government were also involved in running travel businesses. The revenues reaped could be retained for their own use. Therefore, no one was willing to proceed with the separation.

REGULATORY FRAMEWORK FOR TOURISM

During this period of change from planned economy to a market economy, while the former ideology was still predominant it was also breaking down. The formulation of the 'Provisional Regulation on the Administration of Travel Agencies' by CNTA provides a typical example of the influence of the planned economy in the attempt of government agencies to intervene in the operation of enterprises. This regulation classified all travel agencies into one of three categories. Only the Category One travel agencies were allowed to negotiate directly with foreign tour operators. The Category Two agencies were responsible for receiving the tourists organized by those in Category One, and Category Three travel agencies could only run domestic travel business (Han Kehua, 1994). However, ultimately the regulation failed because of the high profitability of running Category One travel agencies and the lack of authority of the CNTA in monitoring its implementation. As a key informant noted 'actually many Category Three travel agencies conducted direct sales and marketing'.

Summary

This was a transitional period when the economic-oriented tourism policy paradigm was formed. During this period, under the new ideological orthodoxies – 'pragmatism', 'economic modernization', 'economic development' – the acute shortage of foreign exchange motivated the new Chinese leadership to consider international tourism as an effective foreign exchange earner. The ample tourism resources in China and restoration of diplomatic relationships with the west also convinced the Chinese leaders that China was ready for the economic development of tourism. The sharp increase of foreign exchange earned by international tourism convinced all the policy actors that tourism was an economic activity. Since the economic function of tourism was being recognized in this period, both political and economic goals were pursued. In institutional terms, the existing institutional arrangements initially were resistant to change which hindered the development of tourism and of institutional change but ultimately they were replaced to meet the new demands.

Period Three 1986–91: tourism as an economic industry

In the previous period, tourism as an economic activity commenced with direct intervention by the top leaders. Tourism development, however, was not placed on the national development agenda. So it was an important step when, in 1986, tourism, as an economic industry, was for the first time incorporated into the Five-Year State Plan for the National Economy and Social Development (Han Kehua, 1994; CNTA, 1995b). The position of tourism in the national economy was the next big issue for the policy-makers

This period is marked by debate and tension between the centrally planned economy and the market-oriented economy as the main model for China.

Marketization advanced incrementally where the market forces were allowed to function but under the planned-economy model. This was defined by the CPC as the 'Planned Commodity Economy'. However, further marketization also caused economic turmoil with an overheated economy and high inflation. This triggered the return of the central plan with austerity measures. Although the retrenched policy stopped the rise of inflation and calmed the overheated economy, China's GDP growth decreased to its lowest level. Subsequently the centralization was reversed and marketization revived. Generally speaking, the planned economy still dominated but was on the wane.

Tourism policy-making developed within the context of this ideological debate. On the basis of past experience the tourism sector, represented by the CNTA, was understood to be market-driven given that international and domestic demand was essentially beyond the scope of the central plan. The role of tourism policy-making therefore, at least in part, was considered to be to nurture the market. There was, however, a gap in conception about its role in the national economy between CNTA and the comprehensive government agencies and to this extent the evolution of the tourism policy paradigm to full marketization was held back by the planned-economy model. Tourism's strong growth and its prospects were insufficient to provide it with recognition.

Background

Policy-oriented learning by tourism agencies

As shown in Table 7.8, China enjoyed double-digit growth in GDP in 1986–8. This required more imports of raw materials, equipment and plant and hence demanded more foreign exchange. But at the same time the decrease in the price of oil in 1985 and 1986, which, together with textiles, was the major export earner, significantly weakened China's foreign exchange earning capacity. From 1986 to 1988, China's foreign exchange reserve was around US$2–3 billion, a sharp decline from over US$8 billion in 1984 (see Table 7.1). In this context the State Council expected tourism to play a more important role in economic development, especially in earning foreign exchange and generating employment (CNTA, 1995b, and interview). A key informant said:

> In 1985 and 1986, the international price of oil decreased greatly, leading to a decrease in the foreign exchange earned by oil. The central government placed increased emphasis on tourism and hoped that tourism could fill the gap in the insufficiency of foreign exchange.

In 1987, the Development Research Centre (DRC) of the State Council, CASS and CNTA jointly undertook the first strategic study of tourism development. Listed as a key study by the state and financed by the National Social Sciences Fund, this research project mainly examined the previous process, existing situation and foreign experience to reach a set of conclusions.

Table 7.8 Proportion of total tourism incomes in China's GDP 1985–2009

Year	International tourism income (US$bn) (a)	Exchange rate (US$ to RMB¥) (b)	International tourism income (RMB¥bn) (c) = (a x b)	Domestic tourism income (RMB¥bn) (d)	Total tourism income (RMB¥bn) (e) = (c + d)	GDP (RMB¥bn) (f)	Proportion (%) (g)=(e)/(f)
1985	1.25	2.94	3.68	8.0	11.68	896.4	1.30
1986	1.53	3.45	5.28	10.6	15.88	1020.2	1.56
1987	1.86	3.72	6.92	14.0	20.92	1196.3	1.75
1988	2.25	3.72	8.37	18.7	27.07	1492.8	1.81
1989	1.86	3.77	7.01	15.0	22.01	1690.9	1.30
1990	2.22	4.78	10.61	18.0	28.61	1854.8	1.54
1991	2.85	5.32	15.16	20.0	35.16	2161.8	1.63
1992	3.95	5.51	21.76	25.0	46.76	2663.8	1.76
1993	4.68	5.76	26.96	86.4	113.36	3463.4	3.27
1994	7.32	8.62	63.10	102.4	165.50	4675.9	3.54
1995	8.73	8.35	72.90	137.6	210.50	5847.8	3.60
1996	10.20	8.31	84.76	163.8	248.56	6788.5	3.66
1997	12.07	8.29	100.06	211.3	311.36	7446.3	4.18
1998	12.60	8.28	104.33	239.1	343.43	7939.6	4.33
1999	14.10	8.28	116.75	283.2	399.95	8206.8	4.87
2000	16.22	8.28	134.30	317.6	451.90	8946.8	5.05
2001	17.79	8.28	147.30	352.2	499.50	9731.5	5.13
2002	20.39	8.28	168.83	387.8	556.63	10517.2	5.29
2003	17.41	8.28	144.15	344.2	488.35	11739.0	4.16
2004	25.74	8.28	213.13	471.1	684.23	13687.6	5.00
2005	29.30	8.19	239.97	528.6	768.57	18308.5	4.20
2006	33.95	7.97	270.58	623.0	893.58	21087.1	4.24
2007	41.92	7.60	318.59	777.1	1095.69	24953.0	4.39
2008	40.80	6.84	279.07	874.9	1153.97	30067.0	3.84
2009	39.70	6.83	271.15	1020.0	1291.15	33535.3	3.85

Source: CNTA, 1985a–2009a; CNTA, 2010b; Wei, 1996; SSB, 1999–2009 and 2010.

First, the study identified that tourism was a 'sunrise' industry. Second, they concluded that tourism was an economic activity with salient cultural characteristics. Third, they took the view that development of tourism was primarily driven by the market and consumption. Fourth, they recognized that both international and domestic tourism can significantly contribute to the national economy in terms of total income, employment and links to other related industries. And fifth, the study advocated expanding tourism from an economic activity to an industry with a development pace exceeding the growth rate of GDP (source: interviews). However, the elevation of tourism to recognition as an industry touched on its position in the national economy and hence required the acceptance and support of the comprehensive government agencies.

In addition to policy research, other sources of policy-oriented learning appeared. With China's further opening to the world, the government took deliberate actions to learn from countries with advanced tourism sectors. As a part of this senior government officials, business leaders and prominent scholars from other parts of the world were appointed to advisory positions in government and industry associations. For example the former First Deputy Prime Minister of Singapore was appointed by the State Council as consultant to the Chinese government on tourism. A team was set up by CNTA to study his recommendations. Similarly Hong Kong business leaders and foreign scholars were elected as honorary advisors to the newly established China Tourism Association. Further, foreign experts from the United Nations World Tourism Organization (UNWTO) and academics were invited to provide consultancy advice. In 1987, the Secretary-General of UNWTO visited Tibet and provided recommendations on its tourism development. Organized by the CNTA, the former head of the British Tourist Authority and academics delivered talks for CNTA and local bureaus. The central government also actively sent delegations overseas for visits and conferences. Government delegations visited both developed and developing regions with rapidly developing and market-led tourism industries, including Singapore, Thailand, the Philippines, Hong Kong, the United States. In 1987, CNTA attended a ministerial conference on tourism in developing countries organized by UNWTO and West Germany (CNTA, 1995b). These learning engagements all helped shape a market-oriented angle.

A slowdown in market growth, a relaxation in domestic investment and a deterioration of tourism quality served to quicken this move to a more market-oriented approach to tourism. When it first opened its doors in 1978, tourists flooded to China almost regardless of quality, varieties and prices. One key informant described it as follows:

> In the initial period of China's opening to the foreign world, international arrivals were not demanding or picky. They felt fine as long as accommodation was available. In fact, there were not as many attractions or recreational facilities as today; not all areas of the Summer Palace and

Forbidden City were opened to tourists. At that time, international tourists just came to see China.

High growth rates of 20 per cent on average were recorded between 1978 and 1987 except for 1982. With excess demand and limited capacity, the government placed first priority on facilities and gave little attention to marketing or market research. Actually under the planned economy, production and distribution were set by central plan and administrative orders and there was no need for marketing and promotion. A key informant said: 'marketing was simply not required in the planned-economy era'. In the mindsets of officials and practitioners, prosperous tourism was taken for granted because of China's particular tourism resources. All that was needed was to expand capacity. Prior to access by domestic investors, the delivery of tourism businesses was monopolized by the 'tourism system' or 'tourism *xitong*'. And front-line employees were knowledgeable, well-trained and stuck to the working codes of those dealing with foreign affairs. Making short-term money was not their goal. Hence service quality was maintained at a satisfactory level. A key informant remarked that: 'tour guides dared not be reckless, they were subject to the disciplines of foreign affairs. However, the foreign affairs ethos has declined since the entry of domestic investors.'

China's tourism capacity expanded after 1984. The number of hotel rooms increased from over 76,900 in 1984 to over 220,000 in 1988. In 1988, there were 1,573 travel agencies (see Tables 7.6 and 7.7). Investment in hotels and travel services established post 1984 came from various government agencies. For example, around 1,900 hotels in 1990 were run by more than 430 government agencies or non-administrative organizations within more than twenty '*xitongs*'. The government agencies in charge of these included the CNTA (i.e. 'tourism *xitong*'), Ministry of Foreign Affairs (i.e. 'foreign affairs *xitong*'), Ministry of Public Security, Ministry of Culture, Office of Overseas Chinese Affairs under the State Council, the All China Federation of Trade Unions and the Communist Youth League (CNTA, 1992b). In accordance with the rule of the '*xitong*', tourism enterprises were administered by the government agencies in charge for their respective '*xitongs*'. In this context the CNTA found it hard to intervene in other '*xitongs*'.

Not all government agencies invested in tourism for commercial reasons. Non-economic motives were diverse, including providing venues for meetings, entertainment, staff welfare and even job opportunities for the children of staff members. For example, the China Industrial and Commercial Bank established country-wide training centres with hotel and recreational facilities. Because of their non-business purposes, such tourism enterprises were eligible for privileges unavailable to others including investment funds and tax advantages and exemptions. The existence of such enterprises, which were offering services to tourists, had three implications. First, they did not, as a matter of course, enhance their service quality. Second, they could operate their business at low prices. Some simply needed to cover their variable costs, leaving fixed costs of buildings and facilities to their supervising agencies. Third, as part of different '*xitongs*', they did not fall within the purview of the CNTA. A further issue was that the employees of such enterprises outside the tourism '*xitong*' were not subject to foreign affairs disciplines and many actively sought material rewards. With the government at the time focusing on quantity rather than quality this meant that service quality could not be maintained. Once the initial flood of demand for tourism in China receded, tourists became more demanding and began to judge quality in China against international standards. As a key informant indicated:

> After 'China fever', repeat or new international tourists became very demanding since their expectation levels were raised. They expected the quality of tourism products in China to be comparable to international levels. They did not expect to suffer from hardship on their tours of China.

Being a long distance from her major international tourism markets made China a relatively high-cost destination in air fares alone. This had the effect of raising quality expectations. From 1986 to 1988, the growth rates of tourist arrivals fell to below the level of 1985 (see Table 7.4) and in 1988, the American market declined for the first time. The situation was compounded the next year when, after the June 4th Incident, total tourist arrivals actually dropped by 22.7 per cent (Table 7.4).

In order to compete, tourism enterprises had no option but to cut prices, leading to a price war among hotels and travel agencies that lasted until the late 1990s. As a result, service quality deteriorated. CNTA acknowledged that quality was at an alarmingly low level. An article by a CNTA official in the *China Tourism News* ('*Zhongguo Luyou Bao*') in September 1989 pointed out that tourist complaints about quality had become increasingly severe, reflecting a large gap between 'hardware' (facilities) and 'software' (quality) (*China Tourism News*, 1989). CNTA envisaged this critical issue in its organizational journal *Tourism Studies* ('*Luyou Diaoyan*'), that poor quality in the tourism industry was reflected in services, professionalism and ethics (CNTA, 1990b). Since then, government and industry have learned that tourist demand is dynamic and beyond administrative control.

The ultimate reason for the decline in quality was ascribed to the lack of institution building, especially market-oriented institutions. In this context a move away from micro control toward 'industry management' became important. Decentralization inside the 'tourism *xitong*' together with relaxation in market access had represented institutional change to the planned-economy model as well as the beginning of the creation of market-oriented institutions. This generated economic incentives and created a range of stakeholders. However, without a corresponding regulatory framework the outcome was a fairly chaotic market place. The CNTA clearly understood this and recognized the need for innovative change. Its proposal was to abandon the notion of the '*xitong*' and establish a system of 'industry management' for the various stakeholders, most of whom were administrative bodies. A key informant acknowledged: 'We saw that many travel businesses were run by non-tourism government agencies or their subordinate enterprises. The traditional "tourism system" could not manage in this situation. Therefore, we initiated the "industry management" measure.' Also,

> In the initial period of the 1980s, the term 'tourism system' was frequently used and referred to. Nevertheless, the 'tourism system' faded away in the late 1980s; the notion of the 'tourism industry' emerged. When funds from foreign and domestic investors were allowed access, the notion of the 'tourism industry' intensified. Although these travel businesses were not under the 'tourism system', they actually existed in the tourism sector.

'Industry management' required central and local administrations to shift from micro control of enterprises in the '*xitong*' to sector management, formulating development plans (or guidelines) and establishing market-oriented institutions with incentives and controls. This approach to 'industry management' sought to enable the CNTA and local tourism administrations to break the rigidity of the '*xitong*' and to manage the whole industry. But its effective implementation depended on the extension of CNTA's authority.

'Industry management' ('*Hangye Guanli*') in this sense was a new idea in line with the developments in market reform. The notion of 'industry' in China was relatively weak. After 1949, under the planned economy, the term 'production departments or units' ('*shengchan bumen*') was used as the official name for China's economic sectors. This reflected the way in which government agencies or departments controlled the production and distribution of their subordinate enterprises. During the Cultural Revolution, the name 'production departments' was replaced by 'battlefronts' ('*zhan xian*') in line with the 'politics-in-command' orthodoxy. In the early reform era, the term '*xitong*' emerged (CNTA, 1996b). '*Xitong*' referred to a model in which government functions, enterprise functions and interest arrangements were institutionalized together. The introduction of 'industry management' demonstrated the extent to which the concept of 'market' had become established in tourism.

For the CNTA, it was considered important to follow international practice in exercising industry management both to obtain the support of foreign investors and to satisfy the demands of international tourists for quality products (CNTA, 1996b). For example, the implementation of a 'hotel star-rating' system followed international norms. A key informant commented: 'the hotel star-rating programme was more scientific and was appreciated by the hotels'. More importantly, the banner of international norms, rather than directly referring to 'market-oriented transformation', made it politically acceptable for both pro-plan and pro-market supporters. In this way the tourism policy paradigm evolved, in the context of a centrally planned model, but with its focus and essence now on marketization.

Policy-oriented learning by comprehensive government agencies

In general, the comprehensive agencies supported the development of tourism as an economic activity. However, their conceptions of its role in the national economy were mixed. As a result, their degree of support for tourism varied in accordance with views emanating from the leaders. One key informant remarked: 'the comprehensive government agencies all supported the development of tourism but their support could not always be relied upon'.

HISTORICAL PRIORITIES

The Chinese government classified economic industries and activities into three sectors: primary (agriculture, fishing, etc.); secondary (heavy and light industry and construction) and tertiary (service industries including tourism) (SSB, 2008). As discussed in Chapter 4, since 1949 the Chinese government had placed priority on industry and agriculture. By 1978 the primary and secondary sectors dominated Chinese output and employment, with the primary sector accounting for 28.1 per cent of GDP and 70.5 per cent of employment, and the secondary sector, headed by heavy industry, contributing 48.2 per cent of GDP and 17.3 per cent of employment (SSB, 2005). The tertiary sector was barely recognized. The background to this industrial structure provided an important context in creating the mindsets of those involved in planning the Chinese economy, especially in the State Planning Commission established in 1950 and its successor bodies. By 1978 most bureaucrats were wedded to the importance of the primary and secondary sectors and to state planning (Lieberthal and Oksenberg, 1988; Saich, 2004). This goes some way to explain why views about tourism were mixed and why non-positive views toward tourism remained even when both international and domestic tourism were demonstrating such strong potential.

TOURISM IN THE NATIONAL ECONOMY

As discussed earlier, travel services and guest houses for international tourists had never been incorporated into China's planned-economy system before 1978 and nor had social hostels which provided basic accommodation for Chinese travellers. In Mao's China, the government strictly controlled social mobility (Lieberthal, 1995; Ogden, 1995), resulting in limited demand for travel. In general, travel services, guest houses and social hostels were seen as a 'non-productive' sector of the economy.

After 1978, while the economic function of tourism began to be recognized, particularly in relation to foreign exchange earnings, it took the decline in the foreign exchange earning capacity of the oil producing sector to prompt the incorporation of tourism into the national economic and social plan. But even with this move its role in the national economy was still viewed with some scepticism and its recognition was still slight compared with the attention devoted to other industries. Basically, as in many other countries, tourism in

China was regarded as insignificant in comparison to industry and agriculture, and modernization of the economy was thought to be associated with industrialization. A key informant revealed that:

> The comprehensive government agencies were accustomed to view tourism in the planned-economy context. In this they attached importance to agriculture and industries and considered tourism as petty and unimportant. Tourism was simply viewed as an activity of 'dining, drinking, enjoyment and amusement' ('*Chi*', '*He*', '*Wan*', '*Le*').

In fact, tourism failed to convince SPC and MoF of its economic significance in the national economy in this period. In 1991, total income from international and domestic tourism accounted for only 1.6 per cent of GDP (see Table 7.8) and although tourism receipts rose sharply from 1978, they contributed most to the local level rather than to central incomes, since the majority of tourism enterprises were owned by local government.

In the era of the planned economy, economic growth was mainly viewed as a supply-side matter flowing from state investment in industry and agriculture. As a demand-driven sector, with demand restrained by the national plan, tourism was not viewed as important. Indeed the Chinese government encouraged people to create and accumulate wealth to provide more resources for development, not to consume it. The political slogan 'production is foremost, life is second' captured the thinking of the time. Hence domestic tourism, as a kind of consumption, was almost considered non-constructive to economic development. It was certainly not conceived as a development vehicle by the comprehensive agencies, even though local authorities increasingly recognized domestic tourism.

One informant further remarked about the societal views of domestic tourism:

> Between 1949 and 1978, the party and government educated the people to live on hardship and to strive for socioeconomic construction, rather than to spend on consumption. The people were inspired to create or accumulate wealth, rather than to consume . . . , touring and recreation were not a correct lifestyle.

and,

> From a political and educational perspective, the government always stressed plain living ('jianku pusu'). And, the Chinese ancestors also regarded 'hardworking' and 'plain living' as virtues, people should save their surpluses. Elders accumulated wealth for the younger generations; parents did so for their children. Neither government nor society recognized 'recreation' and 'touring' as the right kind of consumption. And, touring and recreation were always criticized and condemned in the

past. In the mindset of the people, there was no such notion of 'leisure'; such a kind of consumption was not recognized. Encouragement was not given to 'travel' and 'tour', any surplus money should be saved and then transferred to the state for investment. In the past, people's consumption of books, food and clothing etc were regarded as 'correct consumption', while consumption of travel and leisure were viewed as 'incorrect'.

If this were not sufficient to hold back the recognition of tourism, it was also seen as an activity of the developed world. When a large proportion of China's population still lived in poverty, tourist activity was further associated with a lavish lifestyle and viewed as inadequate for development by the comprehensive agencies. And certainly it was inappropriate under traditional socialist ethics and Chinese values which canonized plain living. As late as 1986 and 1987, the CPC and State Council jointly issued a notice to prohibit leisure travel by government officials through public funds (CNTA, 1995b). As a result, domestic tourism, which does not earn foreign exchange, was not justified as a valid consumption. From the viewpoints of the comprehensive agencies, consumption of daily necessities such as food and clothes was valid. Thus, domestic tourism was regarded as a 'non-productive force'.

To sum up, tourism as an economic activity in this period failed to capture the attention of the comprehensive agencies and generally tourism was unable to demonstrate its economic significance in the national economy. In the context of tourism policy, while 'industry management' became a part of the paradigm, this was not really yet true for market orientation.

Basic tourism policy decisions

It was during this period that tourism was officially declared as an economic activity in the national plan with economic goals as its overt purpose. Tourism was designated as one of the three largest foreign exchange earners (CNTA, 1995b: p.58). Premier Zhao Ziyang remarked on the economic development of tourism on 21 January 1986, when meeting the Director-General of CNTA and other delegates at the National Tourism Works Conference:

> Tourism development by the state has an important meaning, tourism is an important component of China's economic construction and one of three 'pillars' in earning foreign exchange – trade, tourism and the export of labour. Now, we should incorporate tourism into the development plan of government at every administrative level. The state should incorporate tourism into the national plan, as should local government. Tourism should be considered from the perspective of development strategy.
>
> (CNTA, 1995b: p.58)

On 12 April 1986, the National People's Congress endorsed 'The Seventh Five-Year State Plan for National Economy and Social Development (1986–1990)'.

Tourism was for the first time incorporated as an economic activity. The Plan stated clearly 'the state will make a great effort to develop tourism in order to reap more foreign exchange and to promote friendly relations among nations' (CNTA, 1995b: p.60). The political goal of tourism development was also seen as important, but it was now placed after the economic goal and to underpin the economic development of tourism. In addition to the promotion of friendship, the political goal of tourism also shifted to be more defensive in safeguarding China's socialist fabric when faced with the influence of Western ideologies, values, cultures and lifestyles.

In 1986, the State Council, through the State Planning Commission, provided CNTA with RMB¥500 million annually for development for five years, with 30 per cent in grants and 70 per cent in loans. The ratio of grants was later reduced to 18 per cent, considerably reducing its potential impact. Therefore by the end of the 1990s, CNTA had only provided a total amount of around RMB¥120 million for four development projects – Qinhuai River located in Nanjing, Lijiang Project in Guilin, Shaanxi History Museum and Mausoleum of the First Qin Emperor (Terracotta Army). With limited grant aid, CNTA could only assist in relatively small projects such as the construction of toilets in tourist attractions (source: interviews). Indeed, at this time China faced an acute shortage of investment funds and while the allocation of RMB¥500 million demonstrated the commitment of central government, it rested with local government and others to explore funding channels. It was estimated that local government invested roughly RMB¥2–3 billion.

The conservative approach to the tourism development of the first period gradually eased and with the exception of civil aviation, the supply of facilities for tourists gradually began to meet demand by the end of the 1980s. At the same time the tourism development strategy started to shift towards marketing, quality enhancement and industry administration, especially after the June 4th Incident in 1989.

Concrete tourism policy decisions

The emergence of tourism marketing

Without a consensus yet on the establishment of a market economy, the development of market-oriented institutions was only in its early stages. Indeed the initiatives on tourism marketing and industry management later adopted by the CNTA actually originated from local tourism officials. This began in Beijing, which is one of four municipalities directly under central government, with its party secretary appointed as a Politburo member of the CPC. It was here in the mid-1980s that the Director of the Beijing Tourism Administration introduced, for the first time, a marketing campaign – to mark the Year of the Dragon. Given the status of Beijing, this obviously set an example for the CNTA and other local bureaus and so, after the tourism downturn resulting from the June 4th Incident, the CNTA began a series of promotional campaigns.

Institutional changes

The reform of tourism institutions in the previous historical period to a large extent focused on quantity, as a result of which supply generally met demand. However, quality was insufficient in nearly all aspects of tourism. In the hotel sector, there was a significant mismatch between facilities and services, i.e. luxury hotels with poor service quality (*China Tourism News*, 1989). For the travel agencies, complaints about tour guides became more and more acute especially in relation to the demand for tips. To address these issues a number of measures were introduced relating to industry management.

INDUSTRY MANAGEMENT BY CNTA

The absence of quality benchmarks was a main cause of the mismatch between facilities and service quality in the hotel sector. The 'industry management' concept facilitated the building of tourism institutions, but its effective implementation partly depended on whether CNTA would be granted adequate authority. The deterioration of tourism quality and the decline in tourist demand after 1989 meant that this became an urgent matter. In a policy proposal made to the State Council, the CNTA drafted around fifty items relating to the introduction of 'industry management', including the clear delineation of scope and responsibilities. Strong opposition came from about twelve departments and agencies. Notwithstanding this it was generally agreed that CNTA should be given responsibility for the administration of the whole industry, rather than just its own '*xitong*', but in the end details were lacking and 'industry management' tended to be nominal.

THE HOTEL STAR-RATING PROGRAMME

The lack of concrete authority did not mean that the implementation of 'industry management' would fail and nor did it follow that the grant of authority would ensure success. In many ways more important was the extent to which CNTA built up its own authority as a market-oriented agency. Its work in hotel star-rating provides an excellent example of successful development in this regard.

Influenced by poor quality levels internally and by international practice, CNTA began carefully to formulate quality benchmarks for China's tourist hotels. In doing this it proceeded cautiously and with wide consultation. In 1987, a series of seminars to explore domestic opinions were held by CNTA involving hotels, local tourism bureaus, travel agencies and academics. Later, a seminar with Hong Kong hotel practitioners was held to explore the feasibility of a hotel star-rating in China. Subsequently, a senior Spanish tourism official commissioned by UNWTO was invited to conduct consultancy work. After visiting over 110 different hotels in fifteen tourist cities, in-depth discussions were held with CNTA on general guidelines, methods and quality benchmarks and consensus was reached. Finally in 1988, the State Council approved the implementation of 'Star Standard and Star-Rating of Tourist Hotels in the People's Republic of China' (simply the 'Hotel Star-Rating Standards') on a non-mandatory basis. Its non-compulsory feature was crucial in avoiding controversy with other agencies and gaining acceptance. After an experimental implementation in major tourist cities, the system was introduced nationwide in 1990 (CNTA, 1995b).

IDEOLOGICAL REGULATIONS

The Communist Party and government never considered weakening the political goals of tourism, and leaders and senior officials kept alert to its political dimension. In March 1985, the Secretariat Meeting of the CPC remarked: 'Obtaining commissions privately and asking for tips will not increase social wealth. This misconduct is purely for pursuing personal interests and will be detrimental to national interest and prestige' (CNTA, 1995b: p.53).

A Politburo member of CPC, Qiao Shi, attended to the issue of tips and commissions and in November 1986 instructed the CNTA to formulate rules for its prohibition (CNTA, 1995b). The 'Ban on Receiving Commissions and Tips in the Tourism Business' was issued and implemented by the CNTA in 1987 in order to safeguard socialist values and withstand the influence of capitalist business practices. The Chinese government also intensified the use of tourism as a channel to promote Socialist China and to counteract the proliferation of Western ideologies and values. In 1986, the State Council promulgated the 'Administrative Methods on the Internal Television System in Hotels'. According to this, the internal TV system was to promote China's socialism to hotel guests. This stated 'The internal TV system is not only a service provided by the hotels, but also a window for tourists to understand China and our propaganda tool. It should become our frontline in promoting China's socialism' (CNTA, 1995b: p.58).

Summary

This was a period of struggle for tourism. Although it had been realized that both international and domestic tourism were market oriented and consumption driven, based on the past development experience, it was difficult to establish market-oriented tourism policy under the dominance of China's planned economy. The strong market growth of domestic tourism was disregarded. As a result the tourism policy paradigm only saw a partial movement toward the market in the form of international norms, significantly the introduction of 'hotel star-rating', which became a key element in the influence of CNTA.

Since tourism was officially declared as an economic activity in the national plan, the economic goal of tourism became its overt purpose. It was designated as one of the three largest foreign exchange earners.

Period Four 1992–7: tourism as an important industry

Background

As outlined in Chapter 4, the CPC's ideological orthodoxies underwent a major change after 1978. The debates regarding the planned and market economy officially ended in 1992 when CPC formally announced the establishment of the 'Socialist Market Economy'. This cleared the previous impasse and led to a breakthrough allowing tourism to be developed as a 'market-driven' activity. This period therefore is one of change and exploration in the move from economic administration to economic regulation and in deciding how best to achieve market orientation in a Chinese context. The relationship between government agencies and market forces was a particular concern since many of the market forces in China originated in the government agencies and associated organizations. In this sense, except for the recognition of domestic tourism, the essentials of the tourism policy paradigm did not experience significant change, since both the CNTA and the macro-management agencies maintained their role in relation to market forces. In the previous historical period, market-oriented institutionalization had taken place under the banner of international norms and practices. Now the government had no hesitation in launching full institutionalization to establish market mechanisms. However, the institutionalization still lacked clear focus. Eventually the CNTA came to the view that the development and implementation of quality standards was an effective tool in exercising industry management. In summary, this is a preparatory stage for innovations and developments which took place after 1997.

Policy-oriented learning by the CNTA and macro-management agencies

Both the CNTA and macro-management agencies monitored tourism development in the market economy very closely and began to gear their thoughts and approaches to this. The CNTA in particular was concerned with developing effective ways of managing the industry in a market context. A key informant explained it as follows:

> Our policy-making for tourism [CNTA] is a trial-and-error process. Our thinking about tourism, especially domestic tourism, has undergone a transition from the planned economy to the market economy. Nowadays we understand that consumption is good regardless of how people consume. We previously considered that consumption needed to be valid

and correct, [domestic] tourism was not correct consumption; international tourists could come to consume, but domestic people were not encouraged to do so.

Deng Xiaoping's southern inspection tour and the subsequent implementation of the market economy greatly accelerated economic development. China's GDP sharply rose from RMB¥2,664 billion in 1992 to ¥6,789 billion in 1996, a growth of 150 per cent, bringing a corresponding increase in urban disposable income from RMB¥2,027 to ¥4,839 (see Tables 7.8 and 7.9). More leisure time also became available. The State Council adopted the five-day working week in alternate weeks in 1994 and weekly from 1995. All of these factors contributed to the boom in outbound travel and the expansion of domestic tourism which began to show great potential. In 1996, domestic tourists grew to 640 million arrivals, up by 94 per cent from 1992; receipts rose from RMB¥25 billion to ¥163.8 billion, almost double the receipts from international arrivals (see Tables 7.3, 7.5 and 7.8). Domestic tourists became the main market in many regions. Meanwhile self-financed outbound leisure travel also grew and extended way beyond sponsored family travel to Hong Kong and Macau. In 1996, around 5 million outbound tourists spent a total of US$4.5 billion, compared to 2.9 million spending US$2.5 billion in 1992 (CNTA, 1993a–1997a).

Slow growth in the primary and secondary sectors turned attention to the market-driven tertiary sector. 'The Decision to Speed up the Development of the Tertiary Sector' was jointly made by the CPC and the State Council in 1992. Tourism was included as one of the key industries in the tertiary sector, together with insurance, real estate, financial services, insurance etc (CNTA, 1995c: p.4).

The new essentials of the tourism policy paradigm

As a demand-driven sector, tourism generally fitted well with the new market-economy orthodoxy. Perhaps the most important change from the past was the inclusion of domestic tourism, although even changes about this had been flagged in the previous period. For example, in 1986, the CNTA had organized a nation-wide seminar, where, influenced by its importance to local economies, all participating parties had requested a rethink of the 'Three-No' policy decision for domestic tourism. When the ideological orthodoxies shifted and the demand side was formally accepted as a means of development, the importance of domestic tourism was readily acknowledged as addressed by

Table 7.9 Accumulated wealth of Chinese people 1978–2007

Year	GNP (RMB bn)	Growth rate (%)	Annual disposable household income (urban) (RMB) (per head)	Growth rate (%)	Annual disposable household income (rural) (RMB) (per head)	Growth rate (%)	Total savings (RMB bn)	Growth rate (%)
1978	362.4	–	343.4	–	133.6	–	2.6	–
1980	451.8	24.7	477.6	39.1	191.3	43.2	40.0	85.0
1985	898.9	99.0	739.1	54.8	397.6	107.8	162.3	306.2
1986	1,020.1	13.5	899.6	21.7	423.8	6.6	223.8	37.9
1987	1,195.5	17.2	1,002.2	11.4	462.6	9.2	307.3	37.3
1988	1,492.2	24.8	1,181.4	17.9	544.9	17.8	380.2	23.7
1989	1,691.8	13.4	1,375.7	16.4	601.5	10.4	514.7	35.4
1990	1,859.8	9.9	1,510.2	9.8	686.3	14.1	703.4	36.7
1991	2,166.3	16.5	1,700.6	12.6	708.6	3.2	910.7	29.5
1992	2,665.2	23.0	2,026.6	19.2	784.0	10.6	1,154.5	26.8
1993	3,456.1	29.7	2,577.4	27.2	921.6	17.6	1,476.2	27.9
1994	4,667.0	35.0	3,496.2	35.6	1,221.0	32.5	2,151.9	45.8
1995	5,749.5	23.2	4,283.0	22.5	1,577.7	29.2	2,966.2	37.8
1996	6,685.1	16.3	4,838.9	13.0	1,926.1	22.1	3,852.1	29.9
1997	7,314.3	9.4	5,160.3	6.6	2,090.1	8.5	4,628.0	20.1
1998	7,801.8	6.7	5,425.1	5.1	2,162.0	3.4	5,340.7	15.4
1999	8,057.9	3.3	5,854.0	7.91	2,210.3	2.23	5,962.2	11.64
2000	8,825.4	9.5	6,280.0	7.28	2,253.4	1.95	6,433.2	7.90
2001	9,572.8	8.5	6,859.6	9.23	2,366.4	5.01	7,376.2	14.66
2002	10,393.5	8.6	7,702.8	12.29	2,475.6	4.61	8,691.1	17.83
2003	11,674.1	12.3	8,472.2	9.99	2,622.2	5.92	10,361.7	19.22
2004	13,658.4	17.0	9,422.0	11.21	2,936.0	11.97	11,955.5	15.38
2005	18,396.6	34.7	10,493.0	11.4	3,255.0	10.9	14,105.1	18.0
2006	21,180.8	15.1	11,759.0	12.1	3,587.0	10.2	16,158.7	14.6
2007	25,148.3	18.7	13,786.0	17.2	4,140.0	15.4	17,253.4	6.8

Source: SSB, 1996–2008.

the 'Decision to Actively Develop Domestic Tourism' issued by the State Council in 1993:

> The boom and development of domestic tourism has satisfied the increasing needs of our people both materially and spiritually . . . extended consumption choices, promoted related industries and sectors (e.g. transportation, light industry, commerce, building services, gardening and catering), expanded employment, promoted economic-cultural exchanges between the regions, boosted local economies, and so played an active role in socioeconomic development.
>
> (CNTA, 1995c: p.336)

However, some officials still placed more emphasis on international tourism, as reflected by the CNTA (1996b: p.252) that 'some of our comrades still lack an understanding of the significance and role of domestic tourism, they still consider that international tourism is more important than domestic tourism'. While acknowledging the needs of outbound travel, the Chinese government in this period believed that this type of tourism should be controlled, because of its foreign exchange implications, the immaturity of Chinese tourists and possible illegal emigration. A key informant remarked:

> We have three reasons to control the development of outbound tourism. The first is the leakage of foreign exchange. China is a developing country, so foreign exchange is a valuable resource. Secondly, our tourists are largely immature, they may receive unsatisfactory treatment when travelling abroad; if they have travelled domestically, they will be familiar with some travelling arrangements. Thirdly, we are also concerned about possible illegal stays overseas.

Illegal emigration was a real concern. For example, 113 outbound tourists on a trip organized by an agency in Northern China remained illegally in South Korea in 1993. In 1994, a further fourteen tourists were reported as not returning from a tour (CNTA, 1996b: pp.283–4).

In terms of the tourism policy paradigm this period is marked by tourism being formally recognized as a market-oriented and consumption-driven industry within the context of the Socialist Market-Economy Model. Both international and domestic tourism were recognized as important, with international tourism having particular prominence in terms of its foreign exchange earning function, while outbound travel was recognized but not encouraged.

Basic tourism policy decisions

The changes in basic policy decisions began from 1993 when the State Council urged local government to encourage the development of domestic tourism. In the mid-1990s, the CNTA changed the development strategy significantly 'to develop inbound tourism with great endeavour, to develop domestic tourism actively and to develop outbound travel adequately'. This strategy lasted for around a decade until 2005.

Concrete tourism policy decisions

The concrete decisions for tourism were all market oriented. On the demand side they focused on strengthening the marketing efforts of the CNTA; on the supply side, the CNTA explored ways of dealing with market forces. In the previous period, the move toward marketization was partial. Now the CNTA geared its institutional building to deal with a market-driven sector. The question was what kind of market rules should be established. With more and more policy decisions required, there was also need for more coordination with other agencies.

Demand side

In terms of marketing, a number of measures were introduced to stimulate market growth. Starting in 1992, the CNTA launched annual mass promotion campaigns with themes as given in Table 7.10. The CNTA also formulated segmentation strategies. The 'major market' focused on countries with strong growth potential (South Korea in 1994 and Germany in 1995), while the 'niche market' referred to those to which specific products were offered (e.g. the Muslims in the ASEAN countries, high-school students). In order effectively to launch these campaigns, China officially joined the Pacific–Asia Travel Association (PATA) in 1993 and also tried every opportunity to attend or hold exhibitions. The promotional budget also doubled in this period from US$3.2 million to US$6.4 million.

Supply side

As far as supply is concerned, the central government began to reduce its role in the direct investment in and operation of tourist facilities and development, except where deemed necessary. At the same time the CNTA turned its attention toward operating with the market. Given that quality deterioration was a persistent issue, the focus was placed on establishing market institutions that would concentrate on this aspect.

PRODUCT DEVELOPMENT

Recognizing that, for international tourists, resort-based tourism would possibly become more important than sightseeing trips, CNTA initiated the construction of twelve state-level resorts in 1992 designed to combine traditional sightseeing with holidaymaking. This development was readily accepted by the ten central agencies involved, hence implementation was smooth. The sites were

Table 7.10 Thematic tourism marketing launched by the
           CNTA 1992–2010

Years	Marketing themes
1992	Visit China
1993	China Landscape
1994	China Heritage
1995	China Folklore
1996	China Holiday Resorts
1997	Visit China
1998	China City & Country Tour
1999	China Eco-Environments
2000	New Millennium
2001	China Sports & Athletes
2002	China Folks & Festivals
2003	China Cooking
2004	China Lives
2005	Visit China
2006	China Countryside
2007	China Harmony
2008	China Olympics
2009	China Eco-tours
2010	China World Expo Tourism Year
2011	China Cultural Tour

Source: CNTA, 1998b; CNTA's official website (www.cnta.gov.cn).

leased for commercial development attracting both domestic and foreign investment. These twelve resorts are now operational and include the Golden Stone Beach in Dalian, Stone Old Man Holiday Resort in Qindao, Yalong Bay in Hainan and Hengsha in Shanghai. They mainly attract international tourists.

EXPLORATORY ESTABLISHMENT OF MARKET INSTITUTIONS

A number of changes were made to previous regulations more suited to the planned economy. The 'Regulation on the Administration of Travel Agencies' was implemented in 1996 replacing a previous one. This revoked the regulation designating three categories of travel agencies, replacing it with two legal forms of travel businesses – international travel agencies dealing with inbound, out-bound and domestic travel services, and domestic travel agencies confined to internal travel business. Before 1992, foreign investment was only allowed in the hotel sector, now foreign investment was permitted for joint-venture travel agencies within the state-level resorts. Foreign investors were also permitted in the aviation business, jointly with China, including airlines, airports and maintenance but excluding aviation control. The Hainan Airline became the first airline to receive foreign investment. Some fifteen corporations in aircraft maintenance and ground services were established with foreign investment.

As far as quality is concerned the CNTA recognized the importance of this for the future of China's tourism. One of its slogans initiated in the early 1990s, 'services provision should be up to quality', pointed to the underlying concerns that quality was falling short. After the June 4th Incident in 1989, CNTA carried out quality inspections of travel agencies; their licences could be revoked if the products and services offered proved unsatisfactory (CNTA, 1995b). However, there was no substantial improvement in quality during the 1990s. An article published in *China Tourism News* observed an interesting phenomenon that tourism quality varied inversely with the recovery and growth of the market, that is, quality levels declined with market boom and vice versa (Wei, 1996). In addition to 'tourism quality', 'market order' and 'customer satisfaction' also became a part of the institutional logic under the market economy.

In response, the CNTA proposed some more coercive measures. For example, 'The Regulation on Quality Service Guarantee Funds of Travel Agencies' required all agencies to deposit a sum of cash in banks designated by the CNTA as a guarantee of services quality. The 'Tour Guide Registration Measure' was implemented in 1995 to improve the services and competences of tour guides. All tourist guides were required to be registered with only those who passed the CNTA's examination eligible for registration, and complaints from tourists could lead to deregistration. More importantly and interestingly, as a way of operating effectively in a market economy, was the experience of the CNTA in establishing quality standards. The CNTA's experience with the introduction of non-mandatory star-rating had been successful both in attracting voluntary participants and in establishing quality. It had also been successful in establishing the CNTA as the lead body in this field. In 1993 the then Ministry of Domestic Trade (renamed the State Domestic Trade Bureau in 1998) issued the 'Standards Grading for Guesthouses, Hostels and Restaurants' primarily for domestic tourists, that also stretched to tourist hotels. However, this measure failed to obtain industry support both in 1993 and again in 1994. In the meantime the CNTA's successful non-mandatory approach, with the support from the State General Administration of Quality Supervision, Inspection and Quarantine (SGAQSIQ) (i.e. the quality agency), was extended to four sets of quality standards covering cruises on the Yangtze River, tour guides, tour automobiles, and signs and symbols of tourism. The key message for the CNTA was that non-mandatory quality standards provided an effective way of exercising control in a market economy provided the market and industry found them helpful.

Conclusion

This chapter examines the evolution of policy-making and tourism development from the second to fourth periods which all belong to Deng's era. In the second period, from 1978 to 1985, tourism made the transition from being simply a political vehicle to becoming an economic activity, albeit with resistance from the existing tourism institutions. Tourism was formally recognized as an economic industry at the start of the third period, between 1986 and 1991. At this stage tourism began to be accepted as a market-driven activity by the CNTA and industry but, with the planned economy still in place, the shift to the market was partial. The years from 1992 to 1997 represent the fourth period when the policy-making and tourism development began fully to be geared to the market economy and work began in learning how to handle the market economy. This then lays the groundwork for the rapid changes after 1997 covered in Chapter 8.

8　The Collective Leadership era

This chapter covers Period Five from 1997 to the present, referred to as the Collective Leadership era. Alongside the great shifts in China's ideological direction, tourism policy showed enormous change during this period. Notably tourism started to act as a multifunctional strategic sector with political–ideological, diplomatic and socio-cultural dimensions underpinned by economic and market-driven development. At the same time government functions shifted from being dominant to providing guidance to market forces and quality assurance frameworks were developed. The leaders still had the final word in decision-making but local government exercised increasing influence.

Period Five 1997–present: tourism as a multifunctional strategic industry

Background

The period began with the juxtaposition of two different approaches to the role of tourism. The new view sought to justify the promotion of tourism on the basis of its role in boosting economic development. This is reflected in CNTA's policy document 'Tourism as a New Growth Pole of the National Economy' (1999c: p.3) which suggested: 'During the great process of China's economic development and the establishment of the Socialist Market Economy, tourism is increasingly exhibiting its enormous potential as a new growth pole of the national economy.' The more established view emphasized its contribution to the quality of life. This was captured in 2001 by the then General Secretary Jiang Zemin during his inspection visit to Huangshan: 'If every Chinese person could take a tour once a year, many matters in China would get easy' (Wei and Han, 2003).

In a similar vein the official Xinhua News Agency (Xinhua) promoted the leisure economy and leisure travel in 2006 and 2009 in two articles 'The Leisure Society is Coming to You' and 'Get Leisure Affairs Well Done' (Xinhua, 2006f, 2009i). In essence the market and more social approaches complemented each other, with the market mechanism becoming a fundamental means to accomplish social ends. At the same time the social orthodoxy justified the use of the market as the main mechanism for resource allocation. These two orthodoxies, market economy and social harmony, provided the guiding cognitive framework for the policy-makers.

Domestic environment

Domestically this was a period in which China underwent remarkable changes, bringing not only socio-economic improvements but also acute socio-economic and political problems.

SOCIO-ECONOMIC ADVANCES

Generally, socio-economic conditions saw many improvements, reflected in the continuing increase in GNP, disposable incomes and savings (see Table 7.9) as well as in the provision for leisure. Incomes increased over forty-fold between 1978 and 2008 (Xinhua, 2008c). By 2008, China had 1.6 million 'rich' households with annual incomes of RMB¥250,000, a figure predicted to reach 4 million by 2015 (*Hong Kong Wenweipo Daily* (Wenweipo), 8 April 2009). In the wealthiest cities, Beijing, Shanghai, Guangzhou and Shenzhen, standards of living reached a par with the developed world, with urban residents having access to real choice and quality in many areas of life such as catering, entertainment, travel, recreation, fashion and housing. Consumption and expenditure patterns also changed dramatically, with saving for future generations being replaced by saving for self, saving being replaced by consumption, purchasing goods being joined by purchasing of services, and consumption by cash being replaced by consumption on credit. Leisure time also increased. In addition to the five-day working week adopted from the mid-1990s, between 1999 and 2008 the Chinese were also able to enjoy three-day holidays during each of the Lunar New Year, Labour Day and National Day periods. Indeed by rearranging the surrounding weekends, people were actually able to take three one-week holidays, known as 'Golden Weeks' ('*Huangjin Zhou*'). With effect from 2008, the number of Golden Weeks was reduced to two but at the same time statutory holidays were granted for three other traditional Chinese festivals – Qing Ming, Dragon-Boat and Mid-Autumn. The influx of foreign exchange helped to permit relaxation in exchange controls. Since 2003, Chinese outbound travellers have been allowed to take out US$3,000 per trip, instead of the previous allowance of US$2,000. These developments stimulated a further boom in domestic and outbound travel.

SOCIO-ECONOMIC PROBLEMS

The rapid development and transition unavoidably generated a series of socio-economic problems relating, for example, to insufficient aggregate demand, unemployment, economic restructuring, regional imbalance as well as social unrest. If anything, these problems contributed to an increase in the perceived importance of tourism in the economy as well as to its political, socio-cultural and diplomatic roles.

China since the late 1990s had faced insufficient aggregate demand, especially in consumption. After thirty years of rapid economic development, aggregate supply of daily commodities and household appliances broadly satisfied aggregate demand (Zhu, 1998). However, government withdrawal of subsidies from social welfare items such as education, medical services and housing had the effect of restraining other consumption demand (Saich, 2004, Xinhua, 2006k, 2008l, 2008m, 2009j) (*Hong Kong Wenweipo Daily* (Wenweipo), 30 March 2009). This weakness in domestic demand worsened in the financial crisis of 2008 (Xinhua, 2008n), as confirmed by the Minister of the People's Bank of China, who pointed out that consumption remained relatively weak in its contribution to GDP with significant room for expansion (Xinhua, 2008o, 2008p). Indeed the expansion of consumption demand became the focus of China's macro-economic policy after 2008 (Xinhua, 2008q, 2009k; State Council, 2009a, 2010a). In his report submitted to the 2010 Session of the NPC, Premier Wen Jiabao suggested that the 'active expansion of consumption demand' represents one of eight major tasks for the government (State Council, 2010a).

Compared to the primary and secondary sectors, the tertiary sector, including tourism, showed strong potential for development. Employment in the primary sector reduced from 58.5 per cent in 1992 to 39.6 per cent in 2008 and in the secondary sector it remained static at around 26 per cent (SSB, 2009) with heavy military industries accounting for a substantial proportion. With the ending of the cold war and China's opening-up, military production became less necessary. In other words the development potential of the primary and secondary sectors became limited. By contrast the tertiary industries experienced strong growth, with employment increasing from 19.8 per cent in 1992 to 33.2 per cent in 2008 (SSB, 2009). Within this, sectors like tourism were seen to have particularly robust demand (e.g. State Council, 2001).

Population growth and unemployment have traditionally been linked together in China. By 2008 the population totalled 1.3 billion and is still growing and there has been continued growth in the labour force. The official unemployment rate increased continuously from 2.3 per cent in 1992 to 3.1 per cent in 1997 and 4.2 per cent in 2008 (SSB, 1997–2009). This significantly underestimates the true rate because it excludes workers laid off ('*xia gang*') after Enterprise Reform, since they still receive a basic portion of their salary. This issue emerged in the late 1990s and still persists. In June 2006 the Xinhua News Agency reported: 'China is faced with high employment pressure this year and in the coming years' (Xinhua, 2006k). The current economic downturn has added further employment pressures. It was estimated by the government that around 40 million were unemployed in 2009 (*Hong Kong Mingpao Daily* (Mingpao), 19 June 2009). Premier Wen Jiabao acknowledged in his government report submitted to the annual session of the NPC in 2009 that the unemployment problem is 'very serious' (State Council, 2009a).

There are also imbalances in China's development between urban and rural settings and among different provinces. Around 90 per cent of the population living in poverty are in the rural areas (*Hong Kong Wenweipo Daily* (Wenweipo), 9 April 2009). By contrast, one-half of China's multimillionaires live in three regions – Beijing, Shanghai and Guangdong (*Hong Kong Mingpao Daily* (Mingpao), 16 April 2009). The regional imbalance between the eastern (coastal) parts and central, western and northeastern parts are clear. For example, in 2008, the GDP of Jiangsu, Zhejiang and Guangdong in the coastal areas totalled RMB¥3,031, 2,149 and 3,570 billion respectively. The GDP of Gansu, Guizhou and Jilin in the western and northeastern regions amounted to only RMB¥318, 333 and 642 billion (SSB, 2009).

The extent and degree of tension in this period has tended to be greater than in previous periods. Notably conflict has been triggered by socio-economic factors and the associated political background, particularly in relation to high employment, widening development gaps, higher living costs, the re-engineering of state-owned enterprises, alleged administrative misconduct, suspected abuses of power, as well as reported inequalities and corruption. Demonstrations, strikes and other confrontations have been fairly continuous, in some cases even involving demobilized soldiers. For example, the conflict between residents and police in Guangxi in February 2009 was triggered by government land requisition and resulted in the detention of a hundred residents. In June 2009, residents in Jiangxi Province demonstrated at government offices in protest at observed administrative misconduct. In July 2009, employees of a state-owned enterprise in Jilin Province gathered in opposition to the direction that the company was taking.

Some groups have sought assistance from non-government sponsored NGOs or political-social activists to safeguard their interests and others have joined underground religious parties. These have posed challenges for the CPC. Challenges have also come from open expressions of civil opinion through the internet, relating, for example, to social inequalities, nepotism and corruption. In some cases these have prompted government concessions. As an example, in 2009, the authorities required all computers to be installed with filtering software before sale – '*Lu Ba*' – to prevent access to erotic sites. This measure was however perceived as a restriction on information and subsequent opposition eventually resulted in its suspension (*Hong Kong Mingpao Daily* (Mingpao), 1 July 2009). Recognizing the importance of popular opinion, and learning from the experience of the West, the Chinese government is now turning to external consultancies and market research firms to track public opinion. It is against a background of a weakening in the authority of the state that greater consideration has been given to domestic tourism as a tool to influence civil opinion.

International environment

Alongside her economic success, China's international position has shifted dramatically, including greater participation in the international financial system and the use of the RMB as the regional currency. For example, in 2009, Malaysia adopted the RMB in place of the US dollar in its trade with China (*Hong Kong Mingpao Daily* (Mingpao), 5 June 2009). However, this process has not been smooth. Given her history and significantly different state structure and ideology, China's rise has often been seen as a threat. Since the late 1990s, constructive engagement and accompanying friction appear to have been the main themes in relations between China and the US-led Western world. With considerable foreign exchange reserves and an enormous market, China is increasingly expected to provide economic assistance and leadership. But tensions remain, including those related to China's national interests, such as those raised by Germany's invitation to the Dalai Lama and Japan's invitation to the Chinese dissident Rabiye Qadir. In June 2009, Australia objected to Chinese investment in the mining corporation, Rio Tinto (*Hong Kong Mingpao Daily* (Mingpao), 6 June 2009). At the same time Africa has become a source of support for China in international bargaining. In this context China is adjusting her foreign strategy, which in turn provides a diplomatic framework for developments in international and outbound tourism.

Tourism development

In many ways China's socio-economic advance and political stability have outweighed the negative impacts of internal troubles and external friction. Despite short downturns resulting from the Asian Financial Crisis, SARS and current worldwide economic problems, tourism in China under the market economy has seen rapid development, transforming itself from an economic activity to an important industry in the economy. In 2009, the country's foreign exchange earnings from tourism amounted to US$39.7 billion, a threefold growth from 1996 (see Table 7.3 and Table 8.1). The income from domestic tourism rose from RMB¥163.8 billion in 1996 to RMB¥1,020 billion in 2009. With domestic tourism as the main contributor, the proportion of total tourism income in GDP increased in ten years from 1.8 per cent in 1992 to over 5.0 per cent in 2002 (see Table 7.8). This proportion approached that of an officially called 'pillar industry' – a term used by the government to identify a key industry in the national economy (source: interview). The relative size of tourism fell to 3.85 per cent in 2009, but this has not significantly affected its real status in China's economy due to the economic recession and appreciation of the RMB. The growth rate of total tourism income almost has exceeded that of the GDP during the past three decades[1] and tourism is now well rooted in many local economies. Some 80 per cent of China's provinces have recognized it as a 'pillar' or 'backbone' industry (CNTA, 2008d). In 2008, tourism directly employed over 2.7 million people (see Table 8.2). As already noted, globally, in 2009, China's tourism ranked fourth and fifth in international tourist arrivals and tourism receipts (UNWTO 2010b) and the WTTC (2010) estimated that, in 2010, China's tourism ranked second in absolute size and 81st in its relative contribution to the national economy out of 181 countries, with the fastest growth of any nation.

Table 8.1 Foreign exchange from international tourism in China 1978–2009

Year	Total earnings from exports (visibles) (US$ m)	Total earnings from international tourism (US$ m)	Tourism earnings as a percentage of export earnings
1978	9,750	262.90	2.70
1979	13,660	449.27	3.29
1980	18,120	616.65	3.40
1981	22,010	784.91	3.57
1982	22,320	843.17	3.78
1983	22,320	941.20	4.23
1984	26,140	1,131.34	4.33
1985	27,350	1,250.00	4.57
1986	30,940	1,530.85	4.95
1987	39,440	1,861.51	4.72
1988	47,520	2,246.83	4.73
1989	52,540	1,860.48	3.54
1990	62,090	2,217.58	3.57
1991	71,840	2,844.97	3.96
1992	84,940	3,946.87	4.65
1993	91,740	4,683.17	5.10
1994	121,040	7,322.81	6.05
1995	148,780	8,732.77	5.87
1996	151,050	10,200.46	6.75
1997	182,700	12,074.14	6.61
1998	183,760	12,602.00	6.86
1999	194,930	14,099.00	7.23
2000	249,200	16,224.00	6.51
2001	266,098	17,792.00	6.69
2002	325,600	20,385.00	6.26
2003	438,230	17,406.00	3.97
2004	593,320	25,739.00	4.34
2005	761,950	29,296.00	3.84
2006	968,940	33,949.00	3.50
2007	1,217,780	41,919.00	3.44
2008	1,428,500	40,800.00	2.86
2009	1,201,700	39,680.00	3.30

Source: CNTA, 1985a–2010a; SSB, 1999–2009 and 2010.

International, domestic and outbound tourism have demonstrated great growth, especially domestic tourism. In 2009, the number of domestic tourists reached 1.9 billion, up from 640 million in 1996 (see Table 7.5). This represents an average of more than one domestic trip annually for every Chinese resident. Rural residents appear to offer strong growth potential, with travel frequency rates of urban and rural Chinese in 2007 of 1.66 and 1.05 respectively (CNTA, 2008a), this despite disposable incomes of urban residents at RMB¥13,786 per head being more than three times those of rural residents

(RMB¥4,140) (Table 7.9). In 1985, the average expenditure of domestic tourists was RMB¥40 per person. This rose 12.7 times to RMB¥536.3 in 2009. Domestic tourists have become the mainstay of tourism in China. As far as the inbound international market is concerned there was an increase from 51 million arrivals in 1996 to 126 million in 2009; among these, foreign arrivals rose sharply from 6.7 million to 21 million, but the global economic uncertainty has brought decline since 2008 (see Table 7.4). Outbound tourism from China has shown similar fast growth rates. Some 47.7 million outbound travellers spent US$43.7 billion in 2009, compared to US$4.47 billion by 5.06 million outbound travellers in 1996 (CNTA, 2010b).

The new tourism policy paradigm

The changing ideological and national policy context of China has brought with it some significant changes for tourism. Within the state-centric market-

Table 8.2 Tourism employees in China 1981–2008

Year	No. of employees	Growth rate (%)
1981	37,228	–
1982	64,736	73.9
1983	76,789	18.6
1984	98,388	28.1
1985	168,357	71.1
1986	276,463	64.2
1987	356,801	29.1
1988	438,987	23.0
1989	517,363	17.9
1990	619,717	19.8
1991	708,263	14.3
1992	795,942	12.4
1993	876,700	10.1
1994	973,977	11.1
1995	1,115,798	14.6
1996	1,196,749	7.3
1997	1,359,423	13.6
1998	1,830,000	34.6
1999	1,944,867	6.28
2000	2,080,449	6.97
2001	2,006,458	–3.56
2002	2,189,507	9.12
2003	2,423,695	10.70
2004	2,448,751	1.0
2005	2,604,231	6.3
2006	2,713,413	4.2
2007	2,720,476	0.26
2008	2,721,318	0.03

Source: CNTA, 1985a–2009a.

economy model tourism is seen as having a role to play in political–ideological, economic, social-cultural as well as diplomatic terms but above all its market-oriented economic role provides the basis for these broader functions. This market-oriented role is a reflection of the extent to which the position of the government has shifted from being dominant in the planned economy to guiding and regulating in the market economy. As already noted in Chapter 6, the Document of the National Tourism Works Conference 2004 stated:

> We should emphasize the function of tourism as an economic industry; we also should emphasize more the comprehensive functions of tourism in providing employment, promoting Chinese culture and building a socialist spiritual civilization.
>
> (CNTA, 2004b: p.7)

This economic and market-oriented model is seen as the basis for China's tourism development.

During 2000–10, the recognition of tourism has been upgraded from 'a new growth pole' to 'a key industry' in China's national economy. In response to socio-economic problems, in the late 1990s the State Council attempted to identify some industries with substantial potential in terms of market growth, foreign exchange, employment, stimulation of other economic sectors and regional development. These were identified as 'new growth poles of the national economy'. Initially the recommended list did not include tourism. CNTA advocated that tourism's current position and future potential meant that it was well able to fulfil a role as a new growth pole. As such, a series of policy studies and discussions took place among the SPC (NDRC), MoF, CNTA and other relevant agencies. For example, the CNTA undertook studies to investigate the role of tourism in poverty alleviation. These concluded that less developed regions – Xinjiang, Guizhou, Tibet and Inner Mongolia – possessed abundant tourism resources (such as a non-polluted environment and non-ruined ecology), and suggested that tourism development could enhance economic growth in these regions. A significant meeting, 'High-Level Seminar about Tourism and the New Economic Growth Pole', was co-hosted by SPC and CNTA in March 1997. Its participants were all director-equivalent officials from the central agencies closely related to tourism, including the MoF, CASS, the Development Research Centre of the State Council (DRC) and the Budgetary Affairs Commission of the NPC Standing Committee. During this seminar, the strengths and potential of tourism in economic development were well recognized by the macro-management agencies. The view of tourism as an 'insignificant' and 'frivolous' industry was entirely discarded under the Market-Economy Model. Hao Jianxiu, Vice-Minister of the State Planning Commission, commented: 'From its economic scale, number of employees and high development pace, tourism is no longer an unimportant industry, but rather is a significant industry characterized by its solid underpinning by traditional Chinese culture' (CNTA, 1999c: p.87).

A consensus was reached between the CNTA, SPC (SDPC), MoF and academics that tourism was an important tool for economic development. Subsequently in 1998, the State Council formally recognized tourism as 'a new growth pole of the national economy'.

> In the Central Economic Works Conference convened in December 1998, tourism was confirmed as 'a new growth pole of the national economy'. This is another historical moment for tourism following 1986 when it was for the first time incorporated into the state economic and social plan.
>
> (CNTA, 1999c: p.7)

With this upgrade, the purview for tourism in the State Council was transferred from the Vice-Premier overseeing foreign affairs (Qian Qichen) to the Vice-Premier in charge of economic portfolios – Wu Yi (2003–8) and Wang Qishan (2008–present).[2]

Faced with the weakness in aggregate demand, Premier Wen Jiabao called for the expansion of tourism consumption: 'Housing, cars, telecommunication products, tourism, education etc. are becoming the new hotspots of our people's consumption. We should actively promote and appropriately guide them' (CNTA, 2004b: p.6) and 'We should encourage people to enlarge their consumption of tourism, sports and fitness exercise, and cultural activities' (CNTA, 2004b: p.6).

Following its recognition in the economy in 1998, tourism maintained strong and rapid development between 1998 and 2009, with its share in GDP averaging 4 per cent, and reaching 5.29 per cent in 2002 (Table 7.8). As a result the Chinese government conceived that its status could be further elevated, especially in view of its strong recovery after SARS. As a signal, Premier Wen Jiabao addressed the 15th General Assembly of the World Tourism Organization held in Beijing in October 2003, commenting that:

> Since the founding of new China and especially after the implementation of the Economic Reform and Open-door Policy, the Chinese government has placed a high emphasis on tourism. Tourism has experienced continued and rapid development. Tourism in China has become a newly emerging industry characterized by prosperity, vigour and enormous potential. At present, China's international arrivals and international tourism receipts have advanced to the forefront in the world . . . We should foster tourism as a significant industry in China's national economy.
>
> (CNTA, 2004b: p.6)

Subsequently from 2004 to 2006, the Vice-Premier in charge of tourism, Wu Yi, on her inspection trips to several provinces (Liaoning, Zhejiang, Sichuan, Shandong and Hainan) acknowledged that tourism had been an important impetus for economic growth. In the meantime, China's economic strategies further strengthened domestic consumption, which underpinned the expansion of tourism. In 'The Eleventh Five-Year State Plan for National Economy and Social Development' formulated in 2006, the stimulation of internal consumption for the first time became a national policy decision. The Plan indicated that 'the expansion of domestic demand especially consumption demand should be the basic starting point' (NDRC, 2006b). Under the drivers of national policy and tourism performance, tourism was conceived by the government as a key industry, as indicated in 2007 by Wu Yi (CNTA, 2007c) and efforts were made in this direction through national meetings and inspection visits. Eventually in 2008, tourism was recognized by the Chinese government as 'a key industry in the national economy'. Vice-Premier Wu Yi stated: 'The scale of tourism continues to expand, the scope of its services continues to expand, . . . international cooperation further intensifies, tourism has become a key industry in the national economy' (CNTA, 2008b).

Under the global economic downturn after 2008, China has faced a considerable drop in external demand. Domestic tourism has not shown a decline although its annual growth has slowed from 15.5 per cent (tourists) and 24.7 per cent (receipts) in 2007 to 11.1 per cent and 16.4 per cent in 2009 (Tables 7.3 and 7.5). Domestic and outbound travel are still strong areas of consumption demand (Xinhua, 2008e). Between April and July 2009, the current Vice-Premier with responsibility for tourism, Wang Qishan, carried out study and inspection visits to Anhui, Qinhai and Inner Mongolia and called for a 'strategic recognition' of tourism: '[We] should understand about speeding up tourism development from a strategic perspective, and fully exercise its active roles in expanding consumption, adjusting the economic structure, shifting the development modes and promoting employment' (CNTA, 2009d). Subsequently the State Council called for the development of tourism as a 'strategic pillar industry in the national economy', as an upgrade from its place as a 'key industry' recognized in 2008.

In terms of its economic contribution, the major discussion and debate by, for example, the Chinese Academy of Social Sciences (e.g. X.F. Dai, 2005; G.R. Zhang, 2006), has been about foreign exchange issues associated with inbound and outbound tourism. Some have suggested that the foreign exchange earnings function of international tourism is no longer important to China while others have maintained that as a developing nation, foreign exchange earnings from inbound tourism are a source of national wealth. Actually China's total foreign exchange earnings per capita only amounted to US$1,600 in 2009, far below the figures for Hong Kong SAR (US$29,500) or even Japan (US$7,780) (*Hong Kong Mingpao Daily* (Mingpao), 16 July 2009). But it is generally understood by the government and academics that the foreign exchange earning role of tourism is not as pressing as in the 1980s and 1990s and further there are mixed views about foreign exchange being reduced by expenditure on outbound travel. In 2009 the US$43.7 billion of outbound expenditure exceeded the US$39.7 billion earned by inbound tourism. From a non-economic perspective, given the fact that a significant proportion of the population are not wealthy, there is also a view that the rapid growth of outbound tourism does little to help social harmony, although this is countered by a view that since China's wealthy are able to sustain rapid growth, their travel should be politically and socially acceptable. These discussions have led the government to think about outbound tourism rather more broadly to encompass political, social and diplomatic perspectives, in justifying its development.

The government's understanding of its role in the tourism economy has also advanced. It now recognizes its role as guiding and regulating market forces in the form, for example, of providing related infrastructure, stimulating investment and carrying out promotion as well as developing market institutions. Accordingly CNTA retreated from the administration of enterprises to the macro management of the industry. The following paragraph extracted from CNTA's *Handbook of Tourism Standardization Works* reflects the transformation in CNTA's thinking:

> Our economic management under the planned-economy model was basically supply side management; the extreme mode for managing enterprises was rationing. Now the general circumstances are changing, the objective background is now changing, the overall environment is now changing, therefore we should transform from supply side management to demand side management. Demand side management is eventually to manage the market. We should shift from managing enterprises to managing the market.
>
> (CNTA, 1998b: p.14)

Remarkably, the political–ideological and diplomatic considerations of tourism have been significantly re-emphasized since 2000. Especially, envisaging a deepening of social divisions and the rising importance of public opinion, the fourth generation leadership is now integrating socialist values into a new ideological package entitled the 'Socialist Core Values System' (CPC, 2006b; Xinhua, 2006b, 2007a). This is in order to consolidate further the legitimacy and dominance of the CPC and the socialist system, strengthen national cohesion and reconstruct moral norms. Considered as a unique vehicle in promoting socialism and nationalism, domestic tourism has been given a key role in the construction of this 'System'. The promotion of state values through domestic tourism has not only been accorded an official title – 'Red Tourism' – but it has also been brought to the attention of the leadership. In China the colour red usually symbolizes the communist revolution.[3] In this context 'Red Tourism' means self-initiated or officially-organized (e.g. schools, state-owned enterprises, military forces) visits to state-designated places that present sites, histories, relics, experiences, lives and stories related to nationalist movements, anti-aggression wars, communist revolution[4] and socialist development led by the CPC. This physical and non-physical revolutionary heritage has been deliberately preserved since 1949. Equally important,

China's many natural sites and other heritage sites provide tourism resources that can promote pride in Chinese civilization. The Politburo member of the CPC, Ding Guangen, highlighted the functions of tourism in propagandizing the ideological orthodoxies:

> Tourism works are very important. Tourist attractions not only can promote economic development, but are also a crucial frontline in propagandizing socialist thought and achievement. Tourist attractions are an important window for exhibiting our splendid natural scenery, long and brilliant history and culture, and fine national image to domestic and international tourists.
>
> Starting from the height of politics, we have to develop tourist attractions as the significant propaganda frontline.
>
> We should try our utmost to attract more domestic and international tourists to those attractions promoting patriotism so as to expand fully the social influence and to exercise an educational role.
>
> The development of tourism resources and attractions should strengthen socialist, communist, and healthy cultural connotations and should reflect the fine sentiments of cherishing the country, nationality, people and homeland. We should focus on the introduction and presentation of the long history and excellent culture of China, of the fine traditions of hardworking, guileless, ethnic harmony and the solidarity of the Chinese people.
>
> (CNTA, 2002b)

Since 2004, the Standing Committee Member of the Politburo overseeing state ideology, Li Changchun, has delivered speeches on the development of 'Red Tourism' when visiting Hebei, Guangxi, Gansu and Hunan provinces, emphasizing its role in 'political engineering in cementing the CPC's ruling status', 'cultural engineering in constructing advanced socialist cultures' and 'moral education for teenagers' (Xinhua, 2004a). As the chief for ideology, Li's remarks represented the visions of the leadership and boosted to a new level the political utilization of tourism. In the view of government, the promotion of ideological values through leisure-oriented travel is more effective than delivery purely through formal education and organizational learning. Overall, 'Red Tourism' is a new development in China's tourism politics. In addition, the authorities have been aware that tourist products, especially the non-physical aspects such as religious travel, should be ideologically conducive, or at least not detrimental, to China's socialist civilization.

Socially and culturally, domestic and outbound travel have been seen as important elements of leisure time and life quality more generally. Total tourism receipts from the three Golden Weeks between 2000 and 2007 reached RMB¥808 billion (CNTA, 2008d). Travel to remote and culturally distinctive countries (especially European destinations) is among the aspirations of many Chinese. In line with current ideological discourse of the 'fulfillment of the continuously increasing needs of the people', the government has not only recognized leisure travel as representing a current fashion, but also conceived it as an integral part of China's 'well-off society'. General Secretary Hu Jintao remarked: 'We should enforce more competition in the traditional service industries like trade, commerce, catering and tourism etc which generate high employment and are closely related to the daily lives of the people' (CNTA, 2004b: p.6).

In April 2006, at the 'World Leisure High-Level Forum', held in Hangzhou, Vice-Premier Wu Yi presented a keynote speech on actively developing leisure services so as continuously to enhance quality of life. Following this, in June 2006, the CNTA produced an official report that advocated the role of tourism in promoting social integration (CNTA, 2006c). More importantly, domestic and outbound travel have been officially recognized as the right of all Chinese (Nationals' Travel – '*Guomin Luyou*'), indicating official support for leisure travel. This is being carried out through the 'National Leisure Scheme' prepared by the CNTA (Xinhua, 2009d). In summary, these political and socio-cultural considerations reflect deliberate tourism-related responses to some of China's political and social challenges.

Likewise, the diplomatic role of tourism has also been substantially revived. China is now proceeding with her 'quasi-great-power diplomacy' to pursue a more active role in international affairs, on the basis that national strength in terms of resources and attractiveness are essential for future development. Tourism is viewed as an important element in China's foreign strategy. According to the Document of the National Tourism Works Conference 2004, Chairman Jiang Zemin[5] affirmed the significance of tourism in political, economic and foreign affairs:

> Chairman Jiang Zemin specifically listened to the report prepared by the party group of the China National Tourism Administration about the development of China and its recovery and renovation after SARS . . . and fully confirmed the crucial and active roles played by tourism in political, economic and diplomatic realms and in work relating to Hong Kong SAR, Macao SAR and Taiwan.
>
> (CNTA, 2004b: p.6)

Inbound tourism is considered as a distinctive means of nurturing and promoting China's international image and attractiveness, through her physical beauty, ancient civilization and contemporary development. At the same time, after the previous two periods in which it has had a relatively low profile, the traditional role of international tourism in civil diplomacy has been rediscovered as a tool to facilitate international friendship. Formulated in 2007, CNTA's policy document 'Guidelines on the Development of Inbound Tourism with Great Endeavour' presented the understanding of this as follows:

[inbound tourism] has further publicized the great accomplishments of our modernization and the overall image of our nation, and has had positive effects in advancing China's international status.

(CNTA, 2007b)

Inbound tourism is an important component of our tourism sector. . . . It can also play an active role in enhancing friendly intercourse with the people of other countries and regions, publicizing the advanced culture and civilization of China, promoting China's opening and creating a harmonious world.

(CNTA, 2007b)

The Document of the National Tourism Works Conference 2008 further summarized the position that 'tourism has exerted a unique role in serving foreign affairs and measures towards Hong Kong, Macau and Taiwan in our nation' (CNTA, 2008c).

Outbound tourism is also seen as playing an international role. Major powers like the US, UK, France and Japan are recognized as large generators of outbound tourism. For its part China considers that outbound travel can help project a new and positive image for the country and its people, so as to assist the international community in understanding China, building their confidence in the country's development and mitigating fears of perceived threats. The development of outbound travel is also seen as a means of conveying a message to the West that China is attending to the needs and rights of its people. To the extent that expenditure by outbound tourists brings benefits to the host economies, outbound tourism is also seen as providing some support for China in its dealings with other countries. Although against this, even though it is less of a problem than in the past, outbound travel is still associated with defections and illegal emigration. For example, in 2004, around 150 people on a tour run by a travel agency in Beijing were involved in illegal emigration. So the notion that outbound travel should be controlled basically remains unchanged.

Based on the leaders' conceptions and the bureaucratic consensus, the new tourism policy paradigm can thus be summarized as follows:

1   Tourism is an industry that does not matter for national security and survival, but it is an inseparable component of the Economic Reform and Open-door Policy.
2   Tourism is viewed as a multifunctional strategic industry that has political-ideological, economic, social-cultural and diplomatic roles based on its market-oriented economic development.
3   Domestic tourism is recognized as a mainstay in its development.
4   National tourism policy-making is assumed to play the directing role in tourism development, through guiding and regulating market forces.
5   The development of outbound tourism needs to proceed in an orderly fashion; uncontrolled development is not appropriate and should not be encouraged.

Basic tourism policy decisions

As the tourism policy paradigm has advanced, basic policy decisions have also moved forward. In the collective leadership era, tourism has for the first time secured its status at the state level in China. This has meant that the overall position of tourism has been discussed and determined in the national policy-making forum or supported by the relevant national leaders, alongside other industries; such status is underpinned by the performance of tourism and supported by active policy measures.

Tourism at the state level

Tourism is now positioned as a multifunctional strategic sector. At the 2008 National Tourism Conference, the Director-General of CNTA Shao Qiwei urged that it should play its multifunctional roles more fully (CNTA, 2008c). The status of tourism was further upgraded in 2008, to become 'a key industry in the national economy' (CNTA, 2008c). Facing further decline in consumption demand, tourism was designated as one of five consumption drivers at the 2008 Central Economic Works Conference, together with automobiles, housing, services and rural peasants (Xinhua, 2008e).

Goals of tourism development

Though tourism plays multiple roles, its economic contribution is of fundamental importance. Without economic success it would not be supported. Currently, the speeches and instructions of the vice-premiers responsible for tourism all prioritize this. In the policy documents of the National Tourism Works Conference, the economic aspects normally precede other perspectives (CNTA, 2007d, 2008c, 2009e, 2010b). These are to increase income, generate more employment and promote regional economic development. In relation to 'Red Tourism', the political–ideological goals are to strengthen political allegiance to the CPC-led state, to promote socialist values and to enhance nationalism. The policy documents of the National Tourism Works Conferences between 2007 and 2009 reiterate that tourism serves 'China's overall diplomacy' and 'policy measures for Hong Kong, Macau and Taiwan' (CNTA, 2007d, 2008c, 2009e). As for the social and cultural aspects, the goals of domestic tourism are to promote quality of life so as to assist the establishment of a 'Socialist Harmonious Society' and a 'well-off society' (e.g. CNTA, 2007d, 2008c, 2009e).

Tourism development strategy

Although additional weight was given to domestic and outbound tourism in the 2005 CNTA development strategy, inbound tourism still retained its key importance. In the words of the strategy, the intention is 'to develop inbound tourism substantially' and 'fully to boost domestic tourism and develop outbound tourism in an orderly fashion'. Foreign exchange earning potential is no longer as crucial as before but wealth inflow remains important to China as a large developing country. As for domestic tourism this is seen as providing a backbone for the tourism sector as well as having political importance and as from 2009, with the decline in inbound tourism, priority has been given to domestic tourism (CNTA, 2009e, 2010b). For outbound tourism the feelings are more mixed. It is recognized as contributing to the enhancement of the country's national image and providing a positive context for international relations but on the other hand its contributions to outflows of foreign currency and the problems of illegal stays abroad mean that it is not viewed entirely positively. There is also concern that as relatively inexperienced tourists, the Chinese will have unsatisfactory experiences and some public sentiment views outbound travel as luxury consumption highlighting large socio-economic gaps. Until 2006 outbound tourism was in fact controlled because hardly any countries offered individual tourist visas to Chinese citizens. Also China does not encourage individual travel for leisure purposes. This control was effectively continued with the introduction by China in 1999 of the concept of Approved Destination Status (ADS) for group travel. Under ADS China negotiates to approve foreign countries, and territories such as Hong Kong and Macao, as tourist destinations. The ADS agreements normally cover a recognized list of travel agencies in China and the host country including a set of service standards, and the travel companies are made responsible for ensuring that group arrivals and departures take place (e.g. Australian Commonwealth Department of Resources, Energy and Tourism, 2008). Ultimately, however, ADS may not last for much longer as more countries, like those in South Asia in 2006 and 2007 as well as South Africa and Japan from 2009, now offer individual tourist visas.

In 2007, the tourism development strategy was for the first time incorporated into the national development plan, the current 'Eleventh Five-Year State Plan for the National Economy and Social Development' prepared by the NDRC. The position and strategy for tourism development are mainly carried out through national tourism planning, supported by concrete policy decisions. Corresponding to the growing importance of tourism, national tourism planning changed from merely providing a blueprint to outlining an action programme. To ensure that interests and initiatives are properly represented, the CNTA gathers the planning inputs at three levels – central agencies, local government, and academics and industry.

Because of its strategic and multifunctional roles, more and more high-level inputs have been made to enforce the implementation of the basic policy decisions. These include the leaders' initiatives, diplomatic leverage and ideological commitments. In relation to the leaders' initiatives, in 2001 the National Tourism Works Conference was organized by the State Council to mobilize the further development of tourism. During the 2008–9 financial crisis, consumption was thought to hold the key to economic revitalization with tourism used as one of five stimuli. Two top leaders, President Hu Jintao and Premier Wen Jiabao, both emphasized the role of tourism in the expansion of consumption. Hu called for the need to 'put more effort into developing services and tourism consumption'. Wen emphasized the need to 'actively foster the consumption of tourism, culture, sport and health activities, the internet, cartoon animation and other hot spots which are closely related to changes in the provisions for holidays'. These requirements were incorporated into the action plan of the National Tourism Works Conference 2009 (CNTA, 2009e).

In diplomatic terms ADS negotiation has become an important item in China's bilateral and multilateral foreign relations and is strongly influenced by attitudes or support for China's key national interests as well as issues such as destination feasibility. The Chairman of the CNTA acknowledged that the opening of the outbound market is to serve China's foreign policy and strategies (CNTA, 2008c, 2009e). Since 2003 it has been a topic on the agenda of state meetings with leaders of many different countries, such as Cuba, Switzerland, Hungary, Turkey, Malaysia and Zambia as well as the European Union (CNTA, 2004b). Between 2004 and 2010 China's top three leaders (i.e. President, Chairman of NPC Standing Committee and Premier) have been directly involved in not less than twenty ADS negotiations or signing ceremonies (e.g. CNTA, 2010b). For example, Chinese President Hu Jintao announced the ADS agreement with Switzerland in November 2003, while Premier Wen Jiabao announced the opening of the outbound market to eight African countries in December of the same year. This top level involvement has continued with, for example, most recently, in August 2009, President Hu Jintao being present at the signing ceremony for the ADS with Serbia (CNTA, 2009f).

With its growing economic impact on host economies, China's outbound travel, since the mid-2000s, has increasingly been seen as diplomatically important. The ADS offered to the US was a result of the Sino-American Strategic Dialogue in 2008. The Document of the 2009 National Tourism Works Conference commented: 'the implementation of Chinese organized tourists to the US actively assists in facilitating strategic collaboration in US-China relations' (CNTA, 2009e). In relation to Africa, the ADS agreements can be seen in the context of competition among world powers for closer ties. China's support for Africa has included not only financial, technical and human resources but also the opening of outbound travel to African nations. In the Beijing Summit of the Forum on China-Africa Cooperation held in 2006, China announced five cooperative areas with Africa, one of which was tourism; as a result, nine countries obtained ADS. In return, the African nations provided support to China's key national interests. Since Australia became the first nation to obtain ADS in 1999, a total of 139 ADS destinations had been agreed by 2009 (CNTA, 2010b).

Regarding the political goal of tourism, in 2004 Li Changchun, the Chinese leader responsible for state ideology, gave instructions to 'actively develop Red Tourism' (Xinhua, 2004a). This led to a range of concrete policy measures covering planning, product design and infrastructure provision. These are discussed further below.

Concrete tourism policy decisions

Given the rapid development of tourism and the fact that it plays a comprehensive role, there have been a great number of policy decisions during this period dealing with a range of different issues. This has created a challenge for coordination. Different agencies have dealt with different aspects of tourism according to their respective responsibilities and the nature of the issues. As outlined in Chapter 6, almost all initiatives from CNTA, for example, touch on other central government agencies. As a result it cannot always make independent decisions but rather has had to coordinate with the related agencies. Although this coordinated approach to decision-making is evident in previous periods, it is much more prominent in this current period and local forces are also much more prominent.

Demand side: stimulation of inbound and domestic travel

The stimulation of demand is primarily the responsibility of the CNTA which, as explained in Chapter 6, derives its funds from two sources: state appropriation covering administrative expenses and a portion of airport tax used for marketing and development projects. The airport tax began in 1992. Currently, of the airport tax of RMB¥90 per international passenger departure, some RMB¥20 is allocated to CNTA's tourism development fund. This became the 'Tourism Development Foundation' ('*Luyou Fazhan Jijin*') in 2001. MoF regulations limit the Foundation to financing marketing and planning studies and to subsidizing the construction of attractions. In 2003, the MoF transferred administration of the Foundation to CNTA but maintained an auditing and monitoring role. Marketing accounts for the largest item of expenditure, increasing from US$7.25 million in 1998 to US$25 million recently, although this still lags behind competitors such as Thailand, Singapore and Australia (source: interview). In addition to routine funding, the CNTA may also request additional funding from the MoF on an occasional basis. For inbound tourism, a set of promotional campaigns have been used to stimulate market growth. More importantly, tourism marketing has been integrated into China's national propaganda. From 2006 China began marking anniversaries of the establishment of diplomatic relations. In this it launched a series of national celebration campaigns to promote mutual relations and China's image, including, for example, the China-France Cultural Year, China-Russia Friendship Year, China-Italy National Year, China-Japan Year of Sports and Cultural Exchange, China-Spain National Year, China-South Korea Friendship Year and the China-India Tourism Year.

For domestic demand, the CNTA was an initiator of the 'Regulation on Paid Annual Leave' issued by the State Council from January 2008 (State Council, 2007b). So far, however, given the extra operational costs that it creates, especially for small and medium-sized enterprises, this regulation has not been implemented throughout the country. One opinion poll conducted by the China Youth Post in October 2008, suggests that more than 50 per cent of interviewees had not taken their annual leave (Xinhua, 2009m). In addition to economic decline and hesitation by employers, the lack of outside catalysts is another possible reason for the slow development of annual leave. The CNTA is now preparing the 'National Leisure Scheme' ('*Guomin Xiuxian Jihua*'), which is intended to boost Chinese leisure entitlement and utilization. The scheme includes provision for incentives such as tourist coupons, discounts, free products, and leisure tourist routes to stimulate travel. It also encourages leisure travel during the major statutory holidays (Xinhua, 2009d, 2009n, 2009o, 2009p). With the support of the Ministry of Commerce, a scheme of tourism consumption coupons was launched in 2009 in selected cities such as Beijing, Nanjing, Hangzhou and Guangzhou, to stimulate domestic travel. For example, in Nanjing and Guangdong RMB¥20 million was distributed. In Nanjing, the 200,000 randomly selected families can only use these coupons in forty rural travel destinations, while in Guangdong it is only available to those over 55 years of age (*Hong Kong Wenweipo Daily* (Wenweipo), 10 February 2009b and 17 February 2009).

Though there is no initiative for stimulating outbound tourism, interestingly measures have been taken to influence behaviour. A decline in standards of behaviour in China, relating for example to littering, spitting, talking loudly in public, disrespecting local customs and religion has been reflected in the behaviour of some outbound and domestic tourists. The official Xinhua News Agency reported that Chinese tourists had been labelled as 'rude' in some Western nations (Xinhua, 2006l). The Chinese leadership took this very seriously. Viewed by the government as 'representatives of the nation' this sort of behaviour was seen not only not to meet government expectations, but it was also considered to be detrimental to China's image building (Xinhua, 2006m). Under direct instruction from the Standing Committee Member of the Politburo, Li Changchun, the Central Publicity Department of the CPC (CPD) and CNTA promulgated 'Guidelines to Civilized Tourist Behaviour Abroad by Chinese Citizens' and 'The Convention on Civilized Tourist Behaviour by Chinese Citizens during Domestic Travel', and also requested domestic and overseas authorities to give details about such misbehaviour. In 2006 the CPC and CNTA launched a three-year campaign 'The Action Plan to Raise the Civilized Quality of Tourist Behaviour by Chinese Citizens' (CPD and CNTA, 2006; Xinhua, 2006l). Further, unacceptable conduct by Chinese tourists when overseas will be severely punished. For example, anyone found guilty of patronizing prostitutes is to be prohibited from travelling abroad for five years. The authorities are also considering amending the passport law so that such tourists will not again be issued with a passport or be allowed to go abroad.

Supply side: product development and market institutions

On the supply side the central government has basically withdrawn from direct investment and operation in tourism and left these to local government and industry. Direct involvement by the centre has become confined mainly to tourism-related infrastructure as well as certain products and regions where central support is deemed necessary (e.g. central and western China, and ideological products). Market rules including normative quality standards have been the main feature of policy decisions on the supply side.

Since 2000 the state has invested at least RMB¥7 billion in tourism-related infrastructure and in the conservation of the environment and heritage of which a substantial amount has been in the less-developed regions. In this context, with the State Council's approval, the development of tourist attractions and associated facilities in central and western China was incorporated into the master catalogue of projects recommended for investment by the government. Beyond this, for the most part, as far as attractions are concerned, investment and operation by central government has almost disappeared although the CNTA still maintains an influential role in product development through the designation of tourist routes. It is currently preparing and consulting on the first batch of twelve such routes, including the 'Silk Road', 'Great Wall', 'Grand Canal', 'Three Gorges' and 'Yellow River Civilization' to help shape tourism flows and attract investment.

In contrast to other leisure and recreational tourist products, since 2004 the central government has been actively playing an operational role in the development of 'Red Tourism'. A set of guidelines has been jointly formulated by the CPC and the State Council covering goals, planning and investment. There are four key players involved in this. First, the Publicity Department of the CPC's Central Committee (or Central Publicity Department) (CPD) is in charge of designing the contents and promotion as well as directing the media launch. The attractions of 'Red Tourism' are decided and published by the CPD. Up to 2009, four batches of such 'Red Tourism' attractions had been announced amounting to over 350 sites. Some notable ones include the venue of the CPC's first national congress in Shanghai, the Military Museum of the Chinese People's Revolution located in Beijing and China's first nuclear research base in Qinhai Province. Second, NDRC is responsible for infrastructure development. The third player, the CNTA, offers professional support to make these sites accessible to tourists. Lastly the Ministry of Finance arranges the funds. So far over RMB¥1.7 billion has been invested. The central government decided that 'Red Tourism' attractions should be freely open to visitors in phases from 2008. In 2010 such attractions have received more than 1 billion tourists (Xinhua, 2008r; CNTA, 2010f).

The Chinese government is also concerned with making fees for visitor attractions more affordable. Starting in 2008, in order to offer more leisure enjoyment, enhance public welfare and stimulate domestic tourism, the government has provided free admission to all public museums, memorial halls – such as that dedicated to Mao Zedong in Tiananmen Square – and recreational parks at the central and provincial levels. Exceptions to this are some cultural relics and heritage attractions such as the Great Wall, the Forbidden City, the Museum of the Terracotta Army and specialized museums such as the Shanghai Museum of Natural History. Under China's pricing law, the admission fees for such attractions fall into the category of key commodities and services important for national and public interest. The government formulates the prices or pricing ranges for such attractions. As the state's main pricing authority, the NDRC requires local government and individual attractions to take public affordability and welfare into the pricing consideration. The NDRC further has instructed that fee increments should normally take place every three years, with a maximum growth rate of around 30 per cent. Prior to the decision a consultation should be undertaken, with consumer participation. However, notwithstanding these requirements, there are exceptions and regional differences. The admission fees for many main attractions have risen significantly since 2005. For example, the entrance fees for two scenic regions, Zhang Jiajie and Yellow Mountain (i.e. '*Huangshan*') were up by over 50 per cent in 2005. Since 2006, to enforce local compliance, eight central agencies convened by the NDRC, CNTA and MoF have taken regulatory action to lower admission fees to popular attractions (NDRC, 2007a; CNTA, 2008e).

The development of market institutions is proceeding through further market relaxation and the establishment of a quality assurance framework within which non-mandatory quality standards are the building blocks. The Chinese leaders have emphasized the role of standards in enhancing the quality of tourism. At the 2001 National Tourism Works Conference, Premier Zhu Rongji gave instructions that: 'We need to enhance the management and service quality of our tourism, to streamline further the administrative system, to accelerate tourism standardization, and to implement state-level and industry-level standards in tourism facilities, products and services etc.' (CNTA, 2004c).

FURTHER MARKET RELAXATION

Further market relaxation has been granted to both foreign and domestic investors. China started negotiations for membership of the General Agreement on Tariffs and Trade (GATT) (the predecessor of the World Trade Organization), in the mid-1980s, a process speeded up by the adoption of the market economy. Since tourism is a sector that is not seen, significantly, to affect China's national and economic security, it has been used as a kind of concession in exchange for the late and restricted opening of other sectors which are considered as of national importance, such as banking, finance, telecommunications, energy and insurance. China's commitments in tourism cover hotels (including service apartments and restaurants) and travel services. Regarding hotels, China agreed to foreign majority ownership in 2001 and foreign sole ownership by no later than the end of 2003. In travel agencies, China permitted foreign majority ownership in 2003 and sole foreign ownership by no later than the end of 2005. The first fully foreign-owned travel agency was established in 2003 (CNTA, 2004b). More recently this number has increased to seven out of a total of twenty-one travel agencies with foreign investment. Previously not open to them, foreign investors are currently more interested in outbound tourism because of its expanding size and profitable returns. Some tour packages to Africa and North America sell for between RMB¥40,000 and 100,000, almost one-third to two-thirds of annual incomes earned by low-salary earners. In 2009 the CNTA started a trial-run of outbound travel agencies with foreign investment (CNTA, 2009e). Further openness to foreign investment is seen not only to expand the scope of foreign management expertise and technology, but also through competition to compel indigenous businesses to upgrade their quality.

Regulatory and administrative transformation continues. For example, the new 'Regulation on the Administration of Travel Agencies' in May 2009 did away with statutory classification of agencies into international or domestic businesses, although businesses still need to provide higher quality guarantee deposits for outbound tours, than if they offer only inbound or domestic business (CNTA, 1996c, 2001c, 2009g). In the same way, in 2003 CNTA abolished two batches of administrative orders and has limited the scope for administrative approval (CNTA, 2001d, 2008g). All of these measures are designed to make the regulatory and administrative arrangements more transparent, as a response to China's admission to the WTO.

BUILDING THE QUALITY ASSURANCE FRAMEWORK

Building a quality assurance framework has been an important part of the development of the market economy in China. As noted in the previous chapter, the background to this is related to the need for 'tourism quality', and 'customer satisfaction' during a period of rapid growth and change. The emphasis in China on integrity and honesty that emerged in the mid-2000s provided an additional impetus as did the aim to become a member of the WTO.

The first developments took place in the 1980s when, for example, in the travel agency sector the 'Provisional Regulation on the Administration of Travel Agencies' was issued in 1985. This required capital of RMB¥500,000 for Category One travel agencies, RMB¥250,000 for Category Two and RMB¥30,000 for Category Three (State Planning Commission, 1990; Han Kehua, 1994). In the revised versions in 1996 and 2001 the required capital amounts for international travel agencies (inbound, domestic and outbound) and domestic travel agencies (domestic only) were RMB¥1.5 million and RMB¥300,000 respectively (CNTA, 2001c). A later version of this Regulation in 2009 further lowered the requirements to RMB¥300,000 for all businesses (CNTA, 2009g).

In the hotel and guest house sector where capital requirements were more relaxed, with only investments above RMB¥30 million requiring approval from central government (State Planning Commission, 1990; Wei and Shen, 1998), the emphasis on quality was prompted particularly by rapid growth. Investment in hotels expanded significantly during the 1990s, partly influenced by the search for new investment opportunities by sectors such as tobacco, which were facing decline, but also, and more significantly, from the real estate sector. Hotels and guest houses were seen to offer attractive investment opportunities. With the replacement of 'welfare housing' by commercial housing after 1992 (Saich, 2004) there was an expectation of a high demand for commercial housing. As a result significant funds flowed into real estate. In the event, the demand for residential properties was not realized and consequently properties remained unsold. In 1998, there were an estimated 60 million square metres of unsold high-class flats in China. Reconstructed, this would have created 600,000 hotel rooms, approaching the total number of hotel rooms supplied in that year. Each year, from 1994 to 1997, around 300 hotels were directly reconstructed from residential properties. This amounted to nearly 50 per cent of the total hotels built in this period (CNTA, 1998b). These new entrants de facto lacked the professionalism and experience in tourism with consequences for quality levels (CNTA, 1998b).

Pressure on quality also came from social changes in China. Traditional values had obviously been overturned during the Cultural Revolution and change continued during the Reform Era, with its emphasis on material rewards. At the same time Chinese communism itself became less involved in directly guiding moral behaviour (Lieberthal, 2004). As a result, behavioural patterns changed. Tourism was not exempt from the influence of this and plenty of individuals saw tourism as a source of quick or illegal money making. For example, some tour guides sought tips, which was forbidden by regulation and there were also examples of guides influencing the itineraries of tourist groups to ensure they purchased from certain shops in return for a commission. Similarly there were instances of travel agencies being set up and operating without a business licence (CNTA, 1997b). The Document of the National Tourism Works Conference 2004 described the seriousness of quality issues in the tourism industry:

> Recently, we always engage in removing chaos and improving the order of the tourism market . . . but the underlying problems are far from being solved. Some misconduct and illegal behaviour still exists. For example, undertaking businesses and work without obtaining the legal licences in travel agencies, tour guiding, tourist shops and tour buses, and other illegal behavior still cannot be stopped even after many law-enforcing actions. Without approval, some domestic travel agencies deliver international travel businesses; some international travel agencies run outbound travel services; some sales departments of travel agencies are contracted out; some employees take commissions, ask for tips without consent and impose shopping on tourists; this illegal business behaviour and misconduct

exists widely . . . At present, these problems have become negative factors hampering the recovery and rejuvenation of tourism.

(CNTA, 2004b: p.8)

In 2008, the same problem still existed, as described by the Document of the National Tourism Works Conference of that year:

> We have launched a regulatory campaign against serious offences which severely violate market order, including zero-charged tours, advertising misrepresentations, imposed shopping, business fraud etc. A batch of businesses has been inspected and punished. Through such campaigns, preliminary effectiveness has been attained against these serious offences that have breached and disturbed the market rules, and restrained the healthy development of our industry.
>
> (CNTA, 2008c)

With this background the CNTA developed a strong commitment to establish quality assurance mechanisms with the Director-General and senior officials playing crucial roles in their development (source: key informants). This needs to be seen in the context of national concerns. In 2003, for example, Premier Wen Jiabao gave a general instruction to improve business reliability over a five-year period and the Vice-Premier for tourism Wu Yi highlighted the need for business honesty and reliability. The CNTA subsequently started its campaign and in addition to training and publicity it incorporated stronger ethical values of 'honesty', 'trust', 'integrity', 'reliability' and 'goodwill' into its rules and standards. As an example of CNTA's commitment to quality assurance mechanisms, during the formulation of 'Provisional Methods for the Administration of Self-Financed Outbound Travel by Chinese Citizens', the leadership of the CNTA insisted that the principal policy and administrative responsibilities should be vested in the CNTA instead of the Ministry of Public Security. Eventually they succeeded in achieving this:

> Initially some comrades wanted to retreat, and then expected that the Ministry of Public Security would also retreat, so that a status quo could be reached. However, Director-General He Guangwei[6] took a very firm stance. Later, . . . we all found that Director-General He had firmly grasped the principles. We can say that because of our firm stance on the principles we finally obtained authority for the administration of outbound travel.
>
> (CNTA, 1998b: p.22)

> Director-General He Guangwei wrote to the party secretaries and governors of many provinces and explained that the negotiation and clarification with the Ministry of Public Security touched on the issue of 'principle', not on competition for authority.
>
> (CNTA, 1998b: p.21)

Initially institution building for quality assurance relied solely on coercive instruments. Subsequently the CNTA gradually recognized the advantage of developing standards, such as hotel star-ratings, and ensuring their effective adoption across the industry. This has meant the development of a quality assurance framework in tourism. A key informant commented:

> At present, we just have three regulations issued by the State Council; they are 'Regulation on the Administration of Travel Agencies' (1996, 2001 and 2009 versions), 'Regulation on the Administration of Tour Guides' (1999) and 'Regulation on the Administration of Outbound Travel' (1997 and 2002 versions). Our administration of the tourism industry mainly relies on quality standards.

The rules issued by the State Council that usually bear the title of 'Regulation' carry higher legal status and are more coercive than the rules issued by CNTA, with the title 'Administrative Method' or 'Implementation Method'. As noted by the key informant above, at present, there are only three regulations promulgated by the State Council for tourism. These Regulations and Administrative or Implementation Methods generally state the regulatory purpose, stipulate the market access requirements and prescribe the administrative procedures. They provide little in terms of quality standards and perhaps more importantly, in light of China's ambitions in relation to WTO membership, they are insufficient in themselves for the development of the market economy.

The move to a market economy required the transformation of government functions from micro control (i.e. direct intervention in enterprises) to macro management (i.e. industry and market management) through creating appropriate 'rules for the game'. In line with the market economy it was necessary to keep the regulatory approach to a minimum. As a result, standards, often on a non-compulsory basis, became more important. Actually standardization legislation in China began in 1988 to prepare for the market economy, when the CPC proclaimed the development of the commodity economy model. According to the Standardization Law (CNTA, 1998b), standards relating to quality should normally be on a recommended-basis, apart from when they relate to hygiene and safety, covering areas such as food, health, occupational safety, construction and building and environmental protection. Thus the CNTA takes this approach in implementing quality standards. Currently there are twenty-one standards, all voluntary (CNTA, 1998b, 2010b). This is in line with the CPC, which takes the view that market forces can prompt enterprises to become mature and self-accountable (CPC, 1992, 1993). Regulations, on the other hand, easily allow an enterprise to pass its business responsibilities to government in a way that does not fit the market economy. As the Vice-Premier in charge of tourism, Qian Qichen, remarked in 2001, 'on the basis of previous practical experience, a series of tourism rules and standards can

speed up the process of our tourism industry in gearing itself for the world'
(CNTA, 2004c).

The effectiveness and success of the first standards programme, the Star-rating of Hotels, triggered a wide application of quality standards programmes. International star-rating has been widely utilized by hotels and welcomed by consumers. Its adoption in China significantly helped hotels to position themselves for international tourists. As discussed in Chapter 7, the CNTA's success in this has brought the idea of 'star-rating' into more general use in China to include, for example, star-rated restaurants and shops. In its review of the effectiveness of its 'Hotel Star-Rating Programme (Specifications)' the CNTA commented:

> The Hotel Star-Rating Programme is a recommended standard, it is not compulsory for enterprises. So why have the enterprises implemented it? This is because the specification can help them. The specifications in all industries total 18,000, of which, the mandatory specifications amount to approximately 5,000. The State Administration of Quality and Technical Supervision [the forerunner of the SGAQSIQ] commented that the Hotel Star-Rating Programme is one of the best in implementation.
>
> (CNTA 1998b: p.21)

It is interesting to note that the Master Catalogue of Standardization Administration, under the jurisdiction of the State General Administration of Quality Supervision, Inspection and Quarantine (SGAQSIQ), did not initially cover the tourism sector. However, based on its success in tourism together with the growing importance of tourism, the SGAQSIQ endorsed tourism standardization and from 1993 appointed the CNTA as the sole authority in formulating the tourism quality specifications (CNTA, 1998b). In other words tourism has been fully included in the standardization movement and, as has already been noted, the CNTA designed the Catalogue for Tourism Quality Standards in 2000 with specifications under six broad categories: tour operation, accommodation, catering, travel, shopping and amusement. This is now on the SGAQSIQ's file (CNTA, 2000b).

Under the standardization law, there are two kinds of standards: national level and industry level. Approval by the SGAQSIQ is required for the former, with the CNTA responsible for the latter with support from other agencies where required. A further seventeen quality standards are being drafted. A clear theme in all these standards is to enhance competition for quality excellence. For example, the 'Rating and Evaluation for Quality Levels of Tourist Attractions' grades the quality of attractions into five levels with '5A' as the highest. To become a '5A' attraction applications can only be submitted after at least one year at '4A' (CNTA, 2004d, 2005c). The 'Standards for Excellent Tourist Cities' and 'Standards for Competitive Tourist Counties' (rural tourism) all set marks for the awards, with an itemized breakdown. As more and more cities attained the excellent level, the CNTA further formulated the 'Standards for the Best Tourist Cities' (interviews; CNTA, 2007e, 2007f).

W.R. Scott (1987, 2001) argues that the effectiveness of regulation depends on the existence of a relatively clear and unified demand, a mechanism to impose control, a legitimate agent to exercise control and available sanctions. The very comprehensive nature of tourism, the complexity of the tourism sector in China, the fragmented structure of authority and status of the CNTA do not now provide a basis for coercive rules. The fact that tourism developed in China at the same time as the transformation to a market economy was taking place has meant that there is a mixture of public and private involvement in tourism, a variety of quality levels as well as a combination of different views about regulation and quality standards. For example, in 2008, some 40 per cent of hotels were owned by the state, 6 per cent by collectives, 19 per cent by the private sector and 4 per cent by external investors; the remainder were in mixed domestic ownership (CNTA, 2009a). Foreign-owned hotels, geared to the international market, were keen for the government to tighten quality standards in order to raise the quality requirements generally. With this mixture of ownership and particularly with state-owned hotels being the responsibility of different government agencies and operated for different economic and non-economic motives, it would not have been possible for the CNTA, which in any case is a non-cabinet agency, to take a coercive regulatory approach to quality enhancement. For example, between the late 1990s and early 2000s, around 2,500 hotels were owned by different units by the military, judicial, party and government agencies. This has not changed much since 1992, notwithstanding the goal expressed by the General Secretary of the CPC, Hu Jintao, 'to speed up the separation of state-owned enterprises from their supervisory government agencies' (CPC, 2007). In this context, the development and implementation of recommended quality standards and a quality framework has provided the CNTA with an effective way to achieve advances in quality without significant policy disputes with other agencies.

During the process of developing the quality assurance arrangements, those that did not involve any conflict of objectives and interests proceeded smoothly. For example, the 'Standards for Excellent Tourist Cities' hardly touched the interests of other central agencies and with local support they were introduced smoothly. However, where there was a conflict of views that the CNTA was unable to resolve, this typically involved the vice-premier in charge of tourism, sometimes with other vice-premiers, and more recently local support has also been important. The implementation of the 'Rating and Evaluation for Quality Levels of Tourist Attractions' (REQLTA) is a good example. When the CNTA implemented this measure in 1999, four central agencies, the Ministry of Construction (now the Ministry of Housing and Urban–Rural Development), the State Administration of Cultural Heritage, the State General Administration of Environmental Protection (now the Ministry of Environmental Protection) and the State Forestry Administration, not only objected to the State Council against this measure but also refused to allow units under their administration to participate. The CNTA took the view that local support would be on their side. A key informant explained:

We [CNTA] were confident of our success in the implementation of REQLTA because local government supported us. Its application in Tibet was a typical example. At that time, the Tourism Bureau of the Government of the Tibet Autonomous Region initially submitted three tourist attractions to us [CNTA] for evaluation. However with strong opposition from the Local Heritage Bureau [under the state's administrative system for relics and heritage], the Tourism Bureau informed the CNTA in December 1999 of their intended withdrawal. This unexpected development created a dilemma for us, since at that time we were on the way to Tibet to undertake the evaluation; all we could do was wait for further news in Chengdu [the capital city of Sichuan Province] en route to Tibet. We tried to persuade the Tourism Bureau of Tibet that the REQLTA was more concerned with promoting local [tourism] development rather than introducing struggles between agencies, and requested the Bureau to seek support from the Chairman of Tibet [equivalent to provincial governor]. Very quickly on the evening of same day, the Chairman of Tibet expressed his thanks to the CNTA for its support and welcomed its evaluation visits. Tibet submitted a total of six attractions for evaluation ... With local support, divisions between central agencies became less important. With further lobbying by the CNTA, the State General Administration of Environmental Protection and the State Forestry Administration withdrew their opposition, considering that the REQLTA was not actually related to their policy responsibilities. After more than 5 years of implementation, the Ministry of Construction and the State Administration of Cultural Heritage also recognized that the REQLTA has not affected their own administrative systems but rather has enhanced the quality of scenic areas [from the perspective of tourist attractions], and they withdrew their disagreement.

Eventually the REQLTA was successfully adopted nationwide. In January 2000, the Vice-Premier in charge of tourism, Qian Qichen, granted A-Grade Certificates for Attractions to the first batch of awardees.

Conclusion to the five periods

Over the five periods dealt with in this and the preceding chapters it is clear that national tourism policy-making in China has been influenced by various factors, that have arisen through the policy-oriented learning and coordination undertaken by the policy players. At the centre of this process the Chinese tourism policy paradigm has emerged and evolved under the shift of ideological orthodoxies, particularly from the planned economy to the market economy. In summary, Chinese ideological orthodoxies have experienced three shifts. The first was the shift from 'politics-in-command', 'political struggle' and 'class struggle' to 'economic development and modernization'. This shift highlighted the economic function of tourism. The second was from the 'planned-economy model' to the 'market-economy model'. Compared to the first, this one involved a long, complicated and controversial political process. This 'marketization' set the context for the strong market growth of tourism, particularly domestic tourism. The third shift was from the central role of government and with a focus primarily on economic development to a more people-based and comprehensive approach covering political, social, economic as well as environmental issues. In this stage the quality of life of the Chinese people came in for greater attention, and tourism, particularly domestic tourism, was acknowledged as an important element in the quality of life. Also the comprehensive approach highlights the multiple roles of tourism.

The influence of these changes can be seen in the tourism policy paradigm. In the first historical period, from 1949 to 1978, as noted earlier, there was no tourism policy paradigm. The second period, between 1978 and 1985, was transitional, with an economic-oriented tourism policy paradigm emerging. During this period, the acute shortage of foreign exchange led the new Chinese leadership to consider international tourism as a foreign exchange earner. The ample tourism resources in China and the restoration of diplomatic relationships with the West convinced the Chinese leadership that the country was ready for the commercial development of tourism. The sharp increase in foreign exchange earned by international tourism convinced all the policy actors that tourism was an economic activity.

During the third period, between 1986 and 1991, although it had been realized that both international and domestic tourism were market-oriented and consumption-driven, it was also evident that such market-oriented approaches could not occur in the context of the planned economy. As a result the strong market growth of domestic tourism was disregarded. In terms of policy paradigm, there was a partial and incomplete evolution to market orientation, in the form of the adoption of international norms.

The fourth and fifth periods both lead into the market-economy era. Between 1992 and 1996 (the fourth period), the greater acceptance of the market economy meant that tourism policy could foster market-driven tourism. However, this period was largely exploratory and preparatory for the innovations in policy and developments of the fifth period which started in 1997. Influenced by the domestic environment, international circumstances and tourism performance, the tourism policy paradigm became far more people-based and comprehensive as well as market-oriented. In terms of the market, tourism became recognized as a significant means of development and a key industry in the national economy. As far as focus on the people is concerned, the boom in domestic and outbound travel has been viewed as important in enhancing their quality of life. And in its comprehensive approach tourism is now considered from political–ideological, economic, socio-cultural and diplomatic perspectives.

Three decades after the start of the Economic Reform and Open-door Policy, China's economy and society are now increasingly integrating with the outside world and China is feeling the impact of Western ideologies and practices. For the Chinese authorities, some of these deviate from existing socialist and Chinese practices. As far as domestic tourism is concerned, for the policy-makers it can be used to promote national coherence, socialist values and traditional Chinese culture and its rapid development and economic significance can be used as a key development tool. In socio-cultural terms, the popularity of domestic and outbound travel can be utilized to enhance quality of life and social harmony. As a latecomer to the international community, China considers that the international rules are largely those of the Western nations. During the course of continuing international integration, China not only expects to act as a fair player, but also intends to participate actively in the construction of new orders especially with the economic downturn after 2008. In this context international tourism is adopted as a vehicle for building national image and promoting friendship, while the enormous potential of China's outbound tourism can be used as a kind of diplomatic resource to obtain support. The scene is therefore set for tourism policy to cover the comprehensive range of functions that tourism can play in China.

The evolution of the Chinese tourism policy paradigm in every historical period has led to change and development in basic and concrete policy decisions. In the second and third periods, market-oriented tourism was regarded as 'insignificant' and did not have any position in China's state structure. In the current period, tourism has been positioned as a multifunctional and strategic industry. In the first period, only political and diplomatic goals existed, while in the second period both political and economic goals were emphasized. During the third and fourth period, economic goals became dominant. Currently tourism is now seen as important for achieving political-ideological, socio-cultural and diplomatic goals underpinned by a market-oriented economic basis. In the second and third period, only international tourism was given any importance; but since the fourth period international tourism has been joined by domestic and outbound tourism.

Basic policy decisions serve as general guidelines in directing the development of tourism. Implementation of these requires action. What this means is that the tourism policy paradigm, as a set of behavioural beliefs, cannot be implemented unless it can be institutionalized into rules, norms, standard operating procedures and structural forms. In China, apart from marketing and product development strategies, this has particularly found expression in institutional building in terms of regulations and standards which have accounted for the majority of the specific policy actions. Such actions began with institutional building for tourism in the second historical period. This was achieved in the face of some opposition from existing institutions. In the third historical period, the partial evolution of the tourism policy paradigm to marketization also resulted in partial institutionalization in this direction. This took the form of the adoption of hotel star-ratings, to reflect international norms. The fourth period was a trial phase in which the CNTA explored suitable market rules, while in the present period, full market implementation has been achieved with a quality assurance framework based on market principles of quality, market order, customer satisfaction and ethics.

Part III

Four particular regions of China

9 Tourism policy issues in four particular regions

This chapter is about four particular regions of China, namely the two Special Administrative Regions, Hong Kong and Macau, and Tibet and Taiwan. Tibet is included in this chapter because of its distinctive characteristics. Taiwan is included with particular reference to cross-Taiwan Strait relations. Given the breadth and complexity of the issues involved as well as the purpose of this book, the chapter focuses on key policy from China's perspective. The data sources for Hong Kong come from official archives, secondary sources and interviews with representatives from government, the tourist board and an industry association. For Macau, Tibet and Taiwan, the information comes from government documents, secondary literature and quasi-official reports.

Hong Kong and Macau SARs

The sovereignty of Hong Kong and Macau was handed over to China in 1997 and 1999 respectively, when they became special administrative regions (SARs). Under their constitutional documents, the Basic Law, the two SARs enjoy a high degree of autonomy, except for foreign relations and national defence. Adhering to the policy of 'One Country, Two Systems', China's socialist system and practices do not apply. As SARs, the tourism policy issues in these two regions have been characterized by active government intervention and the growing influence of the Chinese state. However, the state forces operate within the existing institutional framework prescribed by the Basic Law. These two factors have ultimately contributed to the prominence of tourism in Hong Kong's economy and its consolidation in Macau.

Hong Kong

Under British rule, the Hong Kong government adhered to a 'positive non-interventionism' policy that favoured laissez-faire management of the economy. Accordingly there was no specific policy decision for the development of travel and tourism. Established in 1952, the Hong Kong Tourist Association (HKTA) (now renamed the Hong Kong Tourism Board (HKTB)) as a statutory public body, was tasked solely with promoting Hong Kong as a tourist destination (HKSARG, 2009b). After the handover this changed, in that the government of the HKSAR (hereafter the HKSARG) formulated a set of long-term goals and strategies to foster its development. This was prompted both by the change in government, with a different ideology, and by the performance of tourism.

In the decade following the handover, the internal and external environment of Hong Kong underwent drastic and remarkable change. Externally, Hong Kong was not only hit by the Asian Financial Crisis and the 2008–9 worldwide economic downturn, but also faced opportunities and challenges from the Mainland economy. These external challenges revealed the weakness of the narrow economic structure that placed over-reliance on financial services and real estate (HKSARG, 1998). Internally, Hong Kong's economy has seen a period of rapid transition. From 1993 to 2003, the services sector experienced growth rates between 2.2 per cent and 7.3 per cent, while manufacturing and construction shrank significantly; for example, the construction sector only grew at an annual average rate of 0.7 per cent in the period (Chong, 2006: p.288). Among services, tourism demonstrated strong growth. Between 1997 and 2009, tourist arrivals increased from 11.27 to 29.59 million, while tourism receipts also rose from HK$72.1 to 162 billion (HKTB, 1997a–2009a; 2002b–2009b).

There have been three key changes in the governing ideology of Hong Kong which have a bearing on tourism development. The first is the incorporation of a long-term vision in government planning and development strategies. The British writer Richard Hughes described Hong Kong before 1997 as 'a borrowed place, a borrowed time' (Hughes, 1968, 1976), highlighting that the time factor stifled the development of Hong Kong before the handover. Since then Hong Kong has rid itself of the time restriction. In his policy speech in 1997, the first Chief Executive of the Hong Kong SAR Tung Chee-hwa remarked:

> Hong Kong has finally broken free from the psychological constraints brought about by the colonial era. We should have the courage to set aside past modes of thought and plan Hong Kong's long term future with new vision.
>
> (HKSARG, 1997: Section 3)

The second change relates to the integration with Mainland China. Hong Kong's economy has, since the 1990s, begun to link closely with her mainland counterpart with production bases gradually moving to the Pearl River Delta (PRD) in Guangdong Province, while management and services are retained locally. After the reunion with China, further integration formally entered the government agenda. Tung Chee-hwa started to extend this from the civil to the institutional sector:

> Strengthening economic co-operation with nearby provinces and cities is of particular importance to the future development of Hong Kong . . . the

SAR Government and the relevant mainland authorities have agreed that the 'Hong Kong and Mainland Major Infrastructure Projects Co-ordinating Committee' be re-established.

(HKSARG, 1997: Section 10)

Similar comments were included in subsequent policy speeches, but a clear breakthrough occurred in 2006 when the Chief Executive Donald Tsang suggested cooperating with the 11th Five-Year State Plan for the National Economy and Social Development, as an active response to its support for Hong Kong's key economic sectors, including tourism.

The third change was the adjustment in the traditional 'positive non-interventionism' philosophy. The Chief Executive Donald Tsang, in an address in 2005 (HKSARG, 2005b), indicated: 'We have a steadfast commitment to promoting economic development' (Section 71) and 'To implement the "Market Leads, Government Facilitates" principle, we will consider delivering more public services through Public-Private-Partnerships' (Section 77).

This new conception represents a substantial change in policy-making characterized by more positive government intervention than ever before, albeit it is assumed to be under the umbrella of 'Big Market, Small Government' (HKSARG, 2005b: Section 72). In this arena, tourism has become an active policy area to boost economic development and structural transformation.

The new environmental stimuli and the ideological shift gave rise to the emergence of a long-term strategy within which tourism has been granted significant status. Overall the government has aimed to maintain and enhance Hong Kong's position as Asia's world city comparable to London and New York in their parts of the world, rather than 'another Chinese city' (HKSARG, 2004: Section 7; 2005b: Section 74). In the meantime the government has also aimed to enlarge Hong Kong's role in China. From an official perspective, quality services are at the core of forging and strengthening its position (HKSARG, 2005a: Section 9), and tourism has a particular role in this. The government envisages tourism as an essential component in Hong Kong becoming a world metropolitan centre:

We have studied the roles of New York and London, which are not only the most cosmopolitan cities in America and Europe respectively, but are also international financial centres, tourist destinations, homes for the headquarters of multi-national corporations and international communication and transportation centres. I believe that Hong Kong too has the potential . . . enjoying a status similar to that of New York in America and London in Europe.

(HKSARG, 1998: Section 17)

and

Hong Kong already possesses many of the key features common to New York and London. For example, we are already an international centre of finance and a popular tourist destination, and hold leading positions in trade and transportation. If we can . . . continue to build on our strengths, we should be able to become world-class. Then, like New York and London . . .

(HKSARG, 1999: Section 44)

Except for the Asian Financial Crisis in 1998 and SARS in 2003, tourism in Hong Kong has enjoyed considerable growth and has significantly contributed to the economy, leading to the government's continuing elevation of its position from 'a stronghold' in 1998 (HKSARG, 1998: Section 44), to 'a major driving force' in 1999 (HKSARG, 1999: Section 32), to 'one of the major economic pillars' in 2001 (HKSARG, 2001: Section 79), and finally, since 2004, to 'one of four core (or pillar) industries' (HKSARG, 2004: Section 19; 2005a: Section 71; 2006: Section 14; 2007: Section 27; 2009a: Section 15). In order to stimulate its development, the government has set clear goals which, through public-private partnerships, are to promote Hong Kong as Asia's premier international city, and to make it a world-class destination for leisure and business visitors and MICE tourism (Meeting, Incentive, Convention and Exhibition). Also in the interests of the public, since 1997 the government has taken on a developmental role in providing attractions, with a number of projects completed as shown in Table 9.1. The government also plays a regulatory role in maintaining and enhancing market order and quality standards in tourism. For example, all travel agents have, since 2002, been required to obtain a licence prior to starting their business (HKSARG, 2009b).

Anticipating the effects of SARS, the central government in Beijing offered the 'Closer Economic Partnership Arrangement' (CEPA) to Hong Kong in June 2003, which lowered entry barriers for eligible Hong Kong businesses to the Mainland market; hotels and travel agents benefited from this. Previously Mainland Chinese were only allowed to visit Hong Kong for leisure in group tours. The Individual Visit Scheme (IVS) under CEPA enables eligible residents in designated cities to travel independently to Hong Kong. IVS arrivals have increased from 35 per cent of all Mainland tourists in 2004 to 57 per cent as of June 2009. As at June 2009, there had been over 40 million visitor arrivals from the Mainland through this scheme (HKSARG, 2009b). Overall, the IVS has put the Mainland market in the lead position of tourists to Hong Kong. The influence from the Chinese state is also reflected in institutional integration. In the 11th Five-Year State Plan for the National Economy and Social Development, the central government indicated support for Hong Kong's four pillar industries – financial services, tourism, logistics and information services – allowing mutual discussion and cooperation to develop.

The Hong Kong SAR has a well-established institutional framework for tourism. Under the Commerce and Economic Development Bureau of the HKSARG, the Tourism Commission established in 1999 is responsible for overall policy, strategy and coordinated development. The Hong Kong

Table 9.1 Government projects for tourism in Hong Kong SAR

Projects

Completed
1   Hong Kong Disneyland
2   Hong Kong Wetland Park
3   Ngong Ping 360
4   The Wisdom Path
5   Avenue of Stars
6   Tsimshatsui Promenade Beautification
7   Central and Western District Enhancement Scheme
8   Enhancement of the Sai Kung Waterfront
9   Lei Yue Mun Minor Improvement
10   'A Symphony of Lights' Light and Sound Show
11   Transport Link in Tsimshatsui East
12   Stanley Waterfront Improvement
13   Enhancement of Dr Sun Yat-Sen Historical Trail
14   Peak Improvement Scheme
15   Enhancement of the Green Tourism Attractions in New Territories

In progress
16   Redevelopment of Ocean Park
17   Visitor Signage Improvement Scheme
18   Aberdeen Tourism Project
19   Enhancement of Footbridges in Tsimshatsui
20   Lei Yue Mun Waterfront Enhancement Project
21   Development of a New Cruise Terminal at Kai Tak

Source: Tourism Commission website, the HKSAR Government (www.tourism.gov.hk).

Tourism Board still retains its primary functions of promoting Hong Kong as a worldwide destination and enhancing the tourist experience. Its members are all appointed by the government, from various sectors. As a functional constituency, tourism holds a seat at the Legislative Council of the SAR. In terms of business, the Hong Kong Hotels Association (HKHA) and the Hong Kong Travel Industry Council (HKTIC) are responsible for self-regulation.

Macau

Unlike Hong Kong, Macau has traditionally had a relatively small economy dominated by gambling. Immediately before the handover, the gaming economy in Macau suffered a considerable downturn from the Asian Financial Crisis. Since 1999, the government of the Macau SAR has successfully led a structural transition from a gaming-led tourism economy to a tourism-led services economy, with substantial support from the central government in Beijing. The Chief Executive of the Macau SAR Government (MSARG) Edmund Hau put forward this initiative in 2002 in this way:

As well as serious consideration of our region's many advantages and attributes, it is clear that an industrial structure is taking shape in Macao with the gaming (tourism) sector[1] as its 'head', and the service industry as its 'body', driving the overall development of other industries [and] to meet this challenge, economic and other departments must prepare well in terms of resource allocation, talent cultivation and ideology.

(MASRG, 2002: p.11)

The government's overall vision is to position Macau as a 'tourism capital of cultures, amusement and conventions'. Over the years, the policy issues and decisions in tourism have revolved around the deregulation in the gaming sector, diversification of tourism components and quality enhancement. Between 1962 and 2001, Macau's gaming sector was almost monopolized by the *Sociedade de Turismo e Diversões de Macau* (STMD), with the sole licence granted by the Portuguese Macau government. By taking the opportunity presented by the expiry of the licence, the SAR Government abolished the gambling monopoly by issuing in 2002 another two licences to Wynn Resorts and Galaxy Casinos. It was expected that this liberalization measure would not only introduce competition, but also support the policy of economic transformation. There were a total of thirty-one casinos in Macau at the end of 2008 (MSARG, 2008b).

Recognizing that reliance on the gaming sector made tourism vulnerable, the government has, since 2000, started to pursue a policy of diversification. In his first policy address the Chief Executive Edmund Ho stated:

Bolstering Macau's identity, shaped through the meeting of eastern and western cultures, will enhance its unique character and attract more tourists. Thus, a prime concern of the Government will be to ensure high quality services, diversified attractions . . . to foster strategic co-operation for regional tourism, diversify tourism promotion and also create the mechanisms for co-ordinating international cultural and sports events and activities.

(MSARG, 2000: pp.13–14)

Master planning is used as an overall instrument to implement this strategy. For diversification, the government explored the historical and cultural appeal of Macau and integrated these elements in building new attractions. Three years after submission, Macau was formally inscribed in UNESCO's World Heritage List in 2005 as the 'Historic Center of Macau'. This makes it the thirty-first such site in China. Appraised by UNESCO as a 'unique testimony to the meeting of aesthetic, cultural, architectural and technological influences from East and West', this inclusion significantly raised the cultural attractiveness of Macau. A series of marketing activities were subsequently launched to promote this, through websites, photographic competitions, TV advertising, and brochures and handbooks. The bill for the 'Law of Cultural Heritage Protection' was completed in 2009 (Ren, 2006, 2009). In addition to cultural elements, the development of the convention business is another strand of diversification. This was announced by the MSARG in 2003, reiterated in 2005 and consolidated in 2006.

> We will fully exploit and strengthen the advantages we have already built in the conference and exhibition industry . . . We will also cooperate closely with the industry as a whole, in order to organize convention and exhibition activities that emphasize effectiveness, uniqueness, professionalism and high quality, and which will ultimately attract even more international buyers and partners.
>
> (MSARG, 2006: pp.14–15)

A set of concrete measures has subsequently been put in place to start development, including the training of specialists, promotion of regional exchange, provision of information and guidance, establishment of a providers' database and organization of major conferences such as the World Cultural Heritage Convention in 2008 and the Developmental Forum and Exhibition for Macau's International Environmental Protection Cooperation also in 2008, as well as marketing Macau as a convention and exhibition centre. As of 2008, Macau had hosted some twenty-eight large-scale international conferences (Ren, 2009). This also chimed well with the government's intention to enhance quality which they view as the key to tourism development. As they express it:

> Under our planned industrial structure, tourism and the gaming industry remain our development priorities. The time is now favourable for building a world-class gaming industry and improving its related services . . . Regarding the development of the tourism industry, the Government will continue to accelerate the construction of tourism 'hardware', promote tourism in a focused and effective manner and, most importantly, enhance the quality of service.
>
> (MSARG, 2003: pp.8–9)

Under SAR Government jurisdiction, the Macau Institute for Tourism (IFT) offers a wide range of professional programmes, specialized courses and vocational training for meeting human resource demands. To ensure compliance with minimum service standards, the Government continues regulatory action against illegal and unethical commercial businesses. In the meantime, it also allocated MOP (Macau currency) $50 million in 2002 for training and associated research related to quality enhancement (Ren, 2003). Like Hong Kong, Macau has also enjoyed the economic benefits from CEPA and its Individual Visit Scheme that took effect from October 2003.

Tourism remains the mainstay of Macau's economy but a decade after the handover, the industry is now more diversified in both supply and demand, and more competitive, viable and sustainable in the face of global competition. In 1999, tourist arrivals totalled 7.4 million, with 56 per cent from Hong Kong. By 2008 this had reached 22.9 million with multiple market sources and rising growth from foreign tourists (i.e. other than the Mainland, Hong Kong and Taiwan) (MSARG, 2008c).

Tibet and Taiwan

As far as the Chinese government is concerned the tourism policy related to both Tibet and cross-Taiwan Straits relations has to be seen in the context of political integration and national union in China.

Tibet

Situated in western China, the Tibet Autonomous Region has a total area of 1.2 million square kilometres, nearly one-eighth of China's total land surface. It borders India, Nepal, Burma, Sikkim and Bhutan with a frontier of 4,000 kilometres. With this strategic location, Tibet is viewed by China as her 'Southwestern Fort'. Over centuries, the lives, religious shrines, customs and festivals of Tibetans have formed a unique culture that appeals to both the internal and outside world (Beijing Review, 2008). But the sensitivities of Tibet's location have been raised for China by forces that have been seeking separation to the extent that it is now a key element in the country's national unity and security. The General Secretary of the CPC, Jiang Zemin, remarked in 1994.

> The works for Tibet occupy a strategic status in our party and state affairs. Our comrades, especially those senior officials in the party and government, must be clearly aware that the stability, development and security of Tibet are concerned with our national stability, development and security.
>
> (*China Tibet News*, 2008)

Because of its national significance, matters relating to Tibet have been institutionalized into China's party-state political structure. The responsible party apparatuses and state administrations comprise the Department of United Front Works of the CPC Central Committee, the State Ethnic Affairs Commission (cabinet agency) and the State Administration for Religious Affairs (non-cabinet central agency), which come together with the regional authorities of Tibet as a policy community. On top of this the Central Tibet Works Conference acts as the nation-wide forum for decision-briefing, brainstorming, consensus building and mobilization. The Conference has met five times between 1980 and 2010.

Compared with equivalent regions in China, Tibet is relatively backward in socio-economic terms and has had a very slow pace of development. In 2008 its GDP totalled RMB¥39.6 billion. This is just 1.1 per cent that of Guangdong Province, one of China's most developed regions. It also lags significantly behind other less developed regions like Xinjiang, Gansu, Guizhou, Qinhai and Qingxia (SSB, 2009). This is largely because Tibet historically has depended on agriculture, stock rearing and handicrafts. The tourism potential of the Himalayas and the centuries-old culture and traditions are now being recognized as development options.

Accordingly, in the last Central Tibet Works Conference, held in 2001, the Chinese leaders put forward initiatives within which tourism was given primary importance. General Secretary Jiang Zemin repeatedly underscored that the stability and development of Tibet mattered for China's core interests, including ethnic union, national security and foreign relations and that these could be strengthened by speeding up economic development and promoting stability. Premier Zhu Rongji stressed the importance of tourism for Tibet's economic development and initiated its development as a 'pillar' industry, alongside the more traditional sectors (*People's Daily*, 2001). Actually Tibet's tourism is also closely tied up with its stability. Acknowledging Tibet's limited capacities, the central government continues to adopt the approach of 'Aiding Tibet' by mobilizing country-wide and state–society support. This approach takes multiple forms, such as favourable policy measures, the provision of resources, technology transfer, the secondment of experts and guidance. Tourism forms an inseparable component in the whole aid programme.

The CNTA organized two study visits to Tibet in 1996 and 2001. In the latest visit, the CNTA suggested its support for master planning, central coordination, education and training, marketing as well as information technology (CNTA, 2001e). Though the CNTA has since 2001 started a programme of help for Tibet (CNTA, 2005b), perhaps the most important decision was from the current CPC General Secretary Hu Jintao, who served as the party chief of Tibet between 1988 and 1992. Faced with insufficiency of tour guides, Hu paid special attention to Tibet's tourism. In 2002 and 2003, he directly instructed the CNTA to help the development of tour guides through the provision of experienced professionals in a kind of mentorship programme, and education and training. Hu remarked:

> The [China] National Tourism Administration should offer support to the team-building of tour guides in Tibet, which can take place in the form of aid [delivered on 17 October 2002].
>
> (CNTA, 2005b)

> Your [CNTA's] plan [i.e. responding to Hu's above instructions] is very good, you are expected to emphasize the implementation. From the long-term perspective, the education institutions in the Mainland can organize Tibetan classes to train tour guides, of which the intakes can be from

the Tibetan graduates in the Mainland's secondary schools [delivered on 21 January 2003].

(CNTA, 2005b)

The CNTA has so far organized eight programmes with over 400 individuals (CNTA, 2009h). The CNTA subsequently proceeded to open a tourism college in the University of Tibet, and to run undergraduate tourism programmes in some selected education institutions in the Mainland, specifically for Tibet. Further, following the Central Tibet Works Conference in 2001 and motivated by the centre, the regional government of Tibet enhanced the contents of the policy document 'to speed up the development of tourism' (originally made in 1996) (CNTA, 2001e) so as further to implement the central decisions. This was of course with support from the local tourism industry, which in 2008 offered eighty-six star-rated hotels and forty-seven travel agencies which, together with other establishments, directly employed over 7,000 people. Running about 1,950 km from Xining in Qinghai Province to Lhasa in Tibet, the Qinghai-Tibet Railway, completed in 2006, has served both to stimulate development and accelerate tourist flows (D.Q. Liu *et al.*, 2007). As a result, tourism in Tibet has experienced fast development since 2001. International arrivals increased from 127,148 in 2001 to 365,370 in 2007, while the international receipts rose from US$46 million to US$135 million during the same period (CNTA, 2001a–2009a).[2]

Cross-Taiwan Strait relations

Although it has always been a part of China, ever since the civil war, when the defeated Guomindang (the Nationalist Party of China) forces retreated there in 1949, Taiwan has been politically separated from the Mainland and relations between the two parts of the country have been strained with communications and travel severely restricted. In the intervening period efforts have been made to relieve the situation. For example, in 1979, the Chinese National People's Congress announced a 'Three Links' policy (direct postal, transportation and trade links), only to be met with Taiwan's 'Three-No' policy (no contact, no compromise and no negotiation). The situation eased in 1987 when the Taiwan side permitted the Taiwanese, especially demobilized soldiers, to visit the Mainland and for two decades to 2008, there were travel flows between the two although largely one-way, from Taiwan and indirect, through third regions, particularly Hong Kong. Actually only the Taiwanese could travel to the Mainland on their own initiative. For their mainland counterparts, their travel was limited to journeys for business, exchange or visiting relatives and then only by invitation. Sightseeing and leisure trips were not permitted. In 2001, Taiwan began to allow entry to residents of the Mainland as a part of visits to other destinations. Furthermore initial 'direct links', including leisure travel, were made between Kinmen and Matsu in Taiwan, and Xiamen on the Mainland, the closest points across the Straits.

This so-called 'Mini Direct Links', was deliberately started on a trial basis, and on a small scale to allow for it to become politically acceptable in Taiwan. From 2003, to accommodate the travel demands for business trips and for the Taiwanese working on the Mainland, air links were introduced. These were, however, restricted to charter flights between designated points, notably Shanghai and Taipei and at specific times of the year, mainly holidays, and with a stopover in a third region, Hong Kong or Macau. Later such services were extended to all Taiwanese on the Mainland, such as students and tourists (CNTA, 1995b; Huang and Huang, 2006, 2009).

The political background to further developments came with the change in the ruling party in 2000 when, after being in power since 1949, the Nationalist Party (GMD) was replaced by the Democratic Progressive Party (DPP). The new administration was strongly supportive of the separation between Taiwan and the Mainland, as a result of which cross-strait relations became increasingly strained. Two developments, however, prompted increases in contact. First, in 2005 the CPC and GMD held their first historic meeting in Beijing after six decades of separation, when agreement was reached to improve the Mainland–Taiwan relations. Second, the people of Taiwan, who had become increasingly prosperous as a result of their economic success, and who had benefited from communications and business ties with the Mainland, recognized the need to take full advantage of the accelerated economic development of the Mainland. These developments put pressure on the ruling DPP to take a more positive stance, such as 'Mini Direct Links' as noted earlier. In 2008, the GMD returned to office and then progress came from the newly elected leader of the authorities of Taiwan, Ma Ying-Jeou, who voiced a pro-'One-China stance' for closer relations with the Mainland. The timing of this, following the tensions of the DPP period of office, and the worldwide economic crisis, which had significantly affected Taiwan, prompted renewed interest in strengthening links with the Mainland as a catalyst for the island's economic redevelopment (Huang and Huang, 2007). Opening Taiwan to tourists from the Mainland was seen as an important part of these economic considerations. It was estimated by the Mainland Affairs Office in Taiwan in June 2008 that opening travel could attract 110 million visitors from the Mainland generating around TWD$60 billion (around US$1.9 billion) in tourism receipts per year (*Hong Kong Wenweipo Daily* (Wenweipo), 12 June 2008). There was also a political angle to this, in that it was thought to be important by the Taiwanese for the Mainlanders to experience their political developments and for Beijing the opening up of tourism was seen as a way to strengthen the economic and social ties between the two sides as a part of ultimate political integration.

The historic breakthrough in Mainland–Taiwan relations came in 2008 when on 13 June, two authorized semi-official organizations, The Association for Relations Across the Taiwan Straits (ARATS) representing the Mainland, and The Straits Exchange Foundation (SEF) on behalf of Taiwan, signed two agreements that introduced full direct links across the Straits. The first of these,

'Agreement on Mainland Residents Travelling to Taiwan Made by the Two Sides of the Taiwan Straits' concerned leisure travel. This first opened thirteen province-equivalent regions for leisure tours to Taiwan on the basis of group travel, with expansion to thirty-one regions in 2010. In the second, 'Key Notes About the Arrangements for Charter Flights Made by the Two Sides of the Taiwan Straits', both sides agreed initially to open a total of thirteen airports for direct flights, five on the Mainland and eight in Taiwan. Both of these initiatives came into effect on 4 July 2008 (*Hong Kong Wenweipo Daily* (Wenweipo), 14 June 2008).

In order to cope with this new travel flow, various policy and administrative measures were introduced by the Chinese government. The CNTA together with the Taiwan Affairs Office of the State Council and the Ministry of Public Security issued a measure under the title 'Administrative Methods for the Travel of Mainland Residents to the Taiwan Region'. In addition to the 'group-in and group-out' requirement, this administrative measure made it clear that no personal or independent activities were allowed during the time in Taiwan. As CNTA's extension arm, the semi-official body – the Association for Tourism Exchanges Across the Taiwan Straits – further issued two supplementary administrative documents: 'Notices to Mainland Residents Travelling to the Taiwan Region' and 'Administrative Methods for Tour Staff in the Travel of Mainland Residents to the Taiwan Region'. Both stipulate that neither the tour staff nor the Mainland residents can engage in any activities that are considered detrimental to Mainland–Taiwan relations (CNTA, 2008h, 2008i).

Between July 2008 and May 2010, a total of over 1 million tourists from the Mainland visited Taiwan; their length of stay was typically six nights with an average expenditure of US$295 per person per day or US$1,800 for the whole stay (CNTA, 2009i, 2010g). With this economic impact, tourism from the Mainland to Taiwan also has developed a political dimension in furthering Beijing's interests. For example, following the visit of the Dalai Lama at the invitation of the DPP Mayor of Kaohsiung, almost all the hotel bookings from the Mainland were cancelled from late August to October 2009, around 4,000 rooms. Similarly some Mainland tour groups also decided temporarily not to travel to southern Taiwan, which is seen as being notably separatist (*Hong Kong Mingpao Daily* (Mingpao), 18 September 2009, 11 October 2009).

Notwithstanding these developments, tourism across the Taiwan Straits has also started to play its role in assisting the political integration. For example, in October 2009, after six decades of separation, the Mainland and Taiwan for the first time appointed semi-official delegates, with their primary functions of promoting cross-straits travel and tourism. The representative from the Mainland is the former division-director of the CNTA, while his counterpart is also a senior civil servant with the authorities of Taiwan. The two offices were formally inaugurated in May 2010 (*Hong Kong Mingpao Daily* (Mingpao), 23 October 2009; CNTA, 2010h).

Conclusion

In conclusion, this chapter briefly examines tourism policy issues in four regions of China in the national context. For Hong Kong and Macau SARs, tourism policy is marked by active and increasing government involvement to support tourism, resulting in the rising importance of tourism particularly in economic terms. The situation in Tibet and cross-Taiwan Straits relations is similar in that tourism is being supported by the public authorities, with important economic implications, but tourism is also, and perhaps primarily, seen in terms of its role of assisting political integration and national union.

Part IV

Theoretical and practical implications

10 Theoretical implications

'You can't go further than China' – Chinese proverb
(cited in Richter, 1989: p.23)

This chapter explores the theoretical implications of this study of policy-making for tourism in China. In particular it considers the issues in relation to the conceptual framework set out in Chapter 3. In doing so it focuses on the period after 1978. As explained, before that date tourism was essentially subordinate to foreign affairs and did not form a separate policy area.

The national tourism policy of China

As outlined in Chapter 3, Chinese tourism policy can be conceptualized as a set of interrelated decisions or non-decisions and actions or inactions formulated and implemented by government. These decisions and actions can be seen as being mutually supportive and complementary, notwithstanding their different purposes and scope. Currently the decisions take a fairly broad view of tourism, to include its political, diplomatic, social, environmental as well as economic dimensions. The tourism policy decisions themselves fall into two broad categories: basic and concrete, the former guiding the latter. In line with the conceptual framework, the basic policy decisions spring from the tourism policy paradigm for China. This provides guidelines for China's tourism development, classified here into three groups: tourism in the context of the state as a whole; the development goals; and the strategies. Its position in the state provides the top-level policy decisions. At this top level tourism is viewed as a strategic component of the country's Economic Reform and Open-door Policy. As far as the development goals are concerned, Chinese tourism policy above all has economic goals but it is also possible to identify political–ideological, socio-cultural and diplomatic goals. In terms of development strategy, since 1978 this can be summed up as: 'to develop tourism with great endeavour' and 'to speed up the development of tourism' with the focus shifting from just international tourism in 1978 to include also domestic and outbound travel.

The basic policy decisions in their turn provide direction for the concrete decisions, which deal with particular problems, issues and opportunities, such as product development or quality enhancement. Most tourism policy decisions occur at this level and they embrace a wide range of issues. In many ways such policy decisions may appear fragmented and disjointed, dealing as they do with such a range of issues, but to the extent that they are dealing with similar problems related to different aspects of tourism they also demonstrate many logical consistencies.

The interrelationships of policy factors

The conceptual framework provides a basis for understanding policy development and change through the interrelationships among the policy factors. Its explanatory abilities rest with whether and how the interrelationships matter in the policy-making process; and if any patterns can be identified.

Interactive coalescence

The experience of China confirms the suggestion that tourism policy-making takes place through the interactive coalescence of policy factors, rather than being driven by any single policy factor. Tourism policy decisions emerge from multiple causes. For example, the policy decision to develop tourism as an economic activity post 1978 was effected by the shift in ideological orthodoxies, the restoration of diplomatic relationships, the shortage of foreign exchange, the initiative of the top leaders and the subsequent building of an economic-oriented tourism policy paradigm. By themselves any one or two factors are insufficient to explain the shift. In the absence of economic development orthodoxy, the economic function of tourism, which previously served political and diplomatic ends, would not have been recognized and justified. Without the shortage of foreign exchange, the foreign currency earning capacity of tourism would not have been highlighted. The economic decisions about tourism, however, could not have started if normal bilateral relationships with the major tourist-generating countries had not been resumed by 1978. In their turn the role played by the authoritative pre-eminent leaders was essential. Only leaders like Deng Xiaoping and Chen Yun had the power to initiate the development of tourism, a politically sensitive decision which at the time lacked bureaucratic consensus. Even so, the effective implementation of policy still rested with the bureaucrats. Their view of tourism only changed slowly from it being seen as a political activity, to an economic activity with concomitant policy decisions relating to foreign exchange earnings and relaxation of market access.

During this process the policy factors interacted. The emergence and formation of the new tourism policy paradigm was credited to economic orthodoxies and tourism performance. Only under the economic development orthodoxy could the commercial role of tourism be acknowledged. But for this to happen it needed the doubtful bureaucrats to be convinced of its foreign exchange earning potential. In this case three key policy factors were at play: ideological orthodoxies, tourism performance and the tourism policy paradigm.

The funnel-of-causality model (King 1973; Hofferbert, 1974; Simeon, 1976; Howlett and Ramesh, 1995, 2003; Howlett *et al.*, 2009) suggests that the policy factors are intertwined in a 'nested' pattern of mutual interaction in which institutions exist within prevailing sets of ideas and ideologies, ideologies within relations of power, and relations of power within a larger social and material environment. This idea of an 'interactive coalescence' concept adds a dynamic and multilateral dimension to the funnel-of-causality model. This supports the comments from Howlett and Ramesh (1995: p.112; 2003: p.132) and Howlett *et al.* (2009: p.100) who suggest that the funnel-of-causality model explains very little in terms of how general forces such as the environmental context, ideologies and economic interests actually function in shaping policy-making. The application of the 'interactive coalescence' concept in China's tourism policy-making context helps to fill this gap.

More importantly, Howlett and Ramesh (1995: p.111; 2003: p.132) as well as Howlett *et al.* (2009: p.99) comment that the greatest weakness of the funnel of causality lies in the absence of exact relationships or causal significance. They further point out that both policy actors and institutions play a crucial role in the policy-making process, even though one may be more significant than another in specific settings; but beyond this they do not provide further theoretical generalization. In general, specific relationships or significant causalities can help unravel the intricacies of interrelationships of policy factors in affecting the policy-making.

Interrelationships and significant causalities

The exploration here is approached in the form of some twelve propositions. According to Reason (1998: p.265), propositions refer to a kind of knowledge about something that is presented in statements and theories. As already explained, China's national tourism policy-making process post 1978 proceeded within two settings. First, China's political economy model shifted from a planned economy to a market economy; the transition has not been fully completed. Second, when the decision was made to commercialize tourism development in 1978, the government lacked the knowledge, professionalism and institutions to start the economic development of tourism. These provide the context for the twelve propositions that are set out and explained in this chapter. A summary of the propositions is grouped under five headings in Table 10.1.

Ideology and the tourism policy paradigm

CHINA'S TOURISM POLICY PARADIGM

Does a policy paradigm exist and function in a tourism context? This empirical examination of national tourism policy-making in China suggests its existence

Table 10.1 Twelve propositions

Propositions

Ideology and the tourism policy paradigm

1　The tourism policy paradigm consists of ideological orthodoxies (i.e. essentials) and tourism-specific essentials.

2　The tourism-specific essentials are configured by ideological orthodoxies, environmental circumstances and tourism attributes.

3　The tourism policy paradigm and its constituent essentials cannot be formed when they are opposite to the reigning ideological orthodoxies of the state.

4　Both ideology and the tourism policy paradigm are based on a systematic set of beliefs that have cognitive (i.e. construct, knowledge) and evaluative (i.e. values) capacities.

5　Ideology and the tourism policy paradigm are interdependent.

Tourism policy paradigm

6　The tourism policy paradigm acts as the hub of the tourism policy-making process.

Tourism policy paradigm and tourism institutions

7　In countries such as China, where the state plays a dominant role, when tourism development starts from nothing and a tourism policy paradigm is entirely absent at the outset, institutionalization of the tourism policy paradigm plays a key role in the policy-making process.

8　The tourism policy paradigm and tourism institutions have a synergistic relationship.

9　When new ideological orthodoxies and a new policy paradigm arise the existing institutions will be antagonistic but political pressures mean that they will eventually change.

Tourism policy players

10　Policy-making in tourism is a political process in which the policy-makers engage in policy-oriented learning and coordination.

11　When ideological orthodoxies, the tourism policy paradigm and the institutions change, the role of the policy actors is of key importance, more so than the existing institutions.

On the whole

12　The inter-relationships of policy factors serve to drive the tourism policy-making process.

and its pervasive significance in influencing China's tourism policy-making. The attributes of China's tourism policy paradigm differentiate it from the policy paradigms examined in previous studies (e.g. P. Hall, 1990, 1993). Notably the experience of China highlights the importance of the ideational dimension in tourism policy-making, which, so far, has had little attention in the existing tourism policy literature. Previous work, in other fields, suggests that ideational factors stand at the core of policy-making, with ideology and the policy paradigm as the two well-established ideational factors although both Hall (1990, 1993) and Menahem (1998), for example, suggest that its structure or contents need further inquiry.

The Chinese tourism policy paradigm can be conceptualized from this study as a set of behavioural beliefs held by the policy-makers towards policy-making and tourism development. In general, it represents a hierarchical and causal system of behavioural beliefs possessing both cognitive and evaluative attributes accepted by the tourism policy-makers. This provides the starting point for the *First Proposition* that the *Chinese tourism policy paradigm consists of ideological orthodoxies (i.e. essentials) and tourism-specific essentials*. These two come together in forming the Chinese tourism policy paradigm. This is set out in some detail in Table 10.2. China's tourism policy paradigm has a solid ideological basis, as the PR China was founded on socialist and communist ideologies. The ideological essentials stand above the tourism-specific essentials and embody socialism, nationalism and traditional Chinese values including, for example, hospitality and friendship, which are largely regarded as given. These are shown as the Ideological Essentials in Table 10.2.

These ideological essentials set the context for the development of tourism. In brief, tourism development in China takes place within the context of Socialism with Chinese Characteristics. Socialism with Chinese Characteristics ultimately aims for the establishment of a harmonious society that will satisfy the people's material and spiritual wants. It places socialist, communist and nationalist values at its core; it insists on people-based, all-round and co-ordinated development with economic modernization as a central theme and it takes a pragmatic approach to development on the basis that it fits the reality of China under a Socialist Market Economy. It also advocates active participation and image building worldwide. Under these ideological essentials, sex tourism, gambling tourism, broadcasting of erotic films in tourist areas, asking for tips, seeking commissions, are all strictly forbidden.

The tourism-specific essentials present the understanding of the policy-makers towards the development of tourism in China. The present tourism-specific essentials cover three causally related aspects: know-why, know-what and know-how, as shown in Table 10.2. 'Know-why' essentials are part of the deep beliefs about tourism development in China and are closely related to its status in the country's state structure. At present, tourism is viewed as an industry that essentially is not important for China's national security and survival but it is considered as inseparable from China's Economic Reform and Open-door Policy. 'Know-what' essentials are based on the understanding about tourism development in China. Tourism is recognized as a market and consumption-driven industry and as an important catalyst for development and economic modernization. Tourism is viewed as having multiple capacities for political–ideological, economic, socio-cultural as well as diplomatic functions. 'Know-how' essentials advise the policy-makers about 'what ought to be done' and 'how it should be done'. Central and local government should guide and prescribe market forces for the most part with normative instruments.

Proposition Two is that *the tourism-specific essentials are configured by ideological orthodoxies, environmental circumstances and tourism attributes.*

Table 10.2 The evolution of the Chinese tourism policy paradigm 1978–present

	Historical Period Two 1978–85	Historical Period Three 1986–91	Historical Period Four 1992–7	Historical Period Five 1997–present
Ideological essentials				
	Tourism development in China should be *conducive* and *contribute* to China's Socialism with Chinese Characteristics (socialist material and spiritual civilizations):	Tourism development in China should be *conducive* and *contribute* to China's Socialism with Chinese Characteristics (socialist material and spiritual civilizations):	Tourism development in China should be *conducive* and *contribute* to China's Socialism with Chinese Characteristics (socialist material and spiritual civilizations):	Tourism development in China should be *conducive* to China's Socialism with Chinese Characteristics (socialist material and spiritual civilizations) **for the establishment of a 'Well-off' and 'Socialist Harmonious Society':**
	– Socialist and communist values at core	– Socialist and communist values at core	– Socialist and communist values at core	– Socialist and communist values at core – **'Socialist Core Values System'**
	– Economic modernization at core;	– Economic modernization at core	– Economic modernization at core	**that also embrace Confucianism and traditional moral values**
	– Nationalism (i.e. national coherence, ethnical union, promotion of traditional Chinese culture and values)	– Nationalism (i.e. national coherence, ethnical union, promotion of traditional Chinese culture and values)	– Nationalism (i.e. national coherence, ethnical union, promotion of traditional Chinese culture and values)	– **People-based, comprehensive and coordinated development, with economic**
	– A pragmatic pace and mode that fits China's realities	– A pragmatic pace and mode that fits China's realities	– A pragmatic pace and mode that fits China's realities	**modernization at the core, to satisfy the rising material and spiritual wants of the Chinese**
	– Under the Central Planned Economy Model	– **Under the Planned Commodity Economy Model**	– **Under the Socialist Market Economy Model being constructed**	– Nationalism and patriotism (i.e. national coherence,
	– Join the world, but not directly challenging the leadership of the United	– Join the world, but not directly challenging the	– Join the world, but not directly challenging the	

States and Soviet Union in world affairs; but unwaveringly safeguarding China's national interests	leadership of the United States and Soviet Union in world affairs; but unwaveringly safeguarding China's national interests	leadership of the US-led Western world in world affairs; but unwaveringly safeguarding China's national interests	ethnical union, promotion of traditional Chinese culture and values) – A pragmatic mode that fits China's realities – **Social harmony** – **Under the Socialist Market Economy Model** (government for economic regulation instead of economic administration) – **Actively participating in the development of world order in multilateralism and taking opportunities in launching initiatives**

Tourism-specific essentials

Know-why aspect	Tourism is an essential component of China's Economic Reform and Open-door Policy	Tourism is an essential component of China's Economic Reform and Open-door Policy	Tourism is an essential component of China's Economic Reform and Open-door Policy	– **In the national context and state structure, tourism is a strategic sector because of its inseparability from China's further openness and integration with the world and national image building** – **But tourism is not of central importance in terms of national/economic security compared with such industries as energy, banking, telecommunications**

continued . . .

Table 10.2 continued . . .

	Historical Period Two 1978–85	Historical Period Three 1986–91	Historical Period Four 1992–7	Historical Period Five 1997–present
Know-what aspect	– Tourism is an economic activity based on foreign exchange earnings – International tourism is more important than domestic tourism since the latter is unable to earn the foreign exchange	– Tourism is an economic activity based on foreign exchange earnings – International tourism is more important than domestic tourism since the latter is unable to earn the foreign exchange *Note:* – Market-oriented essential could not be accepted under the planned economy model	– **Tourism is a market- and consumption-driven industry** – **National policy-making and tourism development should be congruent with the Socialist Market Economy** – **Both international and domestic tourism are important means of development; but international tourism is granted more consideration because of its foreign exchange earning capabilities** – **Development of outbound travel should be controlled; discretionary and reckless development should not be encouraged**	– Tourism is a market- and consumption-driven industry. – **Tourism (both international and domestic) is an important catalyst for all-round and coordinated development, with the focus on the economic perspective** – **Domestic tourism is viewed as its mainstay and has become increasingly important, especially in the face of unstable international demand** – **Tourism is appreciated as a multi-functional industry that has a comprehensive role in China's political-ideological, economic, social-cultural, diplomatic and ecological contexts, on the basis of economic and market-oriented development** – **Starting from the end of**

				– **2009, tourism is further expected to become a 'strategic pillar industry in the national economy'** – **National policy-making and tourism development should be congruent with the Socialist Market Economy Model, in which the state plays the directing role, through guiding and prescribing market forces** – **Development of outbound travel should be at an adequate pace, discretionary development should not be encouraged**
Know-how aspect	– Tourism development should proceed under socialist principles, in Chinese style and within the existing capacities – Central and local tourism administrations should exercise 'tourism xitong' management	– Tourism development should proceed under socialist principles, in Chinese style and within the existing capacities – **Central and local tourism administrations should undertake 'industry management'**	– Tourism development should proceed under socialist principles, in Chinese style and within the existing capacities – **Central and local tourism administrations should undertake 'market management'; with details and apparatuses being explored in this period**	– Tourism development should proceed under socialist principles, in Chinese style – **The government (central and local tourism administrations) should undertake market management. On the demand side, this is to promote domestic and international travel; on**

continued . . .

Table 10.2 continued . . .

	Historical Period Two 1978–85	Historical Period Three 1986–91	Historical Period Four 1992–7	Historical Period Five 1997–present
				the supply side, it is to provide the related infrastructure and facilities, to stimulate and facilitate investment, and to establish/develop market institutions – **Normative instruments are preferred to the coercive instruments in quality assurance**
Institutional logics	– Centralizing the leadership and decentralizing the operations	– **Adoption of prevailing international norms and practices to manage the tourism industry**	– Continuing adoption of the prevailing international norms and practices – **'Quality', 'customer satisfaction' and 'market order'**	– Continuing adoption of the prevailing international norms and practices – 'Quality', 'customer satisfaction' and 'market order' – **Ethical building**

Notes: (1) Interpreted by the authors; (2) It is considered that there was no tourism policy paradigm before 1978, as tourism was a subordinate activity to China's foreign relations. (3) **Bold** type indicates the newly added essentials in the respective historical periods.

As an illustration of this, it is clear from the experience of China that the economic function of tourism in that country could only be justified under the economic-oriented orthodoxy and it was only when this changed that tourism took on a recognized economic role. The fact that it could contribute to foreign exchange earnings did not in itself justify tourism as an economic activity among government and society. Likewise, under the planned-economy model, the demand side was not agreed as a legitimate tool for economic development. As a result a market-oriented policy paradigm failed to form even though tourism had been proved to be a market-driven industry and domestic tourism had exhibited strong market growth. This provides the basis for *Proposition Three* that *the tourism policy paradigm and its constituent essentials cannot be formed when they are opposite to the reigning ideological orthodoxies of the state.* It was only when the CPC's ideological stance became more market-oriented, people-driven and comprehensive, that domestic and outbound tourism, with rapid market growth, became a significant part of China's political economy.

Further to P. Hall's (1990, 1993) and Menahem's (1998) studies, the examination of the Chinese tourism policy paradigm suggests that *both ideology and the tourism policy paradigm are based on a systematic set of beliefs that have cognitive (i.e. construct, knowledge) and evaluative (i.e. values) capacities (Proposition Four).* Both ideology and the policy paradigm have epistemological and evaluative attributes that advocate how a society or a sector of society could be better. In exactly this way the Chinese tourism policy paradigm states how tourism development should proceed. Ideology is like an umbrella embracing the whole of society which provides the broad context for the policy paradigms to play their roles in different sectors. So the policy paradigm resembles a mini-ideology in a sector.

Ideology and the tourism policy paradigm are also interdependent (Proposition Five). State ideology provides the building blocks of the tourism policy paradigm. In the case of China the paradigm springs from the interaction of state ideology, the environmental conditions as well as the attributes of tourism. In the formation of tourism policy the ideological orthodoxies guided the policy actors in their consideration of tourism's attributes and their appropriateness for the needs of the country. At the same time, without its application to a particular sector such as tourism, state ideology has little practical relevance. In this sense there is an interdependency. As an example of this interdependency, in the second historical period after 1978, tourism was viewed by the government as an essential element of China's Economic Reform and Open-door Policy. In this sense it helped underpin the new reigning ideological orthodoxy of 'economic modernization' and 'pragmatism'. Without this change in ideology the tourism policy paradigm could not have emerged. Currently, tourism is conceived as having wider functions, hence addressing and supporting the new reigning orthodoxies. Therefore, the tourism policy paradigm consolidates the dominance of state ideology in a sector and makes the other policy factors vary with ideology and itself.

Tourism policy paradigm

BUILDING THE PARADIGM

The emergence, in the sense of initiation, and formation, in the sense of its acceptance, of a new paradigm or its essentials for tourism in China happened in a rather different way to the way in which, for example, the macroeconomic paradigm shifted in the UK from Keynsianism to Monetarism (P. Hall 1990, 1993). In the UK the shift was prompted by the perceived failure of one paradigm and its replacement by another, brought about by an election which changed the government. In the case of China, there was no introduction of a policy paradigm for tourism as such. Rather the tourism policy paradigm evolved as the state orthodoxies shifted. In part this was influenced by the relatively immature state of tourism itself, viewed as being in a pre-paradigmatic or pre-science phase (P.L. Pearce, 1993; Echtner and Jamal, 1997), compared with economics. In this sense the tourism field probably could not offer the integral thinking to generate policy ideas to compare with Keynesianism and Monetarism. But it can also be linked to the late development of tourism in China, starting from almost zero in 1978, which meant in essence that it began with some basic questions – 'what is tourism?' and 'how do we develop it?'. To answer these questions Chinese scholars first turned to early Western literature, such as McIntosh and Goeldner's (1972) *Tourism: Principles, Practices, Philosophies* and Burkart and Medlik's (1981) *Tourism: Past, Present and Future* (G.R. Zhang, 2003b) and the first strategic study was not conducted until about nine years after China's first steps in modern tourism in 1978. As G.R. Zhang (2003b: p.77) noted, 'in-depth investigations and systematic studies are rare', and 'serious studies of tourism are seldom advocated'. The end result was that the policy paradigm evolved rather than being introduced or being a replacement inside the political system.

THE ROLE OF THE PARADIGM

The tourism policy paradigm acts as the hub of the tourism policy-making process (Proposition Six). The paradigm links the other policy factors together. It serves as the cognitive framework for the policy actors to interpret the environmental conditions for policy proposals. For example, the emergence of the economic-oriented tourism policy paradigm after 1978 brought into focus the inadequacy in the supply of hotels which in turn led to the acceptance of foreign capital and expertise. At the same time, since it was international tourism that was favoured, a policy decision was made to restrict domestic travel and similarly since non-tourism agencies and enterprises were considered as detrimental to the professionalism and interests of the tourism '*xitong*' their access was restricted. Later, under the current paradigm that envisages tourism playing multiple roles, a wider range of tourism-related measures have been brought into play including those related to domestic tourism as a force for socio-economic benefits.

Tourism policy paradigm and tourism institutions

INSTITUTIONALIZING THE POLICY PARADIGM

Based on this study of tourism policy-making it is suggested that *in countries such as China, where the state plays a dominant role, when tourism development starts from nothing and a tourism policy paradigm is entirely absent at the outset, institutionalization of the policy paradigm plays a key role in the policy-making process (Proposition Seven).*

RATIONALE FOR INSTITUTIONALIZATION

Although ideology and a policy paradigm will influence individual and group cognition and values, these are not in themselves sufficient for the policy-makers to achieve their goals. Institutions are important here in establishing rules-based incentives and constraints (Dijk, 1998). Newly formed ideological orthodoxies and policy paradigms cannot be put into practice unless they are institutionalized into rules, procedures and structures. Dijk (1998: p.186) suggests that institutions are the 'practical or social counterpart' of ideologies although *Proposition Eight* goes somewhat beyond this here to suggest that *the tourism policy paradigm and tourism institutions have a synergistic relationship.* To describe the relationship as synergistic emphasizes the point that the building of the institutions closely matches the formation of ideology and the policy paradigm, almost in a natural and spontaneous way. In China's context, when the ideological orthodoxies and policy paradigms became economic oriented, their institutionalization commenced promptly, with, for example, the establishment of a tourism steering group, the reorganization and upgrading of the CNTA and the relaxation of market access, all of which are aspects of institutionalization.

THE POLICY PARADIGM AND INSTITUTIONS: INSTITUTIONAL LOGIC

As a set of guidelines, the institutional logic in a sector directs its participants in carrying out their work (W.R. Scott, 2001). While the policy paradigm presents the beliefs, institutions function through the rules that prescribe behaviour. Institutional logic plays a bridging role between beliefs and behaviour in a way that allows the policy paradigm to be operationalized. In China's context post 1978, the institutional logic of tourism can be summarized as 'centralizing leadership and decentralizing operations', neutrally fitting both the planned and market economies. However, this institutional logic also changed as the policy paradigm evolved. In the period from 1978, for example, centralization covered policy-making and planning, while decentralization was confined to the delegation of administration to local tourism bureaus and the division of responsibilities among state-owned enterprises. Under this institutional logic, the regulatory classification of travel agencies was imposed. In the period from 1986 the market-oriented paradigm did not gain bureaucratic acceptance because the current thinking was rooted in the planned economy. The centralized leadership focused on international norms for its policy-making while decentralization extended to running businesses. In the period after 1992, with the market-oriented paradigm confirmed, the CNTA's industry management became 'market management'; 'quality', 'market order' and 'customer satisfaction' became the institutional logics. For the current period, from 1997, 'ethical codes' have been further incorporated to reinforce institution building.

INSTITUTION BUILDING: INSTITUTIONALIZATION AND ITS DIFFUSION

Institutionalization and institutional diffusion are two facets of institution building. Diffusion of rules or organizational forms reinforces the strength of an existing institutional structure. Hence, institutional diffusion indicates increasing institutionalization (W.R. Scott, 2001). Economic and market-oriented institutionalization in China's tourism development involved the government, enterprises and the market. As with the institutionalization of monetarism in the UK (P. Hall, 1990, 1993), the institutionalization of the tourism policy paradigm in China also began with central government. In China the state was the sole source of any commercial development under the planned economy. The beginnings of this were when the State Council removed tourism from the diplomatic arena and placed the SGATT under its direct jurisdiction, with a tourism leadership group established to oversee the various commissions and ministries. The organizational goals of SGATT and CITS all shifted to economic development.

China is a late adopter of the market economy and tourism itself is a late arrival among China's industries. The institution building and diffusion therefore had to deal with the developing market economy as well as a new industry. There were three dimensions to this. The first was the diffusion of economic and market-oriented rules across the whole sector. Within this, the second was the diffusion of normative practices to enhance quality, maintain market order and protect the consumer. The third, most specific dimension, included, for example, the diffusion of 'modern enterprise' practices through the experience of the Jianguo Hotel, which reinforced institutionalization at the industry level. This diffusion was supported by complementary institution building including, for example, rules such as hotel star-rating standards. These were initially launched by a pilot on a carefully selected sample and then extended until they covered the whole sector.

During this institutionalization process, opposition came from the existing institutions embodying the former opposite ideological orthodoxies. Initially the opposition successfully maintained its position by banning others from access to tourism. This restricted the development of tourism as an economic activity, contrary to the new orthodoxies of market-oriented reform. Notwithstanding the resistance, eventually, the institutions changed. As Simeon (1976) suggests, like policies, institutional arrangements are also subject to change and 'in the long run, if political pressures are sufficiently strong, institutional hurdles can be cleared and institutions changed.' (p. 574). The political pressures in China's case came from the potential stakeholders and leaders. From this *Proposition Nine* is developed that *when new ideological orthodoxies and a new policy paradigm arise, the existing institutions will be antagonistic but political pressures mean that they will eventually change.*

Tourism policy players

THE ROLE OF POLICY PLAYERS IN THE TOURISM POLICY-MAKING PROCESS

Proposition Ten makes the point that *policy-making in tourism is a political process in which the policy-makers engage in policy-oriented learning and coordination.* Policy-oriented learning here refers to the cognitive process undertaken by policy players to comprehend a set of policy factors. The combined effects of the multi-faceted nature of tourism and Chinese-styled bureaucracies means that national tourism policy-making involves a hierarchical and diverse set of policy players, with a fragmented authority structure. In this complex administrative environment the policy-makers develop their cognitive behaviour through policy-oriented learning, within which ideological orthodoxies, the policy paradigm and organizational roles form the interpretation prisms for them to understand their surroundings and to shape the policy initiatives. Coordination between the different authorities is frequently needed to resolve differing views, with the state leaders sometimes intervening in finalizing the decisions. This is particularly true among the leaders, CNTA and the macro-management agencies. Typical examples in the past have included the position of tourism in the national economy and the implementation of the quality services guarantee funds in travel agencies. Of course policy learning and coordination may not follow sequential steps and indeed coordination may go ahead in order to establish the need for a policy initiative. In this sense, these two concepts constitute a kind of theoretical continuum in the policy-making process. Policy learning helps generate policy proposals which lead to the policy decisions which in turn often need coordination before they can be implemented.

From the experience of China it appears that *when ideological orthodoxies, the tourism policy paradigm and the institutions change, the role of the policy actors is of key importance, more so than the existing institutions*; this is *Proposition Eleven*. Lieberthal (1995: p.4) describes China's political regime as being historically characterized by a 'state system [based] on ideological commitment, strong personal leadership at the apex, and impressive nationwide governing bureaucracies' with the strong 'rule of men' traditions. Lieberthal (2004) further points out that China practices 'rule by law', as opposed to the 'rule of law' in the Western democracies. 'Rule of law' makes the law supreme while 'rule by law' makes political and administrative elites paramount and the law an instrument of their governance, although as Lieberthal further acknowledges, no country in fact makes the law totally supreme over political power (p.303). China's 'rule of men' tradition and 'rule by law' practice means that leaders and elites hold sway over the institutions. But more importantly here, it means that during a period of rapid change in ideological orthodoxies and institutions a gap occurs when existing institutions decline but the new institutions have not been fully established. Such an institutional vacuum provides the influential policy players with the opportunity to exercise their own influence in launching paradigm essentials or major policy initiatives or institutional experiments. Examples from China's experience include the top leader putting forward the economic development of tourism in 1978; local elites attempting a marketing campaign in the mid-1980s; bureaucratic elites, in the form of the CNTA, attempting industry management and quality assurance measures.

On the whole

Acknowledging the sheer importance of the policy factors in the model of policy-making developed here, the final proposition, *Twelve*, from the experience of China, is that *the interrelationships of policy factors serve to drive the tourism policy-making process*. Above all it is the policy factors themselves and the ways in which they coalesce which help to understand how and why tourism policies come about.

Conclusion

The theoretical inquiry of this study originated from perceived gaps in the tourism policy literature. In brief the tourism policy-making process appeared to lack well-developed frameworks, approaches and theories (Kerr, 2003). Specifically, the factors affecting tourism policy-making, their interrelationships and the ways in which policy-making was driven, had not been fully explored. Additionally the ideational perspective of tourism policy-making was missing. The conceptual framework used in this book was developed to offer new ways of thinking about policy-making in tourism that would address some of these gaps. By applying the framework to a study of tourism policy-making in China it was hoped both to test the framework and to throw light on developments in that increasingly important tourism country.

The framework was generally found useful and effective in contextualizing China's national policy-making in tourism. Chinese tourism policy-making can be viewed as a series of mutually complementary decisions and actions to develop tourism. The classification of these decisions into basic and concrete areas helps to conceptualize a diverse set of policy behaviours. Chinese national tourism policy-making has been forged by the interactive coalescence of various policy factors. Any single factor such as ideology, power or institutions is not sufficient by itself to determine the policy decisions. Their interaction involves both policy-oriented learning and coordination by the policy players. At the heart lies the tourism policy paradigm. This is very evident in the case of China, where the policy paradigm has had an influence on national tourism policy-making. The Chinese tourism policy paradigm has served as the interpretation framework for the policy actors to understand the environment in which they are operating and has enabled them to generate meanings for their initiatives and decisions. The study of China has revealed that the paradigm consists of ideological orthodoxies and tourism-specific essentials. The tourism policy paradigm formed after 1978 could only be successfully practised if it could be institutionalized into rules, standard operating procedures and structural forms. In this sense China's national tourism policy-making process can be viewed as a process of creating the paradigm – institutionalization – and structuring. With the tourism policy paradigm at their centre, the twelve propositions about the relations and causalities among the policy factors, developed here, help to unravel some of the complexities of tourism policy-making. This goes some way toward filling the theoretical gap in the tourism policy literature.

11   Experiences and lessons

> The political strategy of economic reform: why Gorbachev decided to change the political rules of the game, and why Deng Xiaoping decided to keep them.
>
> Why, then, did China successfully achieve economic reform while the Soviet Union failed?
>
> (Shirk, 1993: p.11 and p.5)

Deng Xiaoping's political logic of launching economic reform by maintaining communist institutions (Shirk, 1993) provides the backdrop against which China's development has taken shape; and tourism is very much a part of this. As something of an experimental field, as envisaged by Deng, tourism started as an economic activity from almost zero in 1978. Yet it has taken only three decades to become a multifunctional strategic industry within China's national economy and state structure. Internationally, tourism is in fourth place in terms of arrivals, fifth in terms of receipts (UNWTO, 2010b: p.7) and with the fastest pace of development (WTTC, 2010: p.5). These achievements prompt the question 'why China works' (*Newsweek* (America), 19 January 2009). This concluding chapter reviews the experiences and lessons from China's tourism development. Under her 'state-centric market' model, China's tourism is typified by 'state direction' at the macro and sector (i.e. industry) levels with a blend of foreign expertise and indigenous inputs at the micro levels. With this combination, the different functions of tourism have been developed so that today, with its basis in its economic contribution, tourism now fulfils political-ideological, economic, socio-cultural and diplomatic missions. This is a long way from the political and diplomatic roles assigned to tourism before 1978.

Experiences

For over six decades China has been a socialist nation governed by the Communist Party and as such some of its experiences may only have direct relevance to existing or former socialist states. However, there is much in China's experience that has more general applicability. Those noted here relate to the ways in which tourism has been kept within the vision of the state leaders;

the central directing role of the state; the utilization of external funding and expertise; the blending of foreign and indigenous inputs; and the ways in which quality standards have been used as a policy tool.

The political infrastructure

The move from the planned economy to the current 'Socialist Market Economy Model' has not changed the key feature of China that the state provides the essential leadership in relation to national goals. The difference between the two models lies more in the way that this is achieved. Except for specific designated sectors, the will of the state is now primarily implemented through the state-defined market rather than through the central imperative plan. At one level the government can been seen to exercise macro management over the economy, run industries of national or public importance, set and oversee prices, and monitor the operation of the private sector. In this sense the state achieves its ends within the regulatory and administrative framework, with considerable support from public ownership. At a more fundamental level and perhaps more pervasively, the CPC is still the dominant political force guiding central government agencies, localities, state-owned enterprises, social organizations, government-sponsored NGOs and community bodies such that the communist-led state–society relationships basically remain the same as before. This sort of political infrastructure enables the state to mobilize the necessary forces to achieve national visions and goals. *Newsweek* in 2009 provides a vivid description from a Western perspective:

> it [China] is the only one that routinely breaks every rule in the economic textbook. There is no truly free market in China, where the state doctors statistics, manipulates the stock markets, fixes prices in key industries, owns many strategic industries outright, and staffs key bank posts with Communist Party members and tells them to whom they should lend, and in what they should invest.
>
> (*Newsweek*, 19 January 2009)

The Chinese-styled market economy may be better described as a 'state-centric market economy'. This feature of China goes some way to explain the efficacy and speed with which it has been able to develop the tourism sector. China's political infrastructure clearly makes it very different from other non-socialist countries for whom the Chinese-style development path is hardly now an option.

The vision of the leaders

As early as in the Qing Dynasty, Chinese imperial rulers began to recognize inbound travel as a primary contact point with the West. As a legacy, this awareness has certainly been an important part of the thinking of their communist successors. International tourism throughout the sixty years of socialist China has been viewed as an important part of the national showcase and a focal point for dealing with foreign influences. This unique status has kept tourism firmly in the sights of the leaders and has ensured that they have been centrally involved in national tourism initiatives. This high profile of tourism with the political leaders in China has clearly given it a significant push in its development, a feature which is often missing in other parts of the world, including western countries where a lack of political interest is often blamed for poor tourism performance.

External investment and expertise

The decision to use external funds and management expertise is one of the most important policy changes made in 1978, particularly since the country had almost no experience or knowledge about running tourism businesses. China's tourism today is almost on a par with international competitors as reflected in the diversity and quality of attractions and facilities. External expertise and investment has significantly shortened the time needed to bring China's tourism up to the standard at which it can easily compete with western tourist destinations. One way of looking at this is that if modern tourism is considered to have begun after the Second World War, then what western countries achieved in sixty years, by drawing on this expertise, China has achieved in thirty years. At the micro level, external capital and expertise have transformed tourism enterprises in all aspects from business philosophy, strategy, marketing, operations, as well as customer service.

Marrying foreign and indigenous processes

Initially the transfer of external thinking and processes did not occur smoothly. Notably the mindset of the bureaucrats and front-line staff remained fixed on previous conceptions of tourism. The joint venture hotels were in fact the first area of business in China to experience depoliticalization, in the sense that the party committee passed business responsibilities to a politically neutral management team of both foreign and local executives. But the party committee still sought to ensure that the foreign investment and business practices took place within China's socialist framework. To this end, it organized party and labour union activities for Chinese staff and provided counselling for native employees opposed to some foreign practices. On the other hand, it also helped to clear misunderstandings by foreign expatriates. Given the importance of internal traditions and practices as barriers to development (Clancy, 1999: p.3), China's experience in attempting to reconcile its need for foreign capital with the maintenance of its own customs, provides examples which have a resonance with other destinations in the processes of development.

Combining generalist and specialist expertise

The close collaboration between the CNTA and the NDRC forms the main administrative driver for the development of tourism in China. This approach not only matches the integration of generalist and specialist expertise found in countries with well-developed tourism sectors, but also parallels the sorts of activities carried out by development agencies with a broad oversight of tourism in many developing countries (Elliot, 1997). In China, this approach has permitted the formation of specialized policy-making expertise for tourism which at the same time has been integrated into the national development and economic policies. One weakness in this, identified by the WTTC (2006), relates to the relatively low bureaucratic rank of the CNTA. The WTTC suggests (2006: p.5) the need 'to elevate tourism to a ministerial portfolio with responsibility for overseeing collateral government agencies/departments that have a direct or indirect links to tourism'. In reality, while the CNTA has ministerial responsibilities that are comparable with similar agencies in other countries, it is not granted full political and administrative authority and lacks full ministry status. This means that the CNTA cannot require compliance from other agencies simply from its official position, but rather needs to work through a process of coordination with them. This has placed a considerable burden of negotiation on the CNTA but at the same time it has also allowed different views and interests to come to the fore. The upgrade of the CNTA to full ministry status is ultimately a question of balance between efficiency and sustainability. The efficiency that would come from the CNTA being able to demand cooperation would likely be at the expense of sustainability which comes from ensuring that a range of views are considered.

In many ways the CNTA is not unusual among NTAs worldwide in having limited powers. This in part reflects that fact that responsibility for tourism is everywhere fragmented among different components of the bureaucracy. The way in which the CNTA has successfully used non-mandatory quality standards as a tool to help develop tourism in China provides a good example of how it has been able effectively to work within its institutional constraints, coordinated with other agencies, in the interests of industry and of the tourist markets. The successful implementation of quality specifications has assisted the CNTA in building up professionalism and recognition, eventually acquiring professional authority in the absence of real political and administrative authority. In setting outcomes rather than determining processes quality benchmarks form an important element of government macro management. The experience with positioning tourism in the national economy also provides a useful example of the ways in which 'policy-oriented learning', in this case learning from weaknesses in Chinese provision and from international experience, has enabled the agencies involved in tourism in China, especially the CNTA and the NDRC, to develop and implement effective policy.

State direction

Government involvement in development happens everywhere regardless of stage of development, or political orientation. Differences lie in the nature, scope and extent of such involvement (P. Hall, 1986; Evans, 1995; Clancy, 1999; Rapley, 2007). The sheer importance for tourism of policy and policy-making has been emphasized by Richter (1989) who suggests that whether it succeeds or fails is largely a function of political and administrative actions, rather than economics or business. This view has subsequently been substantiated by C.M. Hall (1994), C.M. Hall and Jenkins (1995), Wilkinson (1997), C.L. Jenkins and Lickorish (1997) and Harrison (2001b) among others. As far as tourism in China is concerned the model is one of national 'state direction' which is implemented by guiding and regulating market forces. In many ways tourism is different from other sectors in China which typically have a much lower degree of marketization. In this sense, 'state-direction' in tourism is a lighter approach compared to the 'state-driving model' for China more generally. But it is also much heavier than the approaches to the private and market sectors in most non-socialist countries. The state direction for tourism in China includes the provision of infrastructure and facilities, the stimulation of investment, marketing, as well as some elements of product development but not extending to operations. The regulatory role is mainly fulfilled through the establishment and consolidation of market institutions within which the normative quality standards represent a key component. Within a socialist context, in many ways the approach to tourism has been fairly pragmatic in its attempts to develop the sector to reflect the realities of China's characteristics and needs. A typical example is the precedence that was given to inbound over domestic and outbound tourism in the 1980s.

China's tourism development can be placed within two streams of debate from political economy and development studies: modernization versus dependency; and the role of the state in shaping development outcomes (Clancy, 1999). As far as the first is concerned, China's tourism has almost achieved a level of modernization comparable to developed parts of the world. In the meantime, the state still exercises control over the course of development (Goldsworthy, 1988; Bianchi, 2002), while leaving technical and operational aspects to the industry, both indigenous and foreign stakeholders. The debates in the second stream are very much based on successful development stories from East Asia in the 1980s, such as South Korea and Singapore (Hong, 1997). Clearly China differs significantly from these countries in terms of political regime and patterns of pubic-private collaboration, yet there are similarities. Overall, the Chinese state shapes the development outcomes of tourism but has now assigned the management of the micro details to market forces in a state-defined market. Above all this is because China's tourism does not belong to a sector which matters in terms of national security and survival, so like in many other countries market forces are allowed to play a key role.

Quality, ethics and marketing

One of the important lessons from the experience of the development of tourism in China is the need for the inclusion, at the very beginning, of quality and ethical issues alongside the marketing campaigns. The early launch of marketing campaigns certainly helped to create a destination image and market position for China and allowed China and its regions to expand market share. But this then began to expose problems with quality and ethical issues. In part, as noted in Chapters 7 and 8, these were prompted by the arrival into tourism of those previously engaged in other sectors, notably tobacco and real estate, with little real experience of tourism. But it was also exacerbated by a lack of experience in the market economy and changes in Chinese society. The range of issues presented by tourism from food safety, consumer protection, tourist health, tour safety and environmental hygiene has posed particular challenges for tourism in China. In part these have been addressed by measures such as the establishment of quality specifications. More recently, in 2000, a cross-agency coordination forum was set up to provide a coordinated policy and institutional response to the peak season. But it would have been more effective if these had been considered at an earlier stage.

Prospects

Deng Xiaoping's political logic of carrying out reform by sticking to communist institutions has been firmly adhered to by successive leaders. This in essence is viewed as an ultimate source of China's political and social stability and the context within which successful development has taken place including the development of tourism and the service industries. It provides the framework for policy measures. For tourism one of the key developments occurred in late 2009 when the State Council decided to position tourism as 'a strategic pillar industry in the national economy'. This puts tourism in a very prominent position not only to attain a growth of 11 per cent in total tourism incomes for 2009, even in the context of economic austerity (CNTA, 2010b), but also means that it is well placed to maintain the highest level of growth in the world, achieved in 2009 (WTTC, 2010: p.5). Though China's tourism development still faces some issues, such as the manpower shortage, quality instability and ethical standards, these and other issues are being addressed. For example, the CNTA is expanding the quality assurance framework in close collaboration with the quality administration agency. In fact, as measured by tourism satisfaction, service quality has seen a clear improvement (CNTA, 2007g). China is clearly set to strengthen its position as a leading tourism force of the world both in volume and quality terms.

One interesting aspect of China's tourism movements is that foreign tourists only account for around 20 per cent of total inbound arrivals with the remainder coming from Hong Kong, Macau and Taiwan. Given the country's physical and cultural resources there is good reason to think that there is still plenty of scope for China further to differentiate her tourism from other popular destinations and to expand her arrivals. After three decades in which priority has been given to economic modernization, in which tourism has been an important component, much will now depend on the response of China to the changing global landscape in which it is a world player and on internal changes.

Appendix

Academic texts on tourism in China

Lew, A. and Yu, L. (eds.) (1994) *Tourism in China: Geographic, Political, and Economic Perspectives*, Boulder, CO: Westview.

Oakes, T. (1998) *Tourism and Modernity in China*, London; New York, NY: Routledge.

Xu, G. (1999) *Tourism and Local Development in China: case studies of Guilin, Suzhou and Beidaihe*, Richmond: Curzon.

Wen, J.J. and Tisdell, C.A. (2001) *Tourism and China's Development: policies, regional economic growth and ecotourism*, Singapore, New Jersey: World Scientific.

Lew, A.A., Yu, L., Ap, J. and Zhang, G.R. (eds.) (2003) *Tourism in China*, New York: Haworth Hospitality Press.

Zhang, H., Pine, R. and Lam, T. (2005) *Tourism and Hotel Development in China: from political to economic success*, New York: Haworth Hospitality Press/International Business Press (textbook).

Wolfgang, G.A. (2006) *China's Outbound Tourism*, Abingdon: Routledge.

Ryan, C. and Gu, H.M. (eds.) (2009) *Tourism in China: Destination, Cultures and Communities*, New York: Routledge.

Su, X.B., and Teo, P. (2009) *The Politics of Heritage Tourism in China: a view from Lijiang*, Abingdon, New York: Routledge.

Notes

1 Introduction

1 The *Annals of Tourism Research* and *Tourism Management* are the only two journals in the tourism field incorporated into the Social Sciences Citations Index (SSCI).
2 A paper published in *Tourism Tribune* ('*Luyou Xuekan*') – a main tourism academic journal in China.
3 For political and historical reasons, Taiwan has been separated from Mainland China since 1949. Based on the 'One-Country, Two-Systems' policy formulated by the Chinese government, the socialist system and policies of China are not implemented in Hong Kong and Macau where the capitalist system is authorized to practice by Chinese law – The Basic Law.
4 Chinese '*Guanxi*' can be viewed as a blend of personal networks and interpersonal relationships.

2 Context, history and overview

1 AD ('Anno Domini') also equals the CE ('common era').
2 The start date for 'modern times' in China differs from that of the Western world beginning from the fall of the Byzantine Empire in AD 1453.
3 Some Chinese historians also view that 'modern times' in China should start from around AD 1600 when Western civilizations started to impact on China through the Jesuit missionaries.
4 Early historical views in Mainland China consider that China's contemporary era should start from the May 4th Movement in 1919, rather than 1911 (i.e. the establishment of the then 'Republic of China'). Later views suggest that China's 'modern times' came to an end with the collapse of the 'Republic of China' in 1949.
5 Having studied economics at the University of California, Jian Bozan (1898–1968) was a renowned Chinese historian, who served as head of history department and vice-president of Peking University after 1949. He died in the Chinese Cultural Revolution.
6 The Chinese empire was founded by China's first emperor Qin Shihuang in 221 BC, who unified the divided territories and established the centralized dynasty – Qin. The prototype of his centralized monarchy was inherited by successive dynasties and the republican polity.
7 Imperial China lasted for two thousand years until 1911 when the Republic of China (1911–49) was founded by Dr Sun Yat-Sen and other republican revolutionaries.

8 Detailed statistics are provided in Chapters 7 and 8.
9 Exchange rates could only be dated back to 1981 (RMB¥1.7/US$1).
10 The average exchange rate in 2008 was RMB¥6.84/US$1.
11 The average rate dropped from RMB¥8.28/US$1 between 2001 and 2004 to RMB¥6.83/US$1 in 2009.
12 The arrangement for these three weeks was changed by central government in 2008 after which only two-week-long holidays remained. Some local governments like Guangdong Province tried to maintain the original arrangement, so that tourism volumes would not be affected. Further comment is provided in Chapter 8.

3 The conceptual framework

1 In this study, the term 'sector' is used interchangeably with the term 'industry'.

4 Changing national models of China since 1949

1 Qian stepped down from his official positions in 2003.

5 Tourism politics in Mao Zedong's era

1 Overseas Chinese refers to Chinese people who reside in foreign nations but are still Chinese nationals. The situation changed in the 1970s when many such overseas Chinese became foreign nationals.
2 Hong Kong is a special administrative region of China. It was previously under British rule between 1842 and 1997 as a colony. China resumed sovereignty over Hong Kong in 1997. During the colonial era of Hong Kong, Chinese residents could become a British Dependent Territories Citizen (BDTC) or British Nationals (Overseas) (BNO) if they were born in Hong Kong or applied through naturalization. The Chinese government, however, did not recognize their British identities and still regarded them as Chinese nationals.
3 Macau is a special administrative region of China, which was previously under Portuguese rule. China resumed her sovereignty over Macau in 1999. Before the handover, the Chinese government held an identical attitude towards the Chinese residents in Macau as it did to such residents of Hong Kong.
4 The Guomindang (GMD) (Nationalist Party of China) forces retreated to Taiwan in 1949 after losing power in China. Taiwan has since then been separated from the Mainland. Because of mutual hostility and confrontation, there had been no civil exchange between two sides until 1987 when the GMD authorities allowed the Taiwanese to visit the Mainland primarily to see relatives. Between 1949 and 1987, visitors from Taiwan to the Mainland were rare.
5 Civil Diplomacy is called 'Public Diplomacy' in the Western world.
6 China's Cultural Revolution officially broke out on 16 May 1966 when the '16 May Circular' prepared by Mao was issued in the name of the Central Committee of the CPC (Saich, 2004).
7 Born in Hangzhou China, John Stuart was the last US Ambassador to the Republic of China (ROC) (1911–49). He did not retreat with the GMD forces but stayed in Nanjing in an attempt to establish some contact with the new communist regime.
8 Zhou Enlai, as one of the founders of the CPC, served as the Premier of the State Council (i.e. head of government) from 1949 to 1976. He died in 1976.
9 Edgar Snow was an American journalist. Through the arrangement of Song Qingling (Madame Sun Yat-Sen), he visited the revolutionary base of the CPC, Yan-an, in 1936 and interviewed Mao Zedong and other communist leaders. Based

on the visits, he published his best known book, *Red Star Over China*, which introduced China's communist movement to the Western world.

10 Mao aimed to transmit the message to President Nixon that China would welcome his visit.

11 Previously the US government had constantly referred to China as 'communist China'.

12 Located in Shan-an Xi Province, Yan-an was a revolutionary base of the CPC before taking over power in 1949.

13 The 'Three-Anti' Campaign (August 1951–June 1952) targeted the abuse of official positions to engage in corruption, waste and bueaucratism, while the 'Five-Anti' Campaign (January–June 1952) aimed to curb the violation of government regulations by the private business (Saich, 2004: p.35).

14 Liao Zhongkai was a keen supporter of Sun Yen-Sen's alliance policy with Soviet Russia and the CPC. He was assassinated in 1925.

15 It was renamed The Overseas Chinese Affairs Office as a ministry-equivalent agency under the State Council after 1978.

16 Anne Louise Strong (1885–1970) was an American journalist. Like Edgar Snow, she also introduced China's communist movement to the world. She paid a total of six visits to China with the last one in 1958.

17 The breakdown of self-financed tourists is not available.

18 The 'Gang of Four' refers to the political clique formed by four leftist leaders – Jiang Qing (Mao's wife), Wang Hongwen, Zhang Chunqiao and Yao Wenyuan.

6 The national policy-makers

1 The supra-ministerial agency was usually called 'comprehensive agency' in the planned economy, and is now commonly called 'macro-management' agency in the market economy.

2 For example, the presidents of CASS have included Guo Moruo (historian and archeologist), Hu Qiaomu (Mao Zedong's main secretary and later the Politburo member of the CPC).

8 The Collective Leadership era

1 Except for the three abnormal periods: the June 4th Incident in 1989; SARS in 2003 and the current economic turmoil.

2 They were appointed during the 10th and 11th sessions of the NPC and the State Council respectively.

3 It is the colour of the CPC's party flag symbolizing the bloodshed, struggle and sacrifice.

4 Dr Sun Yat-Sen and other Guomindang's leftist leaders are also included.

5 Jiang Zemin stepped down from the General Secretary of CPC in 2002 and remained as the Chairman of the Central Military Commission until 2005.

6 He Guangwei stepped down and Shao Qiwei succeeded to the post of CNTA's Director-General in March 2005. Prior to taking up the post, Mr Shao was Vice-Governor of Yunnan Province of China.

9 Tourism policy issues in four particular regions

1 In the Chinese version of the Policy Address, the gaming sector refers to gaming tourism.

2 The figures for Tibet in 2008 were not used, since this year was considered abnormal due to the outbreak of riots.

Bibliography and sources

1 Han Nianlong served as the Vice-Minister of Foreign Affairs from 1964 to 1982 and then the Chairman of the Chinese People's Association for Friendship with Foreign Countries from 1983.
2 It was under the 'Contemporary China Series' – a state-level publication project approved by the Secretariat of the CPC Central Committee. It covered a wide range of developments in contemporary China after 1949, including but not limited to the political, economic, diplomatic, social, cultural, educational, industrial and regional dimensions.
3 Han Kehua served as the Vice-Minister of Foreign Affairs (1979–81), Director-General (also called Chairman) of the China National Tourism Administration (1981–8) and Standing Committee Member and Vice-Chairman of the Foreign Affairs Committee, the Chinese People's Political Consultative Conference (CPPCC) from 1988.
4 This work was also a component of the 'Contemporary China Series'.

Bibliography and sources

The bibliography and sources used in preparing this work are divided here into a number of sections. The first is the scholarly literature, in English, followed by the Chinese literature. The second are the newspaper articles. The third is the official material, in the form of speeches, policy documents and official reports. In addition, reference has also been made to internet sources, notably Wikipedia, the Free Encyclopedia: English: http://en.wikipedia. org/wiki/Main_Page; Chinese: http://zh.wikipedia.org/zh-tw/Wikipedia:% E9%A6%96%E9%A1%B5)

Section 1: scholarly literature

English

Airey, D. (1983) 'European Government Approaches to Tourism', *Tourism Management*, 4(4): 234–44.

Airey, D. (1984) 'Tourism Administration in the USA', *Tourism Management*, 5(4): 269–79.

Airey, D. and Chong, K. (2010) 'National Policy-Makers for Tourism in China', *Annals of Tourism Research*, 37(2): 295–314.

Akama, J. (1999) 'The Evolution of Tourism in Kenya', *Journal of Sustainable Tourism*, 7(1): 6–25.

Alipour, H. and Kilic, H. (2003) 'An Institutional Appraisal of Tourism Development and Planning: the case of the Turkish Republic of North Cyprus (TRNC)', *Tourism Management*, 26: 79–94.

Almond, G.A. (1988) 'The Return to the State', *The American Political Science Review*, 82(3): 853–74.

Anderson, C.W. (1978) 'The Logic of Public Problems: evaluation in comparative policy research', in D. Ashford (ed.) *Comparative Public Policies*, Beverly Hills, CA: Sage, pp.19–42.

Anderson, J.E. (1979) *Public Policymaking: an introduction*, 2nd edn, Boston, MA: Houghton Mifflin.

Anderson, J.E. (1990) *Public Policymaking: an introduction*, Boston, MA: Houghton Mifflin.

Anderson, J.E. (2003) *Public Policymaking: an introduction*, 5th edn, Boston, MA: Houghton Mifflin.

Andrews-Speed, C.P. (2004) *Energy Policy and Regulation in P.R. China*, The Hague; New York: Kluwer Law International.

Appel, F. and Gagnon, A. (1994) 'Rethinking Corporatism and Comparative Social Science: an old-new approach', in S. Brooks and A. Gagnon (eds) *The Political Influence of Ideas: policy communities and social sciences*, Westport, CT; London: Praeger, pp.15–32.

Arksey, H. and Knight, P.T. (1999) *Interviewing for Social Scientists*, London: Sage.

Arthur, S. and Nazroo, J. (2003) 'Designing Fieldwork Strategies and Materials', in J. Ritchie and J. Lewis (eds) *Qualitative Research Practice: a guide for social science students and researchers*, London; Thousand Oaks, CA: Sage, pp.109–37.

Atkinson, M.M. and Chandler, M.A. (eds) (1983) *The Politics of Canadian Public Policy*, Toronto: University of Toronto Press.

Augustyn, M. (1998) 'National Strategies for Rural Tourism Development and Sustainability: the Polish experience', *Journal of Sustainable Tourism*, 6(3): 191–209.

Australian Commonwealth Department of Resources, Energy and Tourism (RET) (2008) *ADS: code of business standards and ethics*, Canberra: RET.

Babbie, E. (1992) *The Practice of Social Research*, Belmont, CA: Wadsworth Publishing.

Bachrach, P. and Baratz, M.S. (1970) *Power and Poverty, Theory and Practice*, New York: Oxford University Press.

Barone, C.A. (2004) *Radical Political Economy*, Armonk, NY: M.E. Sharpe.

Barrett, P. and Fudge, C. (1981) *Policy and Action*, London: Methuen.

Belsky, J. (2004) 'Contributions of Qualitative Research to Understanding the Politics of Community Ecotourism', in J. Phillimore and L. Goodson (eds) *Qualitative Research in Tourism: ontologies, epistemologies and methodologies*, London; New York: Routledge, pp.273–91.

Berg, B.L. (2004) *Qualitative Research Methods*, 5th edn, Boston, MA: Pearson/Allyn & Bacon.

Berger, P.L. (1976) *Pyramids of Sacrifice: political ethics and social change*, New York: Doubleday.

Bianchi, R.V. (2002) 'Towards a New Political Economy of Global Tourism', in R. Sharpley and D. Telfer (eds) *Tourism and Development: concepts and issues*, Clevedon: Channel View Publications, pp.112–48.

Black, J.A. and Champion, D.J. (1976) *Methods and Issues in Social Research*, New York: John Wiley & Sons.

Bodlender, J. (1991) 'Examples of Tourism Planning', in L.J. Lickorish, A. Jefferson, J. Bodlender and C.L. Jenkins, *Developing Tourism Destinations: policies and perspectives*, Essex: Longman, pp.169–80.

Böhm, A. (2004) 'Theoretical Coding: text analysis in grounded theory', in U. Flick, E.V. Kardorff and I. Steinke (eds) *A Companion to Qualitative Research*, London: Sage, pp.270–5.

Borden, G.A. (1991) *Cultural Orientation: an approach to understanding intercultural communication*, Englewood Cliffs, NJ: Prentice Hall.

Bouden, R. (1986) *Theories of Social Change*, Cambridge: Polity Press.

Bowen, H.E., Daniels, M.J. and Ingram, L. (2006) 'Hybrid Analysis in Tourism Research', *Tourism Recreation Research*, 31(2): 59–66.

Brabant, J.M.V. (1998) *The Political Economy of Transition: coming to grips with story and methodology*, London; New York: Routledge.

Bradford, N. (1994) 'Ideas, Institutions, and Innovation: economic policy in Canada and Sweden', in S. Brooks and A. Gagnon (eds) *The Political Influence of Ideas: policy communities and social sciences*, Westport, CT; London: Praeger, pp.83–106.

Bramham, P., Henry, I., Mommaas, H. and van der Poel, H. (eds) (1993) *Leisure Policies in Europe*, Wallingford, Oxon: CAB International.

Bramwell, B. and Sharman, A. (1999) 'Collaboration in Local Tourism Policymaking', *Journal of Sustainable Tourism*, 26(2): 392–415.

Bramwell, B. and Lane, B. (2004) 'Editorial – A Fragile Recovery and China's Emerging Prominence', *Journal of Sustainable Tourism*, 12(1): 1–3.

Bramwell, B. and Lane, B. (2006) 'Editorial – Policy Relevance and Sustainable Tourism Research: liberal, radical and post-structuralist perspectives', *Journal of Sustainable Tourism*, 14(1): 1–5.

Bramwell, B. and Meyer, D. (2007) 'Power and Tourism Policy Relations in Transition', *Annals of Tourism Research*, 34(3): 766–88.

Braun, D. (1999) 'Interests or Ideas? An Overview of Ideational Concepts in Public Policy Research', in D. Braun and A. Busch (eds) *Public Policy and Political Ideas*, Northampton, MA: Edward Elgar, pp.11–29.

Braun, D. and Busch, A. (eds) (1999) *Public Policy and Political Ideas*, Northampton, MA: Edward Elgar.

Britton, S.G. (1982) 'The Political Economy of Tourism in the Third World', *Annals of Tourism Research*, 9(2): 331–58.

Broham, J. (1996) 'New Directions in Tourism for Third World Development', *Annals of Tourism Research*, 23(1): 48–70.

Brooks, S. (1993) *Public Policy in Canada*, Toronto: McClelland & Stewart.

Brooks, S. and Gagnon, A. (eds) (1990) *Social Scientists, Policy, and the State*, New York: Praeger.

Brooks, S. and Gagnon, A. (eds) (1994) *The Political Influence of Ideas: policy communities and the social sciences*, Westport, CN; London: Praeger.

Browlett, J. (1980) 'Development, the Diffusionist Paradigm and Geography', *Progress in Human Geography*, 4(1): 57–80.

Brunsson, N. and Jacobson, B. (eds) (2002) *A World of Standards*, Oxford: Oxford University Press.

Bude, H. (2004) 'The Art of Interpretation', in U. Flick, E.V. Kardorff and I. Steinke (eds) *A Companion to Qualitative Research*, London: Sage, pp.321–5.

Burkart, A.J. and Medlik, S. (1981) *Tourism: past, present and future*, London: Heinemann.

Busch, A. (1999) 'From "Hooks" to "Focal Points": the changing role of ideas in rational choice theory', in D. Braun and A. Busch (eds) *Public Policy and Political Ideas*, Northampton, MA: Edward Elgar, pp.30–40.

Busch, A. and Braun, D. (1999) 'Introduction' in D. Braun and A. Busch (eds) *Public Policy and Political Ideas*, Northampton, MA: Edward Elgar, pp.1–7.

Busenberg, G.J. (2001) 'Learning in Organizations and Public Policy', *Journal of Public Policy*, 21(2): 173–89.

Cammack, P. (1992) 'The New Institutionalism: predatory rule, institutional persistence, and macro-social change', *Economy and Society*, 21(4): 397–429.

Capano, G. (1999) 'Replacing the Policy Paradigm: higher education reforms in Italy and the United Kingdom', in D. Braun and A. Busch (eds) *Public Policy and Political Ideas*, Northampton, MA: Edward Elgar, pp.61–81.

Caporaso, J.A., and Levine, D.P. (2003) *Theories of Political Economy*, Cambridge: Cambridge University Press.

Carr, W. and Kemmis, S. (1986) *Becoming Critical: education, knowledge and action research*, London, New York: RoutledgeFalmer.

Chambers, D. and Airey, D. (2001) 'Tourism Policy in Jamaica: a tale of two governments', *Current Issues in Tourism*, 4(2–4): 94–120.

Chang, P.H. (1975) *Power and Policy in China*, University Park, PA: Pennsylvania State University Press.

Chang, T.C. (1998) 'Regionalism and Tourism: exploring integral links in Singapore', *Asia Pacific Viewpoint*, 39(1): 73–94.

Chen, J. and Zhong, Y. (2001) 'Are Chinese Still Interested in Politics', in X.B. Hu and G. Lin (eds) *Transition Towards Post-Deng China*, Singapore: Singapore University Press, pp.143–69.

Cheng, J.Y.S. (2001) 'China's Foreign Policy in the Beginning of the Twenty-first Century', in X.B. Hu and G. Lin (eds) *Transition Towards Post-Deng China*, Singapore: Singapore University Press, pp.271–302.

Chhibber, A. (1998) 'Institutions, Policies, and Development Outcomes', in R. Picciotto and E. Wiesner (eds) *Evaluation and Development: the institutional dimension*, New Brunswick, NJ: Transaction Publishers.

Chin, S.S.K. (1979) *The Thought of Mao Tse-Tung: form and content*, Hong Kong: Center for Asian Studies, University of Hong Kong.

China Official Report Publishing House (2004) *China Official Report 2004*, Beijing: China Official Report Publishing House.

Choy, D.J.L. and Yao, Y.C. (1988) 'The Development and Organization of Travel Services in China', *Journal of Travel Research*, 28(1): 28–34.

Choy, D.J.L., Guan, L.D. and Zhang, W. (1986) 'Tourism in PR China: market trends and changing policies', *Tourism Management*, 7(3): 197–201.

Clancy, M.J. (1999) 'Tourism and Development: evidence from Mexico', *Annals of Tourism Research*, 26(1): 1–20.

Clark, B.S. (1991) *Political Economy: a comparative approach*, New York: Praeger.

Clark, B.S. (1998) *Political Economy: a comparative approach*, 2nd edn, Westport, CN: Praeger.

Clark, M., Riley, M., Wilkie, E. and Wood, R.C. (1998) *Researching and Writing Dissertations in Hospitality and Tourism*, London: International Thomson Business Press.

Clements, M.A. and Georgiou, A. (1998) 'The Impacts of Political Instability on a Fragile Tourism Product', *Tourism Management*, 19(3): 283–8.

Coffey, A. and Atkinson, P. (1996) *Making Sense of Qualitative Data*, Thousand Oaks, CA: Sage.

Coleman, W.D. and Skogstad, G. (eds) (1990) *Policy Communities and Public Policy in Canada: a structural approach*, Toronto: Copp Clark Pitman.

Cooper, M. and Flehr, M. (2006) 'Government Intervention in Tourism Development: case studies from Japan and South Australia', *Current Issues in Tourism*, 9(1): 69–85.

Cothran, D.A. and Cothran, C.C. (1998) 'Promise or Political Risk for Mexican Tourism', *Annals of Tourism Research*, 25(2): 477–97.

Cox, R.W. (1981) 'Social Forces, States and World Orders: beyond international relations', *Journal of International Studies*, 10(2): 126–55.

Cox, R.W. (1987) *Production, Power, and World Order*, New York: Columbia University Press.

Crewe, E. and Harrison, E. (1998) *Whose Development?* London: Zed.

Crick, M. (1989) 'Representations of International Tourism in the Social Sciences: sun, sex, sights, savings, and servility', *Annual Review of Anthropology*, 18: 307–44.

Dabb, J.M. Jr. (1982) 'Making Things Visible', in J.V. Maanen (ed.) *Varieties of Qualitative Research*, Beverly Hills, CA: Sage.

Dann, G., Nash, D. and Pearce, P. (1988) 'Methodology in Tourism Research', *Annals of Tourism Research*, 15(1): 1–28.

Decrop, A. (2004) 'Trustworthiness in Qualitative Tourism Research', in J. Phillimore and L. Goodson (eds) *Qualitative Research in Tourism: ontologies, epistemologies and methodologies*, London; New York: Routledge, pp.156–69.

Denzin, N.K. (1978) *The Research Act*, New York: McGraw-Hill.

Denzin, N.K. (1989) *Interpretative Interactionism*, Newbury Park: Sage.

Denzin, N.K. (1998) 'The Art and Politics of Interpretation', in N.K. Denzin and Y.S. Lincoln (eds) *Collecting and Interpreting Qualitative Materials*, Thousand Oaks, CA: Sage, pp.313–44.

Denzin, N.K. (2004) 'Symbolic Interactionism', in U. Flick, E.V. Kardorff and I. Steinke (eds) *A Companion to Qualitative Research*. London: Sage, pp.81–7.

Denzin, N.K. and Lincoln, Y.S. (1994) *Handbook of Qualitative Research*, Thousand Oaks, CA: Sage.

Denzin, N.K. and Lincoln, Y.S. (eds) (1998a) *Strategies of Qualitative Inquiry*, Thousand Oaks, CA: Sage.

Denzin, N.K. and Lincoln, Y.S. (eds) (1998b) *Collecting and Interpreting Qualitative Materials*, Thousand Oaks, CA: Sage.

Denzin, N.K. and Lincoln, Y.S. (1998c) 'Introduction to This Volume', in N.K. Denzin and Y.S. Lincoln (eds) *Strategies of Qualitative Inquiry*, Thousand Oaks, CA: Sage, pp.xi–xxii.

Denzin, N.K. and Lincoln, Y.S (1998d) 'Introduction: entering the field of qualitative research', in N.K. Denzin and Y.S. Lincoln (eds) *Strategies of Qualitative Inquiry*, Thousand Oaks, CA: Sage, pp.1–34.

Denzin, N.K. and Lincoln, Y.S. (1998e) 'The Art of Interpretation, Evaluation, and Presentation', in N.K. Denzin and Y.S. Lincoln (eds) *Collecting and Interpreting Qualitative Materials*, Thousand Oaks, CA: Sage, pp.275–81.

Desforges, L. (2000) 'State Tourism Institutions and Neo-Liberal Development: a case study of Peru', *Tourism Geographies*, 2(2): 177–192.

Devine, F. (2002) 'Qualitative Methods' in D. Marsh and G. Stocker (eds) *Theory and Methods in Political Science*, Basingstoke: Macmillan, pp.197–215.

Dick, P. (2004) 'Discourse Analysis', in C. Cassell and G. Symon (eds) *Essential Guide to Qualitative Methods in Organizational Research*, London; Thousand Oaks, CA; New Delhi: Sage, pp.203–313.

Dieke, P.U.C. (1993a) 'Tourism in the Gambia: some issues in development policy', *World Development*, 21(2): 277–89.

Dieke, P.U.C. (1993b) 'Tourism and Development Policy in the Gambia', *Annals of Tourism Research*, 20(3): 423–49.

Dieke, P.U.C. (ed.) (2000a) *The Political Economy of Tourism Development in Africa*, New York: Cognizant Communication Corporation.

Dieke, P.U.C. (2000b) 'The Nature and Scope of the Political Economy of Tourism Development in Africa', in P.U.C. Dieke (ed.) *The Political Economy of Tourism Development in Africa*, New York: Cognizant Communication Corporation, pp.1–28.

Dijk, T.A.V. (1998) *Ideology: A Multidisciplinary Approach*, London; Thousand Oaks, CA: Sage.

DiMaggio, P.J. (1983) 'State Expansion and Organizational Fields', in R.H. Hall and R.E. Quinn (eds) *Organization Theory and Public Policy*, Beverly Hills, CA: Sage, pp.147–61.

DiMaggio, P.J. and Powell, W.W. (1983) 'The Iron Cage Revisited: institutional isomorphism and collective rationality in organizational fields', *American Sociological Review*, 48: 147–60.

Dirlik, A. and Cheng, P. (1989) *Marxism and Capitalism in the People's Republic of China*, Lanham, MD: University of America Press.

Donaldson, J.A. (2007) 'Tourism, Development and Poverty Reduction in Guizhou and Yunnan', *China Quarterly*, 190 (June): 333–51.

Dredge, D. (2006) 'Policy Networks and the Local Organization of Tourism', *Tourism Management*, 27(2): 269–80.

Dredge, D. and Jenkins, J. (2007) *Tourism Planning and Policy*, Milton, Queensland: John Wiley & Sons.

Dror, Y. (1971a) *Ventures in Policy Sciences: concepts and applications*, New York: Elsevier.

Dror, Y. (1971b) *Design for Policy Sciences*, New York: Elsevier.

Duncan, J.S. (1985) 'Individual Action and Political Power: a structuration perspective', in R.J. Johnston (eds) *The Future of Geography*, London: Methuen, pp.174–89.

Dunleavy, P. (2003) *Authoring a PhD: how to plan, draft, write and finish a doctoral thesis or dissertation*, Basingstoke; New York: Palgrave Macmillan.

Dye, R.T. (1987) *Understanding Public Policy*, 6th edn, Englewood Cliffs, NJ: Prentice Hall.

Dye, R.T. (2002) *Understanding Public Policy*, 10th edn, Upper Saddle River, NJ: Prentice Hall.

Dye, R.T. (2008) *Understanding Public Policy*, 12th edn, Upper Saddle River, NJ: Pearson/Prentice Hall.

Eagleton, T. (1991) *Ideology: an introduction*, London: Verso.

Easton, D. (1965a) *A Systems Analysis of Political Life*, New York: John Wiley & Sons.

Easton, D. (1965b) *A Framework for Political Analysis*, Englewood Cliffs, NJ: Prentice Hall.

Echtner, M.C., and Jamal, T.B. (1997), 'The Disciplinary Dilemma of Tourism Studies', *Annals of Tourism Research*, 24(4): 868–83.

Edelman, M. (1988) *The Symbolic Uses of Politics*, Chicago, IL: University of Chicago.

Edgell, D.L. (1978) 'International Tourism and Travel', in H.F. van Zandt (ed.) *International Business Prospects, 1977–1979*, Indianapolis, IN: Bobbs-Merrill, pp.171–3.

Edgell, D.L. (1990) *International Tourism Policy*, New York: Van Nostrand Reinhold.

Edgell, D.L. (1999) *Tourism Policy: the next millennium*, Urbana, IL: Sagamore Publishing.

Edgell, D.L. (2008) *Tourism Policy and Planning: yesterday, today and tomorrow*, Oxford: Butterworth-Heinemann.

Elliot, J. (1983) 'Politics, Power and Tourism in Thailand', *Annals of Tourism Research*, 10(3): 377–93.

Elliot, J. (1987) 'Government Management of Tourism – a Thai case study', *Tourism Management*, 8(3): 223–32.

Elliot, J. (1997) *Tourism: politics and public sector management*, London; New York: Routledge.

Elster, J. (1989) *Nuts and Bolts for the Social Sciences*, Cambridge; New York: Cambridge University Press.

Evans, P.B. (1995) *Embedded Autonomy: states and industrial transformation*, Princeton, NJ: Princeton University Press.

Fayos-Solá, E. (1996) 'Tourism Policy: a midsummer night's dream?', *Tourism Management*, 17(6): 405–12.

Flick, U. (1998) *An Introduction to Qualitative Research*, London: Sage.

Flick, U. (2004a) 'Design and Process in Qualitative Research', in U. Flick, E.V. Kardorff and I. Steinke (eds) *A Companion to Qualitative Research*, London: Sage, pp.146–52.

Flick, U. (2004b) 'Triangulation in Qualitative Research', in U. Flick, E.V. Kardorff and I. Steinke (eds) *A Companion to Qualitative Research*, London: Sage, pp.178–83.

Flick, U., Kardorff, E.V. and Steinke, I. (eds) (2004a) *A Companion to Qualitative Research*, London: Sage.

Flick, U., Kardorff, E.V. and Steinke, I. (2004b) 'What is the Qualitative Research? an introduction to the field' in U. Flick, E.V. Kardorff and I. Steinke (eds) *A Companion to Qualitative Research*, London: Sage, pp.3–12.

Fontana, A. and Frey, J.H. (1998) 'Interviewing: the art of science', in N.K. Denzin and Y.S. Lincoln (eds) *Collecting and Interpreting Qualitative Materials*, Thousand Oaks, CA: Sage, pp.47–78.

Foucault, M. (1980) *Power/Knowledge: selected interviews and other writings, 1972–1979*, London: Harvester Press.

Francisco, R.A. (1983) 'The Political Impact of Tourism Dependence in Latin America', *Annals of Tourism Research*, 10(3): 363–76.

Friedland, R. and Alford, R. (1991) 'Bringing Society Back In: symbols, practices, and international contradictions', in W. Walter and J.D. Powell (eds) *The New Institutionalism in Organizational Analysis*, London; Chicago, IL: University of Chicago Press, pp.232–63.

Forester, J. (1984) 'Bounded Rationality and the Politics of Muddling Through', *Public Administration Review*, 44: 23–30.

Fox, C.J. and Miller, H.T. (1995) *Postmodern Public Administration*, Thousand Oaks, CA: Sage.

Fridgen, J. (1991) *Dimensions of Tourism*, East Lansing, MI: Educational Institute of the American Hotel and Motel Association.

Gao, D.C. and Zhang, G.R. (1983) 'China's Tourism: policy and practice', *Tourism Management*, 4(2): 75–84.

Gayle, A. (1994) 'Overcrowding Forces Airlines into the Red', *Travel News Asia*, 30 May–12 June.

Gee, C.Y., Maken, J.C. and Choy, D.J.L. (1989) *The Travel Industry*, 2nd edn, New York: Van Nostrand Reinhold.

Gee, C.Y., Maken, J.C. and Choy, D.J.L. (1997) *The Travel Industry*, 3rd edn, New York: John Wiley & Sons.

Geuss, R. (1981) *The Idea of a Critical Theory: Habermas and the Frankfurt School*, Cambridge: Cambridge University Press.

Giddens, A. (1979) *Central Problems in Social Theory: action, structure and contradiction in social analysis*, Cambridge: Polity Press.

Giddens, A. (1984) *The Constitution of Society: outline of the theory of structuration*, Cambridge: Polity Press

Glaster, B.G. and Strauss, A.L. (1967) *The Discovery of Grounded Theory, Strategies for Qualitative Research*, Chicago, IL: Aldine.

Goeldner, C.R. and Ritchie, J.R. (2003) *Tourism: principles, practices and philosophies*, 9th edn, New York; Chichester: John Wiley & Sons.

Goeldner, C.R. and Ritchie, J.R. (2006) *Tourism: principles, practices and philosophies*, 10th edn, Hoboken, NJ: John Wiley & Sons.

Goldsworthy, D. (1988) 'Thinking Politically about Development', *Development and Change*, 19(3): 505–30.

Goodin, R.E. (1996) (ed.) *The Theories of Institutional Design*, Cambridge; New York, NY: Cambridge University Press.

Goodman, D.S.G. (2004) 'The Campaign to "Open Up the West": national, provincial-level and local perspectives', *China Quarterly*, 178: 317–34.

Goodson, L. and Phillimore, J. (2004) 'The Inquiry Paradigm in Qualitative Tourism Research' in J. Phillimore and L. Goodson (eds) *Qualitative Research in Tourism: ontologies, epistemologies and methodologies*. London; New York: Routledge, pp.30–45.

Goulet, D. (1986) 'Three Rationalities in Development Decision-Making', *World Development*, 14(2): 301–17.

Gymen, K. (2000) 'Tourism and Governance in Turkey', *Annals of Tourism Research*, 27(4): 1025–48.

Greener, I. (2001) 'Social Learning and Macroeconomic Policy in Britain', *Journal of Public Policy*, 21(2): 133–52.

Gu, Z. and Thomas, M. (1987) 'The Economic Significance of International Tourism for the People's Republic of China', *Hospitality Education and Research Journal*, 10(2): 145–50.

Guba, E.G. (1990) *The Alternative Paradigm Dialog*, Thousand Oaks, CA: Sage.

Guo, B.G. (2001) 'Old Paradigms, New Paradigms, and Democratic Changes in China', in X.B. Hu and G. Lin (eds) *Transition Towards Post-Deng China*, Singapore: Singapore University Press, 101–17.

Habermas, J. (1972) *Knowledge and Human Interests*, London: Heinemann.

Habermas, J. (1987) *Knowledge and Human Interests*, 2nd edn, Cambridge: Polity.

Haggard, S. and Moon, C. (1989) *Pacific Dynamics: the international politics of industrial change*, Boulder, CO: Westview.

Hall, C.M. (1994) *Tourism and Politics: policy, power and place*, Chichester; New York: John Wiley & Sons.

Hall, C.M. (1998) 'The Institutional Setting – Tourism and the State', in D. Ioannides and K.G. Debbage (eds) *The Economic Geography of the Tourist Industry: a supply-side analysis*, London: Routledge.

Hall, C.M. (1999) 'Rethinking Collaboration and Partnership: a public policy perspective', *Journal of Sustainable Tourism*, 7(3&4): 274–89.

Hall, C.M. (2000) *Tourism Planning: policies, processes and relationships*, Harlow: Pearson Education.

Hall, C.M. (2001) 'Japan and Tourism in the Pacific Rim: locating a sphere of influence in the global economy', in D. Harrison (ed.) *Tourism and the Less Developed World: issues and case studies*, Oxon; New York: CABI, pp.121–36.

Hall, C.M. and Jenkins, J.M. (1995) *Tourism and Public Policy*, London; New York: Routledge.

Hall, C.M., Jenkins, J.M. and Kearsley, G.W. (1997) *Tourism Planning and Policy in Australia and New Zealand: cases, issues and practices*, Roseville, NSW: McGraw-Hill.

Hall, D.R. (1991) *Tourism and Economic Development in Eastern Europe and the Soviet Union*, London: Belhaven Press; New York: Halsted Press.

Hall, D.R. (2000) 'Sustainable Tourism Development and Transformation in Central and Eastern Europe', *Journal of Sustainable Tourism*, 8(6): 441–56.

Hall, D.R. (2001) 'Tourism and Development in Communist and Post-Communist Society', in D. Harrison (ed.) *Tourism and the Less Developed World: issues and case studies*, Oxon; New York: CABI.

Hall, D.R. (2003) 'Rejuvenation, Diversification and Imagery: sustainability conflicts for tourism policy in the Eastern Adriatic', *Journal of Sustainable Tourism*, 11 (2&3): 280–94.

Hall, P. (1986) *Governing the Economy: the politics of state intervention in Britain and France*, Cambridge: Polity Press; Oxford: in association with Basil Blackwell.

Hall, P. (1990) 'Policy Paradigms, Experts, and the State: the case of macroeconomic policy-making in Britain', in S. Brooks and A. Gagnon (eds) *Social Scientists, Policy, and the State*, New York: Praeger, pp.53–78.

Hall, P. (1993) 'Policy Paradigm, Social Learning, and the State: the case of economic policymaking in Britain', *Comparative Politics*, 25(3): 275–96.

Hall, R.H., Clark, J.P., Giordano, P.C., Johnson, P.V. and Roekel, M. (1977) 'Patterns of Interorganizational Relationships', *Administrative Review*, 22(3): 457–72.

Hall, S. (1978) 'The Hinterland of Science: Ideology and the Sociology of Knowledge', in Centre for Contemporary Cultural Studies, *On Ideology*, London: Hutchinson, pp.9–32.

Hall, S., Lumley, B. and McLennan, G. (1978) 'Politics and Ideology: Gramsci', in Centre for Contemporary Cultural Studies, *On Ideology*, London: Hutchinson, pp.45–76.

Ham, C. and Hill, M. (1984) *The Policy Process in the Modern Capitalist State*, New York: St. Martin's Press.

Ham, C. and Hill, M. (1993) *The Policy Process in the Modern Capitalist State*, 2nd edn, New York; London: Harvester Wheatsheaf.

Hamilton, M.B. (1987) 'The Elements of the Concept of Ideology', *Political Studies*, 35(1): 18–38.

Hammersley, M. (1992) *What is Wrong with Ethnography?*, London: Routledge.

Hamrin, C.L. and Zhao, S.S. (eds) (1995a) *Decision-Making in Deng's China: perspectives from insiders*, Armonk, NY: M.E. Sharpe.

Hamrin, C.L. and Zhao, S.S. (1995b) 'Introduction: core issues in understanding the decision process', in Hamrin, C.L. and S.S. Zhao (eds) *Decision-Making in Deng's China: perspectives from insiders*, Armonk, NY: M.E. Sharpe.

Hannam, K. and Knox, D. (2005) 'Discourse Analysis in Tourism Research: a critical perspective', *Tourism Recreation Research*, 30(2): 23–30.

Harding, H. (1984) 'Competing Models of the Chinese Communist Policy Process: toward a sorting and evaluation', *Issues and Studies: a Journal of China Studies and International Affairs*, 20(2): 13–36.

Harding, H. (1987) *China's Second Revolution: reform after Mao*, Washington, DC: Brookings Institution.

Harrison, D. (1992) 'International Tourism and the Less Developed Countries: the background', in D. Harrison (ed.) *Tourism and the Less Developed Countries*, London: Belhaven Press, pp.1–18.

Harrison, D. (1995) 'Development of Tourism in Swaziland', *Annals of Tourism Research*, 22(1): 135–56.

Harrison, D. (ed.) (2001a) *Tourism and the Less Developed World: issues and case studies*, Oxon; New York: CABI.

Harrison, D. (2001b) 'Tourism and Less Developed Countries: key issues', in D. Harrison (ed.) *Tourism and the Less Developed World: issues and case studies*, Oxon; New York: CABI.

Heclo, H. (1974) *Modern Social Politics in Britain and Sweden: from relief to income maintenance*, New Haven, CT: Yale University Press.

Heintz, H. and Jenkins-Smith, H. (1988) 'Advocacy Coalitions and the Practice of Policy Analysis', *Policy Sciences*, 21(2): 263–77.

Henderson, J. (2003) 'The Politics of Tourism in Myanmar', *Current Issues in Tourism*, 6(2): 97–118.

Henderson, K. (1991) *Dimensions of Choice: a qualitative approach to recreation, park and leisure research*, State College, PA: Venture Publishing.

Hendriks, F. (1999) *Public Policy and Political Institutions*, Cheltenham: Edward Elgar.

Henning, D.H. (1974) *Environmental Policy and Administration*, New York: Elsevier.

Hermanns, H. (2004) 'Interview as an Activity', in U. Flick, E.V. Kardorff and I. Steinke (eds) *A Companion to Qualitative Research*, London: Sage, pp.209–13.

Hettne, B. (1995) *Development Theory and the Three Worlds: towards an international political economy of development*, Essex: Longman Scientific and Technical.

Hill, M. (2005) *The Public Policy Process*, 4th edn, Harlow; New York: Pearson Longman.

Hitchcock, M., King, V.T. and Parnwell, M. (eds) (1993) *Tourism in South-East Asia*, London; New York: Routledge.

Hitzler, R. and Eberle, T.S. (2004) 'Phenomenological Life-World Analysis', in U. Flick, E.V. Kardorff and I. Steinke (eds) *A Companion to Qualitative Research*, London: Sage, pp.67–71.

Hobson, J.S.P. and Ko, G. (1994) 'Tourism and Politics: the implications of the change in sovereignty on the future development of Hong Kong's tourism industry', *Journal of Travel Research*, 32(4): 2–8.

Hofferbert, R.I. (1974) *The Study of Public Policy*, Indianapolis, IN: Bobbs-Merrill.

Hoffman, A.W. (1997) *From Heresy to Dogma: an institutional history of corporate environmentalism*, San Francisco, CA: New Lexington Press.

Hofstede, G. (1980) *Culture's Consequences: international difference in work-related values*, Beverly Hills, CA; London: Sage.

Hofstede, G. (2001) *Culture's Consequences: comparing values, behaviors, institutions, and organizations across nations*, Thousand Oaks, CA: Sage.

Hogwood, B. and Gunn, L. (1984) *Policy Analysis for the Real World*, Oxford: Oxford University Press.

Holbig, H. (2004) 'The Emergence of the Campaign to Open Up the West: ideological formation, central decision-making and the role of the provinces', *The China Quarterly*, 178: 335–57.

Holloway, I. and Wheeler, S. (1996) *Qualitative Research for Nurses*, Oxford: Blackwell Science.

Holm-Petersen, E. (2000) 'Institutional Support for Tourism Development in Africa', in P.U.C. Dieke (ed.) *The Political Economy of Tourism Development in Africa*, New York: Cognizant Communication Corporation, pp.195–207.

Holstein, J.A. and Gubrium, J.F. (1997) 'Active Interviewing', in D. Silverman (ed.) *Qualitative Research: theory, method and practice*, London: Sage.

Holstein, J.A. and Gubrium, J.F. (1998) 'Phenomenology, Ethnomethodology, and Interpretive Practice', in N.K. Denzin and Y.S. Lincoln (eds) *Strategies of Qualitative Inquiry*, Thousand Oaks: Sage, pp.137–57.

Hong, S.G. (1997) *The Political Economy of Industrial Policy in East Asia: the semiconductor industry in Taiwan and South Korea*, Cheltenham: Edward Elgar.

Hoornbeek, J.A. (2004) 'Policy-Making Institutions and Water Policy Outputs in the European Union and the United States: a comparative analysis', *Journal of European Public Policy*, 11(3): 461–96.

Hopf, C. (2004a) 'Qualitative Interviews: an overview', in U. Flick, E.V. Kardorff, and I. Steinke (eds) *A Companion to Qualitative Research*, London: Sage, pp.203–8.

Hopf, C. (2004b) 'Research Ethics and Qualitative Research', in U. Flick, E.V. Kardorff and I. Steinke (eds) *A Companion to Qualitative Research*, London: Sage, pp.3–12.

Howarth, D. (1997) 'Complexities of Identity/Difference: black consciousness ideology in South Africa', *Journal of Political Ideologies*, 2(1): 51–78.

Howarth, D. (2000) *Discourse: concepts in the social sciences*, Buckingham; Philadelphia, PA: Open University Press.

Howlett, M. and Ramesh, M. (1995) *Studying Public Policy: policy cycles and policy subsystems*, Toronto: Oxford University Press.

Howlett, M. and Ramesh, M. (2003) *Studying Public Policy: policy cycles and policy subsystems*, 2nd edn, Toronto: Oxford University Press.

Howlett, M., Ramesh, M. and Perl, A. (2009) *Studying Public Policy: policy cycles and policy subsystems*, Don Mill, Ontario: Oxford University Press.

Hu, A.G. (2001) 'Employment and Development: China's employment problem and employment strategy', in X.B. Hu and G. Lin (eds) *Transition Towards Post-Deng China*, Singapore: Singapore University Press, pp.41–81.

Hu, D. (1994) 'China's Quotation System to Go International', *Travel China*, 25 September–9 October: 6.

Hu, X.B. and Lin, G. (eds) (2001a) *Transition Towards Post-Deng China*, Singapore: Singapore University Press.

Hu, X.B. and Lin, G. (2001b) 'Transition Towards Post-Deng China: an introduction', in X.B. Hu and G. Lin (eds) *Transition Towards Post-Deng China*, Singapore: Singapore University Press, pp.1–13.

Huang, J.R. (1999) *The Applicability of Policy-Making Theories in Post-Mao China*, Aldershot; Brookfield, VT: Ashgate.

Hughes, R. (1968) *Hong Kong: borrowed place, borrowed time*, London: Andre Deutsch.

Hughes, R. (1976) *Borrowed Place, Borrowed Time: Hong Kong and its many faces*, 2nd revised edn, London: Deutsch.

Humberstone, B. (2004) 'Standpoint Research: multiple versions of reality in tourism theorizing and research', in J. Phillimore and L. Goodson (eds) *Qualitative Research in Tourism: ontologies, epistemologies and methodologies*, London; New York: Routledge, pp.119–36.

Husserl, E. (1970) *Logical Investigation*, New York: Humanities Press.

Issac, S. and Michael, W.B. (1971) *Handbook in Research and Evaluation*, San Diego, CA: Edits Publishers.

International Union of Official Travel Organizations (IUOTO) (1974) 'The Role of the State in Tourism', *Annals of Tourism Research*, 1(3): 66–72.

Jafari, J. (1988) 'Tourism as the Subject of Doctoral Dissertations', *Annals of Tourism Research*, 15(3): 407–29.

Jafari, J. (1991) 'Tourism Social Science', *Annals of Tourism Research*, 18(1): 1–9.

Jafari, J. and Ritchie, J.R. (1981) 'Towards a Framework for Tourism Education', *Annals of Tourism Research*, 8(1): 13–33.

Jager, S. (2001) 'Discourse and Knowledge: theoretical and methodological aspects of a critical discourse and dispositive analysis', in R. Wodak and M. Meyer (eds) *Methods of Critical Discourse Analysis*, London: Sage, pp.32–62.

Jansen-Verbeke, M. (1989) 'Inner Cities and Urban Tourism in the Netherlands: new challenges for local authorities', in P. Bramham, I. Henry, H. Mommaas and D.V. Poel (eds) *Leisure and Urban Processes: critical studies of leisure policy in Western European cities*, London; New York: Routledge, pp.233–53.

Jenkins, C.L. (1991) 'Tourism Development Strategies', in L.J. Lickorish, A. Jefferson, J. Bodlender and C.L. Jenkins, *Developing Tourism Destinations: policies and perspectives*, Essex: Longman.

Jenkins, C.L. (1994) 'Tourism in Developing Countries: the privatisation issue', in A.V. Seaton, C.L. Jenkins, R.C. Wood, P.U.C. Dieke, M.M. Bennett, L.R. MacLellan, and R. Smith (eds) *Tourism: the state of the art*, Chichester; New York: John Wiley & Sons, pp.3–9.

Jenkins, C.L. (2000) 'Tourism Policy Formulation in the Southern African Region', in P.U.C. Dieke (ed.) *The Political Economy of Tourism Development in Africa*, New York: Cognizant Communication Corporation, pp.62–76.

Jenkins, C.L. and Henry, B.M. (1982) 'Government Involvement in Tourism in Developing Countries', *Annals of Tourism Research*, 9(4): 499–520.

Jenkins, C.L., and Lickorish, L.J. (1997) *An Introduction to Tourism*, Oxford; Boston, MA: Butterworth-Heinemann.

Jenkins, J. (2001) 'Editorial', *Current Issues in Tourism*, 4(2–4): 69–77.

Jenkins, W.I. (1978) *Policy Analysis: a political and organizational perspective*, London: Robertson.

Jenkins-Smith, H.C. and Sabatier, P.A. (1993a) 'The Study of Public Policy Processes', in P.A. Sabatier and H.C. Jenkins-Smith (eds) *Policy Change and Learning: an advocacy coalition approach*, Boulder, CO: Westview, pp.1–9.

Jenkins-Smith, H.C. and Sabatier, P.A. (1993b) 'The Dynamics of Policy-Oriented Learning', in P.A. Sabatier and H.C. Jenkins-Smith, *Policy Change and Learning: an advocacy coalition approach*, Boulder, CO: Westview, pp.41–56.

Jennings, G. (2001) *Tourism Research*, Sydney: John Wiley & Sons.

Jenson, J. (1989) 'Paradigms and Political Discourse: protective legislation in France and the United States before 1914', *Canadian Journal of Political Science*, 22(2): 235–58.

Jepperson, R. (1991) 'Institutions, Institutional Effects, and Institutionalism', in W.W. Powell and P.J. DiMaggio (eds) *The New Institutionalism in Organizational Analysis*, London; Chicago, IL: The University of Chicago Press, pp.143–63.

Jian, B.Z., Shao, X.Z. and Hu, H. (1981) *A Concise History of China*, 2nd edn, Beijing: Foreign Languages Press.

John, P. (1998) *Analysing Public Policy*, London: Continuum.

Johns, N. and Lee-Ross, D. (1998) *Research Methods in Service Industry Management*, London; New York: Cassell.

Jordan, F. and Gibson, H. (2004) 'Let Your Data Do the Talking: researching the solo travel experiences of British and American women', in J. Phillimore and

L. Goodson (eds) *Qualitative Research in Tourism: ontologies, epistemologies and methodologies*, London; New York: Routledge, pp.214–36.

Kamrava, M. (2000) *Politics and Society in the Developing World*, London; New York: Routledge.

Kelle, U. and Erzberger, C. (2004) 'Qualitative and Quantitative Methods: not in opposition', in U. Flick, E.V. Kardorff and I. Steinke (eds) *A Companion to Qualitative Research*, London: Sage, pp.173–7.

Kerr, W.R. (2003) *Tourism Public Policy, and the Strategic Management of Failure*, Oxford: Pergamon.

Kim, S.S. (1998) *China and the World*, 4th edn, Oxford: Westview.

Kincheloe, J.L. and McLaren, P.L. (2005) 'Rethinking Critical Theory and Qualitative Research', in N.K. Denzin and Y.S. Lincoln (eds) *The Sage Handbook of Qualitative Research*, 3rd edn, Thousand Oaks, CA: Sage, pp.303–42.

King, A. (1973) 'Ideas, Institutions and the Policies of Governments: a comparative analysis: part III', *British Journal of Political Science*, 3(4): 409–23.

Kirk, J. and Miller, M.L. (1986) *Reliability and Validity in Qualitative Research*, Beverly Hills, CA: Sage.

Kornai, J. (1992) *The Socialist System: the political economy of communism*, Princeton, NJ: Princeton University Press.

Kosters, M. (1984) 'The Deficiencies of Tourism Science Without Political Science: comment on Richter', *Annals of Tourism Research*, 11(4): 610–12.

Kowal, S. and O'Connell, D.C. (2004) 'The Transcription of Conversations', in U. Flick, E.V. Kardorff and I. Steinke (eds) *A Companion to Qualitative Research*, London: Sage, pp.248–52.

Kuhn, T.S. (1962) *The Structure of Scientific Revolution*, Chicago, IL: University of Chicago Press.

Kuhn, T.S. (1970) *The Structure of Scientific Revolution*, 2nd (enlarged) edn, Chicago, IL: University of Chicago Press.

Kübler, D. (1999) 'Ideas as Catalytic Elements for Policy Change: advocacy coalitions and drug policy in Switzerland', in D. Braun and A. Busch (eds) *Public Policy and Political Ideas*, Northampton, MA: Edward Elgar, pp.116–35.

Kvale, S. (1996) *Interviews: an introduction to qualitative research interviewing*, Thousand Oaks, CA: Sage.

Ladd, E.C. (1989) *The American Polity*, 3rd edn, New York: W.W. Norton.

Lampton, D.M. (ed.) (1987a) *Policy Implementation in Post-Mao China*, Berkeley, CA: University of California Press.

Lampton, D.M. (1987b) 'Chinese Politics: the bargaining treadmill', *Issue and Studies*, 23(3): 11–41.

Lazar, D. (1998) 'Selected Issues in the Philosophy of Social Science', in C. Seale (ed.) *Researching Society and Culture*, London; Thousand Oaks, CA; New Delhi: Sage, pp. 7–22.

Lea, J.P. (1988) *Tourism and Development in the Third World*, London; New York: Routledge.

Legard, R., Keegan, J. and Ward, K. (2003) 'In-depth Interviews', in J. Ritchie and J. Lewis (eds) *Qualitative Research Practice: a guide for social science students and researchers*, London; Thousand Oaks, CA: Sage, pp.138–69.

Leiper, N. (1979) 'The Framework of Tourism: towards a definition of tourism, tourist, and the tourist industry', *Annals of Tourism Research*, 6(4): 390–407.

Leone, R.A. (1986) *Who Profits: winners, losers and government regulation*, New York: Basic Books.

Lertzman, K., Rayner, J. and Wilson, J. (1996) 'Learning and Change in the British Columbia Forest Policy Sector: a consideration of Sabatier's advocacy coalition framework', *Canadian Journal of Political Science*, 29(1): 111–33.

Lew, A. and Yu, L. (eds) (1994) *Tourism in China: geographic, political, and economic perspectives*, Boulder, CO: Westview.

Lew, A., Yu, L., Ap, J. and Zhang, G.R. (eds) (2003) *Tourism in China*, New York: Haworth Hospitality Press.

Lewis, J.W. (1963) *Leadership in Communist China*, Ithaca, NY: Cornell University Press.

Lewis, J.M. (1999) 'The Durability of Ideas in Health-Policy-Making', in D. Braun and A. Busch (eds) *Public Policy and Political Ideas*, Northampton, MA: Edward Elgar, pp.152–67.

Lewis, J. (2003) 'Design Issues', in J. Ritchie and J. Lewis (eds) *Qualitative Research Practice: a guide for social science students and researchers*, London; Thousand Oaks, CA: Sage, pp.47–76.

Lewis, J. and Ritchie, J. (2003) 'Generalising from Qualitative Research', in J. Ritchie and J. Lewis (eds) *Qualitative Research Practice: a guide for social science students and researchers*, London; Thousand Oaks, CA: Sage, pp.263–86.

Leys, C. (1996) *The Rise and Fall of Development Theory*, London: James Currey.

Li, H.R. (1987) 'PR China's Tourism Industry Today and Its Future Development', *Tourism Management*, 8(2): 90–1.

Li, Y.P. (2004) 'Exploring Community Tourism in China: the case of Nanshan Cultural Tourism Zone', *Journal of Sustainable Tourism*, 12(3): 175–93.

Lickorish, L.J. (1991) 'Role of Government and Private Sector', in L.J. Lickorish, A. Jefferson, J. Bodlender and C.L. Jenkins, *Developing Tourism Destinations: policies and perspectives*, Essex: Longman.

Lickorish, L.J., Jefferson, A., Bodlender, J. and Jenkins, C.L. (1991) *Developing Tourism Destinations: policies and perspectives*, Essex: Longman.

Lieberthal, K. (1995) *Governing China: from revolution through reform*, 1st edn, New York: W.W. Norton.

Lieberthal, K. (2004) *Governing China: from revolution through reform*, 2nd edn, New York: W.W. Norton.

Lieberthal, K. and Lampton, D.M. (eds) (1992) *Bureaucracy, Politics, and Decision-Making in Post-Mao China*, Berkeley, CA: University of California.

Lieberthal, K. and Oksenberg, M. (1988) *Policy-Making in China: leaders, structures and processes*, Princeton, NJ: Princeton University Press.

Lin, G. (2003) 'Ideology and Political Institutions for a New Era', in G. Lin and X.B. Hu (eds) *China After Jiang*, Washington, DC: Woodrow Wilson Center Press, pp.39–68.

Lin, G. and Hu, X.B. (2003) *China After Jiang*, Washington, DC: Woodrow Wilson Center Press.

Lincoln, Y.S. and Guba, G.E. (1985) *Naturalistic Inquiry*, Beverley Hills, CA: Sage.

Lindblom, C.E. (1978) *Politics and Markets: the world's political–economic systems*, New York: Basic Books.

Lindblom, C.E. (1968) *The Policy-Making Process*, Englewood Cliffs, NJ: Prentice Hall.

Lindblom, C.E. (1980) *The Policy-Making Process*, 2nd edn, Englewood Cliffs, NJ: Prentice Hall.

Lindblom, C.E. and Cohen, D. (1979) *Usable Knowledge*, New Haven, CT: Yale University Press.

Lindblom, C.E. and Woodhouse, E. (1993) *The Policy-Making Process*, 3rd edn, Englewood Cliffs, NJ: Prentice Hall.

Linder, J. (2003) 'Institutional Stability and Change: two sides of the same coin', *Journal of European Public Policy*, 10(6): 912–35.

Liu, C.X. (1995) 'Tourism Administration Goes Macro', *Travel China*, 7(8): 14.

Liu, G.L. (2001) 'Redefining the Role of the State in Economic Transition', in X.B. Hu and G. Lin (eds) *Transition Towards Post-Deng China*, Singapore: Singapore University Press, pp.83–99.

Liu, Z.H. (1994) 'Tourism Development – A System Analysis', in A.V. Seaton, C.L. Jenkins, R.C. Wood, P.U.C. Dieke, M.M. Bennett, L.R. MacLellan and R. Smith (eds) *Tourism: the state of the art*, Chichester; New York: John Wiley & Sons, pp.20–30.

Livingston, S.G. (1992) 'Knowledge Hierarchies and the Politics of Ideas on American International Commodity Policy', *Journal of Public Policy*, 12(3): 223–42.

Loren, B. and Rawski, T. (eds) (2008) *China's Great Economic Transformation*, Cambridge; New York: Cambridge University Press.

Low, L. (2001) 'Singapore's New Economic Initiatives and Implications for Tourism', in E.S. Tan, S.A.B. Yeoh and J. Wang (eds) *Tourism Management and Policy: Perspectives from Singapore*, New Jersey, London, Singapore, Hong Kong: World Scientific, pp.16–42.

Lowi, T.J. (1972) 'Four Systems of Policy, Politics and Choice', *Public Administration Review*, 32(4): 298–310.

Lowndes, V. (2002) 'Institutionalism', in D. Marsh and G. Stoker (eds) *Theory and Methods in Political Science*, Basingstoke: Macmillan, pp.90–108.

Lukes, S. (1974) *Power: a radical view*, London; New York: Macmillan.

Lynn, M.F. (1993) 'The Development and Impact of Foreign Tourism in China and Thailand', unpublished Master of Arts (MA) thesis, Hong Kong: University of Hong Kong.

Macridis, R.C. (ed.) (1992) *Foreign Policy in World Politics*, 8th edn New York: Prentice Hall.

Malecki, E.J. (1999) 'Knowledge and Regional Competitiveness', paper presented at the International Symposium, Knowledge, Education and Space, Heidelberg, Germany.

March, G. and Olsen, J. (1983) 'The New Institutionalism: organizational factors in political life', *American Political Science Review*, 78(2): 734–49.

March, G. and Olsen, J. (1989) *Rediscovering Institutions*, New York: Free Press.

Marshall, C. and Rossman, G.B. (2006) *Designing Qualitative Research*, Thousand Oaks, CA: Sage.

Masberg, B. and Silverman, L. (1996) 'Visitor Experiences at Heritage Sites: a phenomenological approach', *Journal of Travel Research*, 34(4) (Spring): 20–5.

Mason, J. (2002) *Qualitative Researching*, 2nd edn, London; Thousand Oaks, CA; New Delhi: Sage.

Martinussen, J. (1997) *Society, State and Market*, London; Atlantic Highlands, NJ: Zed Books; Halifax, Nova Scotia: Fernwood Publishing; Pretoria: HRSC/RGN.

Matt, E. (2004) 'The Presentation of Qualitative Research', in U. Flick, E.V. Kardorff, and I. Steinke (eds) *A Companion to Qualitative Research*. London: Sage, pp.326–30.

Matthews, H.G. (1975) 'International Tourism and Political Science Research', *Annals of Tourism Research*, 2(4): 195–203.

Matthews, H.G. (1977) 'Radicals and Third World Tourism: a Caribbean focus', *Annals of Tourism Research*, 5(Special): 20–9.

Matthews, H.G. (1978) *International Tourism: a political and social analysis*, Cambridge, MA: Schenkman.

Matthews, H.G. and Richter, L.K. (1991) 'Political Science and Tourism', *Annals of Tourism Research*, 18(1): 120–35.

Matthews, T. (1980) 'Australian Pressure Groups', in H. Mayer and H. Nelson (eds) *Australian Politics: a fifth reader*, Melbourne: Longman Cheshire.

Mayer, H. and Nelson, H. (eds) (1980) *Australian Politics: a fifth reader*, Melbourne: Longman Cheshire.

McCracken, G.D. (1988) *The Long Interview*, Newbury Park, CA: Sage.

McCulloch, G. (2004) *Documentary Research in Education, History, and the Social Sciences*, London; New York: RoutledgeFalmer.

McDowell, S.D. (1994) 'New Social Movements and Routes to Representation: science versus politics', in S. Brooks and A. Gagnon (eds) *The Political Influence of Ideas: policy communities and social sciences*, Westport, CT; London: Praeger, pp.107–34.

McIntosh, R.W. and Goeldner, C.R. (1972) *Tourism: principles, practices, and philosophies*, Columbus, OH: Grid.

McIntosh, R.W. and Goeldner, C.R. (1990) *Tourism: principles, practices and philosophies*, New York: John Wiley & Sons.

McIntosh, R.W., Goeldner, C.R. and Ritchie, J.R.B. (1995) *Tourism: principles, practices and philosophies*, New York: John Wiley & Sons.

McLellan, D. (1995) *Ideology*, Buckingham: Open University Press.

McNabb, D.E. (2004) *Research Methods for Political Science: quantitative and qualitative methods*, Armonk, NY: M.E. Sharpe.

Meethan, K. (2001) *Tourism in Global Society: place, culture and consumption*, Basingstoke; New York: Palgrave.

Mellor, R.E.H. (1991) 'Eastern Germany (The Former German Democratic Republic)', in D.R. Hall (ed.) *Tourism and Economic Development in Eastern Europe and the Soviet Union*, London: Belhaven Press; New York: Halsted Press.

Menahem, G. (1991) 'Public Policy and Political Interpretations of Socioeconomic Environments', *International Journal of Sociology and Social Policy*, 11(4): 37–61.

Menahem, G. (1998) 'Policy Paradigms, Policy Networks and Water Policy in Israel', *Journal of Public Policy*, 18(3): 283–310.

Meseguer, C. (2004) 'What Role for Learning? The diffusion of privatisation in OECD and Latin American countries', *Journal of Public Policy*, 24(3): 299–325.

Mihalic, T. (2002) 'Tourism and Economic Development Issues', in R. Sharpley and D. Telfer (eds) *Tourism and Development: concepts and issues*, Clevedon: Channel View Publications, pp.81–111.

Miles, M.B. and Huberman, M.A. (1994) *Qualitative Data Analysis: an expanded sourcebook*, Thousand Oaks, CA: Sage.

Mill, R.C. and Morrison, M.A. (1992) *The Tourism System*, Englewood Cliffs, NJ: Prentice Hall.

Mitchell, R.E. and Eagles, P.F.J. (2001) 'An Integrative Approach to Tourism: lessons from the Andes of Peru', *Journal of Sustainable Tourism*, 9(1): 4–28.

Mosedale, J.T. (ed.) (2010) *Political Economy of Tourism*, London: Routledge.

Mowforth, M. and Munt, I. (1998) *Tourism and Sustainability: new tourism in the third world*, London; New York: Routledge.

Nahrath, S. (1999) 'The Power of Ideas in Policy Research: a critical assessment', in D. Braun and A. Busch (eds) *Public Policy and Political Ideas*, Northampton, MA: Edward Elgar, pp.41–60.

Nathan, A.J. (1973) 'A Factionalism Model for CCP Politics', *China Quarterly*, 53: 34–66.

Nathan, A.J. (1976) 'Policy Oscillation in People's Republic of China: a critique', *China Quarterly*, 68: 720–50.

Naughton, B. (2007) *The Chinese Economy: transitions and growth*, Cambridge, MA: MIT Press.

North, D.C. (1996) 'Epilogue: economic performance through time', in Alston, L.J., C. Thrainn and D.C. North (eds) *Empirical Studies in Institutional Change*, Cambridge: Cambridge University Press.

North, D.C. (2004) *Institutions, Institutional Change and Economic Performance*, Cambridge: Cambridge University Press.

Nye, J.S. (2004) *Soft Power: the means to success in world politics*, New York: Public Affairs.

Oakes, T. (1998) *Tourism and Modernity in China*, London; New York: Routledge.

Ogden, S. (1995) *China's Unresolved Issues*, Englewood Cliffs, NJ: Prentice-Hall.

Oksenberg, M. (1972) 'Policy Making under Mao', in M.H. Lindbeck (ed.) *China: management of a revolutionary society*, Seattle, WA: University of Washington Press.

Ostrom, E. (1986) 'An Agenda for the Study of Institutions', *Public Choice*, 48: 3–25.

Oxford University Press (China) (1999) *Oxford Advanced Learner's English-Chinese Dictionary*, extended 4th edn, Hong Kong: Oxford University Press (China).

Pal, L. (1992) *Public Policy Analysis: an introduction*, Scarborough: Nelson Canada.

Paradis, W.T. (2002) 'The Political Economy of Theme Development in Small Urban Places: the case of Roswell, New Mexico', *Tourism Geographies*, 4(1): 22–43.

Parker, I. (2004) 'Discourse Analysis', in U. Flick, E.V. Kardorff and I. Steinke (eds) *A Companion to Qualitative Research*, London: Sage, pp.308–12.

Patton, M.Q. (2002) *Qualitative Research and Evaluation Methods*, 3rd edn, Thousand Oaks, CA: Sage.

Pearce, D.G. (1992) *Tourist Organizations*, New York: John Wiley & Sons.

Pearce, D.G. (1996) 'Tourist Organizations in Sweden', *Tourism Management*, 17(6): 413–24.

Pearce, D.G. (1998) 'Tourism Development in Paris: public intervention', *Annals of Tourism Research*, 25(2): 457–76.

Pearce, P.L. (1993) 'Defining Tourism Study as a Specialism: a justification and implications', *TEOROS International*, 1: 25–32.

Peet, R. and Thrift, N. (1989) 'Political Economy and Human Geography', in R. Peet and N. Thrift (eds) *New Models in Geography: the political economy perspective – Volume II*, London: Unwin Hyman, pp.3–29.

Peters, B.G. (1999) *Institutional Theory in Political Science*, London; New York: Pinter.

Pforr, C. (2006) 'Tourism Policy in the Making: an Australian network study', *Annals of Tourism Research*, 33(1): 87–108.

Phillimore, J. and Goodson, L. (eds) (2004a) *Qualitative Research in Tourism: ontologies, epistemologies and methodologies*, London; New York: Routledge.

Phillimore, J. and Goodson, L. (2004b) 'Progress in Qualitative Research in Tourism: epistemology, ontology and methodology', in J. Phillimore and L, Goodson (eds) *Qualitative Research in Tourism: ontologies, epistemologies and methodologies*, London; New York: Routledge, pp.3–29.

Phillips, S.D. (1994) 'New Social Movements and Routes to Representation: science versus politics', in S. Brooks and A. Gagnon (eds) *The Political Influence of Ideas: policy communities and the social sciences*, Westport, CT; London: Praeger, pp.57–82.

Picciotto, R. and Wiesner, E. (1998) *Evaluation and Development: the institutional dimension*, New Brunswick, NJ: Transaction Publishers.

Pizam, A. (1987) 'Planning a Tourism Research Investigation', in J.RB. Ritchie and C.R. Goeldner, *Travel, Tourism, and Hospitality Research*, New York: John Wiley & Sons, pp.63–76.

Poirier, R.A. (1995) 'Tourism and Development in Tunisia', *Annals of Tourism Research*, 22(1): 157–71.

Poirier, R.A. (1997) 'Political Risk Analysis and Tourism', *Annals of Tourism Research*, 24(3): 675–86.

Powell, W.W. and DiMaggio, P.J. (eds) (1991) *The New Institutionalism in Organizational Analysis*, London; Chicago, IL: The University of Chicago Press.

Prior, L. (2003) *Using Documents in Social Research*, London: Sage.

Pritchard, A. and Jaworski, A. (2005) 'Introduction: discourse, communication and tourism dialogues', in A. Jaworski and A. Pritchard (eds) *Discourse, Communication and Tourism*, Clevedon: Channel View Publications, pp.1–14.

Pye, L. (1981) *The Dynamics of the Chinese Politics*, Cambridge University Press.

Rabinow, P. and Sullivan, W.M. (eds) (1979) *Interpretive Social Science: a reader*, Berkeley, CA: University of California Press.

Radaelli, C.M. (1999) 'The Power of Policy Narratives in the European Union: the case of tax policy', in D. Braun and A. Busch. (eds) *Public Policy and Political Ideas*, Northampton, MA: Edward Elgar, pp.98–115.

Rapley, J. (2007) *Understanding Development*, London: Lynne Rienner Publishers.

Reason, P. (1998) 'Three Approaches to Participative Inquiry', in N.K. Denzin and Y.S. Lincoln (eds) *Strategies of Qualitative Inquiry*, Thousand Oaks, CA: Sage, pp.261–91.

Reichertz, J. (2004) 'Abduction, Deduction and Induction in Qualitative Research', in U. Flick, E.V. Kardorff and I. Steinke (eds) *A Companion to Qualitative Research*, London: Sage, pp.159–64.

Reid, G.R. (2003) *Tourism, Globalization and Development*, London; Sterling, VA: Pluto Press.

Rhodes, R. (1995) 'The Institutional Approach', in D. Marsh and G. Stoker (eds), *Theory and Methods in Political Science*, Basingstoke: Macmillan.

Richins, H. and Pearce, P. (2000) 'Influences on Tourism Development Decision Making: coastal local government areas in Eastern Australia', *Journal of Sustainable Tourism*, 8(3): 207–31.

Richter, L.K. (1983a) 'Tourism Politics and Political Science: a case of not so benign neglect', *Annals of Tourism Research*, 10(3): 313–35.

Richter, L.K. (1983b) 'Political Implications of Chinese Tourism Policy', *Annals of Tourism Research*, 10(3): 395–413.

Richter, L.K. (1985) 'State-Sponsored Tourism: a growth field for public administration', *Public Administration Review*, November/December: 832–9.

Richter, L.K. (1989) *The Politics of Tourism in Asia*, Honolulu, HI: University of
Hawaii Press.

Richter, L.K. (1993) 'Tourism Policy-Making in South-East Asia', in M. Hitchcock,
V.T. King and M. Parnwell (eds) *Tourism in South-East Asia*, London; New York:
Routledge.

Riley, J. (1990) *Getting the Most from your Data*, Bristol: Technical and Educational
Services.

Riley, R.K. (1993) 'Prestige Worthy Leisure Travel Behavior', unpublished Ph.D.
dissertation, Texas: Texas A&M University.

Riley, R. and Love, L.L. (2000) 'The State of Qualitative Research', *Annals of
Tourism Research*, 27(1): 164–87.

Ritchie, J. (2003) 'The Applications of Qualitative Methods to Social Research', in
J. Ritchie and J. Lewis (eds) *Qualitative Research Practice: a guide for social science
students and researchers*, London; Thousand Oaks, CA: Sage, pp.24–46.

Ritchie, J. and Lewis, J. (eds) (2003) *Qualitative Research Practice: a guide for social
science students and researchers*, London; Thousand Oaks, CA: Sage.

Ritchie, J., Spencer, L. and O'Connor, W. (2003) 'Carrying out Qualitative Analysis',
in J. Ritchie and J. Lewis (eds) *Qualitative Research Practice: a guide for
social science students and researchers*, London; Thousand Oaks, CA: Sage,
pp.109–37.

Ritchie, J.R.B. and Goeldner, C.R. (eds) (1987) *Travel, Tourism, and Hospitality
Research*, New York: John Wiley & Sons.

Ritzer, G. and Smart, B. (2001) 'Introduction: theorists, theories and theorizing', in
G. Ritzer and B. Smart (eds) *Handbook of Social Theory*, London; Thousand Oaks,
CA; New Delhi: Sage, pp.1–9.

Rochefort, D. and Cobb, R.W. (1993) 'Problem Definition, Agenda Access, and
Policy Choice', *Policy Studies Journal*, 21(1): 56–71.

Rokeach, M. (1972) *Beliefs, Attitudes and Values: a theory of organization and
change*, San Francisco, CA: Jossey-Bass.

Rokeach, M. (1973) *The Nature of Human Values*, New York: Free Press; London:
Collier-Macmillan.

Rokeach, M. (1979) *Understanding Human Values: individual and societal*, New York:
Free Press.

Roskin, G., Cord, L., Medeiros A. and Jones S. (1997) *Political Science: an introduction*, 6th edn, Upper Saddle River, NJ: Prentice Hall.

Roskin, G., Cord, L., Medeiros A. and Jones S. (2006) *Political Science: an introduction*, 9th edn, Upper Saddle River, NJ: Prentice Hall.

Rubin, H.J. and Rubin, I.S. (1995) *Qualitative Interviewing: the art of hearing data*,
Thousand Oaks, CA: Sage.

Rubin, H.J. and Rubin, I.S. (2005) *Qualitative Interviewing: the art of hearing data*,
2nd edn, Thousand Oaks, CA: Sage.

Ryan, C. and Gu, H.M. (eds) (2009) *Tourism in China: destination, cultures and
communities*, New York: Routledge.

Sabatier, P.A. (1987) 'Knowledge, Policy-Oriented Learning, and Policy Change',
Knowledge, 8: 649–92.

Sabatier, P.A. (1991) 'Towards Better Theories of the Policy Process', *PS: Political
Science and Politics*, 24(2): 144–56.

Sabatier, P.A. (1993) 'Policy Change over a Decade or More', in P.A. Sabatier and H.C. Jenkins-Smith (eds) *Policy Change and Learning: an advocacy coalition approach*, Boulder, CO: Westview, pp.13–39.

Sabatier, P.A. (ed.) (1999a) *Theories of the Policy Process*, Boulder, CO: Westview.

Sabatier, P.A. (1999b) 'The Need for Better Theories', in P.A. Sabatier (ed.) *Theories of the Policy Process*, Boulder, CO: Westview, pp.3–17.

Sabatier, P.A. (2007a) *Theories of the Policy Process*, Boulder, CO: Westview.

Sabatier, P.A. (2007b) 'The Need for Better Theories', in P.A. Sabatier (ed.) *Theories of Policy Process*, Boulder, CO: Westview, pp.3–17.

Sabatier, P.A. and Jenkins-Smith, H.C. (eds) (1993) *Policy Change and Learning: an advocacy coalition approach*, Boulder, CO: Westview.

Sabatier, P.A. and Jenkins-Smith, H.C. (1999) 'The Advocacy Coalition Framework: an assessment', in P.A. Sabatier (ed.) *Theories of the Policy Process*, Boulder, CO: Westview, pp.117–66.

Sabatier, P.A. and Weible, C.M. (2007) 'The Advocacy Coalition Framework: innovations and clarifications', in P.A. Sabatier (ed.) *Theories of the Policy Process*, Boulder, CO: Westview, pp.189–220.

Saich, T. (2004) *Governance and Politics of China*, 2nd edn, New York: Palgrave Macmillan.

Saint-Martin, D. (1999) 'The Formation of the New Entrepreneurial State and the Growth of Modern Management Consultancy', in D. Braun and A. Busch (eds) *Public Policy and Political Ideas*, Northampton, MA: Edward Elgar, pp.82–97.

Samuels, W.J. (2001) 'Technology vis-à-vis Institutions in the JEI: a suggested interpretation', *Journal of Economic Issues*, 11(4): 871–95.

Sarantakos, S. (1998) *Social Research*, 2nd edn, South Melbourne: Macmillan.

Schmidt, C. (2004) 'The Analysis of Semi-structured Interviews', in U. Flick, E.V. Kardorff and I. Steinke (eds) *A Companion to Qualitative Research*, London: Sage, pp.253–8.

Schutz, A. (1964) *Studies in Social Theory*, The Hague: Martinus Nijhoff.

Scott, R. (ed.) (1980) *Interest Groups and Public Policy*, South Melbourne: Macmillan.

Scott, W.R. (1987) 'The Adolescence of Institutional Theory', *Administrative Science Quarterly*, 32: 493–511.

Scott, W.R. (2001) *Institutions and Organizations*, Thousand Oaks, CA: Sage.

Scott, W.R. and Meyer, W.J. (1991) 'The Organization of Societal Sectors: Propositions and Early Evidence', in W.W. Powell and P.J. DiMaggio (eds) *The New Institutionalism in Organizational Analysis*, Chicago, IL: The University of Chicago Press, pp.108–40.

Seale, C. (1999) *The Quality of Qualitative Research*, London; Thousand Oaks, CA; New Delhi: Sage.

Seaton, A.V., Jenkins, C.L., Wood, R.C., Dieke, P.U.C., Bennett, M.M., MacLellan, L.R. and Smith, R. (eds) (1994) *Tourism: the state of the art*, Chichester; New York: John Wiley & Sons.

Self, P. (1985) *Political Theories of Modern Government, Its Role and Reform*, London: George Allen & Unwin.

Selznick, P. (1996) 'Institutionalism "Old" and "New"', *Administrative Science Quarterly*, 41: 270–7.

Sessa, A. (1976) 'The Tourism Policy', *Annals of Tourism Research*, 3(5): 234–47.

Sewell, W.H. (1992) 'A Theory of Structure: duality, agency, and transformation', *American Journal of Sociology*, 98(1): 1–29.

Sharpley, R. (2002) 'Tourism: A Vehicle for Development', in R. Sharpley and D. Telfer (eds) *Tourism and Development: Concepts and Issues*, Clevedon: Channel View Publications, pp.11–34.

Sharpley, R. and Telfer, D. (eds) (2002) *Tourism and Development: concepts and issues*, Clevedon: Channel View Publications.

Sheldon, P. (1990) 'Journals in Tourism and Hospitality', *Journal of Tourism Studies*, 1: 42–8.

Shepsle, K.A. (1989) 'Studying Institutions: some lessons from the rational choice approach', *Journal of Theoretical Politics*, 1(2): 131–47.

Sherman, J.H. (1987) *Foundations of Radical Political Economy*, Armonk, NY: M.E. Sharpe.

Shirk, S.L. (1993) *The Political Logic of Economic Reform in China*, Berkeley, CA: University of California Press.

Short, P. (1999) *Mao: a life*, London: Hodder & Stoughton.

Silverman, D. (1999) *Doing Qualitative Research: a practical handbook*, London: Sage.

Silverman, D. (ed.) (1997) *Qualitative Research: theory, method and practice*, London: Sage.

Silverman, D. (ed.) (2004) *Qualitative Research: theory, method and practice*, 2nd edn, London: Sage.

Simeon, R. (1976) 'Studying Public Policy', *Canadian Journal of Political Science*, 9 (4): 548–80.

Simmons, R.H., Davis, B.W., Chapman, R.J.K. and Sager, D.D. (1974) 'Policy Flow Analysis: a conceptual model for public policy research', *Western Political Quarterly*, 27(3): 457–68.

Simon, H. (1957) *Models of Man*, New York: John Wiley & Sons.

Sindiga, I. (1996) 'Domestic Tourism in Kenya', *Annals of Tourism Research*, 23(1): 19–31.

Sindiga, I. (1999) *Tourism and African Development: change and challenge of tourism in Kenya*, Hampshire: Ashgate.

Singh, S. (2001) 'Indian Tourism: policy, performance and pitfalls', in D. Harrison (ed.) *Tourism and the Less Developed World: issues and case studies*, Oxon; New York: CABI, pp.137–49.

Smith, J.M. (1994) 'Policy Networks and State Autonomy', in S. Brooks and A. Gagnon (eds) *The Political Influence of Ideas: policy communities and the social sciences*, Westport, CT; London: Praeger, pp.33–56.

Smyrl, M.E. (1999) 'When Ideas Get in the Way of Reform', in D. Braun and A. Busch (eds) *Public Policy and Political Ideas*, Northampton, MA: Edward Elgar, pp.136–51.

Smyth, R. (1986) 'Public Policy for Tourism in Northern Ireland', *Tourism Management*, 7(2): 120–6.

Snape, D. and Spencer, L. (2003) 'The Foundations of Qualitative Research', in J. Ritchie and J. Lewis (eds) *Qualitative Research Practice: a guide for social science students and researchers*, London; Thousand Oaks, CA: Sage, pp.1–23.

Sofield, T.H.B. and Li, S.F.M. (1998) 'Tourism Development and Cultural Policies in China', *Annals of Tourism Research*, 25(2): 362–92.

South African Qualifications Authority (SAQA) (2007) *The National Qualifications Framework: an overview*, Pretoria: South African Qualifications Authority.

Spector, M. and Kitsuse, J.I. (1987) *Constructing Social Problems*, New York: Aldine de Gruyter.

Spence, J. (1978) *The Memory Palace of Matteo Ricci*, London: Quercus.

Spence, J. (1999) *Mao*, London: Weidenfeld and Nicolson; New York: Viking.

Spencer, K., Ritchie, J. and O'Connor, W. (2003) 'Analysis: practices, principles and processes', in J. Ritchie and J. Lewis (eds) *Qualitative Research Practice: a guide for social science students and researchers*, London; Thousand Oaks, CA: Sage, pp.199–218.

Spoor, M. (1994) 'Issues of State and Market: from interventionism to deregulation of food markets in Nicaragua', *World Development*, 22(4): 517–33.

Steed, G.P.F. (1988) 'Geography, Social Science, and Public Policy: regeneration through reinterpretation', *Canadian Geographer*, 32(1): 2–14.

Steinke, I. (2004) 'Quality Criteria in Qualitative Research', in U. Flick, E.V. Kardorff and I. Steinke (eds) *A Companion to Qualitative Research*, London: Sage, pp.184–90.

Stevenson, N., Airey, D. and Miller, G. (2008) 'Tourism Policy Making: the policy-makers' perspectives', *Annals of Tourism Research*, 35(3): 732–50.

Stewart, D.W. and Kamins, M.A. (1993) *Secondary Research: information sources and methods*, 2nd edn, Newbury Park, CA: Sage.

Stewart, J. (1992) 'Corporatism, Pluralism and Political Learning: a systems approach', *Journal of Public Policy*, 12(3): 243–55.

Stone, A. and Harpham, E.J. (1982) (eds) *The Political Economy of Public Policy*, Beverly Hills, CA: Sage.

Stone, D.A. (1988) *Policy Paradox and Political Reason*, New York: Harper Collins.

Stone, D.A. (1989) 'Causal Stories and the Formation of Policy Agendas', *Political Science Quarterly*, 104(2): 281–300.

Strauss, A.L. and Corbin, J.M. (1990) *Basics of Qualitative Research: grounded theory procedures and techniques*, Newbury Park, CA: Sage.

Strauss, A.L. and Corbin, J.M. (1998a) *Basics of Qualitative Research: techniques and procedures for developing grounded theory*, Newbury Park, CA: Sage.

Strauss, A.L. and Corbin, J.M. (1998b) 'Grounded Theory Methodology', in N.K. Denzin and Y.S. Lincoln (eds) *Strategies of Qualitative Inquiry*, Thousand Oaks, CA: Sage, pp.158–83.

Stunkel, K.R., and Sarsar, S. (1994) *Ideology, Values and Technology in Political Life*, Lanham, MD: University Press of America.

Su, X.B. and Teo, P. (2009) *The Politics of Heritage Tourism in China: a view from Lijiang*, Abingdon; New York: Routledge.

Tan, E.S., Yeoh, S.A.B. and Wang, J. (eds) (2001) *Tourism Management and Policy: perspectives from Singapore*, New Jersey, London, Singapore, Hong Kong: World Scientific.

Tan, S.Y. (2003) 'Medicine in Stamps: Li Shih-Chen (1518–1593): herbalist of renown', *Singapore Medical Journal*, 44(7): 338–9.

Tang, S.Y., Lo, W.H., Cheung, K.C. and Lo, M.K. (1997) 'Institutional Constraints on Environmental Impact Assessment in Guangzhou and Shanghai', *China Quarterly*, 152: 863–74.

Teiwes, F.C. (1984) *Leadership, Legitimacy, and Conflict in China: from a charismatic Mao to the politics of succession*, London: Macmillan.

Telfer, D.J. (2002a) 'The Evolution of Tourism and Development Theory', in R. Sharpley and D. Telfer (eds) *Tourism and Development: concepts and issues*, Clevedon: Channel View Publications, pp.11–34.

Telfer, D.J. (2002b) 'Tourism and Regional Development Issues', in R. Sharpley and D. Telfer (eds) *Tourism and Development: concepts and issues*, Clevedon: Channel View Publications, pp.112–48.

Tham, E. (2001) 'Regionalisation as a Strategy for Singapore's Tourism Development', in E.S. Tan, S.A.B. Yeoh and J. Wang (eds) *Tourism Management and Policy: perspectives from Singapore*, New Jersey, London, Singapore, Hong Kong: World Scientific, pp.50–4.

Thomas, K. (2004) 'The Research Process as a Journey: from positivist traditions into the realms of qualitative inquiry', in J. Phillimore and L. Goodson (eds) *Qualitative Research in Tourism: ontologies, epistemologies and methodologies*, London; New York: Routledge, pp.197–214.

Thun, E. (2004) 'Keeping Up with the Jones': decentralization, policy imitation, and industrial development in China', *World Development*, 32(8): 1289–308.

Tisdell, C. and Wen, J. (1991) 'Foreign Tourism as an Element in PR China's Economic Development Strategy', *Tourism Management*, 12(1): 55–67.

Tobin, D. (2005) 'Economic Liberalization, the Changing Role of the State and "Wagner's Law": China's development experience since 1978', *World Development*, 33(5): 729–43.

Todaro, M.P. (1989) *Economic Development in the Third World*, 4th edn, London: Longman.

Todaro, M.P. (1997) *Economic Development*, 6th edn, Reading, MA: Addison-Wesley.

Todaro, M.P. (2000) *Economic Development*, 7th edn, Reading, MA: Addison-Wesley.

Torgerson, D. (1986) 'Between Knowledge and Politics: three faces of policy analysis', *Policy Sciences*, 19(1): 33–59.

Towner, J. (1988) 'Approaches to Tourism History', *Annals of Tourism Research*, 15(1): 47–62.

Townsend, W.J. *Robert Morrison: the pioneer of Chinese missions*, London: S.W. Partridge.

Tribe, J. (1997) 'The Indiscipline of Tourism', *Annals of Tourism Research*, 24(3): 638–57.

Tribe, J. (2004) 'Knowing about Tourism: epistemological issues', in J. Phillimore and L. Goodson (eds) *Qualitative Research in Tourism: ontologies, epistemologies and methodologies*, London; New York: Routledge, pp.46–62.

Tsou, T. (1986) *The Cultural Revolution and Post-Mao Reforms*, Chicago, IL: University of Chicago Press.

United Kingdom Foreign and Commonwealth Office (UKFCO) (2009a) *Country Profile: China*, London: UKFCO.

United Kingdom Foreign and Commonwealth Office (UKFCO) (2009b) *The UK and China: a framework for engagement*, London: UKFCO.

United States Department of Defense (2007) *Annual Report to Congress – Military Power of The People's Republic of China 2007*, Washington, DC: US Department of Defense.

United States National Intelligence Council (USNIC) (2008) *The Global Trends 2025: a transformed word*, Washington, DC: USNIC.

United States Department of State (2009) *Background Note: China*, Washington, DC: US Department of State.

Uysal, M., Lu, W. and Reid, L.M. (1986) 'Development of International Tourism in PR China', *Tourism Management*, 7(2): 113–19.

Veal, A.J. (1997) *Research Methods for Leisure and Tourism: a practical guide*, London: Pitman.

Veal, A.J. (2002) *Leisure and Tourism Policy and Planning*, Wallingford; New York: CABI.

Verbole, A. (2000) 'Actors, Discourses and Interfaces of Rural Tourism Development at the Local Community Level in Slovenia: social and political dimensions of the rural tourism development process', *Journal of Sustainable Tourism*, 8(6): 479–90.

Virginie, O. (1990) 'International Tourism in China', *Annals of Tourism Research*, 17(1): 123–32.

Walle, A.H. (1997) 'Quantitative Versus Qualitative Tourism Research', *Annals of Tourism Research*, 24(3): 524–36.

Waller, D.J. (1981) *The Government and Politics of the People's Republic of China*, 3rd edn, London: Hutchinson.

Wang, C.F.J. (2002) *Contemporary Chinese Politics: an introduction*, Upper Saddle River, NJ: Prentice Hall.

Wang, R.C. (2008) 'Editorial – Tourism and Hospitality Management in China', *International Journal of Hospitality Management*, 27(3): 323–4.

Wang, S.S. and Ap, J. (2003) 'Tourism Marketing in the People's Republic of China', in A.A. Lew, L. Yu, J. Ap and G.R. Zhang (eds) *Tourism in China*, New York: Haworth Hospitality Press, pp.217–35.

Wang, Y. and Sheldon, P.J. (1995) 'The Sleeping Dragon Awakes: the outbound Chinese travel market', *Journal of Travel and Tourism Marketing*, 4(4): 41–54.

Wanhill, S.R.C. (1987) 'UK – Politics and Tourism', *Tourism Management*, 8(1): 54–8.

Weiss, J.A. (1989) 'The Power of Problem Definition: the case of government paperwork', *Policy Sciences*, 22: 97–121.

White, C., Woodfield, K. and Ritchie, J. (2003) 'Reporting and Presenting Qualitative Data', in J. Ritchie and J. Lewis (eds) *Qualitative Research Practice: a guide for social science students and researchers*, London; Thousand Oaks, CA: Sage, pp.287–320.

Whiting, A.S. (1992) 'Foreign Policy in China', in R.C. Macridis (ed.) *Foreign Policy in World Politics*, New York: Prentice Hall, pp.222–67.

Wildavsky, E. (1979) *Speaking Truth to Power: the art and craft of policy analysis*, Boston, MA: Little, Brown.

Williams, A.M. and Shaw, G. (eds) (1988) *Tourism and Economic Development: Western European experiences*, London; New York: Belhaven Press.

Williams, A.M. and Shaw, G. (eds) (1991) *Tourism and Economic Development: Western European experiences*, 2nd edn, London; New York: Belhaven Press.

Wilkinson, P.F. (1997) *Tourism Policy and Planning: case studies from the Commonwealth Caribbean*, New York: Cognizant Communication Corporation.

Wilson, C.A. (2000) 'Policy Regimes and Policy Change', *Journal of Public Policy*, 20(3): 247–74.

Winkler, K.J. (1985) 'Questioning the Science in Social Science, Scholars Signal a "Turn to Interpretation"', *Chronicle of Higher Education*, 30(17), 5–6.

Wolf, S. (2004) 'Analysis of Documents and Records', in U. Flick, E.V. Kardorff and I. Steinke (eds) *A Companion to Qualitative Research*, London: Sage, pp.284–9.

Wolfgang, G.A. (2006) *China's Outbound Tourism*, Abingdon: Routledge.

Woon, C.C. (1989) *Tourism Development and Coordination in Peninsular Malaysia: a survey of the government's role*, Hong Kong: Hong Kong Polytechnic.

World Tourism Organization (WTO) (1979) *Role and Structure of National Tourism Administrations*, Madrid: World Tourism Organization (www.world-tourism.org).

World Tourism Organization (WTO) (1980) *Manila Declaration on World Tourism*, Madrid: World Tourism Organzation.

World Tourism Organization (WTO) (1994) *Marketing Plans and Strategies of National Tourism Administrations*, Madrid: World Tourism Organization.

World Tourism Organization (WTO) (1997) 'Travel to Surge in the 21st Century', *WTO News* (November 5): 1–2, Madrid: World Tourism Organization.

World Tourism Organization (WTO) (2001) *Compendium of Tourism Statistics*, Madrid: World Tourism Organization.

World Tourism Organization (UNWTO) (2006a) *Why Tourism?*, Madrid: United Nations World Tourism Organization.

World Tourism Organization (UNWTO) (2006b) *Compendium of Tourism Statistics*, Madrid: United Nations World Tourism Organization.

World Tourism Organization (UNWTO) (2007) *Compendium of Tourism Statistics*, Madrid: United Nations World Tourism Organization.

World Tourism Organization (UNWTO) (2009) *Tourism Highlights: 2009 Edition*, Madrid: United Nations World Tourism Organization.

World Tourism Organization (UNWTO) (2010a) *Why Tourism?*, Madrid: United Nations World Tourism Organization.

World Tourism Organization (UNWTO) (2010b) *UNWTO World Tourism Barometer: Interim Update* (April 2010), Madrid: United Nations World Tourism Organization.

World Travel and Tourism Council (WTTC) (2006) *China, China Hong Kong SAR and China Macau SAR: The Impact of Travel and Tourism on Jobs and the Economy*, London: World Travel and Tourism Council.

World Travel and Tourism Council (WTTC) (2009) *Travel and Tourism Economic Impact: China*, London: World Travel and Tourism Council.

World Travel and Tourism Council (WTTC) (2010) *Travel and Tourism Economic Impact: China*, London: World Travel and Tourism Council.

Wu, G.G. and Lansdowne, H. (eds) (2008) *China Turns to Multilateralism: Foreign Policy and Regional Security*, London: Routledge.

Xu, G. (1999) *Tourism and Local Development in China: case studies of Guilin, Suzhou and Beidaihe*, Richmond: Curzon.

Xu, G. and Kruse, C. (2003) 'Economic Impact of Tourism in China', in A.A. Lew, L. Yu, J. Ap and G.R. Zhang (eds) *Tourism in China*, New York: Haworth Hospitality Press, pp.83–101.

Yabuki, S. (1995) *China's New Political Economy: the giant awakes*, Boulder, CO: Westview.

Yan, J.Q. (1995) 'The Nature of Chinese Authoritarianism', in Hamrin, C.L. and S.S. Zhao (eds) *Decision-Making in Deng's China: perspectives from insiders*, Armonk, NY: M.E. Sharpe.

Yeoh, S.A.B., Tan, E.S., Wang, J. and Wong, T. (2001) 'Tourism in Singapore: an overview of policies and issues', in E.S. Tan, S.A.B. Yeoh and J. Wong (eds) *Tourism Management and Policy: perspectives from Singapore*, New Jersey; London; Singapore; Hong Kong: World Scientific, pp.3–15.

Yin, R.K. (1994) *Case Study Research: design and methods*, Thousand Oaks, CA: Sage.

Yin, R.K. (2003) *Case Study Research: design and methods*, Thousand Oaks, CA: Sage.

Young, R.E. (1989) *A Critical Theory of Education: Habermas and our children's future*, New York: Harvester Wheatsheaf.

Yu, L. (2003) 'Critical Issues in China's Hotel Industry', in A.A. Lew, L. Yu, J. Ap and G.R. Zhang (eds) *Tourism in China*, New York: Haworth Hospitality Press, pp.129–41.

Yu, L., Ap, J., Zhang, G.R. and Lew, A.A. (2003) 'World Trade and China's Tourism: opportunities, challenges, and strategies', in A.A. Lew, L. Yu, J. Ap and G.R. Zhang (eds) *Tourism in China*, New York: Haworth Hospitality Press, pp.297–308.

Zeigler, H. (1980) 'Interest Groups and Public Policy: a comparative, revisionist perspective', in R. Scott (ed.) *Interest Groups and Public Policy*, South Melbourne: Macmillan.

Zeng, B.X., Carter, R.W. and de Lacy, T.D. (2003) 'Short-term Perturbations and Tourism Effects: the case of SARS in China', *Current Issues in Tourism*, 8(4): 306–22.

Zhang, G.R. (1989) 'Ten Years of Chinese Tourism: profile and assessment', *Tourism Management*, 10(1): 51–62.

Zhang, G.R. (1995) 'China's Tourism Since 1978: policies, experiences and lessons learned', in A. Lew and L. Yu (eds) *Tourism in China: geographic, political, and economic perspectives*, Boulder, CO: Westview.

Zhang, G.R. (2003a) 'China's Tourism Since 1978: policies, experiences, and lessons learned', in A.A. Lew, L. Yu, J. Ap and G.R. Zhang (eds) *Tourism in China*, New York: Haworth Hospitality Press, pp.13–34.

Zhang, G.R. (2003b) 'Tourism Research in China', in A.A. Lew, L. Yu, J. Ap and G.R. Zhang (eds) *Tourism in China*, New York: Haworth Hospitality Press, pp.67–82.

Zhang, G.R. and Lew, A.A. (2003) 'Introduction: China's tourism boom', in A.A. Lew, L. Yu, J. Ap and G.R. Zhang (eds) *Tourism in China*, New York: Haworth Hospitality Press, pp.3–11.

Zhang, H., Chong, K. and Ap, J. (1999) 'An Analysis of Tourism Policy Development in Modern China', *Tourism Management*, 20(4): 471–85.

Zhang, H., Chong, K. and Jenkins, C.L. (2002) 'Tourism Policy Implementation in Mainland China: an enterprise perspective', *International Journal of Contemporary Hospitality Management*, 14(1): 38–42.

Zhang, H., Pine, R. and Lam, T. (2005) *Tourism and Hotel Development in China: From Political to Economic Success*, New York: Haworth Hospitality Press/ International Business Press.

Zhang, W.W. (1996) *Ideology and Economic Reform under Deng Xiao Ping: 1978–1993*, London; New York: Kegan Paul International.

Zhao, S.S. (1995) 'The Structure of Authority and Decision: a theoretical framework', in Hamrin, C.L. and S.S. Zhao (eds) *Decision-Making in Deng's China: perspectives from insiders*, Armonk, NY: M.E. Sharpe.

Zheng, S.P. (2001) 'China's Leadership After the 15th Party Congress: changes and implications', in X.B Hu and G. Lin (eds) *Transition Towards Post-Deng China*, Singapore: Singapore University Press, pp.119–42.

Chinese

Bai, S.Y. (1993) *The History of Chinese Communications*, Beijing: Commercial Press.

Chen, J.R. (1987) *A History of the Communication Between China and Foreign Countries*, Hong Kong: Xuejin Publications House.

Chen, Q.Y. (1994) *A Commentary about Li Daoyuan*, Nanjing: Nanjing University Press.

Chen, Q.Y. (2000) *Li Daoyuan*, Shijiazhuang: Huashan Arts Press.

Cheng, Y.S. and Law, K.Y. (eds) (1997) *New Perspectives on Political Sciences: western theories and chinese experiences*, Hong Kong: The Chinese University Press.

Chi, J.C. (1998) *The Two-Decades of Economic Reform and Open-Door: an exploratory study of the tourism economy*, Guangdong: Guangdong Tourism Press.

Chong, K. (2002) 'Tourism in Hong Kong', in G.R. Zhang, X.A. Wei and D.Q. Liu (eds) *The Green Book of China's Tourism – China's Tourism Development: analysis and forecast (2001–2003)*, Beijing: Social Sciences Academic Press (China), Chinese Academy of Social Sciences, pp.357–75.

Chong, K. (2003) 'Tourism in Hong Kong: New Trends and Competitiveness', in G.R. Zhang, X.A. Wei and D.Q. Liu (eds) *The Green Book of China's Tourism – China's Tourism Development: analysis and forecast (2002–2004)*, Beijing: Social Sciences Academic Press (China), Chinese Academy of Social Sciences, pp.393–413.

Chong, K. (2005) 'CEPA and the New Opportunity for Hong Kong's Tourism Development', in G.R. Zhang, X.A. Wei and D.Q. Liu (eds) *The Green Book of China's Tourism – China's Tourism Development: analysis and forecast (2003–2005)*, Beijing: Social Sciences Academic Press (China), Chinese Academy of Social Sciences, pp.382–401.

Chong, K. (2006) 'Tourism Development in Hong Kong under the New Circumstances', in G.R. Zhang, D.Q. Liu and X.A. Wei (eds) *The Green Book of China's Tourism – China's Tourism Development: analysis and forecast (2004–2006)*, Beijing: Social Sciences Academic Press (China), Chinese Academy of Social Sciences, pp. 281–98.

Chong, K. (2007) 'Tourism and Aviation Industry in Hong Kong (2005–2007): analysis and forecast', in G.R. Zhang, D.Q. Liu and R. Song (eds) *The Green Book of China's Tourism – China's Tourism Development: analysis and forecast (2007)*, Beijing: Social Sciences Academic Press (China), Chinese Academy of Social Sciences, pp.295–308.

Chong, K. (2008) 'Hong Kong's Tourism Development (2007–2008): present situation and future perspectives', in G.R. Zhang, D.Q. Liu and R. Song (eds) *The Green Book of China's Tourism – China's Tourism Development: analysis and forecast (2008)*, Beijing: Social Sciences Academic Press (China), Chinese Academy of Social Sciences, pp.486–98.

Cultural Relics Publishing House (2002) *A Succinct Chronological Table of Chinese History*, Hong Kong: Joint Publishing (Hong Kong) Company.

Dai, X.F. (2005) 'A Preliminary Study of Outbound Tourism Policy', in G.R. Zhang, X.A. Wei and D.Q. Liu (eds) *The Green Book of China's Tourism – China's Tourism Development: analysis and forecast (2003–2005)*, Beijing: Social Science Academic Press (China), Chinese Academy of Social Sciences, pp.231–44.

Dai, Z.A (2007) *The Silk Road of the Sea from Monk Fa Xian*, Taipei: Taiwan Commercial Press.

Fang, H. (2008) *The History of Sino-Foreign Communications*, Shanghai: Shanghai People's Press.

Fu, X.Y (2006) *A Commentary about Monk Xuanzhuang*, Nanjing: Nanjing University Press.

Gao, W.Q. (2003) *Later Years of Zhou Enlai*, Hong Kong: Mirror Books.

Hong Kong Commercial Daily (1997) *Directory of Government Structure of China*, Hong Kong: *Hong Kong Commercial Daily*.

Huang, F.C. and Huang, Y.H. (2006) 'Tourism Development in Taiwan (2004–2006)', in G.R. Zhang, D.Q. Liu and X.A. Wei (eds) *The Green Book of China's Tourism – China's Tourism Development: analysis and forecast (2004–2006)*, Beijing: Social Sciences Academic Press (China), Chinese Academy of Social Sciences, pp.310–24.

Huang, F.C. and Huang, Y.H. (2007) 'Tourism Development in Taiwan (2005–2007)', in G.R. Zhang, D.Q. Liu and R. Song (eds) *The Green Book of China's Tourism – China's Tourism Development: analysis and forecast (2007)*, Beijing: Social Sciences Academic Press (China), Chinese Academy of Social Sciences, pp.322–38.

Huang, F.C. and Huang, Y.H. (2009) 'Analysis and Forecast on China's Mainlanders' Travel to Taiwan', in G.R. Zhang, D.Q. Liu and R. Song (eds) *The Green Book of China's Tourism – China's Tourism Development: analysis and forecast (2009)*, Beijing: Social Sciences Academic Press (China), Chinese Academy of Social Sciences, pp.113–26.

Ji, G.M (2005) *Ideology*, Guangxi: Guangxi Normal University Press.

Jian B.Z. (ed.) (1983) *The Outline of Chinese History*, Beijing: People's Press.

Jian B.Z. and Zheng, T.T. (eds) (1983) *The Reference Materials about the General History of China*, Beijing: Zhonghua Book Company.

Jian, B.Z., Qi, S.H., Liu, Q.G. and Nie C.Q. (eds) (2008) *The Chronological Table of Sino-Foreign History*, Beijing: Zhonghua Book Company.

Li, T.G (1998) *Chinese Rites Controversy: History, Literature and Significance*, Shanghai: Shanghai Ancient Books Press.

Li, X.Q. and Zhao, W.B. (2007) 'International Research Progress in China Tourism', *Tourism Tribune*, 22(3): 90–6.

Li, Y.M. (1995) *Research on Mainland China*, Tai Pei: Wunan Books Press.

Li, Y.M (1996) *Methodologies of Communist China Studies*, Tai Pei: Yang-Zhi Cultural Business Co.

Li, Z.T. (2002) *The History of Qing Dynasty*, Shanghai: Shanghai People's Press.

Liu, D.J. (1992) *The Development History of Chinese Literature*, Hong Kong: Joint Publishing (H.K.) Co.

Liu, D.Q, Zhang, G.R. and Song, R. (2007) 'China's Tourism (2006–2007): Highlights and Perspectives', in G.R. Zhang, D.Q. Liu and R. Song (eds) *The Green Book of China's Tourism – China's Tourism Development: analysis and forecast (2007)*, Beijing: Social Sciences Academic Press (China), Chinese Academy of Social Sciences, pp.23–63.

Liu, S.L. (2003) 'Review and Outlook towards the Sino-British Economic and Trade Relationships', *Academic Journal of China Foreign Affairs University*, 4: 77–81.

Luo, G. (1983) *A Biography of Matteo Ricci*, Taipei: Taiwan Student Book Company.

Morrison, E. (ed.) (2008) *Memoirs of the Life and Labour of Robert Morrison*, Zhengzhou: Daxiang (Giant Elephant) Press.

Peng, S.S. (2006) *Development History of World Tourism*, Beijing: China Tourism Press.

Qian, M. (1995) *General Outline of Chinese History*, Taipei: Taiwan Commercial Press (Holding).

Qiu, K. (1994) *Essays about the History of Chinese Communications*, Beijing: People's Communications Press.

Ren, J.Y. (2003) 'Tourism in Macau: Present Situation and Forecast', in G.R. Zhang, X.A. Wei and D.Q. Liu (eds) *The Green Book of China's Tourism – China's Tourism Development: analysis and forecast (2002–2004)*, Beijing: Social Sciences Academic Press (China), Chinese Academy of Social Sciences, pp.414–25.

Ren, J.Y. (2006) 'Tourism Development in Macau (2004–2006)', in G.R. Zhang, D.Q. Liu and X.A. Wei (eds) *The Green Book of China's Tourism – China's Tourism Development: analysis and forecast (2004–2006)*, Beijing: Social Sciences Academic Press (China), Chinese Academy of Social Sciences, pp.299–309.

Ren, J.Y. (2009) 'Macau's Tourism Development (2007–2009)', in G.R. Zhang, D.Q. Liu and R. Song (eds) *The Green Book of China's Tourism – China's Tourism Development: analysis and forecast (2009)*, Beijing: Social Sciences Academic Press (China), Chinese Academy of Social Sciences, pp.357–75.

Tan, S.L. (2004) *Robert Morrison and Sino-Western Cultural Exchanges*, Hangzhou: Chinese Fine Arts Press.

Wang, H.X. (1999) 'Sino-British Economic and Trade Relations Under Mao's Era', unpublished doctoral thesis, Beijing: Party School of the Central Committee of the CPC.

Wei, X.A and Shen, Y.R. (1998) *The Competition and Development in China's Hotel Industry*, Guangdong: Guangdong Tourism Press.

Wu, K.Y. (1989) *Public Policy*, Hong Kong: The Commercial Press (Hong Kong).

Xi, Z.Z. (2002) *A New Catalogue of Ancient Novae and Explorations in the History of Science: self-selected works of academician Xi Zezong*, Shaanxi: Shaanxi Normal University.

Xu, S. (1998) *The Structure and Organizations of the CPC, Government and Military Forces*, Hong Kong: Qi-Lin Books Co.

Yan, J.Q. and Gao, G. (1987) *The History of Ten Years Cultural Revolution*, Hong Kong: Takungpao Press.

You, G.E., Wang, Q., Xiao, D.F., Ji, Z.H. and Fei, Z.G. (eds) (1986) *The History of Chinese Literature*, Hong Kong: China Books Publishing House.

Yu, Y., Lu, Wei and Xiao, X.Z. (2005) *Reform and Development in China: Policy and Performance*, Dalian, China: Dongbei University of Finance and Economics Press.

Zhang, C. (2002) *Comparative Studies of Eastern and Western Cultures: Matteo Ricci's Access and Others*, Hong Kong: City University of Hong Kong Press.

Zhang, G.R. (2006) 'China's Outbound Tourism 2004–2006: analysis and forecast', in G.R. Zhang, D.Q. Liu and X.A. Wei (eds) *The Green Book of China's Tourism – China's Tourism Development: analysis and forecast (2004–2006)*, Beijing: Social Sciences Academic Press (China), Chinese Academy of Social Sciences, pp.65–82.

Zhang, J.M. (1991) *An Introduction to Policy Sciences*, Beijing: The People's University of China Press.

Zhang, S.X. (1982) *The Pioneer of Policy Analysis – Charles Lindblom*, Taipei: Yun-Cheng Cultural Press.

Zhang, X.L. (ed.) (2003) *The Compilation of Historical Materials about the Sino-Western Communications*, Beijing: Zhonghua Book Company.

Zhu, W.H. (1998) *The China Economy in Oversupply*, Hang Zhou: Zhejiang People's Press.

Section 2: newspapers

Hong Kong Apple Daily (2009) 'Chinese Vessels Surrounded the US Naval Ship', Hong Kong: *Hong Kong Apple Daily* (10 March 2009).

Hong Kong Apple Daily (2009) 'Confrontation in the Yellow Sea', Hong Kong: *Hong Kong Apple Daily* (6 May 2009).

Hong Kong Apple Daily (2009) 'Kaohsiung Has Annoyed Beijing and Its Hotels Suffered from the Rooms Cancellation from the Mainland', Hong Kong: *Hong Kong Apple Daily* (18 September 2009).

Hong Kong Mingpao Daily (2009) 'Three Persons Set Fire to Themselves in the Car Prior to the Sessions of NPC and CPPCC', Hong Kong: *Hong Kong Mingpao Daily* (26 February 2009).

Hong Kong Mingpao Daily (2009) 'Around 100 Million of Chinese Suffered from the Psychological Illnesses', Hong Kong: *Hong Kong Mingpao Daily* (8 March 2009).

Hong Kong Mingpao Daily (2009) 'Wang Qishan (Chinese Vice-Premier): the developing countries shall have more say', Hong Kong: *Hong Kong Mingpao Daily* (28 March 2009).

Hong Kong Mingpao Daily (2009) 'The Number of Multimillionaires in China Totals 320,000: capital flowing to Hong Kong', Hong Kong: *Hong Kong Mingpao Daily* (1 April 2009).

Hong Kong Mingpao Daily (2009) 'China Announced the Medical Protection Plan Costing RMB¥ 850 Billion', Hong Kong: *Hong Kong Mingpao Daily* (7 April 2009).

Hong Kong Mingpao Daily (2009) 'Around 200 Million Chinese are not Covered by the Medical Protection', Hong Kong: *Hong Kong Mingpao Daily* (8 April 2009).

Hong Kong Mingpao Daily (2009) 'There are 50,000 Multi-Millionaires in China', Hong Kong: *Hong Kong Mingpao Daily* (16 April 2009).

Hong Kong Mingpao Daily (2009) 'Chinese Can Obtain the Individual Tourist Visa from Japan', *Hong Kong Mingpao Daily* (2 May 2009).

Hong Kong Mingpao Daily (2009) 'Chinese Vessels Confronted with the US Naval Ships Again', Hong Kong: *Hong Kong Mingpao Daily* (6 May 2009).

Hong Kong Mingpao Daily (2009) 'Malaysian Prime Minister Visits China', Hong Kong: *Hong Kong Mingpao Daily* (5 June 2009).

Hong Kong Mingpao Daily (2009) 'Western World Hinders China's Acquisition of Resources', Hong Kong: *Hong Kong Mingpao Daily* (6 June 2009).

Hong Kong Mingpao Daily (2009) 'A Conflict between the Residents and Police Happened in Jiangxi Province', Hong Kong: *Hong Kong Mingpao Daily* (16 June 2009).

Hong Kong Mingpao Daily (2009) 'Unemployed Population Totalled 40 Million in China', Hong Kong: *Hong Kong Mingpao Daily* (19 June 2009).

Hong Kong Mingpao Daily (2009) 'Opposition Caused the Implementation Suspension of the "Green Dam Youth Escort"', Hong Kong: *Hong Kong Mingpao Daily* (1 July 2009).

Hong Kong Mingpao Daily (2009) 'China's Foreign Exchange Per Capita still Lags Behind Hong Kong SAR and Japan', Hong Kong: *Hong Kong Mingpao Daily* (16 July 2009).

Hong Kong Mingpao Daily (2009) 'Recognition of Market Economy Can Enjoy Equal Tariff Treatment', Hong Kong: *Hong Kong Mingpao Daily* (30 July 2009).

Hong Kong Mingpao Daily (2009) 'Kaohsiung Worries About Loss of Mainland Tourists (Arising from Dalai Lama's Visit)', Hong Kong: *Hong Kong Mingpao Daily* (18 September 2009).

Hong Kong Mingpao Daily (2009) 'Mainland Tour Groups Do Not Come to Southern Taiwan', Hong Kong: *Hong Kong Mingpao Daily* (11 October 2009).

Hong Kong Mingpao Daily (2009) 'Two Sides of Taiwan Strait for the First Time Appoint the Semi-Official Delegate After 60 Years', Hong Kong: *Hong Kong Mingpao Daily* (23 October 2009).

Hong Kong Mingpao Daily (2010) 'China's Exports Top the World, Hong Kong': *Hong Kong Mingpao Daily* (8 January 2010).

Hong Kong Mingpao Daily (2010) 'China Jumps to the Second Largest Economy', Hong Kong: *Hong Kong Mingpao Daily* (22 January 2010).

Hong Kong Mingpao Daily (2010) 'China Still Remains as the Largest Debtor of the US National Bonds', Hong Kong: *Hong Kong Mingpao Daily* (27 February 2010).

Hong Kong Mingpao Daily (2010) 'Taiwan's First Tourist Office to Mainland Set up in Beijing (4 May 2010)', Hong Kong: *Hong Kong Mingpao Daily* (5 May 2010).

Hong Kong Oriental Daily News (2009) 'A Hundred People Were Arrested in a Conflict with Police in Guangxi', *Hong Kong Oriental Daily* (26 February 2009).

Hong Kong Oriental Daily News (2009) 'China's Aid to Africa has Drawn Worldwide Attention', *Hong Kong Oriental Daily* (9 June 2009).

Hong Kong Oriental Daily News (2009) 'Japan's Invitation of Rabiye Qadir', *Hong Kong Oriental Daily* (31 July 2009).

Hong Kong Singtao Daily (2009) 'China's External Propaganda Promotes her "Soft Power"', Hong Kong: *Hong Kong Singtao Daily* (27 April 2009).

The Sun Hong Kong, 2009, 'Many Nations Hook in the African Countries', *The Sun Hong Kong* (21 April 2009).

Hong Kong Wenweipo Daily (2008) 'Taiwan Can Earn Annual Incomes of TWD$ 60 Billion from Opening to Mainland Tourists', Hong Kong: *Hong Kong Wenweipo Daily* (12 June 2008).

Hong Kong Wenweipo Daily (2008) 'Agreements Signed for Leisure Travel and Charter Flights between Mainland and Taiwan', Hong Kong: *Hong Kong Wenweipo Daily* (14 June 2008).

Hong Kong Wenweipo Daily (2008a) 'Canada Was Uncomfortable about her Inability in Obtaining the "Approved Destination Status (ADS)"', Hong Kong: *Hong Kong Wenweipo Daily* (19 June 2008).

Hong Kong Wenweipo Daily (2008b) 'Chinese Tourists to France Reduced by 70%, France Appeals for the Removal of "Boycotts"', Hong Kong: *Hong Kong Wenweipo Daily* (19 June 2008).

Hong Kong Wenweipo Daily (2009a) 'Different Income Groups in China by Comparison', Hong Kong: *Hong Kong Wenweipo Daily* (10 February 2009).

Hong Kong Wenweipo Daily (2009b) 'Nanjing City Offered the Rural Travel Coupon', Hong Kong: *Hong Kong Wenweipo Daily* (10 February 2009).

Hong Kong Wenweipo Daily (2009) 'Top Ten Topics of NPC and CPPCC Session of 2009', Hong Kong: *Hong Kong Wenweipo Daily* (16 February 2009).

Hong Kong Wenweipo Daily (2009) 'Guangdong Issued the Tourist Coupons of RMB 20 Million to Stimulate the Consumption of RMB 40 Million', Hong Kong: *Hong Kong Wenweipo Daily* (17 February 2009).

Hong Kong Wenweipo Daily (2009) 'Overseas Acquisitions Increased by 40%, Ranking after Germany', Hong Kong: *Hong Kong Wenweipo Daily* (19 February 2009).

Hong Kong Wenweipo Daily (2009) 'Chinese Purchasing Group of 100 Delegates Go to Europe with the Telecommunications as the Big Buyer', Hong Kong: *Hong Kong Wenweipo Daily* (25 February 2009).

Hong Kong Wenweipo Daily (2009) 'Chinese Purchasing Delegation Signed the Business Agreement of US\$ 2 Billion in the UK', Hong Kong: *Hong Kong Wenweipo Daily* (1 March 2009).

Hong Kong Wenweipo Daily (2009) 'Two Factors Restrain Consumption', Hong Kong: *Hong Kong Wenweipo Daily* (30 March 2009).

Hong Kong Wenweipo Daily (2009) 'China's Rich Households Will Reach 4 Million by 2015', Hong Kong: *Hong Kong Wenweipo Daily* (8 April 2009).

Hong Kong Wenweipo Daily (2009) 'World Bank: a total of 500 million Chinese got themselves alleviated from poverty', Hong Kong: *Hong Kong Wenweipo Daily* (9 April 2009).

Hong Kong Wenweipo Daily (2009) 'Six of Ten Thousand in China are Multi-millionaires', Hong Kong: *Hong Kong Wenweipo Daily* (16 April 2009).

Hong Kong Wenweipo Daily (2009) 'China Increases her Holdings of US National Bonds', Hong Kong: *Hong Kong Wenweipo Daily* (29 July 2009).

Hong Kong Wenweipo Daily (2009) 'Vice Mayor of Tonghua City in the Jilin Province was Appointed as the Chairman of Tonghua Iron and Steel Group', Hong Kong: *Hong Kong Wenweipo Daily* (8 August 2009).

Hong Kong Wenweipo Daily (2009) 'Chinese on Average Spend over RMB¥14,000 Daily in Japan', Hong Kong: *Hong Kong Wenweipo Daily* (23 August 2009).

Hong Kong Wenweipo Daily (2010) 'A List of Senior Officials at the Vice-Minister Rank or Above Facing Penalties for Corruptions', Hong Kong: *Hong Kong Wenweipo Daily* (11 March 2010).

Newsweek (America) (2009) 'Why China Works', New York: *Newsweek* (Forooha Rana, 19 January 2009).

Section 3: government documents and official literature

China

General

The Association for Relations Across the Taiwan Straits (ARATS, Mainland) and The Straits Exchange Foundation (SEF, Taiwan) (2008) *The Agreement on Mainland Residents Travelling to Taiwan Made by the Two Sides of the Taiwan Straits*, Beijing: 13 June 2008.

The Association for Relations Across the Taiwan Straits (ARATS, Mainland) and The Straits Exchange Foundation (SEF, Taiwan) (2008) *Key Notes about the Arrangements for Charter Flights Made by the Two Sides of the Taiwan Straits*, Beijing: 13 June 2008.

Beijing Review (2008) *China's Tibet: Facts and Figures*, Beijing: Foreign Languages Press.

Chen Haosu (2004) *On People to People Diplomacy*, Beijing: The Chinese People's Association for Friendship with Foreign Countries.

Chen Yun (1979) *On the Issues of Plan and Market*, Beijing: Xinhua News Agency.

Chen Yun (1985) *Speech at the National Congress of the Communist Party of China*, Beijing: Xinhua News Agency.

China Tibet News (2008) 'Series of Aid from Three Central Tibet Works Conference', Tibet: *China Tibet News*.

Communist Party of China (CPC) (1949) *Mao Zedong: Report on the Second Plenum of the Seventh National Congress of the Communist Party of China*, Beijing: Xinhua News Agency.

Communist Party of China (CPC) (1951–77) *The Selected Works of Mao Zedong (Volumes 1–5)*, Beijing: People's Press.

Communist Party of China (CPC) (1978) *Communiqué of the Third Plenum of the Central Committee of the Eleventh National Congress of the Communist Party of China*, Beijing: Xinhua News Agency.

Communist Party of China (CPC) (1986) *The Resolution of the Central Committee on the Guidelines in Directing the Building of Socialism Spiritual Civilization*, Beijing: Xinhua News Agency.

Communist Party of China (CPC) (1987) *Marching Alongside the Road of Building Socialism with Chinese Characteristics – Report Made by General Secretary of Central Committee Zhao Ziyang to the Thirteenth National Congress of the Communist Party of China*, Beijing: Xinhua News Agency.

Communist Party of China (CPC) (1990) *Communiqué of the Seventh Plenum of the Central Committee of the Thirteenth National Congress of the Communist Party of China*, Beijing: Xinhua News Agency.

Communist Party of China (CPC) (1992) *To Speed Up the Pace of Economic Reform, Open-door and Economic Modernization, Capturing the Great Triumph of Building Socialism with Chinese Characteristics – Report Made by General Secretary of Central Committee Jiang Zemin to the Fourteenth National Congress of the Communist Party of China*, Beijing: Xinhua News Agency.

Communist Party of China (CPC) (1993) *Decisions on Certain Issues Pertaining to the Building of the Socialist Market Economy Model*, Beijing: Xinhua News Agency.

Communist Party of China (CPC) (1997) *Upholding the Banner of Deng Xiaoping's Theories and Boosting the Work of Building Socialism with Chinese Characteristics towards the 21st Century – Report Made by the General Secretary of Central Committee Jiang Zemin to the Fifteenth National Congress of the Communist Party of China*, Beijing: Xinhua News Agency.

Communist Party of China (CPC) (2002) *Fully Constructing a Well-Off Society, Breaking the New Ground for Socialism with Chinese Characteristics – Report Made by the General Secretary of Central Committee Jiang Zemin to the Sixteenth National Congress of the Communist Party of China*, Beijing: Xinhua News Agency.

Communist Party of China (CPC) (2003) *Communiqué of the Third Plenum of the Central Committee of the Sixteenth National Congress of the Communist Party of China*, Beijing: Xinhua News Agency.

Communist Party of China (CPC) (2004a) *Hu Jintao: The 'Scientific Development Concept' is a New Major Strategic Thought Initiated by our Party*, Beijing: Xinhua News Agency.

Communist Party of China (CPC) (2004b) *The Decision to Enhance the Ruling Capacity of the Communist Party of China*, Beijing: Xinhua News Agency.

Communist Party of China (CPC) (2006a) *The Three Represents*, Beijing: International Department of Central Committee of CPC.

Communist Party of China (CPC) (2006b) *The Decision of the CPC Central Committee on Certain Issues about the Construction of the Socialist Harmonious Society*, Beijing: Xinhua News Agency.

Communist Party of China (CPC) (2007) *Upholding the Great Banner of Socialism with Chinese Characteristics, Striving to Win New Triumph for the Full Construction of a Well-Off Society – Report Made by the General Secretary of the Central Committee Hu Jintao to the Seventeenth National Congress of the Communist Party of China*, Beijing: Xinhua News Agency.

Communist Party of China (CPC) (2010a) *The Important Thoughts of 'The Three-Represents'*, Beijing: Xinhua News Agency.

Communist Party of China (CPC) (2010b) *The Scientific Development Concept*, Beijing: Xinhua News Agency.

Communist Party of China (CPC) (2010c) *The Socialist Core Values System*, Beijing: Xinhua News Agency.

Communist Party of China (CPC) (2010d) *The Constitution of the Communist Party of China*, Beijing: Xinhua News Agency.

Communist Party of China (CPC) (2010e) *List of Meetings Held by the Politburo of the Central Committee of the Communist Party of China*, Beijing: Xinhua News Agency.

Deng Xiaoping (1979) *Adhering to the Four Cardinal Principles*, Beijing: Xinhua News Agency.

Deng Xiaoping (1980) *Implementing the Policy of Readjustment, Ensuring Stability and Unity*, Beijing: Xinhua News Agency.

Deng Xiaoping (1982) *Building Socialism with Chinese Characteristics – Opening Speech made at the Twelfth National Congress of the Communist Party of China*, Beijing: Xinhua News Agency.

Deng Xiaoping (1984) *Building Socialism with Chinese Characteristics*, Beijing: Xinhua News Agency.

Deng Xiaoping (1986) *We Must Firmly Oppose 'Bourgeois Liberalization'*, Beijing: Xinhua News Agency.

Deng Xiaoping (1992a) *Remarks Delivered during the Visit to Shanghai*, Beijing: Xinhua News Agency.

Deng Xiaoping (1992b) *Remarks Delivered in Wuchang, Shenzhen, Zhuhai and Shanghai*, Beijing: Xinhua News Agency.

Han Nianlong[1] (ed.) (1988) *China Today[2]: Foreign Affairs*, Beijing: China Social Sciences Press.

The Information Office of the State Council of PR China (2007) *China in Brief*, Beijing: The Information Office of the State Council.

Jiang Zemin (1993) *Using Comrade Deng Xiaoping's Theories of Constructing Socialism with Chinese Characteristics to Equip Our Party*, Beijing: Xinhua News Agency.

Mao Zedong (1966) *Mao Tse-tung: Four Essays on Philosophy*, Beijing: Foreign Language Press.

Ministry of Foreign Affairs (MoFA) of the People's Republic of China (2009) *The Chronology for China's Establishment of Diplomatic Relationships with Foreign Nations*, Beijing: Ministry of Foreign Affairs.

The National Development and Reform Commission of the PR China (NDRC) (2006b) *The Eleventh Five-Year State Plan for the National Economy and Social Development*, Beijing: NDRC.

The National People's Congress of the PR China (NPC) (1982) *The Organization Law of the State Council*, Beijing: Xinhua News Agency.

The National People's Congress of the PR China (NPC) (1988) *The Standardization Law of PR China*, Beijing: NPC.

The National People's Congress of the PR China (NPC) (1997) *Prices and Pricing Law of the PR China*, Beijing: NPC.

The National People's Congress of the PR China (NPC) (2004) *The State Constitution of the People's Republic of China*, Beijing: Xinhua News Agency.

The National People's Congress of the PR China (NPC) *The Rights and Duties of the NPC Deputies*, Beijing: NPC.

The National People's Congress of the PR China (NPC) *The Definition, Requirements and Scope of NPC Bills*, Beijing: NPC.

The National People's Congress of the PR China (NPC) *The Proposal of the NPC Bill*, Beijing: NPC.

People's Daily (1977) 'Editorial', Beijing: *People's Daily*.

People's Daily (2001) 'The Fourth Central Tibet Works Conference Organized by the CPC Central Committee and State Council', Beijing: *People's Daily*.

People's Daily (2003a) 'The Sino-American Table Tennis Diplomacy', Beijing: *People's Daily*.

People's Daily (2003b) 'President Richard Nixon's Visit and Sino-American Joint Communiqué', Beijing: *People's Daily*.

State Administration of Foreign Exchange of the PR China (SAFE) (2010) *Year-End Foreign Exchange Reserves*, Beijing: State Administration of Foreign Exchange of the People's Republic of China.

The State Council of the PR China (1997) *Regulation on the Organization and Establishment of the State Council*, Beijing: Xinhua News Agency.

The State Council of the PR China (1999) *National Holiday Arrangements*, Beijing: Xinhua News Agency.

The State Council of the PR China (2001) *The Notice of State Council – To Further Speed Up the Development of Tourism*, Beijing: Xinhua News Agency.

The State Council of the PR China (2002) *Regulation on the Administration of Outbound Travel*, Beijing: China National Tourism Administration (CNTA).

The State Council of the PR China (2007a) *National Holiday Arrangements*, Beijing: Xinhua News Agency.

The State Council of the PR China (2007b) *Regulation on Employee Paid Leave*, Beijing: Xinhua News Agency.

The State Council of the PR China (2008) *The Operating Procedures of the State Council*, Beijing: Xinhua News Agency.

The State Council of the PR China (2009a) *Government Report Submitted to the Second Plenary Meeting of 11th National People's Congress*, Beijing: The State Council.

The State Council of the PR China (2009b) *Advice to Speed Up the Development of Tourism*, Beijing: The State Council.

The State Council of the PR China (2010a) *Government Report submitted to the Third Plenary Meeting of 11th National People's Congress*, Beijing: The State Council.

The State Statistical Bureau of the PR China (SSB) (1988–2009) *China Statistical Yearbook*, Beijing: China Statistics Press.

The State Statistical Bureau of the PR China (SSB) (2010) *Statistical Communiqué of PR China 2009*, Beijing: SSB.

Xinhua News Agency (2000) *The Ministerial Coordinating Meeting for Holiday Tourism*, Beijing: Xinhua News Agency.

Xinhua News Agency (2003) *The Grounds in Nurturing the Thoughts of 'Three-Represents'*, Beijing: Xinhua News Agency.

Xinhua News Agency (*People's Daily*) (2004a) *Li Changchun Pays his Inspection Visits to Hebei Province and Requires the Development of 'Red Tourism' with Great Effort*, Beijing: Xinhua News Agency.

Xinhua News Agency (*People's Daily*) (2004b) *Building an Harmonious Society*, Beijing: Xinhua News Agency.

Xinhua News Agency (2005a) *The Author of 'Red Star Over China' – Edgar Snow*, Beijing: Xinhua News Agency.

Xinhua News Agency (2005b) *Corrupt Officials in Escaping, Took Away Funds of US$ 50 billion*, Beijing: Xinhua News Agency.

Xinhua News Agency (2006a) *The Decision on the Certain Issues About the Construction of the Socialist Harmonious Society: The Birth*, Beijing: Xinhua News Agency.

Xinhua News Agency (2006b) *Li Changchun: Boosting the Construction of an Harmonious Culture and Prospering Socialist Culture*, Beijing: Xinhua News Agency.

Xinhua News Agency (2006c) *China's Multi-Lateral Diplomacy under the New Circumstances*, Beijing: Xinhua News Agency.

Xinhua News Agency (2006d) *The Opening Speech delivered by the President Hu Jintao at the Beijing Summit of the Forum on China-Africa Cooperation (2006)*, Beijing: Xinhua News Agency.

Xinhua News Agency (2006e) *Senior Diplomat: support from Africa is requisite to China*, Beijing: Xinhua News Agency.

Xinhua News Agency (2006f) *The Leisure Society is Coming to You*, Beijing: Xinhua News Agency.

Xinhua News Agency (2006g) *Expansion of Departmental Interests Harms the Reform*, Beijing: Xinhua News Agency.

Xinhua News Agency (2006h) *American Renowned Scholar: Confucianism should take precedence when promoting China's 'soft power'*, Beijing: Xinhua News Agency.

Xinhua News Agency (2006i) *Central Foreign Affairs Works Conference Held in Beijing, Hu Jintao (Chinese President) Delivered Important Speeches*, Beijing: Xinhua News Agency.

Xinhua News Agency (2006j) *The Significance of China's Membership Resumption at the United Nations*, Beijing: Xinhua News Agency.

Xinhua News Agency (2006k) *Higher Prices in Four Consumer Products*, Beijing: Xinhua News Agency.

Xinhua News Agency (2006l) *The Poor Behaviour of Chinese Outbound Tourists is Criticized Internally and Overseas*, Beijing: Xinhua News Agency.

Xinhua News Agency (2006m) *Attending to Outbound Travel, Everyone is the Country's Image Ambassador*, Beijing: Xinhua News Agency.

Xinhua News Agency (2007a) *How to Understand the Construction of the Socialist Core Values System*, Beijing: Xinhua News Agency.

Xinhua News Agency (2007b) *Wen Jiabao (Chinese Premier): about the historical tasks in the primary stage of socialism and several issues in our foreign policy*, Beijing: Xinhua News Agency.

Xinhua News Agency (2008a) *The Open-door Policy and Economic Reform over 30 Years: around 400 laws enacted by the National People's Congress*, Beijing: Xinhua News Agency.

Xinhua News Agency (2008b) *Vice Chairman (or Minister) of the National Development and Reform Commission (NDRC) Talked about the Achievements of the Open-door Policy and Economic Reform*, Beijing: Xinhua News Agency.

Xinhua News Agency (2008c) *The Open-door Policy and Economic Reform of 30 Years: Incomes of Urban Chinese Increase 44-fold*, Beijing: Xinhua News Agency.

Xinhua News Agency (2008d) *The Figures about the Open-door Policy and Economic Reform*, Beijing: Xinhua News Agency.

Xinhua News Agency (2008f) *The Chinese Urge the US to Recognize her Full Market Economy Status Promptly*, Beijing: Xinhua News Agency.

Xinhua News Agency (2008g) *Hu Jintao: China's Development Does Not Affect and Threaten Any Country*, Beijing: Xinhua News Agency.

Xinhua News Agency (2008h) *How Sino-Soviet Relationships Split*, Beijing: Xinhua News Agency.

Xinhua News Agency (2008i) *The Origin of Mao Zedong's Final Decision-Making Authority*, Beijing: Xinhua News Agency.

Xinhua News Agency (2008j) *How Had the 'First-Line and Second-Line' System Been Formed before the Cultural Revolution?* Beijing: Xinhua News Agency.

Xinhua News Agency (2008k) *The Official of the National Development Reform Commission Talked about the Revised Arrangements for National Holidays*, Beijing: Xinhua News Agency.

Xinhua News Agency (2008l) *We Need Effectively to Expand Domestic Demand*, Beijing: Xinhua News Agency.

Xinhua News Agency (2008m) *To Understand the Impacts of the Expansion of Consumption on Maintaining Economic Growth*, Beijing: Xinhua News Agency.

Xinhua News Agency (2008n) *How Effectively to Expand Domestic Demand*, Beijing: Xinhua News Agency.

Xinhua News Agency (2008o) *Zhou Xiaochuan: consumption demand is a weak part in the domestic demand of our nation*, Beijing: Xinhua News Agency.

Xinhua News Agency (2008p) *Zhou Xiaochuan: we need first to expand consumption demand when expanding our domestic demand*, Beijing: Xinhua News Agency.

Xinhua News Agency (2008q) *The State Council Announced 10 Policy Measures to Expand Domestic Consumption*, Beijing: Xinhua News Agency.

Xinhua News Agency (2008r) *The Museums and Memorial Halls Nation-wide will be Opened for Free Admission from 2008*, Beijing: Xinhua News Agency.

Xinhua News Agency (2009a) *Foreign Media Concerning Zhou Xiaochuan's (the Governor of the People's Bank of China) Paper that China Challenged the Dominance of the US Dollars*, Beijing: Xinhua News Agency.

Xinhua News Agency (2009e) *National Development and Reform Commission (NDRC): the socialist market economy has been fundamentally established in our nation*, Beijing: Xinhua News Agency.

Xinhua News Agency (2009f) *National Development and Reform Commission (NDRC): the majority of product and service prices are determined by the market*, Beijing: Xinhua News Agency.

Xinhua News Agency (2009g) *Why Did Mao Zedong Select Wang Hongwen as his Successor?*, Beijing: Xinhua News Agency.

Xinhua News Agency (2009h) *The Origin of the Secretariat of the CPC Central Committee and its Authority*, Beijing: Xinhua News Agency.

Xinhua News Agency (2009i) *Get Leisure Affairs Well Done*, Beijing: Xinhua News Agency.

Xinhua News Agency (2009j) *The National Policy Foci on the Expansion of Domestic Demand*, Beijing: Xinhua News Agency.

Xinhua News Agency (2009k) *The Central Government Intensifies Policy Measures to Boost Consumption Demand*, Beijing: Xinhua News Agency.

Xinhua News Agency (2009l) *South Africa Starts to Offer Individual Tourist Visas to Chinese*, Beijing: Xinhua News Agency.

Xinhua News Agency (2009m) *Opinion Poll of Ten Thousands: 90% are Interested in the Citizens Leisure Scheme*, Beijing: Xinhua News Agency.

Xinhua News Agency (2009n) *Guangdong Province first Implements the National Leisure Scheme*, Beijing: Xinhua News Agency.

Xinhua News Agency (2009o) *Our Nation will Start the National Leisure Scheme*, Beijing: Xinhua News Agency.

Xinhua News Agency (2009p) *The CNTA Explains the National Leisure Scheme*, Beijing: Xinhua News Agency.

Xinhua News Agency (2009q) *The CNTA Seeks Feedback on the Draft National Tourist Routes*, Beijing: Xinhua News Agency.

Xinhua News Agency (2010a) *23% of our Population Reach Middle Class*, Beijing: Xinhua News Agency.

Xinhua News Agency (2010b) *The Leaders of the Party and State*, Beijing: Xinhua News Agency.

Xinhua Publishing House (2009) *The People's Republic of China Year-Book*, Beijing: Xinhua Publishing House.

Tourism

Central Publicity Department of the CPC (together with the Ministry of Construction, China National Tourism Administration and State Administration of Religious Affairs) (2000) *Notice to Firmly Prohibit Feudal Activities and Blind Worship in Tourist Attractions*, Beijing: Central Publicity Department (the Office of the Central Spiritual Civilization Steering Committee).

Central Publicity Department of the CPC (The Office of the Central Spiritual Civilization Steering Committee) and China National Tourism Administration (2006) *Action Plan to Raise the Civilized Quality of Tourist Behaviour by Chinese Citizens*, Beijing: Xinhua News Agency.

China National Tourism Administration (CNTA) (1985a–2010a) *The Yearbook of China Tourism Statistics*, Beijing: China Tourism Press.

China National Tourism Administration (CNTA) (1990b) 'Great Achievements and Austere Challenge', *Tourism Studies*, Vol. 4, Beijing: CNTA.

China National Tourism Administration (CNTA) (1992b) *Reform in the Tourism Industry*, Beijing: CNTA.

China National Tourism Administration (CNTA) (1993b) *An Introduction to Tourism*, Beijing: China Tourism Press.

China National Tourism Administration (CNTA) (1995b) *The Chronological Record of The Events in China Tourism Development*, Beijing: CNTA.

China National Tourism Administration (CNTA) (1995c) *Compilation of Tourism Policies and Regulations*, Beijing: CNTA.

China National Tourism Administration (CNTA) (1995d) *The National Tourism Plan in the 9th Five-Year State Plan for the National Economy and Social Development and Outlook to 2010*, Beijing: CNTA.

China National Tourism Administration (CNTA) (1996b) *The Principles and Guidelines of Tourism Industry Administration*, Beijing: Department of Travel Agencies and Hotels Administration, CNTA.

China National Tourism Administration (CNTA) (1996c) *Regulation on the Administration of Travel Agencies*, Beijing: CNTA.

China National Tourism Administration (CNTA) (1997b) *Report on the Development of China's Travel Agencies Sector*, Beijing: Department of Travel Agencies and Hotels Administration, CNTA.

China National Tourism Administration (CNTA) and Ministry of Public Security (1997) *Provisional Methods on the Administration of Outbound Travel*, Beijing: CNTA.

China National Tourism Administration (CNTA) (1998b) *The Handbook of Tourism Standardization Works*, Beijing: CNTA.

China National Tourism Administration (CNTA) (1998c) *Compilation of Tourism Policies and Regulations*, Beijing: CNTA.

China National Tourism Administration (CNTA) (1999b) *Fifty Years of China's Tourism*, Beijing: China Tourism Press.

China National Tourism Administration (CNTA) (1999c) *Tourism as a New Growth Pole of the National Economy*, Beijing: CNTA.

China National Tourism Administration (CNTA) (1999d) *Regulation on the Administration of Tourist Guides*, Beijing: CNTA.

China National Tourism Administration (CNTA) (2000b) *Catalogue of Tourism Standards*, Beijing: CNTA.

China National Tourism Administration (CNTA) (2001b) *The National Tourism Plan in the 10th Five-Year State Plan for the National Economy and Social Development, and Outlook to 2015 and 2020*, Beijing: CNTA.

China National Tourism Administration (CNTA) (2001c) *Regulation on the Administration of Travel Agencies (Revised Version on the Enactment in 1996)*, Beijing: CNTA.

China National Tourism Administration (CNTA) (2001d) *The 17th Administrative Order of CNTA – About the Cancellation of Some Departmental Rules*, Beijing: CNTA.

China National Tourism Administration (CNTA) (2001e) *Study Report about Tourism Development in Tibet*, Beijing: CNTA.

China National Tourism Administration (CNTA) (2002b) *Ding Guangen: Tourist Attractions are the Crucial Frontline in Promoting Socialist Culture (Remarks with the Leaders of Chongqing Municipality)*, Beijing: CNTA.

China National Tourism Administration (CNTA) (2003b) *China's Tourism: A Study of Opening Strategy*, Beijing: Policy and Legal Department, CNTA.

China National Tourism Administration (CNTA) (2003c) *The UNWTO and China's Provincial Tourism Planning*, Beijing: CNTA.

China National Tourism Administration (CNTA) (2004b) 'Document of National Tourism Works Conference 2004', *Tourism Studies*, Volume 1: 2–13, Beijing: CNTA.

China National Tourism Administration (CNTA) (2004c) *Chronology for Tourism Standardization*, Beijing: Policy and Legal Department, CNTA.

China National Tourism Administration (CNTA) (2004d) *Rating and Evaluation for Quality Levels of Tourist Attractions*, Beijing: CNTA.

China National Tourism Administration (CNTA) and the Department of Literature Research of the Central Committee of the Communist Party of China (CPC) (2004) *Discourses of National Leaders on Tourism (1978–2004)*, Beijing: Central Literature Press of China.

China National Tourism Administration (CNTA) (2005b) *To Understand the Deep Meaning of 'Aiding Tibet Programme through Tourism' from the Historical and Development Heights*, Beijing: CNTA.

China National Tourism Administration (CNTA) (2005c) *Provisional Methods for the Administration on Rating and Evaluation of Quality Levels of Tourist Attractions*, Beijing: CNTA.

China National Tourism Administration (CNTA) (2006b) *Travel to Africa Booms with More Chinese Visiting*, Beijing: CNTA.

China National Tourism Administration (CNTA) (2006c) *The Prosperity of Tourism is an Important Reflection of Social Harmony*, Beijing: CNTA.

China National Tourism Administration (CNTA) (2006d) *Tourism Standards*, Beijing: CNTA.

China National Tourism Administration, Ministry of Public Security and Taiwan Affairs Office of the State Council (2006) *Administrative Methods for the Travel of Mainland Residents to the Taiwan Region*, Beijing: CNTA.

China National Tourism Administration (CNTA) (2007b) *CNTA's Guidelines about the Development of Inbound Tourism with Great Efforts*, Beijing: CNTA.

China National Tourism Administration (CNTA) (2007c) *Important Instructions Made by Vice-Premier Wu Yi*, Beijing: CNTA.

China National Tourism Administration (CNTA) (2007d) *The Document of the 2007 National Tourism Works Conference*, Beijing: CNTA.

China National Tourism Administration (CNTA) (2007e) *Standards for Excellent Tourist Cities*, Beijing: CNTA.

China National Tourism Administration (CNTA) (2007f) *Standards for Competitive Tourist Counties*, Beijing: CNTA.

China National Tourism Administration (CNTA) (2007g) *Speech delivered by Vice Premier Wu Yi at the Holiday Tourism Ministerial Coordinating Meeting*, Beijing: CNTA.

China National Tourism Administration (CNTA) (2008b) *The 2008 National Tourism Works Conference Opens, Vice-Premier Wu Yi Presents and Delivers Speech*, Beijing: CNTA.

China National Tourism Administration (CNTA) (2008c) *The Document of the 2008 National Tourism Works Conference (Speeches Delivered by the Chairman of CNTA)*, Beijing: CNTA.

China National Tourism Administration (CNTA) (2008d) *Development of Tourism as a Key Industry in the National Economy – The Interview with Chairman Shao Qiwei of the CNTA by the China Tourism News*, Beijing: CNTA.

China National Tourism Administration (CNTA) (2008e) *The CNTA Together with Other Central Agencies Take Regulatory Action Against Admission Fees for Visitor Attractions*, Beijing: CNTA.

China National Tourism Administration (CNTA) (2008f) *22 CPPCC Members Urge the Legislation of Tourism Law*, Beijing: CNTA.

China National Tourism Administration (CNTA) (2008g) *The 28th Administrative Order of the CNTA – About the Cancellation of Some Departmental Rules*, Beijing: CNTA.

China National Tourism Administration (CNTA) (2008h) *Notices to Mainland Residents Travelling to the Taiwan Region*, Beijing: CNTA.

China National Tourism Administration (CNTA) (2008i) *Administrative Methods for Tour Staff in the Travel of Mainland Residents to the Taiwan Region*, Beijing: CNTA.

China National Tourism Administration (CNTA) (2009b) *Research Fund Allocation Results 2009*, Beijing: CNTA.

China National Tourism Administration (CNTA) (2009c) *Guidance Notes on the Research Topics for the Application for Funds*, Beijing: CNTA.

China National Tourism Administration (CNTA) (2009d) *Vice-Premier Wang Qishan: Understanding about Speeding-Up Tourism Development from the Strategic Height*, Beijing: CNTA.

China National Tourism Administration (CNTA) (2009e) *The Document of the 2009 National Tourism Works Conference*, Beijing: CNTA.

China National Tourism Administration (CNTA) (2009f) *Hu Jintao Attended the Signatory Ceremony for the ADS Agreement with Serbia*, Beijing: CNTA.

China National Tourism Administration (CNTA) (2009g) *Regulation on the Administration of Travel Agencies (New Enactment)*, Beijing: CNTA.

China National Tourism Administration (CNTA) (2009h) *The Notice about the Implementation of 8th Provision of Tour Guides in Aiding Tibet's Tourism*, Beijing: CNTA.

China National Tourism Administration (CNTA) (2009i) *Speeches by the Chairman of CNTA at the Seminar About Mainland Tourists to Taiwan*, Beijing: CNTA.

China National Tourism Administration (CNTA) (2010b) *Document of the 2010 National Tourism Works Conference (Speeches Delivered by the Chairman of CNTA)*, Beijing: CNTA.

China National Tourism Administration (CNTA) (2010c) *Chairman of the Financial and Economic Affairs Committee Shi Xioushi: the legislation of tourism law can promote the sound and sustainable development of tourism*, Beijing: CNTA.

China National Tourism Administration (CNTA) (2010d) *Unifying the Understanding, Updating the Ways and Fully Enhancing Tourism Service Quality*, Beijing: CNTA.

China National Tourism Administration (CNTA) (2010e) *The CNTA Hosted the First Meeting of The Working Group for the Drafting and Legislation of Tourism Law*, Beijing: CNTA.

China National Tourism Administration (CNTA) (2010f) *The 7th Meeting of the Coordinating Group for Red Tourism Development in Beijing*, Beijing: CNTA.

China National Tourism Administration (CNTA) (2010g) *The Number of Mainland Tourists to Taiwan is Expected to Total 1 Million in 2010*, Beijing: CNTA.

China National Tourism Administration (CNTA) (2010h) *Mainland's First Tourist Office to Taiwan Set Up in Taipei (7 May 2010)*, Beijing: CNTA.

China Tourism News (1989) 'Quality: survival and development', Beijing: *China Tourism News* (27 September).

The General Office of the CPC Central Committee and The General Office of the State Council (2004) *The Outline Plan for National Red Tourism Development 2004–2010*, Beijing: The National Development and Reform Commission.

Han Kehua[3] (ed.) (1994) *China Today: tourism industry*,[4] Beijing: Modern China Press.

Han Kehua (2003) *China's Tourism in the New Century*, Beijing: China Tourism Press.

The Ministry of Agriculture and China National Tourism Administration (CNTA) (2009) *Promotion of Rural Tourism to Expand Domestic Demand*, Beijing: CNTA.

The Ministry of Finance of the PR China (MoF) (2001) *Provisional Methods on the Administration of the Tourism Development Foundation*, Beijing: MoF.

The National Development and Reform Commission of the PR China (NDRC) (2006a) *Vice Minister Zhang Mao Visited the China National Tourism Administration*, Beijing: NDRC.

The National Development and Reform Commission of the PR China (NDRC) (2006c) *Outcomes of Tourism-Related Infrastructure Construction by Using State Bonds*, Beijing: NDRC.

The National Development and Reform Commission of the PR China (NDRC) (2007a) *NDRC's Notice to Further Improve the Management of Admission Fees for Visitor Attractions*, Beijing: NDRC.

The Research Office of the State Council (2009) *Implementation of National Tourism Development Strategies to Develop Tourism as a Mega Comprehensive Industry*, Beijing: The State Council Research Office.

The State Development Planning Commission of the PR China (SDPC) (2000) *Impacts on China's Tourism Industry after the Access to the World Trade Organization*, Beijing: Department of Social Development, SDPC.

The State Planning Commission of the PR China (SPC) (1990) *The Handbook of Tourism Economy Works*, Beijing: SPC.

Sun, Shangqing (ed.) (1989) *A Study of the Tourism Economy in China*, Beijing: People's Press.

Wei, Xiaoan (1996) *Tourism Development and Management*, Beijing: Tourism Education Press.

Wei, Xiaoan and Feng, Zongsu (eds) (1993) *China Tourism: industry policy and coordinated development*, Beijing: Tourism Education Press.

Wei, Xiaoan and Han, Jianmin (2003) *Path to Great Tourism Country*, Beijing: Tourism Education Press.

Xinhua News Agency (2008e) *China Confirms the Promotion of Consumption in Five Key Areas*, Beijing: Xinhua News Agency.

Xinhua News Agency (2009b) *Chinese Tourists Luxuriously Touring Japan: making businessmen surprised*, Beijing: Xinhua News Agency.

Xinhua News Agency (2009c) *China Granted 'Approved Destination Status' (ADS) to Canada*, Beijing: Xinhua News Agency.

Xinhua News Agency (2009d) *The CNTA Initiated the 'National Leisure Scheme'*, Beijing: Xinhua News Agency.

Hong Kong and Macau SARs

The Central Government and the Government of Hong Kong Special Administrative Region (HKSARG) (2003) *The Mainland and Hong Kong Closer Economic Partnership Arrangement (CEPA)*, Hong Kong: Hong Kong Trade and Industry Department.

The Government of Hong Kong Special Administrative Region (HKSARG) (1997) *Policy Address 1997*, Hong Kong: HKSARG.

The Government of Hong Kong Special Administrative Region (HKSARG) (1998) *Policy Address 1998*, Hong Kong: HKSARG.

The Government of Hong Kong Special Administrative Region (HKSARG) (1999) *Policy Address 1999*, Hong Kong: HKSARG.

The Government of Hong Kong Special Administrative Region (HKSARG) (2000) *Policy Address 2000*, Hong Kong: HKSARG.

The Government of Hong Kong Special Administrative Region (HKSARG) (2001) *Policy Address 2001*, Hong Kong: HKSARG.

The Government of Hong Kong Special Administrative Region (HKSARG) (2002) *Policy Address 2002*, Hong Kong: HKSARG.

The Government of Hong Kong Special Administrative Region (HKSARG) (2003) *Policy Address 2003*, Hong Kong: HKSARG.

The Government of Hong Kong Special Administrative Region (HKSARG) (2004) *Policy Address 2004*, Hong Kong: HKSARG.

The Government of Hong Kong Special Administrative Region (HKSARG) (2005a) *Policy Address 2005*, Hong Kong: HKSARG.

The Government of Hong Kong Special Administrative Region (HKSARG) (2005b) *Policy Address 2005–2006*, Hong Kong: HKSARG.

The Government of Hong Kong Special Administrative Region (HKSARG) (2006) *Policy Address 2006–2007*, Hong Kong: HKSARG.

The Government of Hong Kong Special Administrative Region (HKSARG) (2007) *Policy Address 2007–2008*, Hong Kong: HKSARG.

The Government of Hong Kong Special Administrative Region (HKSARG) (2008) *Policy Address 2008–2009*, Hong Kong: HKSARG.

The Government of Hong Kong Special Administrative Region (HKSARG) (2009a) *Policy Address 2009–2010*, Hong Kong: HKSARG.

The Government of Hong Kong Special Administrative Region (HKSARG) (2009b) *Hong Kong: The Facts – Tourism*, Hong Kong: Tourism Commission.

The Hong Kong Tourism Board (HKTB) (1997a–2009a) *A Statistical Review of Hong Kong Tourism*, Hong Kong: HKTB.

The Hong Kong Tourism Board (HKTB) (2002b–2009b) *Tourism Expenditure Associated to Inbound Tourism*, Hong Kong: HKTB.

The Government of Macau Special Administrative Region (MSARG) (1999) *Tourism Statistics*, Macau: MSARG.

The Government of Macau Special Administrative Region (MSARG) (2000) *Policy Address 2000*, Macau: MSARG.

The Government of Macau Special Administrative Region (MSARG) (2001) *Policy Address 2001*, Macau: MSARG.

The Government of Macau Special Administrative Region (MSARG) (2002) *Policy Address 2002*, Macau: MSARG.

The Government of Macau Special Administrative Region (MSARG) (2003) *Policy Address 2003*, Macau: MSARG.

The Government of Macau Special Administrative Region (MSARG) (2004) *Policy Address 2004*, Macau: MSARG.

The Government of Macau Special Administrative Region (MSARG) (2005) *Policy Address 2005*, Macau: MSARG.

The Government of Macau Special Administrative Region (MSARG) (2006) *Policy Address 2006*, Macau: MSARG.

The Government of Macau Special Administrative Region (MSARG) (2007) *Policy Address 2007*, Macau: MSARG.

The Government of Macau Special Administrative Region (MSARG) (2008a) *Policy Address 2008*, Macau: MSARG.

The Government of Macau Special Administrative Region (MSARG) (2008b) *Macau Gaming History*, Macau: Gaming Inspection and Coordination Bureau.

The Government of Macau Special Administrative Region (MSARG) (2008c) *Tourism Statistics 2008*, Macau: MSARG.

The Government of Macau Special Administrative Region (MSARG) (2009) *Policy Address 2009*, Macau: MSARG.

The Government of Macau Special Administrative Region (MSARG) (2010) *Policy Address 2010*, Macau: MSARG.

Index

Page numbers in *italics* indicate illustrations

Commission of the European
Communities (CEC) 67
Communist Party of China *see* CPC
conceptual framework *41*
concrete tourism policy decisions 44–5,
167–76, 186–8, 193–5, 214–24, 245,
246
consumer culture 107
coordination 80–2, 83, 136
corruption 108
CPAFFC (Chinese People's Association
for Friendship with Foreign
Countries) 117
CPC (Communist Party of China) 17,
24, 26, 32, 33–5, 88, 109–10, 112,
120; Central Committee of 34;
governing of nation 136; structure
and organization of 34–5; *see also*
National Party Congress
CPPCC (Chinese People's Political
Consultative Conference) 35–6, 137,
147
Cultural Revolution (1966–76) 27,
90–1, 96, 99, 108, 111, 118, 121, 122,
123, 130, 131, 132–3, 134, 170, 182,
194
Current Issues in Tourism 3

Dalai Lama 31, 201, 240
democratic centralism 121–2
Democratic Progressive Party (DPP)
239
Deng Xiaoping 35, 90, 128, 133, 134,
139, 246, 262; role in tourism
development 157; southern inspection
tour 103, 104, 190; speeches on
economic development of tourism
157, *158–9*
Deng Xiaoping's era 25, 27–9, 87,
93–106; **Period Two** (1978–85)
99–101, 153–76, 195–6, 225; basic
tourism policy decisions 162, 165–7;
concrete tourism policy decisions
167–76; domestic tourism 162, *165*,
167; Economic Reform and Open-
door Policy 100, 156; enterprise
reform 174–5; foreign exchange
reserves 154–5, *155*; foreign relations
156–7; influence of leaders 157–60;
institutional development 167–73,
176, 226; Jianguo Hotel's enterprise
management model 174–5; regulatory
framework for tourism 176; relaxation
of market access 169–73, 181;

tourism resources 155; tourist arrivals
162, *163–4*, 172; upgraded leadership
arrangements 168–9; **Period Three**
(1986–91) 101–3, 176–89, 196, 225,
226; basic tourism policy decisions
185–6; concrete tourism policy
decisions 186–8; domestic tourism
184–5, 188; emergence of tourism
marketing 186–7; hotel star-rating
programme 187–8; ideological
regulations 188; incorporation of
tourism into Five-Year State Plan
176, 185–6; industry management
181–2, 185, 186, 187; institutional
changes 187–8; learning from other
countries 179; policy-oriented
learning by comprehensive
government agencies 183–5; policy-
oriented learning by tourism agencies
177–82; political goal of tourism 186;
role of tourism in national economy
183–4; tourism capacity 180; tourism
quality 181, 187; tourist arrivals 181,
187; **Period Four** (1992–7) 103–6,
189–95; basic tourism policy
decisions 192–3; concrete tourism
policy decisions 193–5; development
of the tertiary sector 190; domestic
tourism 190, 192–3; exploratory
establishment of market institutions
194–5; marketing 193, *194*; new
essentials of the tourism policy
paradigm 190–1; outbound travel 190,
192; policy-oriented learning by
CNTA and macro-management
agencies 189–90; product
development 193–4; quality of
tourism 195; resort-based tourism
193–4; socio-economic and tourism
development 190; tourism as an
economic activity 139, 140, 144–5,
153–76, 185, 195–6; tourism as an
economic industry 176–89, 196;
tourism as an important industry
189–95; transition from planned-
economy model to market-economy
model 98–105, 176–7, 189, 224–5
Denzin, N.K. 12
Department of Investigation 126
descriptive model 9
Desforges, L. 11
Destutt de Tracy, Antoine 59
Development Research Centre (DRC)
37, 138, 149, 177